DUF

Trees of East Texas

Trees of East Texas

by Robert A. Vines

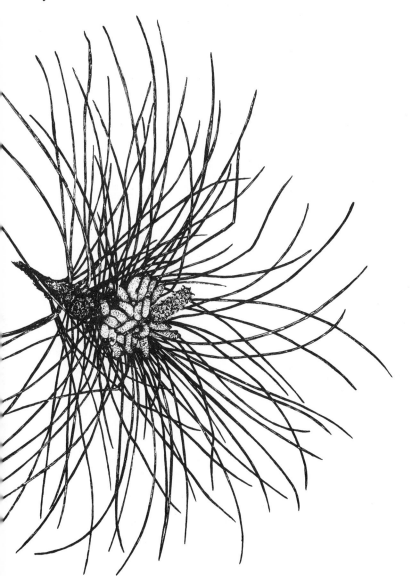

University of Texas Press, Austin & London

Library of Congress Cataloging in Publication Data

Vines, Robert A   1907–
    Trees of east Texas.

    Includes index.
    1. Trees—Texas—Identification. I. Title.
QK484.T4V52   582'.1609'764   76-54789
ISBN 0-292-78016-8
ISBN 0-292-78017-6 pbk.

Printed in the United States of America

Set in Primer types by G&S Typesetters, Inc.

This book is dedicated to my wife,

RUBY VALRIE VINES,

who has shared thirty-nine years of

wonderful botanical adventures with me

Contents

Acknowledgments

Special thanks are acknowledged herewith to the staffs of various herbaria for the loan of plant materials for study. Without such assistance this work would have been impossible. These include the United States National Herbarium, United States National Arboretum, New York Botanical Garden, Missouri Botanical Garden Herbarium, Harvard University Gray Herbarium, Southern Methodist University Herbarium, Chicago Museum of Natural History Herbarium, and University of Texas Herbarium.

Marshall Conring Johnston of the University of Texas Botany Department has been very helpful in providing plant material, but most helpful of all has been the book he coauthored with Donovan Stewart Correll, *Manual of the Vascular Plants of Texas*. This excellent work substantiated and clarified many things for me.

Also, I wish to give special thanks to Cornelius H. Muller for his advice on the revision of the oaks of Texas. George Avery of Miami, Florida, has been very helpful in providing information on the subtropical plants.

My thanks should also go to the various artists who prepared the illustrations, namely Sara Kahlden Arendale, Margaret Beggins, Pat Beggins, Jan Milstead, Felicia Bond, and Michele Cox.

Introduction

The purpose of this field guide is to identify by full descriptions and illustrations all the native and naturalized trees of the east Texas zone. The very nature of a field guide, however, limits the amount of material it can contain and still be easily carried and used in the field. Because of this limitation, detailed data on the varieties, horticultural forms, propagation, and medicinal uses of the trees have been omitted. The reader who seeks a more in-depth discussion is referred to the author's *Trees, Shrubs and Woody Vines of the Southwest,* upon which this guide is based.

East Texas is considered to be the state's richest area botanically. More species of plants have been recorded in this area than in any other. A combination of adequate rainfall, good soils, and a moderate climate due to the low altitude and southern location favors the development of a large arborescent flora or numerous tree species.

WHAT IS A TREE?

A native tree is one which grows without cultivation. A naturalized tree is one which is introduced from other regions but escapes cultivation and grows freely. A somewhat general definition of a tree has been suggested by some authorities but is not accepted by all. The definition often given is that a tree is a plant with a single woody trunk at least four inches in diameter four feet above the ground, with a definite branched crown, and with a height not less than twelve feet.

This rule may have some exceptions because some trees may have several trunks growing from the base, and some are tall enough but fail to attain the stipulated trunk diameter. Also, some shrubs are treelike but have a number of stems rising from the base. Under unfavorable conditions of soil or climate a true tree may become shrublike, or in favorable circumstances a shrub may become treelike. Also, some species are fast growing and reach maximum tree size much quicker than other species. Individual trees vary within the same species as to size.

CONSERVATION IMPORTANCE

It is recognized that east Texas sustains the largest forest zone in the state, and that forest products are considered the most important industry of the area. However, in recent years farming, ranching, and recreational activities have cleared much of the forest land. Fortunately, much progress has been made in creating a harmonious land-use program, as evidenced by extensive tree planting, which has done much to help stabilize the forest industry. Actually, good native stands are much scarcer than in former years, but improved selective tree farming has helped to keep up with the high demand.

Many organizations have contributed to the over-all land-use program and forest conservation: federal bureaus, state agencies, district and county governments, timber producers, processors, and wood products manufacturers. The Texas Parks and Wildlife Department has coordinated the wildlife and park management. It should certainly be fully recognized that trees are of great value for purposes other than providing wood products. Humans, animals, and birds eat the seeds, fruit, and sap. Trees furnish drugs, dyes, and resins, prevent erosion, are good sound barriers, reinstitute the oxygen content in the air, and are much used for street, park, and home beautification and shade. All these uses are justifiable reasons for forest conservation.

EAST TEXAS TREE ZONES DEFINED

For the purposes of this publication the east Texas tree zone has been divided into three sections (see map 1): Pineywoods section (A), Post Oak Savannah section (C), and Upper Gulf Coast Prairie section (B).

Pineywoods Section (A)

The largest timber producing area in the state, the Pineywoods extends into Texas from Louisiana, Arkansas, and Oklahoma. It includes approximately 43 counties and 15 million acres, with an altitude of 50 to 500 feet above sea level. The soils are usually acid, light to dark gray sands or sandy loams. The rainfall and temperature of this section are indicated on map 2. The forest is not a continuous unbroken unit but is separated into many ecological areas according to plant species. There are many diverse habitats of pine and hardwood stands, upland prairies, cypress swamps, bogs, seeps, and dense bay-gall, yaupon, and titi thickets. Hence the name of Big Thicket was historically applied to the forest. It is very fitting that part of it has been set aside as a national park.

Many streams dissect and drain the area. Pine is the principal timber tree, including Longleaf, Shortleaf and Loblolly species. Also, the introduced Slash Pine has been widely planted over the area. The hardwoods include many kinds of oak, ash, elm, hickory, sweet gum, black gum, and so on. The two plant families with the most species are the oaks and the hawthorns. The hawthorns are usually small trees of little commercial value, but they are important for furnishing humans, birds, and animals with food from the fruit and some are very ornamental.

However, the nature of this great forest is changing, producing more pine in proportion to hardwoods. One problem of the area is that the predominantly sandy, somewhat sterile soil does not have the strength to develop hardwoods as large as do heavier soils. In fact, much of the cutting is now for plywood or pulp, instead of saw log timber. Also, many of the hardwoods are along streams, and the creation of reservoirs by dams has flooded these areas.

Post Oak Savannah Section (c)

The Post Oak Savannah area covers 26 counties and 9 million acres and merges into the Pineywoods on the east. The elevation is from 300 to 800 feet. The upland soils are light colored, acid sands or sandy loams. The bottomland soils are light brown to dark gray, acid sandy loams to clays. The area has less rainfall and a slightly higher elevation than the Pineywoods. A considerable amount of open prairies blend into the Blackland Prairies on the west. There are a number of oaks, principally Post Oak and Blackjack Oak, elms, hickories, and

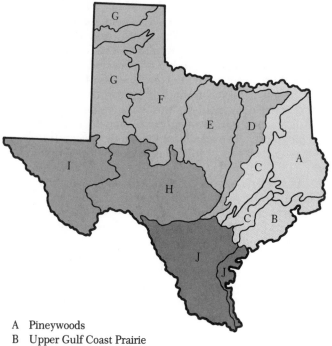

A   Pineywoods
B   Upper Gulf Coast Prairie
C   Post Oak Savannah
D   Blackland Prairies
E   Cross Timbers and Prairies
F   Rolling Plains
G   High Plains
H   Edwards Plateau
I   Trans-Pecos
J   South Texas Plains

Map 1.   Texas Tree Zones

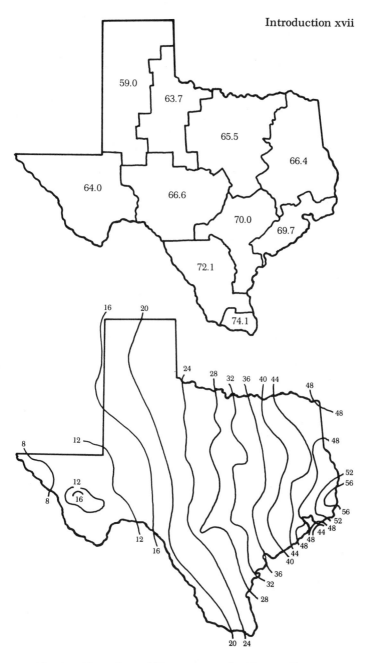

Map 2. Mean Annual Temperatures by Climatic Divisions
(1941–1970)
Mean Annual Precipitation by Climatic Divisions
(1941–1970)

the mesquite invading from the west. Along streams and low places are found pecans, hickories, and walnuts.

Upper Gulf Coast Prairie Section (B)

The Gulf Coast Prairies follow the Texas coast from the Sabine River to the Rio Grande. However, the upper section contains about half of the total acreage, or about 6 million acres. The width varies, and the elevation is from 150 feet downward to the Gulf. The soils are acid sands, sandy loams, and clays and are not generally very permeable, so that water stands. The area is predominantly grassland, with salt marshes near the Gulf shores. It is predominantly ranch or farm land. However, the forested southern ends of the Post Oak Savannah and Pineywoods follow along the edges of the many bayous and rivers which cut through the coastal prairies, and many of the same species occur. However, the clays, level terrain, and poor drainage limit their spread. Westward there are coastal forests along the basins of the Brazos, Colorado, and Lavaca rivers and on the flood plains of the Guadalupe, San Antonio, and Nueces rivers. The coverage of this book ends along the lower Nueces River, near Corpus Christi, but a number of southwestern-type trees intrude eastward from the lower Rio Grande region.

Trees of East Texas

Taxodiium Family (Taxodiaceae)

Common Bald Cypress

Taxodium distichum Rich. [A, B, C]

FIELD IDENTIFICATION. Deciduous conifer growing in swampy grounds, attaining a height of 130 ft and a diameter of 8 ft. It is reported that some trees have reached an age of 800–1,200 years. The trunk is swollen at the base and separated into narrow ridges. Curious cone-shaped, erect structures called "knees" grow upward from roots of trees growing in particularly wet situations. Branches horizontal or drooping.

FLOWERS. March–April, staminate cones brownish, 3–5 in. long; stamens 6–8, with filaments enlarged and anthers opening lengthwise; pistillate cones solitary, or 2–3 together, clustered in the leaf axils, scaly and subglobose; scales shield-shaped, with 2 ovules at the base of each.

FRUIT. Ripening October–December, cone globose, closed, rugose, ¾–1 in. in diameter, formed by the enlargement of the spirally arranged pistillate flower scales; scales yellowish brown, angular, rugose, horny, thick; seeds 2-winged, erect, borne under each scale, dispersed by water or wind; large crops occur every 3 to 5 years with lighter crops between.

LEAVES. Deciduous, alternate, 2-ranked, ½–¾ in. long, flat, sessile, entire, linear, acute, apiculate, light green, lustrous, flowering branches sometimes bear awl-shaped leaves, deciduous habit unusual for a conifer.

TWIGS. Green to brown, glabrous, slender, flexible, often deciduous.

BARK. Gray to cinnamon-brown, thin, closely appressed, fairly smooth, finely divided by longitudinal shallow fissures.

WOOD. Light or dark brown, sapwood whitish, straight-grained, moderately hard, not strong, very durable, weighing 28 lb per cu ft, not given to excessive warping or shrinking, easily worked; heart often attacked by a fungus, the disease being known as "peck."

RANGE. Texas, Oklahoma, Arkansas, and Louisiana; eastward to Florida, northward to Massachusetts, and west to Missouri.

REMARKS. The genus name, *Taxodium*, is from the Greek and means "yewlike," in reference to the leaves, and the species name, *distichum*, means "two-ranked" and also refers to the leaves. Other vernacular names are White Cypress, Gulf Cypress, Southern Cypress, Tidewater Red Cypress, Yellow Cypress, Red Cypress, Black Cypress, Swamp Cypress, and Sabino-tree. Cypress wood is used for boatbuilding, ties, docks, bridges, tanks, silos, cooperage, posts, shingles, interior finishing, car construction, patterns, flasks, greenhouses, cooling towers, stadium seats, etc. It is very durable in contact with soil and water. It is easily worked and takes a good polish. The knees are sometimes made into souvenirs, and the cone resin used as an analgesic for wounds. The conical erect knees serve as a mechanical device for anchoring the tree in soft mud, and some authorities believe that the knees also aerate the roots. The seeds are eaten by a number of species of birds, including wild ducks. Common Bald Cypress is often planted for ornament and has been in cultivation in Europe since about 1640. Fossil ancestors of Bald Cypress, at one time, covered the greater part of North America in company with the ginkgoes, sequoias, and incense-cedars. At present it is concentrated in the swamps of the southern states and middle to lower Mississippi Valley. Florida has about one-third of the total amount of acreage of Common Bald Cypress.

Pine Family (Pinaceae)

Slash Pine

Pinus elliottii Engelm. [A]

FIELD IDENTIFICATION. A rapid-growing tree attaining a
height of 100 ft, with a diameter of 3 ft. The trunk is clean,
straight, and symmetrical, and the branches heavy, horizontal, or ascending, to form a handsome round-topped head.
The root system reaches a depth of 9–15 ft.

FLOWERS. Borne January–February before the new leaves.
Staminate inflorescences in short many-flowered, purplish
brown clusters, young pistillate cones cylindrical and ¾–
1½ in. long; pistillate cones solitary, lateral, pinkish, ovate,
long-peduncled.

FRUIT. Cone borne on a peduncle ¾–1 in. long, persistent
until the following summer, lateral, symmetrical, variable in
size, 2–6 in. long, 2–3½ in. wide when open, ovoid to ovoid-
conic, rich brown, shiny; scales flat, thin, flexible, apex
lustrous-varnished, armed with a minute recurved prickle;
seeds about ¼ in. long with a wing ¾–1 in. long; seed body
almost triangular, sides full and rounded, dorsally ridged,
gray to black or mottled, shell thin and brittle; wing rather
thin and transparent; cotyledons 5–9.

LEAVES. Stout, stiff, in 2–3-leaved clusters (mostly 2), enclosed at base in a persistent, membranous sheath, 5–10 in. long (rarely longer or shorter), rather dark, lustrous green, marked with numerous bands of stomata on each face, deciduous at the end of the second year. The heavy, shiny green foliage differs from the associated Longleaf Pine with its coarser, rather bluish green foliage. Loblolly Pine, like Longleaf Pine, has 3 bluish green leaves in a cluster, but has smaller leaves than Longleaf Pine or Slash Pine.

TWIGS. Stout, orange to brown, leaves tufted at the ends; buds with silvery brown scales, loose at the apex; terminal bud large, reddish brown, elongating in spring into a straight, stout, light gray "candle," about as thick as a pencil. (Longleaf Pine has a larger bud and candle 1 in. or more in diameter.)

BARK. On mature trees ¾–2 in. thick, separating into large flat plates deeply furrowed between, surfaces breaking into scales which are thin, papery, and reddish to orange or silvery. Fairly similar to the Longleaf Pine. Differing from Loblolly Pine in being less deeply furrowed.

WOOD. Yellow to dark orange or brown, sapwood nearly white; coarse-grained, strong, tough, stiff, hard, durable, weighing about 45 lb per cu ft, seasons easily, strong in endwise compression, moderately high in shock resistance, holds nails and screws well, glues well, low in ability to take and hold paint. Considered to be the hardest, strongest, and heaviest of all commercial conifers in the United States.

RANGE. Rolling lands of the southern coastal plains. Replacing Longleaf Pine of the lowlands. Sandy-loam soils of swamps and along streams. In Louisiana in St. Tammany, Washington, Tangipahoa, and Livingston parishes; eastward to Florida and Georgia.

REMARKS. The genus name, *Pinus*, is the classical name, and the species name, *elliottii*, honors its discoverer, Stephen Elliott (1771–1830), botanist and banker of South Carolina.

Slash Pine is often planted for ornament along highways in the South. The wood has a wide variety of uses, such as crossties, posts, poles, joists, flooring, railroad cars, veneers, tanks, silos, boxes, baskets, crates, planing-mill products, excelsior, agricultural implements, paving blocks, woodenware and novelties, shipbuilding and boatbuilding, fuel, paper pulp, mine timbers, bridges and trestles, and general rough construction of warehouses and factories. Large amounts of resin and turpentine are obtained from the gum for use as naval stores.

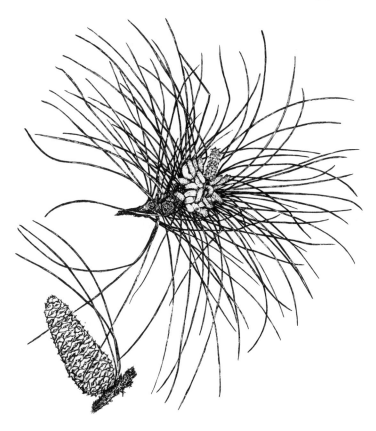

Loblolly Pine

Pinus taeda L. [A, B, C]

FIELD IDENTIFICATION. Handsome conifer attaining a height of 170 ft and a diameter of 6 ft.

FLOWERS. Staminate flowers yellowish green or violet, spirally arranged in slender inflorescences about 2 in. long; involucral scales 10–13, overlapping; stamens almost sessile, anthers 2, opening lengthwise; pistillate cone ovate, about ½ in. long, yellowish green, also spirally arranged in scaly catkins, each scale with 2 ovules at the base.

FRUIT. Ripening September–November, the spirally arranged imbricate scales of the pistillate inflorescences harden to form a cone; cone persistent, ripening in 2 years, 3–5 in. long, elongate-oblong or ovoid, reddish brown, sessile, scales thickened at the apex and bearing short incurved or straight spines; seeds 2 on each scale, rhomboid, mottled brown, about ½ in. long, attached to a thin wing about ¾ in. long.

LEAVES. Persistent, in clusters of 3, rarely a few in pairs, glaucous, light to dark green, rigid, slender, 3-sided, 5–10 in. long, sheath about ½ in. long.

TWIGS. Stout, reddish brown, scaly.

BARK. Reddish brown, rough, thick, deeply furrowed, scaling into coarse, large segments with large, appressed, papery scales.

WOOD. Streaky yellow and brown, coarse-grained, resinous, soft, brittle, weighing 34 lb per cu ft.

RANGE. Over wide areas on low grounds. East Texas and Louisiana; eastward to Florida and north into southeastern Oklahoma, southern half of Arkansas, southern Tennessee, Georgia, South Carolina, North Carolina, Virginia, Maryland, and Delaware.

REMARKS. The genus name, *Pinus*, is the old Latin name. The species name, *taeda*, is for the resinous wood. Other vernacular names are Frankincense Pine, Black Pine, Lowland Shortleaf Pine, Torch Pine, Slack Pine, Sap Pine, Swamp Pine, Bastard Pine, Long-straw Pine, Indian Pine, Long-shucks Pine, Fox-tail Pine, Shortleaf Pine, Rosemary Pine, and Old-field Pine. The date of earliest cultivation is 1713. The wood is used for lumber, cooperage, pulp, boxes, crossties, posts, and fuel. Loblolly Pine is not usually worked for turpentine, because the flow of gum is checked quickly and labor costs are too high. Razorbacks do not injure the saplings of Loblolly Pine as much as those of Longleaf Pine.

Shortleaf Pine

Pinus echinata Mill. [A, B, C]

FIELD IDENTIFICATION. Valuable coniferous tree to 110 ft, and 2 ft in diameter. The branches are whorled and the crown is rather short and pyramidal to oblong.

FLOWERS. March–April, staminate inflorescences borne in larger clusters, sessile, about ¾ in. long, yellowish brown to purple; pistillate in small clusters of 2–3 cones with stout peduncles, about ¼ in. long, rosy pink, with scaly bracts and inverted ovules.

FRUIT. Maturing the second year October–November, persistent on the branches, cone solitary or a few together, sessile or short-stalked, borne laterally, reddish brown, 1½–2½ in. long, ovoid to oblong-conic; scales separating at maturity, woody, thickened at apex, armed with sharp but weak spines which are often deciduous; seeds 2 on each scale, brown marked with black, triangular, about ¾ in. long, bearing an oblique wing about ½ in. long.

LEAVES. Needlelike, from persistent sheaths, usually 2 in a cluster, sometimes 3, 3–6 in. long, slender, flexible, dark

bluish green, persistent. A ton of straw contains about 14.2 lb of nitrogen and 5.4 lb of phosphoric acid. Pine straw protects the soil and increases the moisture-holding capacity.

TWIGS. Stiff, rough, stout, brittle, glaucous, brownish to greenish purple at first, later dark reddish brown to purple.

BARK. Thick, brownish red, broken into large, angular, scaly plates with small appressed scales and coarse fissures.

WOOD. Variable in color and quality, yellow, orange, or yellowish brown, sapwood lighter, coarse-grained, fairly heavy, medium-hard, not as resinous as other yellow pines, weighing 38 lb per cu ft.

RANGE. Forming dense stands, doing best on uplands or foothills. East Texas, Oklahoma, Arkansas, and Louisiana; eastward to Florida, northward to New York, and west to Illinois.

REMARKS. The genus name, *Pinus*, is the ancient Latin name, and the species name, *echinata*, refers to the hedgehoglike, or echinate, bristly needles. Vernacular names are Yellow Pine, Rosemary Pine, Forest Pine, Old-field Pine, Bull Pine, Pitch Pine, Slash Pine, and Carolina Pine. The wood is valuable because of its softer and less resinous character. It is used for general construction, exterior and interior finishing, planing-mill products, veneer, cooperage, excelsior, boxes, crates, agricultural instruments, low-grade furniture, posts, poles, woodenware, toys, etc. A number of species of birds and rodents feed on the seeds.

Longleaf Pine

Pinus palustris Mill. [A, B]

FIELD IDENTIFICATION. Coniferous tree to 125 ft, and a diameter to 4 ft. Trunk straight and tall with few branches.

FLOWERS. Cones February–April, staminate cones purple, 2–3½ in. long, borne on conspicuous scaly, clustered inflorescences; stamens short-filamented, anthers 2, opening lengthwise; pistillate cones reddish purple, bearing spirally arranged scales, each scale with 2 ovules at base.

FRUIT. Ripening September–October, cone large, dry, reddish brown, subsessile, conical-oblong or cylindrical, slightly curved, 6–12 in. long; the scales much thickened and bearing at the apex a short, recurved spine; seeds mostly triangular, blotched, ridged, ¼–½ in. long with an oblique, thin wing about 1½ in. long.

LEAVES. Borne in terminal, plumelike clusters, needles in bundles of 3, flexible, slender, shiny, dark green, 3-sided, 10–15 in. long, sheaths long. Plants 3–12 years of age almost grasslike in leaf appearance.

TWIGS. Stout, scaly, orange-brown, buds long, white-silvery, scaly.

BARK. Smooth, thin-scaled, separating into large reddish brown plates with coarse fissures.

WOOD. Very desirable, resinous, heavy, hard, strong, tough, durable, coarse-grained, yellow, yellowish brown or orange, sapwood whitish, weighing about 44 lb per cu ft.

RANGE. Mostly in pure stands on deep sandy land. Texas and Louisiana, eastward to Florida and northward to Virginia. In Texas west to the valley of the Trinity River. Rare, if at all, in Oklahoma and Arkansas.

REMARKS. The genus name, *Pinus*, is the classical Latin name, and the species name, *palustris*, refers to the marshy

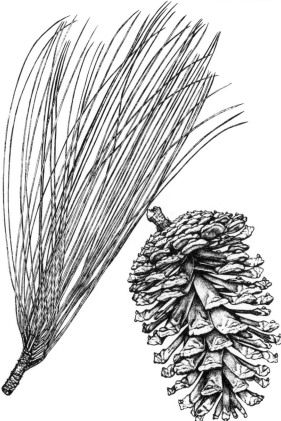

habitat. Vernacular names are Georgia Pine, White Rosin-tree, Pine Broom, Southern Pine, Yellow Pine, Hard Pine, Texas Yellow Pine, Pitch Pine, Fat Pine, Heart Pine, Turpentine Pine, and Florida Pine.

The seeds of Longleaf Pine are eaten by at least 10 species of birds and by many rodents. Razorbacks are very destructive to Longleaf Pine, eating the seeds and the thick, succulent root bark of young seedlings and saplings. Goats also do considerable damage to young plants. After cuttings, the new seedling should be allowed 5 years or so to become established. When the saplings are 5–8 ft high moderate grazing in the area by horses, cattle, or mules can be maintained without appreciable damage. Longleaf Pine is resistant to fire. During hot dry years southern pine beetles cause damage, and pine sawyers sometimes infest dead or felled trees. The wood is very desirable because of its strength and durability. It is used for a great variety of purposes, especially for interior finishing, flooring, fencing, piling, paper pulp, bridges, ties, heavy construction timbers, fuel, charcoal, and shipbuilding. The date of its earliest cultivation is 1727.

Cypress Family (Cupressaceae)

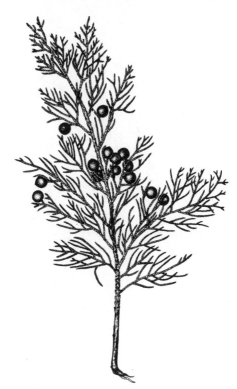

Eastern Red-cedar

Juniperus virginiana L. [A, B, C]

FIELD IDENTIFICATION. Evergreen tree of variable shape, attaining a height of 50 ft or rarely more. Leaves of two kinds, either scalelike and appressed, or awl-shaped and spreading.

FLOWERS. March–May, dioecious, catkins small and terminal; staminate catkins oblong or ovoid; stamens 10–12, golden brown, pollen sacs 4; female cones globular; scales spreading, fleshy, purplish, bearing 1–2 basal ovules.

FRUIT. Ripening September–December, cone berrylike, on straight peduncles, pale blue, glaucous, subglobose, ¼–⅓ in. in diameter, sweet, resinous; seeds 1–2, ovoid, acute, 1/6–1/8 in. long, smooth, shining.

LEAVES. Of two kinds; one kind scalelike, appressed, glandular, dark green, acute or obtuse, about 1/16 in. long, 4-ranked; the other awl-shaped, sharp-pointed, glandless, glaucous, ½–¾ in. long; some of the leaves are intermediate between the two forms.

TWIGS. Reddish brown, round or angled.

BARK. Light reddish brown, separating into long fibrous strips; trunk more or less fluted and basally buttressed.

WOOD. Red, sapwood white, knotty, light, brittle, soft, even-textured, compact, weighing about 30 lb per cu ft, shrinks little, very resistant to decay.

RANGE. Growing in all types of soil, on hilltops or in swamps. Almost throughout the eastern United States. West into Texas, Oklahoma, Arkansas, Kansas, Nebraska, and North and South Dakota.

REMARKS. *Juniperus* is the classical name, and the species name, *virginiana*, refers to the state of Virginia. Other names are Red Savin, Carolina Cedar, Juniper-bush, Pencil-wood, and Red Juniper. The capital of the state of Louisiana, Baton Rouge (Red Stick), gets its name from the red wood. The wood is used for novelties, posts, poles, woodenware, millwork, paneling, closets, chests, and pencils. The aromatic character of the wood is considered to be a good insect repellent. The extract of cedar oil has various commercial uses. The tree is host to a gall-like rust which in certain stages attacks the leaves of apple trees. Twig-laden bagworm cocoons are also frequent on the branches. A few borers attack the tree, and it suffers greatly from fire damage. It is sometimes used in shelter-belt planting, and has been cultivated since 1664. The fruit is eaten by at least 20 species of birds and the opossum.

Southern Red-cedar

Juniperus silicicola (Small) Bailey [A, B, C]

FIELD IDENTIFICATION. Pungent evergreen tree sometimes attaining a height of 50 ft, with a trunk to 2 ft in diameter. Branches spreading when the tree grows in the open to form a broad irregular crown. The upper branches usually erect and the lower pendulous. When crowded by other trees the branches form a more symmetrical, narrower, pointed crown. The root system is rather shallow.

FLOWERS. Generally opening in March, minute, dioecious, axillary or terminal; staminate cones usually terminal, solitary, oblong-ovoid, 1/8–1/4 in. long; stamens 10–12, filaments enlarged with yellow scalelike rounded connectives, usually with 8 pollen sacs at the base; pistillate cones ovoid, scales at base persistent, acute, some ovulate with 1–2 ovules opposite the scales, scales later fusing with the fleshy fruit.

FRUIT. Berrylike, persistent, succulent, formed by the coalescence of the flower scales, subglobose to short-oblong, 1/12–1/6 in. in diameter, dark blue, glaucous when ripe, skin thin, flesh sweet and resinous; seeds 1–2, ovate, acute, prominently ridged.

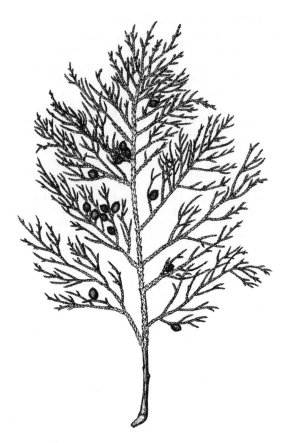

LEAVES. Minute, sessile, persistent, opposite, or in whorls of 3, acute or acuminate, dorsal surface with a conspicuous oblong gland; leaves sometimes of 2 kinds; either linear-subulate and sharp-pointed, or scalelike, ovate, imbricate and appressed.

TWIGS. Slender, flexuous or curved on the lower branches, young ones green, soon light reddish brown or eventually gray, the older leaves becoming brown, woody, and persistent.

BARK. On the older branches and trunk reddish brown, thin, separating into long fibrous strips.

WOOD. Dull red, sapwood lighter, close-grained, light, soft, fragrant, very durable.

RANGE. River swamps, stream and creek margins in low woods. Eastern and southeastern Texas and Louisiana; eastward to Georgia and Florida and northward to South Carolina.

REMARKS. The genus name, *Juniperus*, is the classical name. The species name, *silicicola*, refers to its growing in sandy soils. Also known as Red-cedar and Eastern Red-cedar. The tree is slow growing, long-lived, and very desirable for ornamental purposes. The wood is commercially important, but the supply is considerably diminished.

Southern Red-cedar is distinguished from Eastern Red-cedar by the former having a usually irregular-shaped crown and lower pendulous branches, by the much smaller fruit (1/12–1/6 in. in diameter), and by its growth in low wet grounds. However, some authors maintain that these differences are not distinct enough to merit a specific rank for it. Southern Red-cedar has been listed by some authors under the names of *J. barbadensis* L. and *J. lucayana* Britt.

Palm Family (Palmae)

Louisiana Palm

Sabal louisiana (Darby) Bomhard [A, B, C]

FIELD IDENTIFICATION. An arborescent palm often confused with *S. minor* when in juvenile form. The trunk averages 3–6 ft tall (rarely, to 18 ft), usually exhibiting three zones: (1) a region of roots at the base, but occasionally an additional root development occurs fairly high on the trunk, indicating some previous high water level; (2) a narrow girdle of grayish brown, rough bark; (3) a boot area below the leaf crown. Trunk diameter (bark only) rarely more than 27 in., and usually less.

FLOWERS. June–July, or even delayed until the following spring, borne in 4–6 spadices, stiff, erect; spathes 20 or more, long-pointed, tubular, overlapping, covering the length of the axis of the inflorescence, upper ones sterile, basal ones fertile; inflorescence thrice compound, some as long as 3 ft; some of the lower panicles may flower but the rest may be abortive.

Individual flowers white, sessile, 1/5–1/4 in. high, spirally placed above the rachillae at rather regular intervals, spaced several millimeters apart. Subtended by two unequal bracteoles, the base of the smaller one being partially enclosed by the larger; calyx about 1/12 in. high, cylindric and thick below, 3-angled, with 3 short, triangular, unequal, slightly carinate, thin, nerved lobes; corolla more or less united with the stamens into a short pseudotube at base; petals 3, broadly ovate, 1/8–1/7 in. high, ½ in. broad at base, thin, involute, minutely serrulate, thickened and hooded at apex, auricled at base, 5–7-nerved; stamens 6, the alternate shorter than the opposite that are adnate to the petals; filaments

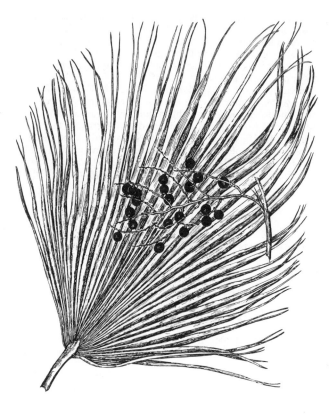

subulate-lanceolate, dorsiventrally flattened; anthers bright yellow, introrse, short-saggitate, 1/25 in. long, anther sacs somewhat unequal; pistil comprised of 3 carpels, 1/8–1/6 in. long, about 1/25 in. or more broad at the enlarged ovary base, stylar portion 3-angled, apex truncate.

FRUIT. Ripening in November, brown to black, suborbicular, averaging about 2/5 in. in diameter; seeds reddish brown, sublustrous, enclosed in a thin integument, micropyle lateral.

LEAVES. Palmate, comparatively thin, bluish green, attaining a width of 80 in.; rachis winged below and supporting the lower one-third of the blade, then deeply split into 2 halves beyond; segments 36–50, splitting the outer half or two-thirds of the blade, acuminate, rather stiff, the apices usually bifid and flaccid, margins of younger segments often with threadlike fibers; hastula flat, platelike, asymmetrical, averaging about 1½ in. long; petiole unarmed, longer than the blades, upper surface concave, lower surface rounded, margin very sharp and faintly denticulate toward the base; the two boot halves erect or ascending, persistent; an interesting character of this species is the peculiar collapse of the dying leaves at the juncture of the petiole and blade, giving a half-closed-umbrella effect.

RANGE. In Louisiana along Bayou Sauvage, north of Chef Road; Frenier Beach, west shore of Lake Pontchartrain; Bayou Bienvenue; Bayou Vermilion; Bayou des Allemands; east of Berwick Bay on bayous Black and Chacahoula, and south of it on Bayou Shaffer. In Texas a stand was discovered by the author containing about 20 plants, one with a trunk 18 ft in height. This stand is located 8 miles west of Brazoria on the Brazoria–Cedar Lane cutoff road; other locations of Texas stands are on the bottom lands of the Lavaca River west of Lolita; 4 miles south of Cleveland within sight of the bridge (U.S. Highway 59) that crosses the East Fork of the San Jacinto River; north of Rockport, eastern shore of Copano Bay; on the Blanco River south of Blanco; on Hog Bayou, about 8 miles south of Port Lavaca; isolated stands are also known from Alabama and Florida.

REMARKS. The genus name, *Sabal*, is of uncertain origin. The species name, *louisiana*, is for the state of Louisiana, where it is found in greatest abundance. This palm has long been unrecognized as a distinct species and has been linked historically with both *S. minor* and *S. palmetto*. Diverse opinions still exist as to its relationship.

Dwarf Palm

Sabal minor (Jacq.) Pers. [A, B, C]

FIELD IDENTIFICATION. A palm without a trunk, the leaves fanlike and arising in a crown from a subterranean rootstock.

FLOWERS. May–June, on the coast of the Gulf of Mexico, spadix 2–8 ft high from a long spathe, erect or ascending; secondary flowering panicles 4–11 in. long from sheaths 1–5 in. long which are split on one side, striate and acuminate; ultimate flowering divisions 4–20, 3–6 in. long; flowers small, numerous, perfect, sessile or nearly so, 2/16–3/16 in. long, subtended by one or more minute bracts; calyx-lobes 3, lobes unequal, about 1/25 in. long, rounded; petals 3, erect, white, elliptic, concave, apex obtuse or rounded, about 1/12 in. long; stamens 6 (sometimes fewer); filaments flattened, broadened at base and adnate to the corolla, slightly longer than the petals; anthers yellow, ovate-saggitate, about 1/25 in.; pistil included, columnar, stigma small and truncate; gynoecium of 3 carpels, usually developing only one.

FRUIT. Drupe on a peduncle ⅛ in. long or less, subglobose, slightly broader than long, ¼–⅓ in. in diameter, black, remnants of the short style basal; seed coat thin and membranous; seed solitary, white, lustrous, hard, bony, flattened at base.

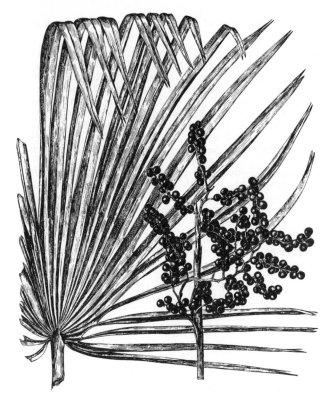

LEAVES. Clustered from the base, flabellate (fanlike), suborbicular, 2–8 ft in diameter, pale green or glaucous; segments shallowly cleft at apex, almost as long as the leaf or much shorter, mostly entire on the margin or more rarely with filiferous threads, midribs very short, petioles shorter than the blades, ligules ⅜–¾ in.

RANGE. Wet alluvial ground in Texas and Louisiana; north to Oklahoma, Arkansas, and North Carolina. Abundant in the river bottoms and swamps of southern Louisiana, and in Texas west to the valley of the Colorado River.

REMARKS. The genus name, *Sabal*, is of obscure meaning, and the species name, *minor*, refers to this palm's dwarf, or trunkless, stature. Also known locally under the names of Dwarf Palmetto, Blue Palm, Blue Stem, and Swamp Palm. It is occasionally browsed by cattle. Although rather attractive, it is usually not cultivated for ornament.

Much botanical controversy has been waged concerning the relationship between the Dwarf Palm and the Louisiana Palm, *S. louisiana* (Darby) Bomhard. For a discussion of this problem the reader may refer to the description of the Louisiana Palm.

Lily Family (Liliaceae)

Aloe Yucca

Yucca aloifolia L. [A, B, C]

FIELD IDENTIFICATION. A plant to 10 ft, with a simple or
branched stem.

FLOWERS. In a stout, conic, showy, white panicle 1–1½ ft
high and 6–10 in. wide; panicle usually set ¼–½ within
the upper leaves; peduncles and pedicels minutely puberulent or glabrous; individual flower pedicels ½–1 in. long,
mostly flexed downward; sheathing bracts ¼–½ in. long,
lanceolate-ovate, acuminate; mature flowers not spreading,
petals 3 and sepals 3, approximately the same color, shape,
and size, semiconcave, oblong-elliptic, apex acute or obtuse,
base slightly rounded or cuneate, many-veined, waxy white,
sometimes purplish at base, 1–1¼ in. long, ⅓–½ in. wide;

pistil with lower style stout, columnar, greenish, ½–¾ in. long, of 3 united carpels; stigmatic portion about ⅛ in. long, whitish, 3-angled; stamens 6, erect or nearly so, surrounding the pistil, about ½ in. long, white, flattened, puberulent; anther sessile, yellow, falcate, 1/25–1/16 in. long.

FRUIT. Capsule 1½–2 in. long, ¾–1 in. wide, oblong or slightly larger toward the apex, apex abruptly obtuse or rounded, 3-parted by broad, flat troughs between the valves, glabrous, light green at first, black to purplish at maturity, pulpy, indehiscent.

LEAVES. Daggerlike, closely spiraled, stiff, crowded, spreading, deflexed and usually deciduous below but sometimes persistent, flattened or slightly concave, light green, 12–20 in. long, 1–1½ in. wide; widest at the middle or slightly below; gradually narrowed toward the apex and base; apex stiff, ending in a stiff, sharp, dark brown spine; leaf margin sharp with minute, erose teeth.

STEMS. Simple or branched, usually 3–6 ft high, rarely to 10 ft, leaves on upper stems spreading and stiff, on older plants lower leaves persistent, but reflexed and brown.

RANGE. Usually on sand dunes or shell mounds close to the coast. Louisiana; east to Florida, and north to Virginia. Also in Mexico and the West Indies. Escaped from cultivation on the Texas coast.

REMARKS. Yuca (*Yucca*) is the native Haitian name for the *Manihot* genus, erroneously applied to this group of plants. The species name, *aloifolia*, refers to the *Aloe*-like leaves.

Propagation of Aloe Yucca may be made from seeds, offsets, or cuttings from stems or rhizomes. The leaves were used in pioneer days for string or twine to hang up cured meats.

Trecul Yucca

Yucca treculeana Carr. [B, C]

FIELD IDENTIFICATION. Tree 5–25 ft, with a simple trunk or with a few stout spreading branches at the top, crowned by large symmetrical heads of radiating sharp-pointed leaves. The plant sometimes occurs as a thicket-forming shrub.

FLOWERS. Maturing December–April, borne in a large dense, showy glabrous or puberulous panicle 1½–4 ft long; pedicels ½–3 in.; bracts ovate to lanceolate, often spinescent at apex, varying from 1 in. at base of pedicels to 1 ft at base of main stem, becoming dry, thin, and papery; flowers creamy white, rather globose, later expanding broadly, the 6 segments ovate to ovate-lanceolate, acute to acuminate at apex, waxy, brittle, thin, 1–2 in. long; stamens 6, filaments slightly papillose above, usually finely and shortly pubescent below, about as long as the pistil; pistil ¾–1⅓ in. long, ovary

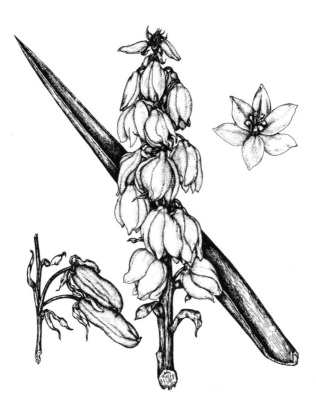

slender and oblong-cylindric; style very short (1/8–2/5 in.); stigmas 3, abruptly spreading, nearly horizontal at anthesis, deeply lobed.

FRUIT. Capsule indehiscent, 2–4½ in. long, about 1 in. thick, reddish brown or later black, oblong-cylindric, rather abruptly contracted at the acute or acuminate apex, surfaces often with fissures or deeply cleft, filaments and perianth often persisting, heavy and thick-walled, 3-celled, flesh sweetish and succulent; seeds numerous, flat about 1/16 in. thick, 1/8–¼ in. broad, with a narrow border to the rim.

LEAVES. In large radiating clusters, bluish green, length 2½–4 ft, 1–3½ in. wide, usually straight, concavo-convex, apex acute to short-acuminate, with a brown or black, short, sharp spine, margin entire, rigid, inner surface rather smooth, outer surface scabrous to the touch; dead leaves hanging below the crown and long-persistent.

BARK. Dark reddish brown, on older trunks ¼–½ in. thick, with shallow or deep irregular fissures. The intervening ridges broken into thin oblong plates with small appressed scales.

WOOD. Light brown, spongy, fibrous, heavy, not easily cut.

RANGE. Well-drained hillsides, chaparral regions, or open flats near the Gulf of Mexico. From the shores of Matagorda Bay, Texas, westward and southward along the coast to Brownsville. From San Antonio in Bexar County, westward to the Rio Grande and Pecos River. In Mexico in Nuevo León, Tamaulipas, Durango, and Coahuila.

REMARKS. The genus name, *Yucca*, is from a native Haitian name. The species name, *treculeana*, is in honor of A. A. L. Trecul (1818–1896), who in 1850 took the plant to France from Texas. Also known under the vernacular names of Spanish Dagger, Spanish Bayonet, Don Quixote Lance, Pita, Palma Pita, Palma de Dátiles, and Palma Loca. The plant is a handsome ornamental for use in central or coastal Texas or Louisiana and is sometimes grown in southern Europe. The leaves are very tough and were used in frontier days for making twine or rope. The blossoms were made into pickles or cooked like cabbage. The spines on the leaves are used by the Mexican people to jab the wound of a snake bite and induce bleeding. In this manner much of the poison is carried away. The Chihuahua Indians fermented the fruit of various species of *Yucca* to make an intoxicating beverage. The trunks are sometimes used for posts, and the leaves for thatch, in making huts. It is also reported that the seeds have purgative qualities.

Moundlily Yucca

Yucca gloriosa L. [A, B, C]

FIELD IDENTIFICATION. A low caespitose, simple or few-branched, treelike dune plant, 6–15 ft and 4–6 in. in diameter, usually with dead leaves to the base.

FLOWERS. In late summer to autumn, panicles showy, narrow, on scapelike simple stalks 2–4 ft long; flowers pendulous, large, perfect, white or occasionally purplish; sepals and petals 3 each, oblong-lanceolate, apex obtuse or acute, 1½–2 in. long, slightly united at base, deciduous; stamens 6, hypogynous, about as long as the ovary; ovary slightly lobed, 6-sided, with 3 spreading stigmatic lobes, 3-celled, ovules numerous.

FRUIT. Stipe short and stout; capsule pendulous, 2–3¼ in. long, about 1 in. in diameter, oblong-ovoid, 6-ribbed, constricted at or near the middle, cuspidate; outer coat black, thin and leathery, indehiscent, pulpy; seeds ¼–⅓ in. long, lustrous, black, thin, flattened, slightly margined.

LEAVES. Numerous, stiff, straight, firm, erect, spreading, broadly linear, apex rigidly spine-tipped, base somewhat constricted, gradually narrowed upward, nearly flat or concave near apex, margin with a few minute teeth when young and

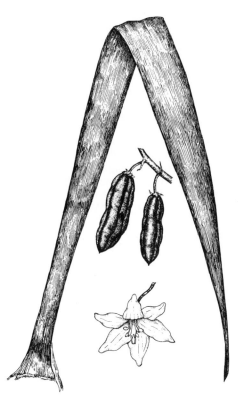

a few threads when old, glaucous green, sometimes reddish-tinged.

RANGE. On coastal dunes, known from Breton Island, Louisiana, and Mississippi. Also cultivated in its many forms in south Texas and other Gulf Coast states. Persistent about old gardens and waste places. Probably only indigenous as a species on the coastal dunes of South Carolina, Georgia, and northeastern Florida.

REMARKS. The genus name, *Yucca*, is from a native Haitian name. The species name, *gloriosa*, refers to the beauty of the flowers. Known also under the names of Spanish Bayonet and Sea Island Yucca.

Curve-leaf Yucca

Yucca recurvifolia Salisb. [A, B, C]

FIELD IDENTIFICATION. Plant with a leafy stem 3–6 ft, simple or branched.

FLOWERS. Borne in a narrow panicle which is elevated only slightly above the leaves on a scapelike stem; perianth 6-parted; calyx of 3 white or greenish sepals; corolla of 3 similar petals; stamens 6, shorter than the perianth, filaments enlarged above, anthers sagittate; gynoecium of 3 united carpels; style stout and shouldered; ovules numerous in the cavity of each carpel.

FRUIT. Capsule oblong, indehiscent, erect, 6-ribbed or -winged (wings mostly infolded over the nectarial grooves), 1–1¾ in. long; seeds numerous, thin, margined, dull, about ¼–⅓ in. long, albumen not ruminated.

LEAVES. Numerous, crowded, closely alternate, green, pliable, recurved, surface nearly plane, often slightly plicate above, about 2 in. wide, margin narrowly yellow or brown, often with a few microscopic teeth, at maturity entire or slightly filiferous.

RANGE. Usually in sandy soil of the Gulf Coast plain from eastern Louisiana eastward to Florida and Georgia.

REMARKS. The genus name, *Yucca*, is an old Haitian name, probably incorrectly applied to this plant. The species name, *recurvifolia*, refers to the recurved, flaccid leaves. The plant may be propagated from seeds, offsets, stem, or rhizome cuttings.

Willow Family (Salicaceae)

White Poplar

Populus alba L. [A, B, C]

FIELD IDENTIFICATION. Tree attaining a height of 100 ft, with a trunk diameter of 3–4 ft. Sometimes spreading by root-suckers to form thickets in old fields or about abandoned dwelling sites. Recognized by the conspicuous white-tomentose undersurface of the leaves.

FLOWERS. Borne in pendulous catkins, pistillate about 2 in., slender, stigmas 2, each deeply 2-parted; staminate 1½–4 in.; scales dentate, fringed with long hairs; stamens 6–10 (usually about 8).

FRUIT. Capsule narrowly ovoid, 1/8–1/5 in. long, tomentose, 2-valved; seeds minute, numerous, with a tuft of long silky, white hairs.

LEAVES. Simple, alternate, rather variable, on vigorous shoots palmately 3–5-lobed, the lobes also coarsely toothed or with additional small lobes, base rounded to subcordate, blades

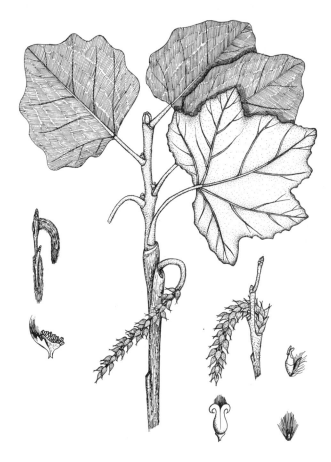

2⅓–5 in. long, upper surface dark green, lower surfaces
conspicuously white-tomentose; on older branches leaves
often smaller, ovate to elliptic-oblong; margin sinuate-
dentate; petioles terete, densely tomentose; young twigs and
branches also white-tomentose.

BARK. Greenish gray to white, usually smooth on branches or
young trunks, toward the base of old trunks roughened into
firm dark ridges.

WOOD. Reddish to yellowish, sapwood nearly white, tough
but light and soft.

RANGE. Adapted to many soil types, on dry, well-drained
sites in the sun. Grown for ornament in Texas, New Mexico,
Oklahoma, Arkansas, Louisiana, and more or less throughout
the United States. A native of central and southern Europe
to western Siberia and central Asia.

REMARKS. The genus name, *Populus*, is the ancient Latin name, and the species name, *alba*, refers to the white under-surface of the leaves. The tree is also known under the vernacular name of Abele. White Poplar has long been grown for ornament. It is very conspicuous because of the contrasting white and green leaf surfaces. However, the white under-surfaces catch soot and dust easily and become unsightly in some localities. The tree grows rapidly, transplants easily, prunes well, and has few insects or fungus pests, but is short-lived.

Black Poplar

Populus nigra var. *italica* Du Roi [A, B, C]

FIELD IDENTIFICATION. A tree 40–80 ft high with a very narrow, spirelike crown and many erect branches and twigs. The short, ridged, buttressed trunk is 2–3½ ft in diameter. Bark thick and gray-brown, or almost black on old trunks, deeply and irregularly furrowed.

FLOWERS. Borne in April–May before the leaves and dioecious; the staminate in sessile, dark red cylindrical catkins about 3 in. long; pistillate catkins shorter, and the staminate trees more numerous than the pistillate. Calyx none; corolla none; stamens 20–30 with white filaments and purple anthers; stigmas 2, bifid.

FRUIT. Pistillate catkins to 6 in. long in fruit.

LEAVES. Simple, alternate, 2–3¾ in. long, and somewhat broader than long; shape broad-deltoid; apices abruptly acuminate; margin finely but bluntly crenate-serrate; texture thick and firm; upper surface dark green and lustrous; lower surface paler; golden yellow in autumn. Petioles slender, laterally compressed, ½ in. long.

TWIGS. Slender, long, flexible, glabrous, shining yellow, becoming gray. Pith rather small, 5-angled, brownish. Terminal bud conical, slightly angled, taper-pointed, glutinous, about ⅓ in. long. Lateral buds smaller, appressed. Leaf scars broad; bundle scars 3, sometimes compound; stipule scars present.

RANGE. A native of Europe and West Asia. Cultivated for many years in various countries.

REMARKS. The genus name, *Populus*, is the classical name. The species name, *nigra*, is for the blackish trunk of old trees. The variety name, *italica*, refers to its growth in Italy on the Plains of Lombardy. Rows of these tall slender trees are conspicuous and effective in formal plantings. It is rapid growing and is sometimes used for windbreaks. The wood is light, soft, easily worked, not likely to splinter, weak,

not durable, light red-brown, with thick, nearly white sap-wood.

Eastern Cottonwood

Populus deltoides Marsh. [A, B, C]

FIELD IDENTIFICATION. Tree to 100 ft high and 8 ft in diameter. The trunk is often rather short, the branches massive, the top rounded, and the root system spreading and shallow.

FLOWERS. February–May, borne in separate staminate and pistillate catkins; staminate catkins densely flowered, 1½–2 in. long, ½–¾ in. wide, disk oblique and revolute; stamens 30–60, filaments short, anthers large and red; pistillate catkins at first 3–3½ in. long, loosely flowered; bracts brown,

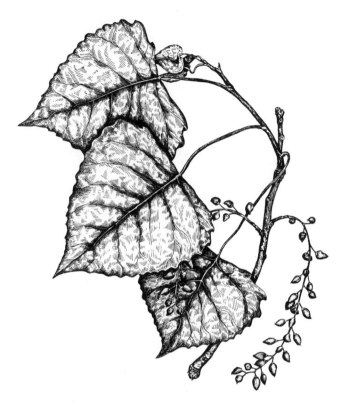

glabrous, apex fimbriate; disk ovoid, obtuse, enclosing about one-third of ovary, ovary sessile, style short, stigmas 2–4, large, spreading, laciniately lobed.

FRUIT. Ripening May–June, racemose, 8–12 in. long at maturity, capsules on slender pedicels 1/8–2/5 in., ovoid to conical, acute, about ¼ in. long, 1-celled, 3–4-valved; seeds numerous, small, brown, oblong-obovoid, buoyant with cottony hairs when the capsule ruptures. The minimum seed-bearing age about 10 years and maximum about 125. The seed averages 10–30 seeds per capsule, with an average of 3,032,000 seeds per lb. The commercial purity is about 40 percent, with a soundness of 95 percent. Germination averages 60–90 percent.

LEAVES. Simple, alternate, deciduous, broadly deltoid-ovate, margin crenate-serrate, apex abruptly acute or acuminate, base truncate to heart-shaped or abruptly cuneate, blades 3–7 in. long, about as broad; upper surface light green, glabrous, lustrous, main vein stout, yellow to reddish; lower surface paler and glabrous with primary veins conspicuous; petiole smooth and glabrous, flattened, stipules linear.

TWIGS. Yellowish to brown or gray, stout, angular, lenticels prominent; buds ovoid, acute, resinous, brown, about ½ in. long or less, laterals much flattened; leaf scars triangular or lunate, with 3 bundle marks, pith star-shaped.

BARK. Thin and smooth on young branches or trunks, green to yellow; older trunks gray to almost black with flattened, confluent broad ridges broken into closely appressed scales.

WOOD. Dark brown, sapwood white, weak, soft, weighing about 24 lb per cu ft, moderately weak in bending, weak in endwise compression, low in shock resistance, moderately easy to work with tools, takes paint well, easy to glue, warps and shrinks considerably, low in durability, below average in ability to stay in place, nails easily, does not split easily.

RANGE. Eastern Cottonwood is found in rich, moist soil, mostly along streams. It and its varieties occur over practically the entire United States east of the Rocky Mountains. Texas, New Mexico, Oklahoma, Arkansas, and Louisiana; eastward to Florida and northward into Canada.

REMARKS. The genus name, *Populus*, is the ancient name given by Pliny, and the species name, *deltoides*, refers to the triangular shape of the leaf. Other vernacular names are Carolina Poplar, Necklace Poplar, Water Poplar, Southern Cottonwood, Yellow Cottonwood, and Alamo. Alamo is the Spanish name for the tree, and was also the name given the famous Texas fort which was surrounded by the trees. "Remember the Alamo" was the battle slogan of the Texas-Mexico War. The tree is often planted for ornament and for erosion control in dune-fixing. The air-borne cottony seeds are undesirable at fruiting season. The leaves flutter rapidly and make a rustling sound in the wind because of the flexible flattened petiole. The tree sprouts from the stumps and roots, is easily storm damaged, is easily fire damaged when young, is much attacked by fungi, and grows rapidly. The foliage is known to be browsed by cattle, black-tailed deer, and cottontail. The seeds are eaten by rose-breasted grosbeak and evening grosbeak. The wood is used for paper pulp, cases and crates, tubs and pails, excelsior, veneer for plywood, musical instruments, dairy and poultry supplies, laundry appliances, and fuel.

Gulf Black Willow

Salix nigra Marsh. [A, B, C]

FIELD IDENTIFICATION. A rapidly growing tree sometimes attaining a height of 125 ft.

FLOWERS. April–May, dioecious, borne in many-flowered catkins preceding the leaves or with them; staminate catkins

cylindrical, slender, 1–2 in. long; bracts obtuse, yellow, hairy below; stamens 3–7, filaments hairy below, anthers yellow; pistillate catkins 1½–3 in. long; bracts deciduous; pistil solitary, style short, the 2 stigmas thickened.

FRUIT. May–June, borne on slender spreading pedicels, capsule light brown, conic-ovoid, sharp-pointed, glabrous, ¼–⅛ in. long, splitting into two valves; seeds minute, green, pilose with long hairs.

LEAVES. Simple, alternate, deciduous, blades 3–6 in. long, ¼–¾ in. wide, narrowly lanceolate; apex long-attenuate and sometimes falcate; base rounded, acute; margin finely glandular-serrate; green above and paler below, glabrous or puberulent along the veins, or pubescent when young; petiole short, puberulent; stipules variable, either large, persistent, semicordate, pointed, and foliaceous, or small, ovate, and deciduous.

TWIGS. Slender, brittle, reddish brown.

BARK. Light brown to black, rough, deeply fissured, ridges dividing into thick shaggy scales, rich in tannin.

WOOD. Light brown, soft, light, weak, not durable, weighing 27 lb per cu ft.

RANGE. In wet soil, Texas, Louisiana, Oklahoma, and Arkansas. Reaching its largest size on the banks of the Brazos, San Bernard, and Colorado rivers in Texas; east to North and South Carolina, north to New Brunswick, and west to North Dakota.

REMARKS. The genus name, *Salix*, is the classical Latin name, and the species name, *nigra*, refers to the black bark. Vernacular names are Scythe-leaved Willow, Swamp Willow, and Pussy Willow. The bark was formerly used as a home remedy for fever ailments. The wood is used for artificial limbs, charcoal, toys, doors, fuel, cheap furniture, boxwood, and excelsior.

Sand-bar Willow

Salix interior Rowlee [A, B, C]

FIELD IDENTIFICATION. A slender, upright shrub forming thickets by stolons, or a small tree to 30 ft.

FLOWERS. Dioecious, April–May on leafy twigs. Staminate and pistillate catkins slender, cylindric, linear, borne on different plants; staminate catkins terminal or axillary, dense, ¾–2 in. long, about ⅓–⅜ in. broad; stamens 2, exserted, filaments distinct, hairy at base; pistillate catkins loosely flowered, 2–3 in. long and about ¼ in. broad; scales light yellow, hairy, ovate to obovate, entire or erose; ovary short-stalked, oblong-cylindric, silky-hairy when young, less hairy or glabrous later; stigmas 2, subsessile, lobed; young capsule with long white silky hairs.

FRUIT. Capsule matures in April, sessile or short-peduncled, narrowly ovoid-conic, gradually narrowed to a blunt apex, 1/6–1/4 in. long, brownish, glabrous or villous, 1-celled, splitting into 2 reflexed valves; seeds minute, attached to long white hairs, buoyant in the wind.

LEAVES. Deciduous, alternate, blades 2–6 in. long, ⅛–⅓ in. wide, linear-lanceolate, sometimes falcate, thin, apex acuminate, base gradually narrowed into a short petiole, margin with remote, denticulate, glandular teeth, main vein prominent; upper surface dark green and glabrous or puberulent along the main vein; paler and pubescent beneath; petioles 1/8–3/16 in., pubescent; stipules small or absent. Young leaves silky-hairy beneath.

TWIGS. Slender, erect, green to brown or red, glabrous or puberulent and sometimes glaucescent.

BARK. Green to gray or brown, smooth; on older trunks furrowed and broken into closely appressed scales; lenticels sometimes large and abundant.

WOOD. Soft, light, reddish brown, sapwood pale brown, weighing 31 lb per cu ft, little used except for fuel or charcoal.

RANGE. The species is found in alluvial soil along streams and lakes over a wide area; Texas and Louisiana coast, and north through Arkansas and Oklahoma to Canada and Alaska. Also in northern Mexico in the states of Nuevo León, Tamaulipas, and Coahuila.

REMARKS. The genus name, *Salix*, is the classical Latin name, and the species name, *interior*, refers to the plant's inland distribution along water courses. It was formerly listed under the scientific names of *S. longifolia* Muehl. and *S. fluviatilis* Sarg. Known under the vernacular names of Riverbank Willow, Osier Willow, Shrub Willow, Long-leaf Willow, Narrow-leaf Willow, Red Willow, and White Willow.

Babylon Weeping Willow

Salix babylonica L. [A, B, C]

FIELD IDENTIFICATION. Cultivated tree attaining a height of 50 ft. The drooping twigs give the tree its name.

FLOWERS. April–May, catkins small, appearing on short lateral leafy branches; staminate catkins to 1⅝ in. long and ¼–⅓ in. wide on peduncles ⅜–⅝ in. long (pistillate catkins smaller); bracts ovate-lanceolate, yellowish, obtuse, deciduous; stamens 3–5, free, pubescent at base; style almost none.

FRUIT. Capsule ovoid-conic, sessile or nearly so, glabrous, style almost absent, stigmas minute.

LEAVES. Alternate, narrowly lanceolate, apex long-acuminate, base narrowed, margin serrulate, at first somewhat silky pubescent, glabrous with maturity, lower surface glaucous, blade length 3–7 in., width ¼–½ in., sometimes curling; stipules wanting or if present lanceolate and 1/12–1/3 in. long.

TWIGS. Slender, glabrous, elongate, drooping, green at first, later yellowish or brownish.

RANGE. Grows best in damp sandy soils near water courses. In Texas, Arkansas, Oklahoma, and Louisiana; eastward to

Florida, northward to Virginia and Connecticut, and westward to Michigan. A native of north China, cultivated throughout North America below an altitude of 3,500 feet.

REMARKS. The genus name, *Salix*, is the classical name. The species name, *babylonica*, refers to its once-presumed west Asiatic origin, but this is a misnomer because it is a native of China.

The tree of the biblical reference (Psalms 127:1–2) is now known to be the willowlike Euphrates Poplar, *Populus euphratica* Oliv. Babylon Weeping Willow sometimes escapes cultivation by the distribution of its twigs. It is known as the Garb Willow, Napoleon Willow, and Weeping Willow.

Coastal Plain Willow

Salix caroliniana Michx. [A]

FIELD IDENTIFICATION. Shrub or small tree to 30 ft, and 18 in. in diameter. Branches spreading or drooping to form an open irregular crown. Closely related to Black Willow, *S. nigra* Marsh, and known to hybridize with it. However, Black Willow leaves are green beneath and Coastal Plain Willow leaves are very glaucous.

FLOWERS. May–June, buds single-scaled, expanding with the leaves; catkins terminal, slender, lax, narrow-cylindric, to 4 in. long; scales yellow, ovate to obovate, apex rounded or obtuse, densely villose-pubescent; glands of staminate flowers lobulate or forming a false disk; stamens 3–12, exserted, separate, filaments hairy at base, anthers yellow; gland of pistillate flower clasping the base of the pedicel; ovary stipitate, ovoid-conic, acute; style short, 2-lobed.

FRUIT. Capsule ovoid-conic, 1/6–1/4 in. long, granular-roughened, abruptly long-pointed, remnants of the 2 persistent stigmatic lobes almost sessile, base with pedicel to ¼ in.; seeds numerous, silky-hairy.

LEAVES. Involute in the bud, simple, alternate, deciduous, length 2–7 in., width ⅜–1⅓ in., lanceolate to lanceolate-ovate, sometimes falcate, apex acuminate or acute, base gradually narrowed on young leaves, on older ones often rounded; upper surface bright green and glabrous; lower surface whitened or glaucous, somewhat puberulent when young, glabrous later, veins yellowish, delicate, margin finely serrate; petioles ⅛–½ in. long, densely hairy, glandless; stipules usually small on normal leaves, on vigorous shoots large (to ¾ in. wide), foliaceous, conspicuous, ovate to reniform, mostly serrate above the middle.

TWIGS. Slender, yellowish to reddish brown or grayish, more or less pubescent, eventually glabrous; winter buds small, brown, lustrous.

BARK. Reddish brown to gray, ridges broad, fissures deep, conspicuously checkered, breaking into closely appressed scales.

WOOD. Dark reddish brown, sapwood nearly white, light, soft, not strong.

RANGE. Mostly along gravelly banks and shores of streams or lakes or in low woods. Texas, western Arkansas, eastern Oklahoma, and Louisiana; east to Florida, north to Maryland, and west to Kansas.

REMARKS. The genus name, *Salix*, is the classical Latin name, and the species name, *caroliniana*, refers to the states of Carolina. Also known under the vernacular names of Ward Willow and Carolina Willow. The scientific terminology of this willow has been very confused. The following names have been applied from time to time: *S. occidentalis* Bosc. *ex* Koch, *S. longipes* Shuttl., *S. nigra* var. *wardii* Bebb, *S. occidentalis* var. *longipes* (Anderss.) Bebb., *S. wardii* Bebb, *S. marginata* Wimm. *ex* Small, *S. amphibia* Small, *S. longipes* var. *venulosa* (Anderss.) Schneid., *S. longipes* var. *wardii* (Bebb) Schneid., *S. harbisonii* Schneid., *S. chapmanii* Small, and *S. floridana* Chapm.

Brittle Willow

Salix fragilis L. [A]

FIELD IDENTIFICATION. An introduced, rapid-growing tree
40–90 ft tall and 3 ft in trunk diameter, but usually smaller.
The brown branches obliquely ascending.

FLOWERS. Aments appearing with the leaves, slender, lax,
1–3 in. long; 1/3–2/5 in. wide; on leafy peduncles 1/3–1 1/4
or 2 in. long, bearing 2–5 small leaves. Flower scales oblong,
greenish yellow, crisp-villous, deciduous. The staminate tree
is reported to be rare in America.

FRUIT. Capsules narrowly conic, 2-valved, glabrous, 1/6–1/5
in. long; pedicels about 1/25 in. long; styles about 1/35 in.
long; stigmas short, notched. The seed is often sterile.

LEAVES. Simple, alternate, large, narrowly lanceolate to
lanceolate; 3–7 in. long; 3/4–3 2/5 in. wide; apices long-
acuminate; margin finely glandular-serrate; upper surface

glabrous and dark green; lower surface glaucescent or glaucous, glabrous at maturity. Petioles 1/3–2/5 in. long, usually with 2 glands at base of blade.

TWIGS. Green to dark red or brown to gray later, glabrous, very brittle at base and deciduous in winds. Stipules absent, or small, semicordate, and early deciduous. Buds medium size and pointed.

RANGE. Native of Europe and introduced into America in early times for ornament, hedges, shade, and gunpowder charcoal. It frequently escapes cultivation in the east, and some are found in northeast Texas.

REMARKS. The genus name, *Salix*, is an ancient name. The species name, *fragilis*, refers to the brittle character of the twigs. It is reported that a stake cut from a tree and driven into the ground will soon establish itself. *S. fragilis* var. *decipiens* is a variety with yellow twigs, buds black in winter, and leaves smaller and brighter green.

Wax-myrtle Family (Myricaceae)

Southern Wax-myrtle

Myrica cerifera L. [A, B, C]

FIELD IDENTIFICATION. Crooked evergreen shrub, but sometimes a tree to 40 ft.

FLOWERS. Borne March–April, with staminate and pistillate catkins on different plants. Staminate catkins oblong, cylindric, ¼–¾ in.; scales acute, ovate and ciliate; stamens 2–8, yellow, anthers 2-celled, reddish yellow; pistillate catkins short, ovoid; ovary 2–4-scaled at base; stigmas 2, slender and spreading.

FRUIT. Drupe maturing September–October, spikes short; bracts deciduous; drupes persistent, about ⅛ in., globose, light green, covered with granules of bluish white wax; seed pale, minute, solitary.

LEAVES. Simple, alternate, tardily deciduous; 1½–5 in. long, ¼–¾ in. wide, oblanceolate to elliptic, apex acute or rounded, cuneate or narrowed at base and decurrent on the short stout petiole, margin entire or coarsely serrate above the middle, shining above, resinous with orange-colored glands beneath, aromatic when crushed.

TWIGS. Reddish brown to gray, young parts with early-deciduous orange-colored glands.

BARK. Gray, or grayish green, smooth, compact, astringent.

WOOD. Light, brittle, soft, fine-grained, dark brown, sapwood lighter, weighing 35 lb per cu ft.

RANGE. Sandy swamps or low acid prairies. Eastern Texas, Oklahoma, Arkansas, and Louisiana; eastward to Florida and north to New Jersey.

REMARKS. The genus name, *Myrica*, is the ancient name of the tamarisk, and the species name, *cerifera*, refers to the waxy fruit. Vernacular names are Waxberry, Spice-bush, Candleberry, Bayberry, Sweet-oak, and Tallow-shrub. The fruit is eaten by about 40 species of birds, especially bob-white quail and turkey. It was first cultivated in 1699, and makes a desirable ornamental. Candles were formerly made by boiling the waxy blue berries. The bark and leaves are reputed to have medicinal properties. Southern Wax-myrtle is closely related to the Dwarf Wax-myrtle, *M. pusilla*, which is smaller and spreads by underground runners.

Bayberry Wax-myrtle

Myrica pensylvanica Lois. [A]

FIELD IDENTIFICATION. Half-evergreen, divaricately branched shrub to 9 ft.

FLOWERS. Dioecious, the catkins appearing after the leaves; staminate catkins ¼–¾ in., oblong-cylindric; stamens 2–4 on short filaments about 1/25 in., anthers erect, 2-celled, base of stamens attached to a hairy, ovate, acute or rounded bract about 1/16 in.; pistillate catkins axillary, short-oblong, smaller than the staminate catkins, not bristly, bracts ovate and acute.

FRUIT. Drupe persistent, globose, about ¼ in. in diameter, waxy-granular, white, resinous, in crowded clusters.

LEAVES. Alternate, half-evergreen, blades 2–4 in. long, ½–1½ in. broad; oblong, oblanceolate, elliptic or lanceolate, generally of broad type; margin mostly entire, slightly revolute, occasionally with a few low, coarse, remote teeth near the apex; apex obtuse, acute or rounded; base gradually narrowed; young leaves with white hairs above and below; older leaves dark green and semilustrous above, glabrous or

finely pubescent along the veins; lower surface pale and dull green, inconspicuously white-hairy along the veins with minute, scattered, brown, peltate scales (scales more noticeable under magnification); leaves not conspicuously reduced in size toward branch tips (as in *M. cerifera*); petioles 1/5–1/2 in.

TWIGS. Gray, stout, glabrous, somewhat glandular-scaly.

BARK. Grayish brown, smooth, tight.

RANGE. Usually in sandy, boggy soils. East Texas and Louisiana; eastward to Florida, north to Connecticut and Pennsylvania, and on the shores of the Great Lakes. Rare in east Texas, specimens collected in Angelina County State Park at Boykin Springs, also on the banks of the San Jacinto River near Humble, Texas.

REMARKS. The genus name, *Myrica*, is the ancient name of the tamarisk, and the species name, *pensylvanica*, refers to the state of Pennsylvania, where it grows abundantly. Vernacular names in use are Waxberry, Tallow Bayberry, Small Waxberry, Northern Bayberry, Tallow-shrub, Swamp Candleberry, Candlewood, Candle-tree, and Tallow-tree.

Bayberry Wax-myrtle has some value for erosion control in dry, sterile soil. However, it is most widely known as a source of bayberry wax. The wax occurs in fine granules on the white fruit and is obtained by steeping the fruit in boiling water and skimming off the wax for candlemaking. The wax is also used for the manufacture of soap in Europe. It contains a substance known as "palmitin." The leaves and berries are sometimes substituted for bay leaves in flavoring stews and soups.

The seeds of Bayberry Wax-myrtle number about 55,500 seeds per lb. They are known to be eaten by about 40 species of birds, particularly by the ruffed grouse and bobwhite quail.

Corkwood Family (Leitneriaceae)

Corkwood

Leitneria floridana Chapm. [B]

FIELD IDENTIFICATION. Swamp-loving shrub or tree attaining a height of 20 ft.

FLOWERS. Dioecious, staminate catkins clustered, many-flowered, 1–2 in. long; stamens 3–12, subtended by triangular to ovate, scalelike bracts; filaments incurved, slender, anthers oblong, 2-celled; pistillate catkins few-flowered,

shorter than the staminate; pistil surrounded by 3–4
glandular-fringed bractlets; style flattened, recurved, inwardly stigmatic; ovary pubescent, 1-celled, ovule solitary.

FRUIT. In clusters of 2–4, flattened, about ¾ in. long, ¼–⅓
in. wide, oblong, pointed at apex, rounded or acute at base,
rugose, reticulate, dry, brown; seed light brown, flattened.

LEAVES. Alternate, entire, firm, oblong, or elliptic-lanceolate,
apically acute, obtuse or acuminate, basally narrowed, blades
3–6 in. long, 1–3 in. wide, when young pubescent above and
densely tomentose below, when mature bright green, glabrous or pubescent above, villose-pubescent below; petioles
⅓–1¼ in. long, villose-pubescent.

BARK. Gray to brown, ridges narrow, fissures shallow.

TWIGS. Reddish brown to gray, glabrous, finely furrowed,
lenticels numerous, leaf scars semilunate.

WOOD. Pale yellow, soft, close-grained, exceedingly light, about 12½ lb per cu ft.

RANGE. Rare in Texas. Reported from Velasco and West Columbia. Also on railroad embankments in the vicinity of Port Arthur and High Island. Eastward to Florida and north to Georgia and Missouri.

REMARKS. The genus name, *Leitneria*, is in honor of the German naturalist E. F. Leitner, and the species name, *floridana*, refers to the early so-called Floridian Provinces of the southeastern states. The exceedingly light wood is used to float fishing nets.

Walnut Family (Juglandaceae)

Eastern Black Walnut

Juglans nigra L. [A, B, C]

FIELD IDENTIFICATION. Tree to 125 ft with a rounded crown.

FLOWERS. May–June, staminate and pistillate flowers on same tree; staminate catkins 2–5 in. long, stout, stamens 20–30, sessile, calyx 6-lobed, lobes oval and pubescent; bracts triangular, brown-tomentose; pistillate flowers in 2–5 flowered spikes, about ¼ in. long; stigmas 2, plumose, yellowish green; style short on a subglobose ovary; calyx-lobes acute, ovate, green, pubescent.

FRUIT. Ripening September–October, solitary or clustered, subglobose; husk yellowish green, thick, papillose, indehiscent, 1½–2½ in. in diameter; nutshell hard and bony; nut dark brown to black, compressed, corrugated, 4-lobed at base, oily, sweet, edible.

LEAVES. Pinnately compound, 1–2 ft long, yellowish green, deciduous; petioles puberulent; leaflets 11–23, sessile or short-stalked, ovate-lanceolate, acute or acuminate, rounded or subcordate at base, inequilateral, serrate, glabrous above, pubescent below, 3–5 in. long, 1–2 in. wide.

BARK. Grayish brown, black, or reddish, fissures deep, ridges broad, rounded, and broken into close scales.

WOOD. Very beautiful, dark rich brown, sapwood white, durable, strong, heavy, hard, close-grained, is easily worked, glues well, does not warp, shrink, or swell much, takes a good polish, weighs 38 lb per cu ft. The whitish sapwood is sometimes stained to match the color of the heartwood to bring a better price.

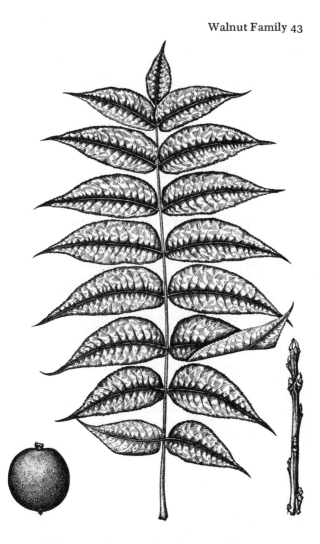

RANGE. Oklahoma, Arkansas, Louisiana, and Texas; east to Florida, north to Minnesota, New York, and Ontario; and west to Nebraska.

REMARKS. The genus name, *Juglans*, is from the Latin *Jovis glans*, meaning "acorn [or any nut of similar shape] of Jove," and the species name, *nigra*, refers to the dark wood. The wood is used in making superior furniture, cabinets, veneers, musical instruments, interior finish, sewing machines, caskets, coffins, posts, railroad crossties, and fuel. Large amounts were used for gunstocks during the Civil War and World War I. Trees about 12 years old begin to bear nuts. Confections and cakes are made from the nuts, which were also a favorite with the American Indians. Squirrels are fond of the large nuts. The tree makes a fine ornamental because of its shape and beautiful large leaves. Black Walnut and English Walnut are known to hybridize. Eastern Black Walnut is sometimes planted in shelter belts, and has been cultivated since 1686. It is a rapid grower and is usually found mixed with other hardwoods.

Pecan

Carya illinoensis (Wangh.) K. Koch [A, B, c]

FIELD IDENTIFICATION. Tree to 150 ft, with a broad rounded crown. The largest of all hickories.

FLOWERS. March–May, borne in staminate and pistillate catkins on same tree, subject to frost damage; staminate in slender, fascicled, sessile catkins 3–6 in. long; calyx 2–3-lobed, center lobe longer than lateral lobes; stamens 5–6, yellowish; pistillate catkins fewer, hairy, yellow, stigmas 2–4.

FRUIT. Ripening September–October, in clusters of 2–10, persistent; husk thin, aromatic, splitting along its grooved sutures into 4 valves at maturity; nut oblong to ellipsoid, cylindric, acute, bony, smooth, reddish brown, irregularly marked with darker brown, 1½–3½ in. long; seed deeply 2-grooved, convoluted on surface.

LEAVES. Alternate, deciduous, odd-pinnately compound, 9–20 in. long; leaflets 9–17, sessile or short-stalked, oblong-lanceolate, falcate, acuminate at apex, rounded to cuneate and inequilateral at base, doubly serrate on margin, 4–8 in. long, 1–2 in. wide; aromatic when crushed, dark green and glabrous above, paler and glabrous or pubescent beneath; rachis slender, glabrous or pubescent.

TWIGS. Reddish brown, stout, pubescent, lenticels orange-brown.

BARK. Grayish brown to light brown under scales; ridges flattened, narrow, broken, scaly; fissures narrow, irregular.

WOOD. Reddish brown, sapwood lighter, coarse-grained, heavy, hard, brittle, not strong, weighing 45 lb per cu ft, inferior to other hickories.

RANGE. Rich river-bottom soils. Texas, Oklahoma, Arkansas, and Louisiana; eastward to Alabama, and north to Kansas, Iowa, Indiana, and Tennessee.

REMARKS. The genus name, *Carya*, is the ancient name for walnut, and the species name, *illinoensis*, refers to the state of Illinois, the tree at one time having been called Illinois Nut. It is widely planted as an ornamental and for its sweet edible nuts. The wood is not important commercially but is occasionally used for furniture, flooring, agricultural implements, and fuel. The nut is valuable to wildlife, being eaten by a number of species of birds, fox squirrel, gray squirrel,

opossum, raccoon, and peccary. The bark and leaves are sometimes used medicinally as an astringent. Pecan is a rather rapid grower for a hickory and is long-lived but is subject to bark beetle attacks. It has been cultivated since 1766.

Shellbark Hickory

Carya laciniosa (Michx. f.) Loud. [A]

FIELD IDENTIFICATION. Tree attaining a height of 120 ft, with short, stout limbs and a narrow crown. A specimen at Big Tree State Park, Missouri, has been reported with a circumference of 12 ft 9 in., a height of 128 ft, and a spread of 70 ft.

FLOWERS. April–June, borne in separate staminate and pistillate catkins on the same tree; staminate catkins in threes, 5–8 in.; bracts linear-lanceolate, acute, scurfy-tomentose;

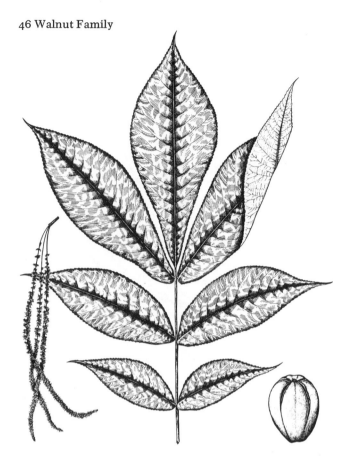

calyx 3-lobed, central lobe longer than lateral ones; stamens 3–10, hairy, yellow, anthers emarginate; pistillate in 2–5-flowered spikes, tomentose; bracts longer than calyx-lobes; stigmas short.

FRUIT. Ripening September–November, solitary or 2–3 together, ellipsoid to globular, depressed at apex, 1–3 in. long; hull light to dark orange-brown, hard, woody, ¼–½ in. thick, dehiscent along the 4 ribs; nut yellowish white, ellipsoid to obovoid or globose, usually rounded and flattened at ends but sometimes pointed at apex, somewhat compressed, bony, hard, thick-shelled; kernel sweet. Largest of all hickory nuts.

LEAVES. Large, 1–2 ft long, alternate, deciduous, odd-pinnately compound of 5–9, usually 7, leaflets; leaflets ovate to oblong-lanceolate or acute at apex, cuneate or rounded and inequilateral at base, finely serrate on margin; dark green, glabrous and shiny above; pale green beneath and velvety pubescent when young, glabrous later; terminal leaflet petioled, lateral leaflets sessile or nearly so; petiole and rachis pubescent or glabrous with age.

TWIGS. Stout, dark brown to reddish orange, lenticels elongate.

BARK. Gray, separating into long, thin, shaggy plates hanging loosely.

WOOD. Dark brown, sapwood lighter, close-grained, hard, strong, tough, heavy, very flexible, weighing 50 lb per cu ft.

RANGE. Northeast Texas, Oklahoma, Arkansas, and Louisiana; east to Alabama, and north to Nebraska, Minnesota, Iowa, Kansas, Delaware, and Ontario.

REMARKS. The genus name, *Carya*, is the ancient name for walnut, and the species name, *laciniosa*, refers to the deep furrowing and splitting of the bark. Vernacular names are King Nut, Bottom Shellbark, Big Shellbark, and Thick Shellbark. The wood is used as is that of other hickories, particularly for tool handles, baskets, and fuel. The large nuts are edible and sweet but are considered to lack the flavor of the Shagbark Hickory. The tree is long-lived, slow growing, hard to transplant, and subject to insect damage. It is rather similar in appearance to the Shagbark Hickory but has larger leaves and nuts and the bark is somewhat less shaggy in appearance. However, the two species are known to hybridize.

Shagbark Hickory

Carya ovata (Mill.) K. Koch [A, B]

FIELD IDENTIFICATION. Tree attaining a height of 100 ft, with an oblong crown and shaggy bark. A specimen in Turkey Run State Park, Indiana, has been reported with a trunk diameter of 9 ft 8 in., a height of 127 ft, and a spread of 50 ft.

FLOWERS. Appearing March–June, borne in separate staminate and pistillate catkins; staminate catkins in threes after the leaves appear, 4–5 in. long, slender, green, hairy-glandular; bract ovate-lanceolate and longer than the ovate and acute calyx-lobes; stamens 4, reddish yellow, hairy; pistillate catkins 2–5-flowered, rusty-tomentose.

FRUIT. Ripening September–October, very variable in size and shape. Borne 1–3 together, 1–2½ in. long, oval to subglobose or obovoid, depressed at apex; hull blackish to reddish brown, glabrous or hairy, ¼–½ in. thick, splitting freely to the base into 4 valves along the grooved sutures; nut light brownish white, oblong-obovate, somewhat compressed, usually prominently 4-angled, barely acute, or rounded, or truncate at apex; rounded at base, shell thin; kernel light brown, aromatic, sweet, edible.

LEAVES. Alternate, deciduous, 8–17 in. long, odd-pinnately compound of 3–5 (rarely 7) leaflets; lateral leaflets sessile

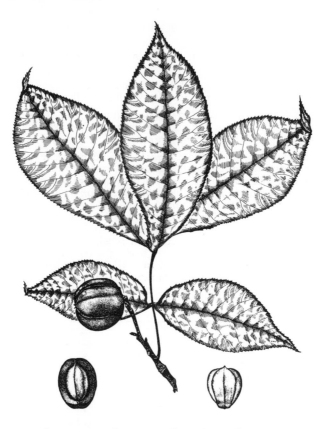

or nearly so, ovate-obovate or elliptic-lanceolate, acuminate at apex, cuneate and unequal at base, serrate on margin, yellowish green and glabrous above, paler and glabrous or hairy beneath, 4–7 in. long, 2–3 in. wide; terminal leaflet stalked, terminal leaflet and the upper pair of leaflets considerably larger than the lower pairs; rachis and petiole glabrous or pubescent.

TWIGS. Orange-brown, stout, glabrous or pubescent.

BARK. Gray, conspicuously exfoliating into long shaggy strips.

WOOD. Light brown, sapwood lighter, close-grained, heavy, hard, strong, tough, flexible, weighing 52 lb per cu ft.

RANGE. East Texas, Oklahoma, Arkansas, and Louisiana; east to Alabama, north to Maine and Quebec, and west to Minnesota, Michigan, and Nebraska.

REMARKS. The genus name, *Carya*, is the ancient name for walnut, and the species name, *ovata*, refers to the ovate-shaped leaflets. Vernacular names are Scaly Bark Hickory, White Hickory, Upland Hickory, Red Heart Hickory, Sweet-

walnut, and White-walnut. The tree is long-lived, slow growing, and subject to insect attacks. The wood is used for fuel,
tool handles, baskets, wagons, and other general uses. This
nut, next to the pecan, is the best of any American tree and
is the common hickory nut of commerce.

Water Hickory

Carya aquatica (Michx. f.) Nutt. [A, B, C]

FIELD IDENTIFICATION. Water-loving tree attaining a height
of 100 ft, with an irregular, narrow crown. A specimen near
Camden, South Carolina, has been reported to be 120 ft high,
with a trunk circumference of 10 ft 7 in., and a spread of
68 ft.

FLOWERS. In separate staminate and pistillate catkins on
the same tree, staminate catkins hairy, 2½–3 in., solitary or
in threes, pubescence yellow-glandular; stamens usually 6,

anthers yellow-pubescent; calyx-lobes almost equal in length; pistillate catkins 2–10-flowered.

FRUIT. Often clustered, ovoid or obovoid, conspicuously flattened in comparison with other hickories, 1–1½ in. long, about 1 in. wide; hull thin, shallowly 4-winged, splitting from the base, yellow-pubescent; nut very flat, reddish, angled and corrugated, thin-shelled; seed bitter, dark reddish brown.

LEAVES. Alternate, deciduous, odd-pinnately compound, 9–15 in. long, composed of 7–15 leaflets; leaflets lanceolate-ovate, often falcate, long-acuminate, the laterals unequally cuneate at base, serrate, 3–5 in. long, ½–1 in. wide, dark green and glabrous above, pubescent or glabrous beneath; rachis and petiole puberulent to pubescent.

TWIGS. Reddish brown or gray, tomentose at first, glabrous later, lenticels pale.

BARK. Grayish brown, tinged with red; scales small, thin, and brittle.

WOOD. Dark brown, sapwood lighter, heavy, hard, brittle, close-grained, weighing 46 lb per cu ft.

RANGE. East Texas, Oklahoma, Arkansas, and Louisiana; also eastward to Florida and north to Illinois, Missouri, and Virginia.

REMARKS. The genus name, *Carya*, is the ancient name for walnut, and *aquatica* refers to the tree's wet habitat. Vernacular names are Bitter Pecan, Swamp Hickory, and Water Pignut. The wood, rather inferior to that of other hickories, is hard to work and is used in small amounts for fuel, posts, and props. The nuts have been found in the stomachs of mallard duck and wood duck.

Mockernut Hickory

Carya tomentosa Nutt. [A, B, C]

FIELD IDENTIFICATION. Tree to 100 ft, with rather short limbs and a broad or oblong crown. A specimen has been reported from Turkey Run State Park, Indiana, with a circumference of 9 ft 6 in., a height of 146 ft, and a spread of 52 ft.

FLOWERS. April–May, borne in separate staminate or pistillate catkins; staminate catkins 3-branched, 4–5 in. long, yellowish green, hairy; bracts ovate to lanceolate, hairy, much longer than calyx-lobes; stamens 4, with red, hairy anthers; pistillate in 2–5-flowered hairy spikes; bracts ovate and acute, longer than bractlets and calyx-lobes; stigmas dark red.

FRUIT. Ripening September–October, solitary or paired, very variable in size and shape, usually obovoid, globose, or

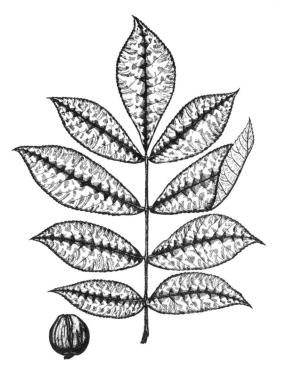

ellipsoid, 1–3½ in. long, acute at apex, rounded or rarely
with a short necklike base; hull dark reddish brown, woody,
hairy or nearly glabrous with yellow resinous dots, 4-ribbed,
dehiscent down the deep ribs to the middle or near the base,
about ⅛–¼ in. thick; nut variable in shape, obovoid-oblong
to globose or ovoid, rounded at base, acute or acuminate at
apex, slightly flattened, noticeably or obscurely 4-ridged,
brownish white or reddish, shell thick and hard; kernel dark
brown, small, shiny, sweet, edible.

LEAVES. Alternate, deciduous, 8–24 in. long, odd-pinnately
compound of 5–9 (usually 7) leaflets; lateral leaflets sessile
or nearly so, oblong to lanceolate or obovate, acute to acuminate at apex, rounded or broadly cuneate at base and inequilateral, serrate on margin; shiny yellowish green above,
paler beneath and clothed with brownish orange hairs,
glandular and resinous, fragrant when crushed, 5–8 in. long,
2–5 in. wide, terminal leaflets and upper pairs generally
larger than lower pairs; rachis and petiole glandular-hairy.

TWIGS. Stout, grayish brown to reddish, hairy at first but
more glabrous later; buds distinctively large and tomentose.

BARK. Gray, close and rough but never shaggy, ridges
rounded and netted, separated by shallow fissures.

WOOD. Dark brown, sapwood lighter, close-grained, heavy,
hard, strong, tough, flexible, weighing 51 lb per cu ft.

RANGE. Texas, Louisiana, Arkansas, and Oklahoma; east to Florida, and north to Nebraska, Ontario, Iowa, Illinois, Michigan, and Maine.

REMARKS. *Carya* is the ancient name for walnut, and the species name, *tomentosa*, refers to the tomentose hairs of the leaves. Vernacular names are Whiteheart Hickory, White Hickory, Red Hickory, Black Hickory, Whitebark Hickory, Hardbark Hickory, Bigbud Hickory, Bullnut Hickory, and Fragrant Hickory. It is long-lived, is a rapid grower when young, will sprout from the stump, and is subject to insect damage. The foliage is occasionally browsed by white-tailed deer. The wood is important commercially and is used for vehicle parts, handles, fuel, and agricultural implements. The nut is sweet and edible but used in smaller quantities than other edible species.

Bitternut Hickory

Carya cordiformis (Wangh.) K. Koch [A, B, C]

FIELD IDENTIFICATION. Tree attaining a height of 100 ft, with stout limbs and a broad spreading head. Tree in West Feliciana Parish, Louisiana, has been reported to be 171 ft high, with a trunk 12 ft 6 in. in circumference.

FLOWERS. April–May, staminate and pistillate catkins separate but on the same tree; staminate catkins in threes, 3–4 in. long, reddish-hairy, bracts ovate and acute; calyx 2–3-lobed; stamens 4, anthers yellow and hairy; pistillate catkins mostly in ones or twos, sessile.

FRUIT. September–October, solitary or paired, obovoid to subglobose, about ¾–1 in. long; husk yellow-scaled, thin, 4-winged above the middle and splitting to somewhat below the middle; nut globose to ovate, small, smooth, white, thin-shelled, abruptly pointed into a conical beak, slightly flattened; kernel convoluted and bitter to taste.

LEAVES. Alternate, deciduous, 6–12 in. long, odd-pinnately compound of 7–11 leaflets on a pubescent or glabrous rachis; leaflets ovate-lanceolate, some falcate, sessile or nearly sessile, terminal leaflets petioled, acuminate at apex, cuneate or rounded at base, serrate on margin, shiny green and glabrous above, paler and glabrous or pubescent beneath, 3–6 in. long, 1–2 in. wide; rachis slender and pubescent; leaflets are generally smaller and more slender than those of other species of hickories.

TWIGS. Winter buds scurfy, bright yellow; twigs greenish brown to reddish brown, lustrous, pubescent at first and glabrous later, stout; lenticels numerous and pale.

BARK. Grayish brown, smooth for a hickory, with thin scales in the flattened ridges, furrows shallow.

WOOD. Reddish brown, heavy, hard, strong, tough, weighing 47 lb per cu ft. Used for the same purposes as other hickories, but wood considered to be somewhat inferior.

RANGE. In moist woods of bottom lands; east Texas, Oklahoma, Arkansas, and Louisiana; east to Florida, north to Minnesota, Maine, and Ontario.

REMARKS. The genus name, *Carya*, is the ancient name for walnut, which is close kin to the hickories, and the species name, *cordiformis*, means "heart-shaped," in reference either to the fruit or the base of the leaflets. Vernacular names are Swamp Hickory, Pig Hickory, White Hickory, Pignut Hickory, and Red Hickory. The wood is used for wheel stock, handles, and fuel. It was first cultivated in the year 1689. It is perhaps the most rapid grower of all hickories and sprouts from the stump. It is suitable as a good park and shade tree and is often used as a potted stock for grafting pecan varieties.

Black Hickory

Carya texana Buckl. [a, b, c]

FIELD IDENTIFICATION. Tree attaining a height of 80 ft, with short, crooked branches forming a narrow crown.

FLOWERS. Borne in separate staminate and pistillate catkins, staminate catkins 2–3 in. long with acuminate bracts considerably longer than the calyx-lobes; stamens 4–5 with somewhat hairy anthers; pistillate catkins 1–2-flowered and red-hairy on all parts.

FRUIT. Hull of nut 1¼–2 in. in diameter, puberulent, subglobose to obovoid, or sometimes with a short basal neck, splitting at sutures to the base with valves 1/12–1/6 in. thick; nut globose, or obovoid, somewhat compressed, rounded at base, suddenly narrowed to an acute apex, 4-angled along upper part especially, reddish brown, reticulate-veined, shell about ⅛ in. thick; kernel small, rounded, sweet.

LEAVES. Alternate, deciduous, 8–12 in. long, odd-pinnately compound of 5–7 (usually 7) leaflets; leaflets sessile or nearly so, 4–6 in. long, lanceolate to oblanceolate or obovate, acuminate or acute at apex, cuneate and somewhat inequilateral at base, serrate on margin; dark green, shiny, and usually glabrous above; paler and rusty-pubescent below, especially when young, later becoming more glabrous; petioles rusty-hairy when young. The occurrence of rusty hairs and white scales on buds and young parts is a conspicuous feature.

TWIGS. Rusty-pubescent and reddish brown at first, grayish brown and glabrous later.

BARK. Dark gray to black, ridges irregular, broken into deep fissures.

WOOD. Brown, sapwood paler, hard, tough, brittle, used chiefly for fuel.

RANGE. The species, *texana*, and its variety, Arkansas Black Hickory, are distributed through east and southcentral Texas and Louisiana; north to Oklahoma, Arkansas, Indiana, Illinois, Missouri, and Kansas.

REMARKS. The genus name, *Carya*, is the ancient name for walnut, and the species name, *texana*, refers to the state of Texas. Some of the vernacular names for it are Buckley Hickory and Pignut Hickory. The thick shell makes the nut almost impossible to extract, but hogs sometimes crack them. Wood used for fuel.

Nutmeg Hickory

Carya myristicaeformis (Michx. f.) Nutt. [A, B, C]

FIELD IDENTIFICATION. Tree attaining a height of 100 ft, with a narrow open crown.

FLOWERS. Borne in separate staminate and pistillate catkins, staminate catkins 3–4 in., covered with brown scurfy pubescence; bracts ovate to oblong; stamens 6, with yellow anthers; pistillate catkins oblong, also with brown pubescence.

FRUIT. Usually solitary, 1–1⅔ in. long, ellipsoid to obovoid, covered with yellowish brown scurfy pubescence; hull very thin, distinctly 4-ridged at the sutures, splitting nearly to the base; nut small, bony, ellipsoid, acute or rounded at ends, smooth, reddish brown, often marked with blotches or bands, shell thick, resembling a nutmeg; kernel sweet but astringent.

LEAVES. Alternate, deciduous, odd-pinnately compound, 7–14 in. long, composed of 5–9 leaflets; leaflets oblong, lanceolate to ovate-lanceolate, the lateral ones sometimes ovate to obovate, acute or acuminate, unequally rounded or cuneate at the base, sharply serrate, dark green and nearly glabrous above, pubescent to glabrous and lustrous silvery white beneath, thin and firm, short-stalked or almost sessile, 4–5 in. long, 1–1½ in. wide; petioles slender and pubescent.

TWIGS. Grayish brown to reddish brown, covered with small golden brown scales.

BARK. Dark brown to reddish; scales small, thin, appressed.

WOOD. Light brown, sapwood lighter, close-grained, tough, strong.

RANGE. Nowhere abundant, but scattered from east Texas to Louisiana and Alabama; north to South Carolina and west to Oklahoma and Arkansas.

REMARKS. *Carya* is the ancient name for walnut, and the species name, *myristicaeformis*, means "shaped like myristicae or nutmegs." Another vernacular name is Bitter Waternut. The tree is difficult to transplant and is seldom seen in cultivation. The wood is considered inferior to that of other hickories and is of little commercial importance.

Swamp Hickory

Carya leiodermis Sarg. [A]

FIELD IDENTIFICATION. Tree attaining a height of 80 ft, with a rounded crown.

FLOWERS. Opening after the leaves, in staminate and pistillate catkins 4–5 in. long; staminate catkins pubescent; bracts lanceolate-ovate, glandular-hairy, longer than the ciliate calyx-lobes; stamens 4, hairy, anthers red; pistillate spikes few-flowered, shorter, pubescent, stigmas short.

FRUIT. Solitary or clustered, obovoid or globose, 1½–2 in. long, about 1¼ in. in diameter, little-compressed, or occasionally depressed, at apex; husk fairly thick (about ¼ in.), white-scaly, splitting along the 4 sutures to base; nut

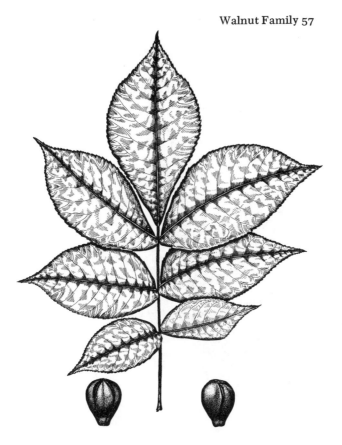

obovoid or ellipsoid, rounded at ends, reddish or brown, smooth, thin-shelled; kernel small and sweet.

LEAVES. Alternate, deciduous, 12–14 in. long, composed of 7 (rarely 5) leaflets; leaflets oblong-obovate to lanceolate, acuminate at apex, cuneate and inequilateral at base, serrate on margin; dark green, glabrous and shiny above; paler and slightly pubescent beneath; 4–5 in. long, and 2–2½ in. wide; lateral leaflets sessile or nearly so, terminal one short-stalked; distal leaflets larger than proximal ones; petiole and rachis pubescent at first and glabrous later.

TWIGS. Slender, grayish brown.

BARK. Grayish brown, close, rather smooth.

WOOD. Light reddish brown, sapwood paler, hard, strong, used for same purposes as that of other hickories.

RANGE. The species, *leiodermis*, is distributed from Mississippi to Louisiana and east Texas, and north into Arkansas.

REMARKS. The genus name, *Carya*, is the ancient name for walnut. The species name, *leiodermis*, refers to the smooth leaf surfaces.

Ruddy Swamp Hickory, *C. leiodermis* var. *callicoma* Sarg., is a variety having bright red young leaves and a thinner husk to the fruit. It occurs with the species, and has been found on the Neches River near Beaumont, Texas.

Pignut Hickory

Carya glabra (Mill.) Sweet [A]

FIELD IDENTIFICATION. Tree with a narrow, oblong crown, and somewhat pendulous branches. Known to attain a height of 120 ft. A specimen from near Crosswicks, New Jersey, has been reported with a circumference of 14 ft 9 in.

FLOWERS. April–May, borne in separate staminate and pistillate catkins on the same tree, staminate catkins 3-branched, 2–2½ in., yellowish green; bracts hairy; stamens 4, anthers yellow; pistillate few-flowered, calyx unequally 4-lobed; stigmas short.

FRUIT. Ripening September–October, variable in size and shape, but usually pear-shaped to ovoid, often with a neck-like base, somewhat compressed, about 1¼ in. long and ¾ in. wide; hull tardily dehiscent along 2–4 sutures, or sometimes not at all, about 1/16 in. thick; nut obovate, short-beaked, compressed, not ridged; bony, brownish, thick-shelled; kernel small, usually sweetish but astringent, sometimes bitter.

LEAVES. Alternate, deciduous, 8–12 in. long, odd-pinnately compound of 5 (rarely 3–7) leaflets; leaflets sessile or nearly so, lanceolate-obovate or ovate, acute or acuminate at apex, rounded or cuneate at base, serrate on margin, yellowish green and glabrous above, paler and glabrous or pubescent on veins beneath, terminal leaflet and upper pair larger than lower pairs; rachis and petiole usually glabrous.

TWIGS. Reddish brown, glabrous or nearly so, dotted with pale lenticels.

BARK. Gray, close, ridges narrow and scaly.

WOOD. Brown, sapwood lighter, heavy, hard, strong, tough, elastic, 51 lb per cu ft.

RANGE. Eastern Texas, Louisiana, and Arkansas; eastward to Florida, north to Maine, and west to Ontario and Michigan.

REMARKS. The genus name, *Carya*, is the ancient name of walnut, and the species name, *glabra*, refers to the smooth character of the leaves and petioles. Vernacular names are Broom Hickory, Switch Hickory, Black Hickory, Red Hickory, White Hickory, Brown Hickory, and Switchbud Hickory. The wood is used for fuel, tool handles, wagons, and agricultural implements. Settlers made brooms from the tough, flexible wood. The tree is slow growing and hard to transplant.

Birch Family (Betulaceae)

Hazel Alder

Alnus serrulata (Ait.) Willd. [A, B, C]

FIELD IDENTIFICATION. Irregularly shaped shrub or slender tree to 20 ft.

FLOWERS. Borne in separate staminate and pistillate catkins; staminate catkins in clusters of 2–5, 2–4 in. long, cylindric, drooping, bracts subtending the flowers; stamens 3–6; pistillate catkins in clusters of 2–3, about ¼ in. long, green to purple; bracts 3-lobed, each subtending 2–3 pistils.

FRUIT. About ¾ in. long, ovoid, a conelike aggregation of woody bracts, each subtending a nutlet; nutlet small, ovate, flattened, sharp-margined, less than ⅛ in. long.

LEAVES. Alternate, simple, deciduous, thick, blades 1–5 in. long, obovate to oval, obtuse or rounded at apex, acute or cuneate at base, sharply serrulate on margin, rather dark green on both sides, veiny and somewhat pubescent or glabrous beneath; petioles glabrous or pubescent, ⅓–½ in. long; stipules oval, deciduous.

TWIGS. Reddish brown or orange, pubescent at first, glabrous later, slender.

BARK. Gray, smooth, thin, slightly roughened with age.

WOOD. Light brown, soft, brittle, weighing 29 lb per cu ft.

RANGE. In wet soil along streams. East Texas, Louisiana, Oklahoma, and Arkansas; east to Florida, north to Maine, and west to Minnesota.

REMARKS. The genus name, *Alnus*, is the classical name of the alder, and the species name, *serrulata*, refers to the finely toothed leaves. This species was formerly known as *A. rugosa* (Du Roi) Spreng., which is a name better applied to *A. incana* (L.) Moench, a European species. Vernacular names are Common Alder, Smooth Alder, Tag Alder, Green Alder, Red Alder, Speckled Alder, and American Alder. The bark yields tannic acid and is an astringent. It was formerly used in the treatment of intermittent fever. The fruit is eaten by a number of species of birds. Hazel Alder is sometimes planted to prevent erosion on stream banks.

River Birch

Betula nigra L. [A, B, C]

FIELD IDENTIFICATION. Tree commonly of wet ground to 90 ft high, with dull reddish brown bark peeling off in curly thin flakes.

FLOWERS. Staminate catkins clustered, sessile, 1–3½ in. long; scales brown and shining; stamens 2, bifid; pistillate catkins cylindric, about ½ in. long; scales ovate, green, pubescent, ciliate; ovary sessile, with 2 spreading styles.

FRUIT. Strobile oblong-cylindric, about 1½ in. long and ½ in. thick, erect, borne on peduncles ½ in. long; scales 3-lobed; nutlet about ⅛ in. long, ovoid-obovate with a thin reniform wing, ripening April–June.

LEAVES. Simple, alternate, deciduous, rhombic-ovate, acute, cuneate at base, doubly serrate or some lobed with double serrations, blades 1½–3½ in. long, 1–2 in. wide, lustrous dark green above, tomentose beneath; petioles tomentose, slender, averaging about ½ in. long.

BARK. Reddish brown or grayish, marked by darker elongate lenticels, peeling into conspicuous papery strips.

WOOD. Light brown, hard, strong, close-grained, weighing 36 lb per cu ft.

RANGE. Texas, Oklahoma, Arkansas, and Louisiana; north to Massachusetts and west to Minnesota and Kansas.

REMARKS. *Betula* is the ancient classical name of the birch, and the species name, *nigra*, means "black," but no reason can be found for the name. Vernacular names are Red Birch, Water Birch, and Black Birch. The wood is used for furniture, woodenware, wagon hubs, and fuel. The seeds are sometimes eaten by birds and the foliage is browsed by white-tailed deer. Sometimes cultivated as an ornamental along streams or ponds and is also used for erosion control. It has been cultivated since 1736.

American Hornbeam

Carpinus caroliniana Walt. [A, B, C]

FIELD IDENTIFICATION. Small crooked tree attaining a height of 35 ft, with a fluted gray trunk and pendulous branches.

FLOWERS. April–June, staminate and pistillate flowers separate but on same tree; staminate flowers green, borne in linear-cylindric catkins, 1–1½ in.; scales of catkin triangular-ovate, acute, green below, red above; stamens numerous, filaments short and 2-cleft; pistillate catkins about ½ in.; flowers with hastate bracts which develop into a 3-lobed green involucre; styles slender, stigmas 2.

FRUIT. August–October, nutlet about ⅓ in. long, ovoid, acute, nerved, borne at base of a 3-lobed foliaceous bract, many together forming loose pendent clusters 3–6 in. long. The middle lobe of the bract is lanceolate and entire or dentate, and much longer than the lateral lobes which are usually incised-dentate on one side.

LEAVES. Simple, alternate, deciduous, sometimes falcate, acute or acuminate at apex; base rounded, wedge-shaped, or heart-shaped, often somewhat inequilateral; margin sharply double-serrate, teeth glandular except at base; dull bluish green and glabrous above, paler and hairy in axils of the veins below; petioles about ⅓ in. long, slender, hairy; stipules ovate-lanceolate, hairy, reddish green.

TWIGS. Slender, zigzag, gray or red.

BARK. Smooth, tight, thin, bluish gray, sometimes blotched with darker or lighter gray (some gray blotches may be due to crustose lichens), trunk fluted into musclelike separations.

WOOD. Light brown, sapwood lighter, strong, hard, tough, heavy, close-grained, weighing about 45 lb per cu ft.

RANGE. East Texas, Oklahoma, Arkansas, and Louisiana; east to Florida, north to Virginia, and west to Illinois.

REMARKS. The genus name, *Carpinus*, is the classical name for hornbeam, and the species name, *caroliniana*, refers to the states of Carolina. Vernacular names are Blue-beech, Water-beech, Lean-tree, and Ironwood. The wood is used for golf clubs, handles, fuel, mallets, cogs, levers, and wedges. The seed is eaten by at last 9 species of birds. The tree has been cultivated since 1812.

Woolly American Hop-hornbeam

Ostrya virginiana (Mill.) K. Koch. var. *lasia* Fern. [A, B, C]

FIELD IDENTIFICATION. Tree with grayish brown bark, attaining a height of 60 ft.

FLOWERS. Monoecious, staminate catkins 1–3 at ends of branches, 1½–3 in. long; scales triangular-ovate, acuminate, nerved, ciliate, green to red; stamens 3–14, filaments short and forked, anthers villous; pistillate catkins small, usually solitary, slender, about ¼ in. long; scales lanceolate, acute, ciliate, hirsute and red above, developing into pubescent-nerved bladdery sacs; ovary 2-celled.

FRUIT. In conelike imbricate clusters 1½–2 in. long; pe-

duncles hairy, about 1 in. long; each papery sac about ¾ in. long, ⅔–1 in. wide, ellipsoid, strongly tomentose at apex; nuts enclosed in the sac, small, ovoid, brown, faintly ribbed, about ¼ in. long.

LEAVES. Simple, alternate, deciduous, blades 2½–4½ in. long, 1½–2½ in. wide, ovate, or oblong-lanceolate, apex acute or acuminate, base rounded, heart-shaped, or wedge-shaped, often inequilateral, margin sharply and doubly serrate, glabrous and yellowish green above, hairy and paler below, turning yellow in autumn; petioles about ¼ in. long, hairy; stipules acute, rounded, ciliate, hairy, about ½ in. long.

TWIGS. Terete, crooked, slender, yellow-orange to brown, pubescent.

BARK. Grayish brown, broken into small, narrow, oblong, shreddy scales.

WOOD. Hard, strong, tough, close-grained, durable, light brown to white, sapwood lighter, weighing 51 lb per cu ft.

RANGE. In rich, moist woods. East Texas, Oklahoma, Arkansas, and Louisiana; eastward to Florida; and the northern variety to Ontario, west to Minnesota and Nebraska. The exact overlapping distribution of the southern and northern varieties is not known.

REMARKS. The genus name, *Ostrya*, is the ancient Greek name, and the species name, *virginiana*, refers to the state of Virginia. Vernacular names are Ironwood, Leverwood, Deerwood, Hardhock, and Indian-cedar. The wood is used for posts, golf clubs, tool handles, mallets, and woodenware. The fruit is eaten by at least 5 species of birds. The tree is rather slow growing but has possibilities as an ornamental; has been cultivated since 1690.

The east Texas form appears to be the southern variety, *lasia*, described by Merritt Lyndon Fernald and varying from the northern variety mostly by pubescence of leaves, petioles, and twigs. The northern variety, *O. virginiana* var. *glandulosa*, has glandular hairs on young parts.

Beech Family (Fagaceae)

The author is greatly indebted to the authors of the following two publications for much of the information on the Beech family: Cornelius H. Muller, *The Oaks of Texas, Contributions from the Texas Research Foundation*, vol. 1, part 3 (Renner, 1951); Donovan Stewart Correll and Marshall Conring Johnston, *Manual of the Vascular Plants of Texas* (Renner: Texas Research Foundation, 1970).

American Beech

Fagus grandifolia Ehrh. [A, B, C]

FIELD IDENTIFICATION. Beautiful tree attaining a height of 120 ft, with a rounded top and spreading branches. Easily sprouting from the roots to form thickets.

FLOWERS. April–May after the leaves unfold in separate staminate and pistillate clusters; staminate in globose heads, about 1 in. in diameter, pendent on hairy peduncles 1–2 in. long; stamens 8–10 with green anthers; pistillate flowers in clusters of 2–4 borne on short hoary peduncles ½–1 in. long; calyx campanulate, 4–5-lobed, hairy; pistil composed of a 3-celled ovary and 3 inwardly spreading stigmatic styles.

FRUIT. Ripening September–November, borne on stout hairy peduncles, composed of burlike involucres ½–¾ in. long with straight or recurved prickles, full-grown at midsummer

but becoming brown and persistent on the branches, splitting into 4 valves to release a pair of small brown, 3-angled, sweet nuts, dispersed after first frost, good seed crops every 2–3 years.

LEAVES. Simple, alternate, deciduous, straight-veined, ovate-oblong; acuminate at apex, cuneate to rounded or cordate at base, coarsely serrate on margin; when mature glabrous and dark green above; paler and pubescent, especially in the axils of veins beneath; 3–6 in. long; petioles 1/6–1/2 in., hairy; stipules ovate-lanceolate to linear.

TWIGS. Slender, zigzag, green and hairy at first, later glabrous and orange to yellow or reddish brown; lenticels oblong and orange-colored.

BARK. Light gray, often mottled, smooth.

WOOD. Varying shades of red, sapwood lighter, close-grained, hard, strong, tough, difficult to cure, not durable, weighing 43 lb per cu ft.

RANGE. Eastern Texas, Louisiana, Arkansas, and Oklahoma; eastward to Florida, north to Nova Scotia, and west to Wisconsin, Michigan, Illinois, and Missouri.

REMARKS. The genus name, *Fagus*, is from an old Greek word referring to the edible nuts, and the species name, *grandifolia*, refers to the large leaves. Vernacular names are Red Beech, Ridge Beech, and White Beech, also Beechnut. The tree is a very desirable one for ornamental planting, but grass has a difficult time growing under the dense foliage. It was first cultivated in the year 1800. It is long-lived, is free of disease, and sprouts easily from the roots to form thickets. The wood is sold commercially for chairs, tool handles, shoe lasts, flooring, cooperage, crates, spools, brush backs, toys, and fuel. The small sweet edible nuts are sometimes gathered and sold in the markets in the northern states and Canada and are a source of vegetable oil and swine feed. They are eaten by many species of birds and by raccoon, opossum, porcupine, gray fox, red fox, and white-tailed deer.

Allegheny Chinquapin

Castanea pumila (L). Mill [A, C]

FIELD IDENTIFICATION. Thicket-forming shrub or tree with slender spreading branches and a round top, sometimes attaining a height of 50 ft.

FLOWERS. Both staminate and pistillate catkins on same tree; some catkins all staminate, and some with both staminate and pistillate flowers; staminate catkins cylindric, slender, hoary-tomentose, 2½–6 in. long, ¼–⅓ in. in diameter; calyx small, 6-lobed; stamens 8–20 with 2-celled anthers; pistillate flowers generally in threes, or scattered toward base of catkins, and staminate flowers toward the tip; involucre prickly, sessile or short-stalked; ovary imperfectly 6-celled; styles linear, exserted with small stigmas.

FRUIT. In spikelike clusters; burs formed by the prickly involucre and 1–1½ in. in diameter; spines of bur in crowded clusters, slender and basally tomentose or glabrous; bur opening by 2–3 valves to expose the nutlet; nutlet solitary, small, shiny brown, round-ovoid, pointed and somewhat pubescent at the apex; kernel sweet and edible.

LEAVES. Alternate, simple, deciduous, blades 3–4 in. long, 1½–2 in. wide, elliptic-oblong to oblong-obovate, acute at the apex, unequal and rounded or broadly cuneate at the base; margins coarsely serrate with pointed teeth; upper surface glabrous, yellowish green, lower velvety white pubescent; petioles short, stout, flattened, pubescent at first, glabrous later, ¼–½ in. long; stipules yellowish green, ovate to lanceolate or linear, pubescent.

TWIGS. Green to reddish brown or orange-brown, pubescent at first, glabrous later.

BARK. Smoothish, reddish brown, furrows shallow, ridges flat with platelike scales.

WOOD. Dark brown, coarse-grained, light, hard, strong, durable, weighing 37 lb per cu ft.

RANGE. East Texas, Oklahoma, and Louisiana; eastward to Florida, north to New Jersey, and west to Missouri.

REMARKS. The genus name, *Castanea*, is for a town in Thessaly, and the species name, *pumila*, is for the tree's small stature. The tree is generally too small for commercial use but is occasionally used for posts, railroad crossties, and fuel. The sweet nuts are sometimes gathered for the market and are eaten by a number of birds and mammals.

Ashe Chinquapin

Castanea ashei Sudw. [A]

FIELD IDENTIFICATION. Shrub or small tree to 30 ft high, with usually several trunks from the base, and a broad round-topped head.

FLOWERS. In slender cylindric catkins; staminate catkins about 5 in. long; stamens 8–20, conspicuous, exserted on long filaments with small yellow anthers; calyx bell-shaped, 6-lobed, yellowish green, pubescent; pistillate flowers on the lower part of bisexual catkins in little clusters of 2 or 3 with spiny involucres; sterile stamens often present; ovary 6-celled with spreading linear styles.

FRUIT. Borne in subglobose brown burs about 1 in. long; spines of bur short, stubby, pubescent, in rather distant clusters; bur dehiscent into 2–4 valves to expose the nuts; nuts solitary, ovate, lustrous brown, point pubescent and often stellate; kernel sweet; edible.

LEAVES. Alternate, simple, deciduous, firm, elliptic to narrowly obovate, acute or rounded at apex, narrowly rounded at base, coarsely serrate on margin, dark green and glabrous above, gray-downy beneath, about 3 in. long and 1½ in. wide, but sometimes larger on young twigs.

TWIGS. Yellowish brown, slender, gray-tomentose, especially when young.

BARK. Rather smooth, brownish gray, ridges flat and broad, furrows shallow.

WOOD. Hard, strong, tough, not large enough for commercial use.

RANGE. Thickets on hillsides. East Texas, Arkansas, and Oklahoma; east to Florida and north to Virginia.

REMARKS. The genus name, *Castanea*, is for a town in Thessaly, and the species name, *ashei*, is in honor of W. W. Ashe

(1872–1932), a dendrologist of the U.S. Forestry Service. This species may be confused with the Allegheny Chinquapin, but the leaves are usually smaller and narrower, and the burs have shorter, stubbier pubescent spines in less crowded clusters. However, some authors feel that Ashe Chinquapin is not a species but only a variety of Allegheny Chinquapin, and have accepted the name of *C. pumila* var. *ashei* Sudw. Ashe Chinquapin may be distinguished from Florida Chinquapin by the gray-tomentose undersurface of the leaf. Florida Chinquapin is lustrous and smooth and only occasionally thinly tomentose.

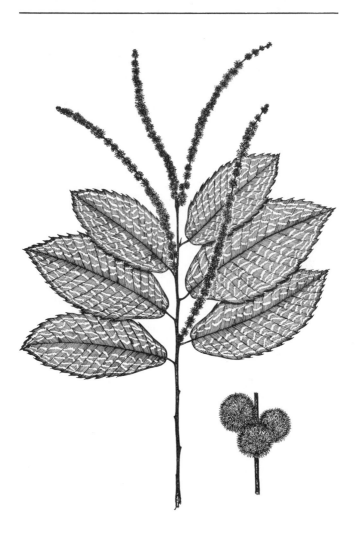

Common Chinquapin

Castanea alnifolia Nutt. [A]

FIELD IDENTIFICATION. A stoloniferous shrub to 10 ft or more.

FLOWERS. March–June; staminate aments erect-ascending, slender, greenish yellow, pale pubescent, the small clusters interrupted and somewhat fragrant; pistillate aments as long or longer than the staminate, borne near the branch ends, with 10–12 interrupted involucres usually near the middle.

FRUIT. From subglobose to short-oblong, 1–7 on a peduncle, from ¾–1¼ in. in diameter, brown-tomentose to tawny, closely set; spines scattered, pubescent, divided into branches at base; scales splitting into 2–4 valves. Nuts 1–3, shape ovoid, terete, acute; color chestnut brown, shiny; about ⅓ in. in diameter; ½–¾ in. long; flesh sweet.

LEAVES. Shape narrowly-elliptic to oblong-obovate; apices acuminate or rounded; base narrowed to cuneate or rounded; length 3–4¾ in.; width 1–2 in.; upper surface green and glabrous; lower surface light green, from tomentose at first to glabrous later; margin sinuate-toothed with apiculate teeth, the straight parallel veins ending in the teeth. Texture thin and glabrous. Petioles stout, glabrous, about 1/12 in. long.

TWIGS. Slender, reddish brown, pilose to glabrous later.

RANGE. In open woodlands or in thickets. Eastern Texas, Louisiana, Mississippi, Alabama, Georgia, and Florida; northward to Arkansas, and along the coast of North Carolina.

REMARKS. The genus name, *Castanea*, is for a town in Thessaly. The species name, *alnifolia*, refers to the alderlike leaves. A treelike form is listed as *C. alnifolia* var. *floridana* Sarg. However, the tree form and the stoloniferous thicket-forming form seem to intergrade, and in some regions they are difficult to distinguish.

Florida Chinquapin

Castanea alnifolia var. *floridana* Sarg. [A]

FIELD IDENTIFICATION. Tree to 40 ft high, with spreading branches forming a narrow crown; often with many trunks from the base.

FLOWERS. Borne in 2 kinds of catkins on same tree, one kind bearing all staminate flowers, and the other bearing staminate flowers on the distal part and pistillate on the proximal; staminate, catkins 4–5 in. long, cylindric, pubescent; stamens 8–20, exserted with 2-celled anthers; calyx 6-lobed; androgynous catkins with pistillate flowers below the middle,

bearing prickly involucres and a 6-celled ovary terminating in linear exserted styles.

FRUIT. A bur formed from the spiny involucre, ¾–1¼ in. in diameter, globose or short-oblong, tomentose; spines stout, pubescent, fascicles somewhat scattered with bald spots between; bur splitting into 2–3 valves to expose the nut; nut ovoid, shiny brown, acute, ½–¾ in. long; kernel sweet, edible.

LEAVES. Alternate, simple, deciduous, oblong-obovate to elliptic, acute at apex, rounded or cuneate at base, shallowly bristle-toothed on margin, thin, dark green and glabrous above, lighter green and glabrous below, or some showing a thin tomentum, 3–4 in. long, 1–1¾ in. wide; petiole stout and glabrous.

TWIGS. Reddish brown, slender, pubescent or glabrous.

BARK. Smoothish, ridges flat, furrows shallow.

WOOD. Hard, strong, durable, brownish.

RANGE. Rich moist soil of thickets or roadsides. Eastern Texas, Louisiana, and Oklahoma; eastward to Florida and northward to North Carolina.

REMARKS. The genus name, *Castanea*, is for a town in Thessaly; the species name, *alnifolia*, refers to the alderlike leaves; the variety name, *floridana*, refers to the Floridian habitat.

Chinquapins are rather similar in appearance but may be distinguished chiefly by the leaf pubescence and spines of the fruit. The Allegheny Chinquapin has no rootstocks, it has leaves with velvety-white tomentum beneath, and the bur spines are rather long, slender, and glabrous, or sparsely pubescent. Florida Chinquapin has bur spines which are sparser and shorter, and the leaves glabrous and lustrous or only thinly tomentose beneath. Ashe Chinquapin has even shorter, stubbier, and more pubescent spines than Florida Chinquapin, and the leaves are gray-downy beneath.

Overcup Oak

Quercus lyrata Walt. [A, B, C]

FIELD IDENTIFICATION. Tree attaining a height of 100 ft, and a diameter of 2–3 ft. Branches small, crooked, often drooping, forming an open, irregular head. When growing in swamps the base often buttressed.

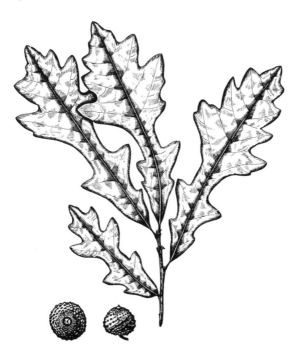

FLOWERS. March–April, staminate and pistillate catkins on the same tree; staminate clusters loosely flowered, 3–6 in. long, slender, hairy; calyx yellow, hairy, irregularly lobed, lobes acute; pistillate catkins sessile, or on peduncles ⅛–¾ in., solitary or a few together; peduncles and bracts tomentose; style short, stigmas recurved.

FRUIT. Acorn annual, sessile or short-peduncled, solitary or in pairs, ovoid or depressed-globose, base broadly flattened, chestnut brown, ½–1 in. high, about 1 in. broad, nearly or quite covered by the cup; cup hemispheric or spheroid, depressed, 3/5–1 1/5 in. broad, 2/5–4/5 in. deep, tomentose, thin, ragged, often splitting at the apex, thicker toward the base; scales reddish brown, ovate, acute, lower coarse and thickened, marginal ones small, thin, and appressed.

LEAVES. Alternate, simple, deciduous, thin, obovate-oblong, blades 3–10 in. long, 1–4 in. wide, apex acute to acuminate or rounded, base cuneate or attenuate, margin with lobes very variable, usually 7–9, rounded, acute or acuminate, middle lobes generally broadest, sinuses deep and broadly rounded; upper surface dark green, glabrous and lustrous; lower surface white-tomentose or glabrate later; petioles ⅓–1 in., glabrous or pubescent.

TWIGS. Slender, green and pubescent at first, later grayish brown and glabrous; buds about ⅛ in. long, ovoid, obtuse, chestnut brown; stipules deciduous and subulate.

BARK. Gray to brown or reddish, broken into irregular ridges with thin flattened scales.

WOOD. Dark brown, sapwood lighter, durable, hard, strong, tough, close-grained, weighing about 51 lb per cu ft.

RANGE. On wet, poorly drained clay soils. East Texas, Oklahoma, and Arkansas; east to Florida, north to New Jersey, and west to Missouri.

REMARKS. The genus name, *Quercus*, is the ancient classical name, and the species name, *lyrata*, refers to the lyrate-pinnatifid leaves. Other vernacular names are Water White Oak, Swamp White Oak, Swamp Post Oak, and White Oak. The wood is used for the same purpose as the true White Oak, *Q. alba*. The trees are slow growing, long-lived, generally free from insects and disease, and resistant to disease. Overcup Oak was first introduced into cultivation about 1786. The young plants are browsed by deer and cattle.

Bur Oak

Quercus macrocarpa Michx. [A, B, C]

FIELD IDENTIFICATION. Tree to 150 ft, with heavy spreading limbs and a broad crown.

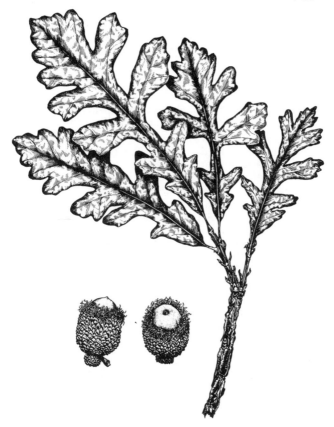

FLOWERS. Borne in staminate and pistillate catkins; staminate catkins 4–6 in. long, yellowish green; calyx deeply 4–6-lobed, hairy; pistillate flowers sessile or nearly so, solitary or a few together; involucral scales ovate, red, tomentose; stigmas red.

FRUIT. Acorn very large, variable in size and shape, sessile or short-stalked, solitary or paired; ¾–2 in. long, ellipsoid to ovoid, apex pubescent; cup subglobose or hemispheric, thick, woody, tomentose, enclosing one-half to three-fourths of nut; scales imbricate, thick, upper scales with awnlike tips to produce a fringed border on the cup, giving a mossy appearance.

LEAVES. Simple, alternate, deciduous, obovate-oblong, 5–9-lobed, lobes separated by very deep sinuses; terminal lobe usually largest and obovate with smaller lobes or coarse teeth, apex usually rounded; base cuneate from smaller lobes; blades 6–12 in. long, 3–6 in. wide; dark green, lustrous and glabrous above, paler and pubescent beneath; petioles stout, pubescent, ⅓–1 in.

TWIGS. Light brown and pubescent, later becoming dark brown and glabrous, and sometimes with corky ridges; terminal buds reddish brown, pubescent, ovoid, obtuse, about ¼ in. long.

BARK. Light gray, or reddish brown, thick, deeply fissured and broken into irregular narrow flakes.

WOOD. Dark or light brown, close-grained, heavy, hard, strong, tough, durable, weighing about 46 lb per cu ft.

RANGE. Not apparently at home on the Atlantic and Gulf Coast plains, but on higher grounds. Central and east Texas, Oklahoma, Arkansas, and Louisiana; east to Georgia, north to Nova Scotia, and west to Manitoba, Kansas, and Wyoming.

REMARKS. The genus name, *Quercus*, is the ancient classical name, and the species name, *macrocarpa*, refers to the large acorn. Vernacular names are Mossycup Oak and Overcup Oak. The wood is similar to that of White Oak and is used for baskets, lumber, ties, fences, cabinets, ships, and fuel. The acorns are greedily eaten by squirrels and white-tailed deer, and young plants are browsed by livestock. A narrow-leaved and small-fruited variety of Bur Oak has been given the name of Q. *macrocarpa* var. *olivaeformis* Gray. A dwarf form of Bur Oak known as Bur Scrub Oak, Q. *macrocarpa* var. *depressa* (Nutt.) Engelm., is found in Minnesota, South Dakota, and Nebraska and has acorn cups about 2/5 in. wide, slightly fringed, innermost scales caudate-attenuate; acorns ovoid, about 2/5 in. long. It is usually 3–8 ft high with corky branches. However, many intermediate forms occur between it and the species.

White Oak

Quercus alba L. [A, B, C]

FIELD IDENTIFICATION. Large tree to 150 ft, with a broad open head.

FLOWERS. Appearing with the leaves April–May, staminate and pistillate on the same tree; staminate catkins solitary, hairy, about 3 in. long; calyx yellow, pubescent, with acute lobes; stamens 6–8; pistillate catkins usually solitary, 2–3-flowered, about ½ in. long, red; involucral scales hairy, ovate; calyx-lobes acute, ovate; styles erect, short.

FRUIT. Ripening September–October. Acorn sessile or short-stalked, solitary or in pairs; nut ellipsoid-ovoid, light brown, lustrous, ¾–1 in. long, enclosed to one-fourth its length in cup; cup bowl-shaped, scales woody-tuberculate, thickened, somewhat fused, closely appressed, acorn maturing the first season. Minimum commercial seed-bearing age 30 years, optimum 50–100, maximum 150. Good crops about every 3 years, with light crops intervening.

A form sometimes
known as Q. *alba*
forma *pinnatifida*

LEAVES. Alternate, simple, deciduous, oblong-obovate, 5–9
in. long, 7–11-lobed; lobes oblique, rounded, elongate, the
terminal lobe usually shallowed, 3-parted; leaf base cuneate;
bright green and glabrous above, paler or glaucous below.

TWIGS. Slender, reddish brown to gray, glabrous; terminal
buds about 3/16 in. long, subglobose, glabrous, brown; leaf
scars half-moon–shaped, pith stellate in cross section.

BARK. Light gray, or reddish brown beneath the flat loose
ridges, which are separated by shallow fissures.

WOOD. Light brown, hard, strong, heavy, close-grained, durable, weighing about 46 lb per cu ft.

RANGE. On bottom lands, rich uplands, and gravelly ridges.
East Texas, Oklahoma, Arkansas, and Louisiana; east to
Florida, north to Maine, Ontario, and Minnesota, and west
to Nebraska.

REMARKS. The genus name, *Quercus*, is the classical name,
and the species name, *alba*, refers to the white bark. Vernacular names are Stave Oak, Fork-leaf White Oak, and
Ridge White Oak. The wood is used for fuel, ties, baskets,
cabinets, barrels, tools, furniture, and construction work.
The dried, powdered inner bark of this and other oaks has
some medicinal value because of the quercitanic acid it
contains. It is used almost solely as an astringent wash, or
occasionally as an injection in leucorrhea or hemorrhoids.
Indians ground the acorns into meal and poured water

through it to leach out the tannin before baking into bread. Squirrel, white-tailed deer, wild turkey, and bobwhite quail eat the acorns, and livestock browse the foliage. White Oak is very desirable for park and street planting and is rather free of insect pests, but is somewhat difficult to transplant. It has been in cultivation since 1724.

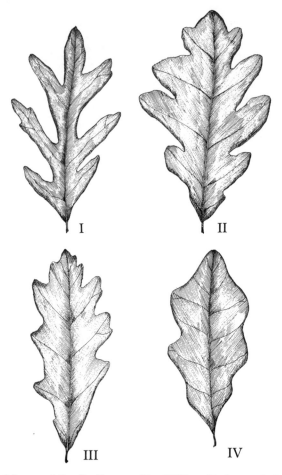

Leaf forms of *Q. alba* L., noted by William Trelease: I, *Q. alba* forma *typica*, is a widely distributed form; II, *Q. alba* forma *latiloba*, has leaves divided usually less than halfway to the midrib into broad rounded lobes and appears to be a common form from east Texas and eastward; III, *Q. alba* forma *sublyrata*, is an intermediate somewhat lyre-shaped form; IV, *Q. alba* forma *repanda*, has leaves with shallow sinuses and acorns usually short-stalked.

Chinquapin Oak

Quercus muhlenbergii Engelm. [A, C]

FIELD IDENTIFICATION. Narrow, round-topped tree rarely over 60 ft.

FLOWERS. In separate staminate and pistillate catkins on the same tree; staminate catkins 3–4 in. long, hairy; calyx 5–6-lobed, yellow, hairy, ciliate, lanceolate; stamens 4–6, filaments exserted; pistillate catkins sessile, short, tomentose; calyx 5–6-lobed; stigmas red.

FRUIT. Acorns mostly solitary or in pairs, sessile or short-peduncled, broadly ovoid, brown, shiny, ½–¾ in. long, enclosed about half its length in the cup; cup thin, bowl-shaped, brown, tomentose; scales of cup appressed, obtuse to acute or cuspidate; kernel sweet, edible.

LEAVES. Alternate, simple, deciduous, 4–6 in. long, 1–3½ in. wide, oblong to lanceolate or obovate, acute or acuminate at apex, cuneate to rounded or cordate at base; margin with coarse, large, acute, mucronate, often recurved teeth; dark green, lustrous and glabrous above; paler gray-tomentulose and conspicuously veined beneath; petiole slender, ½–1 in.

TWIGS. Slender, hairy or glabrous, reddish brown to gray, terminal buds orange to reddish brown, ovoid, acute.

Bray Chinquapin Oak

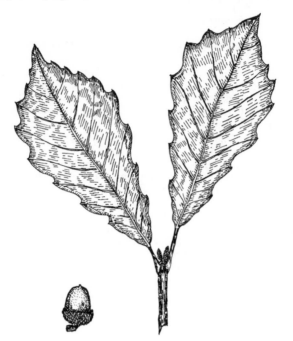

BARK. Light grayish brown, broken into narrow, loose plates.

WOOD. Reddish brown, sapwood lighter, close-grained, durable, hard, heavy, strong, weighing 53 lb per cu ft.

RANGE. Well-drained uplands. Texas, Louisiana, Oklahoma, and Arkansas; east to Florida, north to Maine, and west to Ontario, Michigan, Wisconsin, and Nebraska. In Mexico in Coahuila and Nuevo León.

REMARKS. The genus name, *Quercus*, is the classical name of the oak tree, and the species name, *muhlenbergii*, is in honor of G. H. E. Muhlenberg (1753–1815), botanist and minister in Pennsylvania. Other vernacular names are Pin Oak, Shrub Oak, Scrub Oak, Yellow Oak, Chestnut Oak, Rock Oak, and Chinkapin Oak.

Chinquapin Oak sprouts from the stump, grows rather rapidly, and is fairly free of insects and disease. The wood is used for posts, ties, cooperage, furniture, and farm implements. Bray Chiquapin Oak, Q. *muhlenbergii* var. *brayi* (Small) Sarg., is somewhat similar and is found on the Edwards Plateau and into west Texas, and south into Mexico. It has nuts sometimes to 1¼ in. long, and deeper cups to 1 in. in diameter. However, these differences are not distinct, and it is now considered by some botanists as only a form instead of a variety.

Dwarf Chinquapin Oak

Quercus prinoides Willd. [A]

FIELD IDENTIFICATION. Slender shrub, or more rarely a small tree to 15 ft, with a trunk diameter of 1–4 in. Usually growing in thicket-forming clumps on rocky hillsides. Closely related to the Chinquapin Oak, Q. *muhlenbergii*, but differing in its shrubby stature, smaller leaves with generally shorter petioles, deeper acorn cups, with thicker scales, and shorter stamens.

FLOWERS. Borne April–May in separate staminate catkins and pistillate catkins; staminate catkins 1–2½ in. long, pendent, cylindric, loosely and remotely flowered, perianth densely hairy, lobes thin, scarious, ovate to oblong; stamens numerous, exserted, filaments short, anthers large and short-oblong; pistillate flowers solitary or paired, sessile, stigmas yellowish red.

FRUIT. Ripening September–October, maturing the first season, often abundant, acorn covered one-half or more by the cup, chestnut brown, ovoid to ellipsoid, apex obtuse or rounded, 2/5–1 in. long; cup sessile or nearly so, hemispheric, thin, deep, ½–¾ in. wide; scales appressed, pale brown, densely hairy, finely tuberculate, triangular-ovate to oblong-lanceolate, apex obtuse to truncate, acorns average about 400 per lb; sweet and edible.

LEAVES. Alternate, simple, deciduous, blades 2–6 in. long, width 2–3 in., obovate to oblanceolate or elliptic, apex acute or short-acuminate, base cuneate, margin undulate-serrate; teeth 3–7 to each side, large, short, acute or obtuse; upper surface olive green to bright green, lustrous, glabrous; lower surface much paler, finely gray-pubescent to tomentulose; veins conspicuous and rather straight; petiole slender, channeled, ¼–¾ in., sparsely puberulent or glabrous; leaves brilliant red in autumn.

TWIGS. Young reddish brown and puberulent to glabrous, older ones gray and glabrous; bark of older limbs and trunk dark brown to gray, broken into flat, scaly, checkered ridges and shallow furrows.

RANGE. Dwarf Chinquapin Oak is found in sunny sites, often in rocky or acid sandy soil. Northeast Texas, Oklahoma, and Arkansas; east to Alabama, north to Vermont, and west to Minnesota and Kansas.

REMARKS. The genus name, *Quercus*, is the ancient classical name. The species name, *prinoides*, refers to its resemblance, especially in the leaves, to *Q. prinus*. It also has the vernacular names of Scrub Chestnut Oak, Dwarf Chestnut Oak, Running White Oak, and Chinquapin Oak. It was introduced into cultivation about 1730. The acorn is known to be eaten by a number of species of birds and mammals, including the gray squirrel and ruffed grouse, and the foliage is browsed by cottontail.

Swamp Chestnut Oak

Quercus prinus L. [A, B, C]

FIELD IDENTIFICATION. Long-lived tree attaining a height of 100 ft, with a compact narrow head.

FLOWERS. Borne April–May. Arranged in separate staminate and pistillate catkins; staminate catkins slender, hairy, 3–4 in.; calyx 4–7-lobed, hairy, green; pistillate catkins few-flowered, involucral scales tomentose; stigmas red.

FRUIT. Ripening September–October. Acorn sessile, or stalked, solitary or paired, ovoid-oblong, ¾–1½ in. long, shiny brown, set one-third to one-half its length in the cup; cup bowl-shaped, thick; scales hard, stout, ovate, acute, reddish brown.

LEAVES. Simple, alternate, deciduous, obovate-oblong, acute or acuminate at apex, cuneate or rounded at base, undulately crenate on margin, glabrous and lustrous green above, paler and pubescent beneath, blades 4–8 in. long, 1½–4 in. wide; petioles about ¾ in.

TWIGS. Smooth, reddish brown to gray later.

BARK. Pale gray, broken into shaggy strips which are reddish beneath, furrows deep.

WOOD. Light brown, heavy, tough, hard, strong, close-grained, durable.

RANGE. In greatest abundance and size on the coastal plain, generally in moist soil. Texas, Arkansas, and Oklahoma; east to Florida, north to Delaware, and west through Indiana and Illinois to Missouri.

REMARKS. The genus name, *Quercus*, and the species name, *prinus*, are both classical names applied to certain oaks of Europe. Vernacular names are Cow Oak, Basket Oak, Michaux Oak, Swamp White Oak, and Swamp Oak. The tree has been in cultivation since 1737. The wood is used for posts, tools, baskets, splints, cooperage, boards, veneer, and fuel. The acorns are eaten by mourning dove, wild turkey, and white-tailed deer, and the leaves frequently browsed by livestock.

Post Oak

Quercus stellata Wangh. [A, B, C]

FIELD IDENTIFICATION. Shrub or tree to 75 ft, with stout limbs and a dense rounded head.

FLOWERS. Appearing with the leaves March–May, borne on
the same tree in separate catkins; staminate in pendent catkins 2–4 in. long; calyx yellow, hairy, 5-lobed; lobes acute,
laciniately segmented; stamens 4–6, anthers hairy; pistillate
catkins short-stalked or sessile, inconspicuous; scales of involucre broadly ovate and hairy; stigmas red, short, enlarged.

FRUIT. Ripening September–November. Acorns maturing the
first season, sessile or short-stalked, borne solitary, in pairs,
or clustered; acorn oval or ovoid-oblong, broad at base, ½–
¾ in. long, striate, set in cup one-third to one-half its length;
cup bowl-shaped, pale and often pubescent within, hoary-
tomentose externally; scales of cup reddish brown, rounded
or acute at apex, closely appressed.

LEAVES. Simple, alternate, deciduous, oblong-obovate, blades
4–7 in. long, 3–4 in. wide, 5-lobed with deep rounded sinuses; lobes usually short and wide, obtuse or truncate at
apex; middle lobes almost square and opposite giving a
crosslike appearance to the leaf; terminal lobe often 1–3
notched; base of leaf cuneate or rounded; dark green, rough
and glabrous above, paler and tomentose beneath; leathery
and thick; petioles short, usually ½–1 in., pubescent.

TWIGS. Brown, stout, pubescent to tomentulose, or becoming
glabrous later; buds 1/16–1/8 in. long, subglobose, brown.

BARK. Gray to reddish brown, thick, divided into irregular
fissures with platelike scales.

WOOD. Light to dark brown, durable, heavy, hard, close-
grained, difficult to cure, weighing about 52 lb per cu ft.

RANGE. Post Oak is distributed in the Edwards Plateau of Texas, adjacent Oklahoma, and Arkansas; east to Florida, north to New England, and west to Iowa and Kansas.

REMARKS. The genus name, *Quercus*, is the classical name; the species name, *stellata*, refers to the stellate hairs of the leaves and petioles. Vernacular names are Iron Oak, Cross Oak, Branch Oak, Rough Oak, and Box Oak. The wood is used for railroad crossties, fuel, fence posts, furniture, and lumber; the acorns are eaten by deer, javelina, and wild turkey.

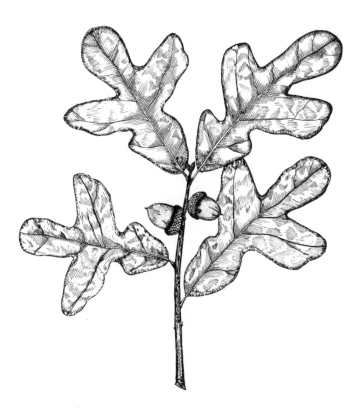

Sand Post Oak

Quercus margaretta Ashe [A, B, C]

FIELD IDENTIFICATION. A low, branched shrub 4–10 ft high, forming thickets in sand by means of stolons, or in other instances assuming the form of a tree to 40 ft tall. The bark light gray, thick, rough, and furrowed.

FLOWERS. The staminate in aments 3–4 in. long; calyx hirsute, yellowish, with 5 segments laciniately cut. Pistillate catkins sessile or short-peduncled; scales of the involucre broadly ovate, hirsute; stigmas red.

FRUIT. Annual, solitary or paired, short-peduncled or sessile; acorns about one-half included in cup; ⅓–⅝ in. long; ⅓–½ in. broad; shape ovoid, color light brown, glabrous. Acorns cup ½–¾ in. broad; 1/6–2/5 in. deep, shallowly to deeply cup-shaped, with the bases rounded; scales of cup oblong to ovate to obovate; apices narrowed and loosely appressed, densely short-pubescent.

LEAVES. Simple, alternate, deciduous; membranous or thickened; length 2–5¾ in.; width 1¼–4 in.; shape obovate to oblong or elliptic; apices broadly rounded; bases rounded to cuneate; margins 2–3-lobed on each side; sinuses broad or narrowed, but rounded at the bottom; lobes truncate or rounded (sometimes on same branch or tree), simple or obscurely toothed or undulate with revolute margins; upper surface glabrate or with scattered stellate hairs, shiny green; lower surface more or less densely stellate-tomentose, with age remaining pubescent or later glabrate or some slightly glaucous. Petioles 1/8–3/5 in. long, tomentose or glabrate later.

TWIGS. Grooved, 1/15–1/10 in. thick, dull brown and glabrous, or when young stellate with scattered hairs; lenticels small; buds ovoid, acute, ⅛–¼ in. long; 1/12 in. broad; scales closely imbricated, color reddish brown, at first pubescent but later glabrate; margins sometimes ciliate; stipules about 1/5 in. long, subulate, pubescent, soon caducous.

RANGE. Said to be the common Post Oak of the south Atlantic and Gulf states. In sandy soils of eastern and central Texas, western Louisiana (Natchitoches and Caddo Parishes), Mississippi, Alabama, Georgia, Florida; northward to Virginia, Oklahoma, and Arkansas.

REMARKS. The genus name, *Quercus*, is an ancient name. The species name, *margaretta*, is for Margaret Henry Wilcox, the late Mrs. W. W. Ashe. In some areas the dominant form is a stoloniferous shrub, known as Q. *stellata* var. *margaretta* Sarg.; in others it is a small tree. On the areas of contact, hybrids of Q. *margaretta* and Q. *stellata* are found with intermediate characteristics.

Bottom Land Post Oak

Quercus similis Ashe [A, B, C]

The following description is adapted from that of Correll and Johnston, *Manual of the Vascular Plants of Texas*, p. 476.

FIELD IDENTIFICATION. A moderate to large tree, closely resembling Q. *stellata*.

FLOWERS. Pistillate catkins 1/12–2/5 in. long, 1–3-flowered.

FRUIT. Acorn annual, solitary or paired, moderate-sized, short-peduncled, very similar to Q. *stellata*.

LEAVES. Simple, alternate, deciduous, thin and membranous, about 4¾ in. long and 3¼ in. broad (or as small as 2 in. long or as large as 6¼ in. long); shape obovate; with usually 2 pairs of lateral lobes with the apical pair somewhat clavate, but the blade scarcely cruciform; margin minutely revolute; base varying from narrow to cuneate or rounded; lower surface grayish and minutely stellate-puberulent; upper surface glossy green and glabrous at maturity. Petioles 1/8–2/5 in. long, pubescent like the twigs.

TWIGS. Only slightly fluted, 1/12–1/8 in. thick, persistently gray-puberulent to velvety-tomentulose, buds 1/12–1/8 in.

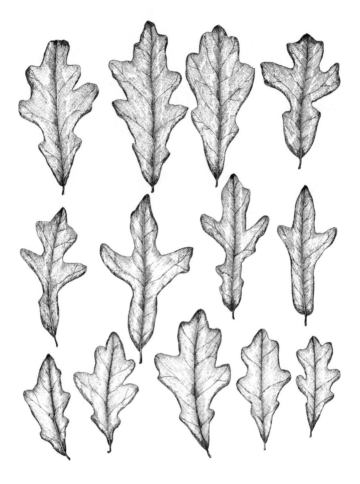

Leaf variations
of *Q. similis* Ashe

long, ovoid, brown, pubescent. Stipules 1/8–1/5 in. long,
subulate, pubescent, caducous or only those of the terminal
buds persistent.

RANGE. Reported to be the common Post Oak of wet bottom
lands in east Texas, south Arkansas, and Louisiana; east
to South Carolina. The upper terraces of some streams,
particularly in Louisiana, exhibit intermediate forms between
Q. *similis* and Q. *stellata* to which Q. *mississippiensis* Ashe
is applicable.

However, some authors feel that the latter should be relegated to the status of a variety under the name of Delta
Post Oak, Q. *stellata* var. *mississipiensis* (Ashe) Little. Also
that the entity known as Q. *similis* Ashe should be of varietal
standing under the name of Q. *stellata* var. *similis* Ashe, or
that it be listed as only a synonym of Q. *stellata*.

However, the author might make a general comment
based on field observation. The so-called Post Oak of the
river-bottom lands of east Texas, and eastward, does present a different appearance in foliage forms from the typical cruciform-shaped leaves of the upland Post Oak. Therefore, there could be some real validity for the name of Q.
similis Ashe.

The variability of Q. *stellata* Wangh., so great over its
wide range, plus its propensity to hybridize so abundantly,
has given rise to many names and has created considerable
diverse opinions among taxonomists.

REMARKS. The genus name, *Quercus*, is an ancient name,
and the species name, *similis*, refers to the species' similarity
to Q. *stellata*.

Boynton Oak

Quercus boyntoni Beadle [A, C]

This description follows that of Cornelius H. Muller, "The
Distribution of *Quercus boyntoni*," *Madroño* 13 (1956): 222.

FIELD IDENTIFICATION. Rhizomatous shrubs 8 in. to 9 ft tall,
trailing or sometimes semierect.

FLOWERS. Staminate catkins 1¼–2⅓ in. long, fulvous-
glandular-puberulent and stellate-pubescent, the puberulent
anthers well exserted from the ciliate perianth; pistillate
catkins about 1/5 in. long, about 3-flowered, and subsessile,
densely fulvous-pubescent.

FRUIT. Annual, solitary or paired on peduncles 1/12–2/5 in.
or rarely 1 2/5 in. long; cups 2/5–1/2 in. broad, 1/5–2/5 in.
high, deeply cup-shaped or more shallow, the scales densely
fulvous or silvery-tomentulose, the bases moderately or
markedly thickened, the thin apices closely appressed; acorns

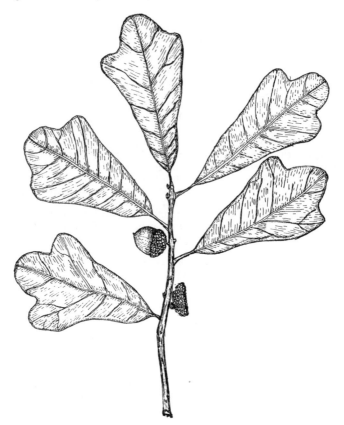

2/5–3/5 in. long, 1/4–2/5 in. broad, broadly or narrowly ovoid, the ends broadly rounded, brown and minutely puberulent, especially about the apex, about one-half or one-third included.

LEAVES. Deciduous or subevergreen, thin and rather soft, 2–4¾ in. long, ¾–2⅓ or rarely 3¼ in. broad, cuneate to oblanceolate, obovate or oblong, characteristically roundly 3-lobed at the broad apex or sometimes 5-lobed above the entire cuneate base; margins minutely cartilaginous-revolute; upper surface glossy, in youth sparingly glandular-puberulent and with scattered stellate hairs, at length glabrate or the stellate pubescence persistent especially about the midrib; lower surface dull, persistently fulvous-glandular-puberulent and stellate pubescent or the pubescence silvery, the veins about 6–8 on each side, very irregular and with some intermediates, those passing into the lateral lobes very prominent, slightly raised above and prominently so beneath, markedly and irregularly branching and anastomasing. Petioles 1/5–2/5 in. long, moderately slender, persistently pubescent like the twigs.

TWIGS. About 1/12–1/8 in. thick, densely fulvous-tomentulose with a mixture of simple appressed glandular hairs and moderately spreading stellate hairs, the pubescence darkening and persisting through the second season, buds 1/12–1/8 in. or even 1/6 in. long, ovoid, acute or sometimes rounded, russet, sparingly pubescent; stipules deciduous 1/8–1/5 in. long, subulate, sparsely hairy.

RANGE. Usually growing in deep sandy soil in the valley of creeks. Reported in Texas in Angelina County. Also reported from Etowah County, Alabama, at about the summit of Lookout Mountain, near Gadsden. Probably also to be found in other areas between the Alabama and Texas locations.

REMARKS. The genus name, *Quercus*, is the ancient Latin name. The species name, *boyntoni*, is for Frank Ellis Boynton. Sometimes listed as *Q. stellata* var. *boyntoni* Sarg.

Drummond Post Oak

Quercus drummondii Liebm. [A, c]

The following description is based on that of Muller, *The Oaks of Texas*, p. 51.

FIELD IDENTIFICATION. Small or medium-sized trees.

FLOWERS. Borne in catkins, those of the staminate 2–2⅓ in. long, loosely flowered, sparsely villous. Pistillate catkins on short peduncles or almost sessile, the subsessile involucres borne singly or in pairs.

FRUIT. Acorns annual, solitary or paired, borne on short glabrous peduncles to ⅓ in. Long or subsessile. Body of acorns ⅝–¾ in. long, about ⅓ in. broad; shape narrowly ovoid or elliptic, glabrous and light brown, one-third to one-half of body included.

LEAVES. Simple, alternate, deciduous; texture thick and leathery; length to 4¾ in.; width to 3½ in.; shape obovate, deeply incised (½–⅔ the distance to the midrib) by narrow or even closed sinuses, rarely the sinuses rounded; lobes 2 or 3 on each side, oblong, rounded or truncate to clavate; upper surface with sparse stellate hairs, with maturity shiny and glabrate; lower surface villous or loosely tomentose with stellate hairs, at maturity persistently pubescent or finally glabrate; the midrib and veins with persistent pubescence. The lateral veins spreading, irregular, and terminating into the lobes. Petioles about ½ in. long, at first stellate-pubescent, some persistently pubescent, others becoming glabrate.

TWIGS. Light brown, 1/12–1/6 in. thick, with spreading stellate hairs; lenticels light and small at first, with age more prominent; buds 1/6–1/3 in. long; shape broadly or narrowly ovoid, obtuse or acute; color dull red or brown, glabrous, sparingly brown-pubescent near the apex.

RANGE. In deep sand belts of central Texas and eastward. In Austin, Bexar, Caldwell, Guadalupe, Medina, Robertson, Tarrant, and Wilson counties.

REMARKS. The genus name, *Quercus*, is an ancient name, and the species name, *drummondii*, honors Thomas Drummond (1780–1835), Scotch botanical explorer.

Q. *drummondii* is separated from the closely related Q. *margaretta* Ashe by the fact that the former is a moderately sized tree and the latter is a shrub or small tree with running stolons. Also. Q. *drummondii* has twigs about ⅛ in. in diameter; the leaves are very thick and leathery with strongly revolute margins. Q. *margaretta* has twigs usually about 1/12 in. in diameter, and the leaf margins are flat or slightly revolute.

Some synonyms of Q. *drummondii* are Q. *stellata* var. *drummondii* (Liebm.) Trel., Q. *stellata* var. *araniosa* (Ashe) Sarg. × Q. *pseudomargaretta* Trel.

Durand Oak

Quercus sinuata Walt. [A, B, C]

FIELD IDENTIFICATION. A tree attaining a height of 60 ft,

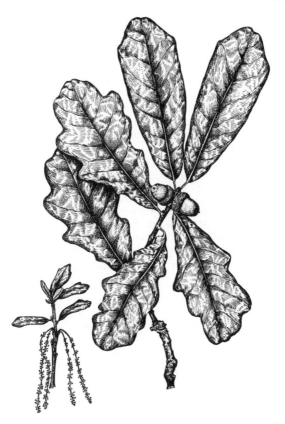

with a trunk diameter of 30 in. The bark gray and flaky
with broad thin scales. This species has been referred to
under the name of Q. *durandii* Buckl. for many years, but it
has been ascertained that the name Q. *sinuata* Walt. has
precedence, as listed in Muller, *The Oaks of Texas*, p. 65.

FLOWERS. Pistillate catkins about 1/5 in. long, usually 2-
flowered on minutely stellate peduncles.

FRUIT. Acorns solitary or paired on peduncles about ⅓ in.
long, or subsessile. Cups about ¾ in. broad and ⅓ in. high,
saucer-shaped or shallowly cup-shaped, flat or rounded at
base, margin not enrolled; scales of cup narrowly ovate,
only moderately thickened basally; apically loosely appressed, silvery-puberulent all over, the margins dark red.
Acorns to 3/5 in. or more long or broad, elliptic to subro-
tund, glabrous except immediately above the apex, tan, one-
fourth or less included in the cup.

LEAVES. Simple, alternate, deciduous; texture firm; length
to 5⅓ in.; width to 2½ in.; shape obovate to oblanceolate;
apices broadly rounded; base cuneate or somewhat rounded;
margin entire to regularly or irregularly sinuate toothed

or lobed; margins minutely revolute; upper surfaces when young sparsely minute-stellate, with maturity glabrate and glossy green; lower surfaces noticeably whitened, or less so later. Petioles to ⅓ in. long, somewhat stellate or glabrous.

TWIGS. About 1/12–1/6 in. thick, when young sparsely stellate-pubescent; later glabrate and gray with minute lenticels.

RANGE. East Texas forests along rivers, and eastward to South Carolina. Westward to the edge of the Edwards Plateau in Texas.

REMARKS. The genus name, *Quercus*, is the ancient classical name. The species name, *sinuata*, refers to the leaf margins being regularly or irregularly sinuate toothed or lobed. It has also been listed as *Q. austrina* Small and *Q. durandii* var. *austrina* (Small) Palmer. Another vernacular name is Bastard Oak. In central Texas, on limestone soils, and in northeast Mexico a variety has been named *Q. sinuata* var. *breviloba* (Torr.) C. H. Mull.

Limestone Durand Oak

Quercus sinuata var. *breviloba* (Torr.) C. H. Mull. [c]

FIELD IDENTIFICATION. Straggling shrubs or small trees with

gray flaking bark. This variety has been long listed under the name of Q. *durandii* var. *breviloba* (Torr.) Palmer, but it has been determined that the name of Q. *sinuata* var. *breviloba* (Torr.) C. H. Mull. has precedence. Reference is made to Muller, *The Oaks of Texas*, p. 66.

FLOWERS. Staminate catkins to 3¼ in. long, finely rather loosely flowered, tomentulose, the anthers moderately or only slightly exserted; pistillate catkins ⅛–⅓ in. long, 1–3-flowered, densely short-tomentose.

FRUIT. Acorn annual, solitary or paired, subsessile or on a pubescent peduncle to ⅓ in. long; acorn cups to ½ in. long and ⅓ in. high, goblet-shaped or shallowly cup-shaped, base rounded or constricted; margins thin, smooth, simple; cup scales ovate, obtuse, the tomentose bases slightly or sharply keeled and thickened, the puberulent apices thin, closely appressed, dark reddish brown. Acorns to ⅝ in. long and ⅜ in. broad, ovoid to elliptic, glabrous, light brown, ¼ enclosed in the cup.

LEAVES. Simple, alternate, deciduous; texture thin to firm; to 3¼ in. long and 1½ broad, or often smaller; shape obovate to oblanceolate or oblong, usually broadest above the middle; apices broadly rounded; bases cuneate or obtuse or some gradually narrowed; margin entire to irregularly toothed or moderately lobed; upper surface glabrous and lustrous; lower surfaces duller, canescent with appressed, minute, stellate puberulence, or in shade forms green and only slightly puberulent or glabrous. Petioles 1/12–1/8 in. long, glabrous or pubescent like the twigs.

TWIGS. Subterete or channeled, to ⅛ in. thick; color grayish brown, glabrous or minutely stellate-tomentulose; lenticels minute; buds 1/12–1/8 in. long, broadly ovoid, obtuse or acute, glabrous or sparsely pubescent, dark reddish brown or grayish brown; stipules rather promptly caducous, 1/8–1/5 in. long, filiform-ligulate, pubescent.

RANGE. Wooded limestone hills of central Texas and northeast Mexico. The related species Q. *sinuata* Walt. occurs in moist river bottoms of south and east Texas.

REMARKS. The genus name, *Quercus*, is the ancient classical name. The species name, *sinuata*, refers to the sinuate leaf margins, and the variety name, *breviloba*, to the short leaf lobes. Other names which have been used are Q. *breviloba* (Torr.) Sarg., Q. *obtusifolia* var. *breviloba* Torr., Q. *annulata* Buckl., Q. *san-sabeana* Buckl., Q. *brevilobata* Sarg., and Q. *breviloba* forma *argentata* Trel.

Live Oak

Quercus virginiana Mill. [A, B, C]

FIELD IDENTIFICATION. Evergreen tree to 60 ft, with a wide-spreading crown and massive limbs close to the ground.

FLOWERS. Staminate and pistillate borne in separate catkins on same tree; staminate catkins hairy, 2–3 in. long; calyx yellow, with 4–7 ovate lobes; stamens 6–12, filaments short, anthers hairy; pistillate catkins fewer, on pubescent peduncles ⅓ in. long; scales and calyx-lobes hairy; stigmas 3, red.

FRUIT. Acorn on peduncles ¼–4 in. long, in clusters of 3–5; nut ellipsoid-obovoid, brownish black, shiny, ⅓–½ in. long; enclosed about one-half its length in the cup; cup turbinate, light reddish brown, hoary-tomentose; scales of cup ovate, acute, thin, appressed.

LEAVES. Simple, alternate, persistent, coriaceous, dark green and lustrous above, paler and glabrous to pubescent beneath; very variable in size and shape, 2–5 in. long, ½–2½ in. wide, oblong or elliptic or obovate; apex rounded or acute, base cuneate, rounded or cordate, margin entire and often revolute, sometimes sharp-dentate, especially toward the apex; petioles about ¼ in. long, stout, glabrous or puberulent.

TWIGS. Grayish brown, glabrous, slender, rigid; terminal buds ovate to subglobose, about 1/6 in. long, light brown; leaf scars half-mooned–shaped.

BARK. Dark brown to black (in some varieties gray), furrows narrow and interlacing, scales closely appressed, small.

WOOD. Light brown, sapwood lighter, close-grained, tough, hard, strong, heavy, weighing about 59 lb per cu ft, difficult to work.

RANGE. This species is usually found in sandy-loam soils but may also occur in heavier clays. In Texas, Oklahoma, and Louisiana. In Louisiana it reaches its largest size in the vicinity of New Orleans and the lower delta area. It extends eastward to Florida and north to Virginia.

REMARKS. The genus name, *Quercus*, is the classical name, and the species name, *virginiana*, refers to the state of Virginia. The wood is used for hubs, cogs, shipbuilding, or any other purpose where a hard and strong wood is required. The tree is often planted in the southern states for ornament along avenues. It is comparatively free of insect pests and diseases and can stand considerable salinity, often growing close to the sea. The bark was formerly much used in the production of tannin, and acorn oil was much used in cooking by the Indians. Live Oak seems to be susceptible to soil types, and produces dwarf varieties and diverse leaf forms under certain conditions. The fruit seems to vary least in the varieties.

Scrub Live Oak

Quercus fusiformis Small [B, C]

FIELD IDENTIFICATION. A shrub or tree to 36 ft tall. Very similar in habit to Q. *virginiana* Mill., and, although it appears distinct in the western part of its distribution (beyond the Edwards Plateau area and into Mexico), on its eastern range it seems to pass into this species with many intermediary variants.

FLOWERS. Similar to that of Q. *virginiana* Mill.

FRUIT. Borne on peduncles ¾–2⅓ in. long, solitary or several together. The cups much constricted basally and flaring upward. Acorn elongate, fusiform or subfusiform, brown, shiny.

LEAVES. Simple, alternate, evergreen; length ¾–2⅓ in. or more; width ⅓–1¼ in.; shape narrowly oblong; margins entire or toothed and strongly revolute.

RANGE. Limestone outcrops on the coastal plain uplands, abundant on the limestone hills west to the Pecos River and south along the east face of the mountains through Coahuila, Nuevo León, and Tamaulipas. The type from Kerr County, Texas.

REMARKS. The genus name, *Quercus*, is the ancient Latin name. The species name, *fusiformis*, refers to the shape of the acorn. Some authors prefer to maintain it as a variety under the name of Q. *virginiana* var. *fusiformis* (Small) Sarg.

Dwarf Live Oak

Quercus minima (Sarg.) Small [B]

The interpretation of Q. *oleoides* var. *quaterna* C. H. Muller, as presented by Muller, *The Oaks of Texas*, p. 76, and

Robert A. Vines in *Trees, Shubs and Woody Vines of the Southwest*, p. 171, has been superseded in interpretation by Correll and Johnston, *Manual of the Vascular Plants of Texas*, p. 483. The following description follows the latter work but is rearranged according to the standard outline of the present publication.

FIELD IDENTIFICATION. A shrub from 8 in. to 6 ft tall, in sandy soils, or hybridizing with other species to form small to medium-sized trees.

FLOWERS. The staminate catkins rather loosely flowered, ½–2 in. long; borne on a fulvous-stellate, tomentulose peduncle; calyx pubescent; anthers exserted. Pistillate catkins 1¼–4 in. long, several-flowered. The peduncle fulvous-pubescent, but later more glabrate.

FRUIT. Acorns solitary or paired on peduncles 1/5–1 1/5 in. long. The acorn body about 3/5–4/5 in. long and ⅓–½ in. thick, glabrous and usually glossy brown, about one-fourth to one-third included in the cup. Acorn cup about 2/5–3/5 in. broad; about 1/3–3/5 in. high; or some more variable; usually deeply goblet-shaped and suddenly constricted at base; scales somewhat strongly thickened at base; surfaces silvery-tomentose, the reddish apices puberulent or glabrous.

LEAVES. Simple, alternate, evergreen and very variable in shape on different plants. Characteristically with two general leaf types with the texture hard and coriaceous. The lower leaves usually larger and toothed or lobed; 1¾–4½ in. long and ¾–2 in. broad; shape broadly oblanceolate to narrowly obovate; margin slightly revolute, coarsely and irregularly toothed in the upper half or full length; apices obtuse or acute; base broadly cuneate; upper surface glabrous and lustrous or sparingly stellate about the base of the midrib; lower surface densely or sparsely silvery appressed-stellate-puberulent, this persistent or on some of the broad lower leaves, variously deciduous, the midrib and principal veins glabrous. The upper leaves usually narrowly oblong and entire, tending to hold their pubescence more persistently than the broad upper ones; length of the narrow forms ¾–3 in.; width 1/5–3/5 in.; shape oblanceolate, entire or few-toothed near the acute or rounded apex; base narrowly cuneate. Veins 4–12 on each side, but usually more on the narrower leaves, much-branched and anastomasing, but prominent beneath. Petioles 1/25–1/5 in. long, stellate-pubescent.

TWIGS. Densely silvery or fulvous-stellate-tomentulose, finally glabrate and dark red, 1/15–1/12 in. thick. Buds about 1/15 in. long, subglobose, shiny red, sparingly pubescent, quickly caducous.

RANGE. Along the Texas Gulf coast. Often in deep sand behind the beach areas. In Aransas, Brazoria, Calhoun, Jackson, Jefferson, Nueces, Victoria counties, and probably others. Eastward along the coast to Florida and North Carolina.

REMARKS. The genus name, *Quercus*, is the ancient name. The species name, *minima*, refers to its size as a shrub, except where hybridization occurs with other larger oaks.

Some synonyms are considered to be Q. *virens* var. *dentata* Chapm., Q. *virginiana* var. *minima* Sarg., Q. *oleoides* var. *quaterna* C. H. Mull. It is likewise stated that the type of Q. *oleoides* var. *quaterna* C. H. Mull. has been relegated to be a synonym of Q. *fusiformis* Small.

Willow Oak

Quercus phellos L. [A, B, C]

FIELD IDENTIFICATION. Tree to 130 ft, and 6 ft in diameter, with a rounded or broad-oblong crown.

FLOWERS. Borne in spring in separate staminate and pistillate catkins; moderately close-flowered, hairy, yellowish green, with 4–5 acute calyx-lobes, anthers oval and exserted; pistillate flowers usually solitary, occasionally in pairs, glabrous peduncles 1/25–1/8 in. long, 1–3-flowered; scales and calyx hairy; stigmas red, slender, recurved.

FRUIT. Maturing in 2 years, solitary or in pairs, sessile, or on short peduncles to 1/5 in. long; acorn subglobose to ovoid,

2/5–3/5 in. long, nearly as broad as long, densely puberulent or glabrate later, yellowish to dull brown, sometimes striate, about one-fourth of base enclosed in cup; cup 2/5–3/5 in. broad, 1/6–1/3 in. high, saucer-shaped, shallow, margin not inrolled, enveloping only the base of the acorn; scales closely appressed, imbricate, small, thin, ovate, greenish brown, finely tomentose. Acorns averaging about 600 per lb.

LEAVES. Revolute in the bud, alternate, simple, deciduous, linear-lanceolate to elliptic, entire on margin, apex acute and bristle-tipped, base cuneate or narrowly rounded; light to dark green and glabrous above, or slightly pubescent on the midrib; lower surface paler and glabrous or pubescent along the midrib, blade length 2–5 in., width 1/3–1 in.; petioles stout, 1/25–1/4 in. long, tomentose at first and glabrate later.

TWIGS. Reddish brown and pubescent at first, gray and glabrous later, slender, fluted; buds brown, ovoid to lanceolate, apex acute, 1/12–1/6 in. long, scales mostly glabrous and ciliate; stipules caducous, 1/4–1/3 in. long, filiform, villous.

WOOD. Light brown, close-grained, soft, moderately strong, not durable, weighing 46 lb per cu ft, of rather low quality in comparison with that of other oaks.

RANGE. Willow Oak grows usually on rich, wet bottom lands of clays or loams. Eastern Texas, Oklahoma, Arkansas, and Louisiana; eastward to Florida, north to New York, and west to Illinois.

REMARKS. The genus name, *Quercus*, is the classical Latin names of the oaks, and the species name, *phellos* ("cork"), is the ancient Greek name of Q. *suber* L., Cork Oak. Other local names are Water Oak, Peach Oak, Sandjacks Oak, Red Oak, Swamp Oak, Swamp Willow Oak, and Pin Oak. Willow Oak is often called Pin Oak in many sections of the South, but that name should apply to the true Pin Oak, Q. *palustris* Muenchh. The author has never seen the true Pin Oak in Texas outside of cultivation. However, there is a remote possibility that the true Pin Oak may extend far enough southward to reach into the northeastern corner of the state. Other oaks which are apt to be confused with the Willow Oak are Laurel Oak, Bluejack Oak, Water Oak, and Diamond-leaf Oak. Willow Oak makes an exceedingly handsome ornamental tree and has been cultivated since 1723. The wood is somewhat inferior to that of other commercial oaks but is used for fuel, charcoal, ties, shingles, sills, planks, and general construction. The acorns are eaten by wild turkey, bobwhite quail, dove, jay, gray fox, and squirrel.

Bluejack Oak

Quercus incana Bartr. [A, B, C]

FIELD IDENTIFICATION. Shrub or tree to 35 ft, with stout crooked branches.

FLOWERS. In spring, in staminate and pistillate catkins; staminate catkins clustered, 2–3 in. long, hairy; calyx-lobes 4–5 in. ovate, acute, red to yellowish green; stamens 4–5, yellow; anthers apiculate; pistillate catkins on stout, tomentose, short peduncles; scales and calyx-lobes of pistillate flowers tomentose, stigmas dark red.

FRUIT. Maturing the second season, sessile or short-stalked, globose to ovoid, sometimes flattened, brown with grayish pubescence, often striate, about ½ in. long, set in a shallow cup one-third to one-half its length, kernel bitter; cup shallow, saucer-shaped; scales imbricate, thin, ovate, tomentose, reddish brown.

LEAVES. Alternate, simple, deciduous, entire (or rarely 3-dentate at the apex), oblong-lanceolate to elliptic, distinctly grayish green, densely tomentose beneath, smoother above, cuneate or rounded at base, acute or rounded at the apex, apiculate, 2–5 in. long, ½–1½ in. wide; petiole ¼–½ in. long, stout.

TWIGS. Gray to dark brown, slender, smooth.

BARK. Grayish brown to black, broken into small blocklike plates.

WOOD. Reddish brown, close-grained, hard, strong.

RANGE. Usually in dry sandy pinelands of east Texas, Louisiana, Oklahoma, and Arkansas; north and east to North Carolina and Virginia.

REMARKS. The genus name, *Quercus*, is the ancient classical name, and the species name, *incana*, refers to the grayish green tomentum of the leaves. Vernacular names are Upland Willow Oak, High-ground Willow Oak, Sandjack Oak, Turkey Oak, and Cinnamon Oak. The trunk is generally too small to be of much value except for fuel or posts.

Laurel Oak

Quercus laurifolia Michx. [A, B, C]

FIELD IDENTIFICATION. Dense, round-topped tree attaining a height of 100 ft.

A diamond-leafed
variation from east Texas

FLOWERS. Staminate and pistillate catkins borne separately
on same tree in spring. Staminate catkins clustered, red,
hairy, 2–3 in. long; calyx 4-lobed, pubescent; pistillate catkins short-stalked with brown hairy involucral scales; calyx-
lobes acute; stigmas red with short spreading styles.

FRUIT. Acorn usually solitary, sessile or subsessile, ovoid to
hemispheric, dark brown, about ½ in. long, enclosed about
one-fourth its length in the cup; cup thin, saucer-shaped,
reddish brown, with appressed ovate scales.

LEAVES. Alternate, simple, deciduous in the North, half-
evergreen in the South, elliptic, or oblong or occasionally
obovate and lobed, sometimes falcate; leaves on young
shoots or young plants often variously cut and lobed. Apex
acute and apiculate, base narrowed, deep shiny green and
glabrous above, paler and lustrous beneath, blades 2–6 in.
long, ½–1 in. wide; petioles yellow, stout, rarely more than
¼ in. long.

TWIGS. Reddish brown to gray, glabrous, slender.

BARK. When young nearly smooth, dark brown tinged with
red, when older dark gray to black, furrows separated by
flat ridges.

WOOD. Reddish brown, coarse-grained, heavy, hard, strong,
weighing 48 lb per cu ft, warps easily.

RANGE. In low grounds, eastern and coastal Texas and Louisiana; east to Florida and north to South Carolina and Virginia.

REMARKS. The genus name, *Quercus*, is the classical name of the oak tree, and the species name, *laurifolia*, refers to the laurellike foliage. Vernacular names are Water Oak, Willow Oak, and Live Oak. The tree is often cultivated for ornament in the South. The wood is mostly used for fuel and charcoal.

Laurel Oak forms part of a very complex group including the Willow Oak, Water Oak, and Diamond-leaf Oak. There is considerable variation and hybridization. Botanical authors do not agree on the exact relationship of these species. For example, the Diamond-leaf Oak (*Q. obtusa* [Willd.] Ashe) is now considered to be a broadleaf form of Laurel Oak (*Q. laurifolia* Michx.) with the leaves typically broadest across the middle (diamond-leaf) or with margins entire or slightly wavy (or short-lobed in young leaves); apex acute to rounded and apiculate and a cuneate base. Also, there is considerable diversity of opinion between the names of *Q. laurifolia* Michx. and *Q. hemisphaerica* Bartr. (see description of *Q. hemisphaerica*).

Coastal Laurel Oak

Quercus hemisphaerica Bartr. [B]

There is a considerable diversity of opinion among taxonomists concerning the differences between *Q. hemisphaerica* Bartr. and *Q. laurifolia* Michx. They are so closely related that they are very difficult to separate by any constant set of dependable diagnostic characteristics. However, there are a few colonies in the coastal sands of Aransas County, in the vicinity of Rockport, Texas, and forming mottes on the sandy prairies which possibly could be designated as *Q. hemisphaerica*. The following description of *Q. hemisphaerica* is adapted from Correll and Johnston, *Manual of Vascular Plants of Texas*, p. 486.

FIELD IDENTIFICATION. Shrubs or small trees to 30 ft tall.

FLOWERS. Catkins and fruit similar to *Q. laurifolia* but smaller.

FRUIT. Acorns 1/25–1/15 in. long. Cups 1/25–1/15 in. broad, 1/8–1/6 in. high.

LEAVES. Evergreen, highly variable; ½–3¼ in. long; ⅓–1½ in. broad; shape narrowly oblong to obovate; apices usually acute and aristate-tipped; base rounded to cordate or sometimes cuneate; margin entire or variously apically toothed or basally lobed, the teeth and lobes aristate; margins

markedly revolute; upper surface minutely and sparsely puberulent, glossy green; lower surface similar to upper, but dull, more densely and persistently puberulent near the base. Petioles 1/12–1/8 in. long, rose-colored becoming red with maturity, pubescent as the twigs.

TWIGS. Very stiff, 1/25–1/8 in. thick, round or only slightly fluted, dark reddish brown, gray the second season, densely fulvous-stellate the first season. Buds 1/8–1/6 in. long; 1/12–1/8 in. broad; very acute; nearly glabrous and dark reddish brown; stipules deciduous, 1/6–1/5 in. long, ligulate, villous.

RANGE. Sandy woodlands, sometimes forming mottes on sandy prairies, often dominating stream terraces, along the Gulf Coast in Texas; east to the Atlantic.

REMARKS. The genus name, *Quercus*, is an ancient name. The species name, *hemisphaerica*, refers to the rounded acorn. A hybrid has been named Q. *hemisphaerica* × Q. *falcata*. It differs from Q. *hemisphaerica* in having large variable leaves 2–6¾ in. long and ⅝–4¾ in. broad; shape entire to undulate or deeply and irregularly lobed; lower surface persistently pubescent or merely with axillary tufts. Acorns densely puberulent; cups deep bowl-shaped, the scales densely tomentose. Differing from Q. *falcata* in the

A common lobe-leafed
variant of Aransas County

less-lobed thick leaves with sparse pubescence beneath,
acorns subglobose. In various sites with Q. *hemisphaerica*
east of the San Antonio River near the Gulf Coast in Texas.

Water Oak

Quercus nigra L. [A, B, C]

FIELD IDENTIFICATION. Tree attaining a height of 80 ft, with
a round top and grayish black bark. Leaves variously shaped,
wedge-shaped and entire at the apex, or 3-lobed at apex, or
variously cut into oblique bristle-tipped lobes.

FLOWERS. Appearing with the leaves in spring in separate
staminate and pistillate catkins; staminate catkins clustered,
2–3 in. long; calyx 4–5-lobed, pubescent; pistillate catkins
short-peduncled, scales rusty-hairy; stigmas red.

FRUIT. Ripening September–October. Acorn sessile or short-peduncled, solitary or paired, globose-ovoid, ⅓–⅔ in. high, light yellowish brown, often striate, usually somewhat pubescent, flat at base, enveloped in cup one-third to one-half its length; cup shallow, saucer-shaped, thin, reddish brown, pubescent; scales small, thin, closely appressed, imbricate.

LEAVES. Simple, alternate, persistent, variously shaped; typically entire, obovate or spatulate; with a rounded or 3-lobed apex; margins on some leaves often with deep, oblique, bristle-tipped lobes, a variety of shapes frequently appearing on the same twig or on different twigs; blades 2–4 in. long, 1–2 in. wide, upper surface lustrous green and glabrous, lower surface lighter and glabrous, or pubescent in vein axils; petioles short and stout. Leaves half-evergreen in the southern Gulf Coast area.

TWIGS. Slender, glabrous, reddish gray; buds ovoid, acute, angled, reddish brown, ⅛–¼ in. long.

BARK. Grayish black to light brown, bark so tightly appressed as to appear almost smooth, ridges flattened and thin.

WOOD. Light brown, sapwood lighter, close-grained, heavy, hard, strong.

RANGE. In low woods or borders of streams or swamps. From the Colorado River of Texas eastward through Louisiana to Florida, northward into Oklahoma, Arkansas, and Missouri, and on the Atlantic Coastal Plain to New Jersey.

REMARKS. The genus name, *Quercus*, is the classical name, and the species name, *nigra*, refers to the black bark. Vernacular names are Bluejack Oak, Duck Oak, Pin Oak, Spotted Oak, Barren Oak, Punk Oak, and Possum Oak. The wood is used for fuel, crossties, and poles. Water Oak is extensively planted as a street shade tree in the South and is subject to attack by mistletoe. Trident Water Oak, *Q. nigra* var. *tridentifera* Sarg., is a variety described as having leaves more acute at the apex, but this character does not appear to be constant, and it has been relegated to the status of a synonym of Water Oak.

Blackjack Oak

Quercus marilandica Muenchh. [A, B, C]

FIELD IDENTIFICATION. Shrub, or round-topped symmetrical tree attaining a height of 60 ft and a diameter of 2 ft.

FLOWERS. With the leaves in spring, in staminate or pistillate catkins; staminate catkins clustered, loosely flowered, slender, hairy, yellowish green, 2–4 in. long; stamens 3–12, filaments filiform, anthers exserted; calyx thin, pubescent, reddish green, 4–5-lobed; pistillate flowers solitary or paired, 1/8–1/5 in. long, pubescent to glabrate, peduncles rusty-tomentose and short; styles recurved, stigmas red.

FRUIT. Acorn ripening in 2 years, solitary or in pairs, sessile or on peduncles 1/8–2/5 in. long; light brown, enclosed one-third to two-thirds in cup, 3/5–4/5 in. long, ½–¾ in. high, often striate, ovoid-oblong to subglobose, pubescent; cup thick, turbinate, 3/5–4/5 in. broad, bases rounded or suddenly constricted; scales of cup imbricate, loose, obtuse, ovate to oblong, thin.

LEAVES. Simple, alternate, deciduous, stiff, coriaceous, broadly obovate to clavate, margin revolute; apex, 3-lobed to entire or dentate, bristle-tipped, base rounded, cordate or cuneate; upper surface dark green, glossy and glabrous (or young leaves tomentose and hairy along the veins); lower surface semiglabrate or scurfy and yellow-hairy, veins conspicuous, length 3–7 in., width 2–5 in.; petioles ½–¾ in., stout, glabrous or pubescent; stipules caducous, ¼–⅓ in., glabrous or pubescent.

TWIGS. Grayish brown, stout, stiff, densely tomentose at first, glabrous later; buds 1/6–1/3 in. long, ovoid to lanceolate, apex acute, reddish brown, slightly or densely tomentose.

BARK. Dark brown or black, broken into rough, blocklike plates.

WOOD. Dark brown, sapwood lighter, heavy, hard, strong, weighing 46 lb per cu ft.

RANGE. Usually on dry, sandy, sterile soils. Central Texas, Oklahoma, and Arkansas; eastward through Louisiana to Florida, north to New York, and west to Minnesota, Michigan, Illinois, and Kansas.

REMARKS. The genus name, *Quercus*, is of classical origin, and the species name, *marilandica*, refers to the state of Maryland. Also known by the vernacular names of Iron Oak, Black Oak, Jack Oak, Barren Oak, and Scrub Oak. The wood is used mostly for posts, fuel, and charcoal, and the acorns are sought by wild turkey and white-tailed deer.

Southern Red Oak

Quercus falcata Michx. [A, B, C]

FIELD IDENTIFICATION. An open, rounded tree, forming a broad top and attaining a height of 80 ft. Leaves very variable, 3–7-lobed (or 5–13 lobes in some varieties), lobes often falcate, brownish white-tomentose beneath.

FLOWERS. March–May, staminate and pistillate catkins borne separately on same tree; staminate catkins clustered, tomentose, 3–5 in. long; calyx-lobes 4–5, round, thin, hairy; pistillate flowers solitary or several together, borne on downy peduncles; scales of involucre with reddish tomentum; calyx-lobes acute.

FRUIT. Solitary or in pairs, sessile or short-peduncled, small, globular or hemispheric, orange-brown; often striate, pubescent, about ½ in. long, enclosed to one-third its length in

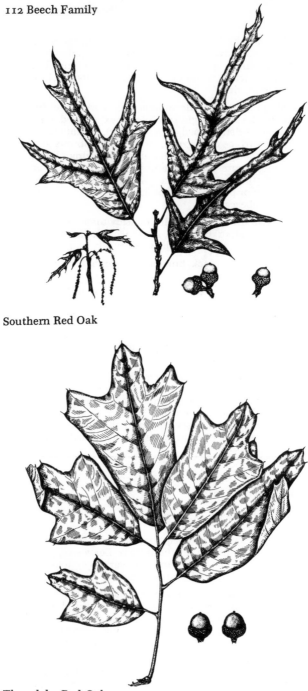

Southern Red Oak

Three-lobe Red Oak

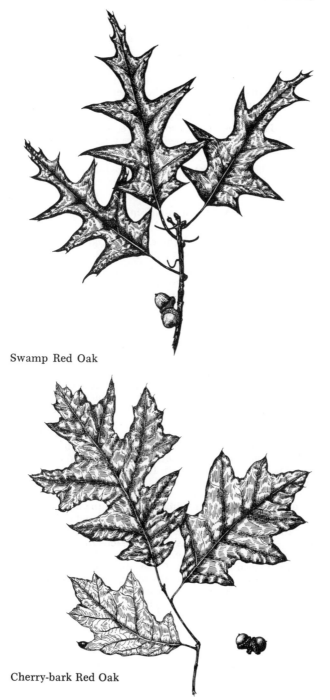

Swamp Red Oak

Cherry-bark Red Oak

the shallow, saucer-shaped, thin cup; cup scales reddish, pubescent, ovate-oblong, acute or rounded at apex; matures during the second season.

LEAVES. Simple, alternate, deciduous, very variable in shape and lobing, ovate-oblong to obovate, with usually 3–7 bristle-tipped lobes (usually 3-lobed in the variety *triloba*, but numerous lobes in the varieties *pagodaefolia* and *leucophylla*); lobes often falcate, slender, narrowed, rounded or cuneate at the base; dark green and lustrous above, paler with brown to grayish white tomentum beneath; leaf blades 6–7 in. long, 4–5 in. wide; petioles slender, flattened, 1–2 in.

TWIGS. Reddish brown, stout, pubescent at first, later glabrous; terminal buds ⅛–¼ in. long, ovoid, acute, reddish brown.

BARK. Grayish black, broken into deep fissures and appressed scales.

WOOD. Light red, sapwood lighter, coarse-grained, durable, heavy, hard, strong, weighing 43 lb per cu ft.

RANGE. The typical species of Southern Red Oak occur from the Brazos River of Texas eastward through Louisiana to Florida, Oklahoma, and Arkansas and northward to New York, Pennsylvania, Ohio, and Illinois.

REMARKS. *Quercus* is an old classical name, and the species name, *falcata*, refers to the scythe-shaped leaves. Vernacular names are Spanish Oak, Turkey Oak, Pagoda Oak, and Cherry-bark Oak. The tree is often planted for ornament, and the wood is used for general purposes, rough lumber, and furniture (chairs and tables). The bark is excellent for tanning and is used as an astringent in medicine.

Red Oak Complex: The former name of Q. *rubra* L., meaning "Red Oak," has for many years been a vague and confusing term applying to a complex of northern and southern oaks. It was suggested that the name be replaced by Q. *falcata* Michx., as applying to Southern Red Oak and Q. *borealis* Michx., as applying to Northern Red Oak.

Southern Red Oak, Q. *falcata*, is in itself a very variable species, and not all botanists agree as to the exact status of some of its variations. The difficulty lies in the unstable character of the species and its tendency to produce intergrading forms over wide areas.

The first variety, known as the Three-lobe Red Oak, Q. *falcata* var. *triloba* (Michx.) Nutt., is a form in which the leaves are 3-lobed at the apex. Other differences between it and the species are negligible. However, the number of 3-lobed leaves on different trees varies considerably. Some trees have practically all leaves 3-lobed, some trees perhaps half, and others very few. Some botanists conclude, therefore, that this 3-lobed form is not constant enough to warrant a special varietal name.

A second variety, now known as Swamp Red Oak, Q. *falcata* var. *pagodaefolia* (Ell.) Ashe, is described by some botanists as a separate species (Pagoda Oak, Q. *pagoda* Raf.).

However, a varietal standing does seem to fit the tree better than species rank. The fruit and flowers are similar to the typical species, but the leaves are distinctly pagoda-shaped, with 5–13 lobes, and have a cuneate or truncate base. Also, the bark has a tendency to be tighter and resemble the bark of Wild Cherry, hence giving it the name of Cherry-bark Oak in some areas.

The third variety, known as the true Cherry-bark Red Oak, Q. falcata var. leucophylla (Ashe) Palmer & Steyerm., is very closely allied to the Swamp Red Oak. In fact, if the Swamp Red Oak were given a species name, then the Cherry-bark Red Oak would fall into a varietal classification under it. It has similar acorns and cherrylike bark, but the leaves have somewhat more irregular lobes and the lower surface is more or less white-tomentose. The lower leaves on Cherry-bark Oak-trees resemble those of Black Oak leaves in shape.

Black Oak

Quercus velutina Lam. [A, B, C]

FIELD IDENTIFICATION. Stout tree attaining a height of 90 ft, with a spreading open crown. Bark dark brownish black. Leaves cut into usually 7 oblique lobes with sinuses of different depths.

FLOWERS. April–May, appearing with the leaves in staminate and pistillate catkins; staminate catkins clustered, tomentose, 3–6 in. long; calyx hairy with acute lobes; stamens 4–12; pistillate catkins a few together on short tomentose peduncles; bracts ovate; stigmas red.

FRUIT. Maturing September–October, acorn solitary or paired, sessile or short-stalked, ovoid-oblong or hemispheric, brown, often striate, pubescent, ½–1 in. long, one-half to three-fourths of length enclosed in cup; cup turbinate, light brown, pubescent or glabrous, ¾–1 in. broad; scales closely appressed toward base of cup but loose and spreading near the rim—a diagnostic feature distinguishing it from other similar oaks.

LEAVES. Simple, alternate, deciduous, oval-obovate, usually with 7 oblique bristle-tipped lobes, middle lobes longest, apex acuminate or acute, base cuneate or truncate, surface dark green and lustrous; paler below and either pubescent or glabrous, tufts of hairs in axils of veins; 4–10 in. long, 3–7 in. broad; petioles 3–6 in., stout, yellow, glabrous or puberulous.

TWIGS. Reddish brown, stout, tomentose at first, glabrous later.

BARK. Dark brown to black, ridges flattened with platelike scales between deep fissures; inner bark orange-yellow, bitter.

WOOD. Reddish brown, sapwood paler, coarse-grained, strong, heavy, hard, weighing about 43 lb per cu ft, not commercially distinguished from other Red Oaks.

RANGE. Apparently not at home on the Gulf Coast plain. Often on poor, dry, sandy, heavy clay, or gravelly soils. Eastern Texas, Louisiana, Oklahoma, and Arkansas; eastward to Florida, north to Maine, and west to Ontario, Wisconsin, and Iowa.

REMARKS. The genus name, *Quercus*, is the classical name, and the species name, *velutina*, refers to the velvety pubescence of the lower leaf surface. Vernacular names are Dyers Oak, Spotted Oak, Yellow-bark Oak, Yellow Oak, and Quercitron. The inner bark yields a tannin and a yellow dye for woolen goods. It is also a source of quercitannic acid, which has medicinal uses. However, because of the large amount of tannin, the bark is less often used in medical practice than White Oak bark. The drug is officially known as Quercus Cortex and is used mostly as a mild astringent.

The wood of Black Oak is used for rough lumber, crossties, and fuel, or generally for the same purposes as Red Oak, not generally being separated from it in the lumber trade. Black Oak is seldom used for ornamental planting, because it lacks the brilliant fall coloring of some of the other oaks. It is rather slow growing and trees over 200 years of age are seldom seen. It has been cultivated since 1802.

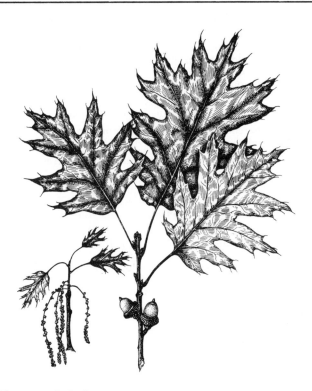

Shumard Oak

Quercus shumardii Buckl. [A, B, C]

FIELD IDENTIFICATION. Tree attaining a height of 120 ft, with an open head and stout spreading branches. Leaves 5–9-lobed, usually 7-lobed, green and glabrous on both sides except for tufts of hairs in the axils of the veins beneath. Distinguished from Southern Red Oak by the smoothness and lobing, the Southern Red Oak having leaves densely pubescent beneath and irregularly lobed. Also, Southern Red Oak has much smaller acorns than Shumard Oak.

FLOWERS. Borne in spring on separate staminate and pistillate catkins; staminate catkins slender, 6–7 in. long, usually clustered; calyx-lobes 4–5, hairy; stamens 4–12; pistillate flowers solitary or paired, peduncles pubescent; involucral scales ovate, pubescent, brown or greenish; stigmas red.

FRUIT. Acorn sessile or short-stalked, solitary or paired, ovoid to oblong-ovoid, pubescent or glabrous, sometimes striate,

¾–1 in. long, ½–1 in. wide, set only at base in shallow, thick cups; cup covering one-fourth the length of acorn; scales appressed, imbricate, thin or tuberculate, acuminate.

LEAVES. Simple, alternate, deciduous, obovate, or elliptic-oblong, cut into 7–9 more or less symmetrical lobes, lobes sometimes lobulate and bristle-tipped, sinuses broad and varying in depth. The leaves of upper and lower branches often vary considerably in the number and length of lobes. Upper surface dark green, glabrous and lustrous, lower surface paler and glabrous with tufts of axillary hairs; petioles glabrous, grayish brown.

TWIGS. Grayish brown, glabrous; branches smooth.

BARK. Gray to reddish brown, smooth or broken into small tight interlacing ridges.

WOOD. Light reddish brown, close-grained, hard, strong, weighing 57 lb per cu ft.

RANGE. Moist hillsides or bottom lands in clay soils. Central Texas, Oklahoma, and Arkansas; eastward through Louisiana to Florida, northward to Pennsylvania and west to Kansas.

REMARKS. The genus name, *Quercus*, is the classical name, and the species name, *shumardii*, refers to Benjamin Franklin Shumard (1820–1869), state geologist of Texas. Vernacular names are Spotted Oak, Leopard Oak, and Spanish Oak. The wood is not commercially distinguished from that of the other Red Oaks and is used for veneer, cabinets, furniture, flooring, interior trim, and lumber. It is a beautiful tree with a symmetrical leaf design and, being rather free from insects and diseases, could be more extensively cultivated for ornament.

Nuttall Oak

Quercus nuttallii Palmer [A]

FIELD IDENTIFICATION. Tree attaining a height of 120 ft, with a diameter of 3 ft. Small trees have a rather narrow pyramidal crown which becomes broad, open, and wide-spreading with age. The upper branches are ascending and the lower horizontal or drooping. The trunk is often branched close to the ground, and older trees are almost always strongly buttressed.

FLOWERS. Borne in separate staminate and pistillate catkins similar to those of Red Oak.

FRUIT. Acorn and cup variable in size and shape; sessile or short-stalked, oblong-obovoid, length ¾–1¼ in., width ½–1 in., light to dark reddish brown, usually striate, apex rounded and narrowed, at first scurfy but later shiny, enclosed about

one-fourth to one-half of length in a hemispheric or turbinate cup; cup about 5/8 in. broad, gray-puberulent, abruptly
continued into a conspicuous (1/12–3/16 in. long) neck at
the base, which is an important diagnostic feature.

LEAVES. Very variable in size and shape, simple, alternate,
deciduous, rather symmetrically 5–7 lobed, the lobes horizontal or slightly ascending, the central pair usually longer
and broader, usually terminating in 2–5 bristly teeth and
commonly abruptly squared or angular; terminal lobe either
entire, acuminate, and bristle-tipped, or 3-toothed with the
middle tooth much larger than the others and all bristle-
tipped; smaller and lower lobes triangular, acuminate, and
more or less entire (particularly in the small leaves in the
upper part of the crown), sinuses wide, deep, obtuse or angu-
larly rounded, base cuneate to truncate, length of blade 4–8
in., width 2–5 in., upper surface dull dark green and glabrous, lower surface paler and glabrous or with tufts of pale
hair in the axils of the main veins, thin but firm; petioles
slender, glabrous, 3/4–2 in. long; winter buds pubescent to

glabrous, ciliate, ovoid, acute to acuminate, about ¼ in. long; autumnal leaves yellow or dull light brown, rarely red.

TWIGS. Young ones glabrous, olive green to reddish brown, later brown to gray.

BARK. On young trees greenish brown, tight, smooth, often shiny; on older trees very close, hard, firm, ½–1 in. thick; fissures shallow, irregular and narrow; ridges broad, flat and gray-scaly; light to dark gray or brownish to black, often with small excrescences, warts, or burls.

WOOD. Reddish brown, sapwood yellowish brown, hard, heavy, mineral stains common, checks excessively. The short trunk and many horizontal or drooping branches result in many pin knots in the logs.

RANGE. Usually in low, poorly drained clay, silty clay, or occasionally loamy flats in both first and second bottom lands. Also sometimes on fairly well-drained clay ridges of first bottoms. Not usual in permanent swamps but more common in shallow swags and drains. On the Gulf Coast plain or adjacent provinces. Eastern Texas, Louisiana, Mississippi, Alabama, Oklahoma, Arkansas, and southeastern Missouri.

REMARKS. The genus name, *Quercus*, is the classical name for the oak. The species name, *nuttallii*, is in honor of Thomas Nuttall (1786–1859), an English-born American botanist and ornithologist. It is also known under the name of Red Oak, is not segregated from it in the lumber trade, and is of considerable commercial value. Other names for it are Smooth-bark Red Oak, Tight-bark Red Oak, Yellow-butt Oak, Striped Oak, Red River Oak, and Pin Oak. The tree has more than average susceptibility to fire injury and fungus damage. It is also subject to leaf beetle and grub infestation in damaged or waning specimens. A variety of Nuttall Oak has been given the name of *Q. nuttallii* var. *cachensis* Palmer. It has smaller, short-oblong or depressed conic acorns included about ⅓ in. in the cup, length 3/5–3/4 in., width 1/2–2/5 in. In Arkansas in the bottoms of the Cache River.

Nuttall Oak is easily confused with the Northern Pin Oak, *Q. palustris* Muenchh., especially in Arkansas, where the ranges of the two overlap.

Elm Family (Ulmaceae)

Sugar Hackberry

Celtis laevigata Willd. [A, B, C]

FIELD IDENTIFICATION. Tree attaining a height of 100 ft, with a spreading round-topped or oblong crown.

FLOWERS. In spring, monoecious-polygamous, small, inconspicuous, greenish, borne on slender glabrous pedicels; staminate fascicled; calyx 4–6-lobed, (usually 5), lobes ovate-lanceolate, glabrous or pubescent; stamens 4–6; pistillate flowers solitary or 2 together, peduncled; ovary 1-celled, surmounted by 2 stigmas.

FRUIT. Drupe ripening in late summer, pedicel ¼–½ in., subglobose-obovoid, orange-red to black, about ¼ in. in diameter, flesh thin and dry, sweetish; seed solitary, pale brown, roughened. Fruit pedicel often longer than the leaf petiole.

LEAVES. Simple, alternate, deciduous, ovate-lanceolate, often falcate, long-acuminate at apex, rounded or wedge-shaped and inequilateral at base, entire or a few teeth near apex, thin, light green and glabrous above, paler and smooth beneath, conspicuously 3-veined at base beneath, 2½–4 in. long, 1–2½ in. wide.

TWIGS. Light green to reddish brown, somewhat divaricate, lustrous, glabrous or pubescent.

Small Sugar Hackberry

BARK. Pale gray, thin, smooth or cracked, with prominent warty excrescences.

WOOD. Yellowish, close-grained, soft, weak, weighing 49 lb per cu ft.

RANGE. The species is found in Texas, Arkansas, Oklahoma, and Louisiana; east to Florida, and north to Missouri, Kansas, Indiana, and Virginia. Also in Nuevo León, Mexico.

REMARKS. *Celtis* is a name given by Pliny to a sweet-fruited African lotus. The species name, *laevigata*, means "smooth." The wood is used to a limited extent for furniture, flooring, crating, fuel, cooperage, and posts. The dry sweet fruit is eaten by at least 10 species of birds. The tree is often used for street planting in the lower South.

This species seems to present a considerable number of local variations which have caused some botanists to name a number of varieties, while other botanists feel that the distinctions are too slight. Some of these are as follows:

Texas Sugar Hackberry, *C. laevigata* var. *texana* (Scheele) Sarg., is scattered in Texas and extends over the Edwards Plateau limestone area to the west. It has leaves which are ovate-lanceolate, acuminate, mostly entire, rounded or cordate at the base, glabrous above and pubescent beneath with axillary hairs; fruit orange-red with pedicels longer than the petioles; branches gray to reddish brown and pubescent.

Uvalde Sugar Hackberry, *C. laevigata* var. *brachyphylla* Sarg., is a form with thicker and shorter leaves, found on the rocky banks of the Nueces River, Texas.

Scrub Sugar Hackberry, *C. laevigata* var. *anomala* Sarg., is a sandy-land shrub of Callahan County, Texas, having oblong-ovate, cordate leaves and dark purple, glaucous fruit.

Texas Sugar Hackberry

Net-leaf Sugar Hackberry

Small Sugar Hackberry, *C. laevigata* var. *smallii* (Beadle) Sarg., is a small tree with sharply serrate, acuminate, somewhat smaller leaves. It occurs from the Gulf Coast plain north to North Carolina and Tennessee.

Arizona Sugar Hackberry, *C. laevigata* var. *brevipes* Sarg., is an Arizona variety with ovate, mostly entire leaves 1½–2 in. long, yellow fruit, and glabrous reddish brown branchlets.

Net-leaf Sugar Hackberry, *C. laevigata* var. *reticulata* (Torr.) L. Benson, is considered by some botanists as a distinct species, but others feel that it has such close affinities it should be classed as a variety of the Sugar Hackberry with xerophytic tendencies. The flowers and fruit are similar except for more pubescence on the fruit pedicel. The leaves are smaller, broadly ovate, yellowish green, stiff, coriaceous, entire or serrate, conspicuously reticulate-veined beneath, the veins are pubescent beneath, and the leaf petiole is densely pubescent. As a tree it is rarely over 30 ft and quite often it is only a large shrub. Subsequently it may be found that Arizona Sugar Hackberry is a synonym of Net-leaf Sugar Hackberry. West Texas to California; north to Colorado, Utah, Washington, and Oklahoma; and south into Mexico. In Texas generally on limestone hills west of the Colorado River. Occasionally on shell banks near the Gulf as far east as Houston.

Common Hackberry

Celtis occidentalis L. [A, C]

FIELD IDENTIFICATION. Tree attaining a height of 120 ft, with a rounded crown. The gray bark bears corky warts and ridges.

FLOWERS. In spring with the leaves, perfect or imperfect, small, green, borne in axillary, slender-peduncled fascicles, or solitary; staminate fascicles few-flowered; calyx 4–6-lobed, lobes linear-oblong; stamens 4–6 (mostly 5); no petals; pistillate flowers usually solitary or in pairs; ovary sessile, ovoid, with 2 hairy reflexed stigmas.

FRUIT. Drupe variable in size and color, globose or subglobose to ovoid, orange-red turning dark purple, ¼–½ in. long, persistent; flesh thin, yellow, sweetish, edible; seed bony, light brown, smooth or somewhat pitted, pedicels longer than leaf petioles.

LEAVES. Simple, alternate, deciduous, ovate to elliptic-ovate, often falcate, short acuminate or acute, oblique at base with one side rounded to cuneate and the other somewhat cordate, usually coarsely serrate but less so near the base, 3-nerved at base, light green and glabrous above (or rough in var. *crassifolia*), paler green and soft pubescent or glabrous be-

neath, blades 2½–4 in. long, 1½–2 in. wide; petioles slender, glabrous, about ½ in. long. The leaves are broader in proportion to width, not as long taper-pointed, more serrate on margin, and drupes larger than in Sugar Hackberry.

TWIGS. Green to reddish brown, slender, somewhat divaricate, glabrous or pubescent.

BARK. Gray to grayish brown, smooth except for wartlike protuberances.

WOOD. Yellowish white, coarse-grained, heavy, soft, weak, weighing 45 lb per cu ft.

RANGE. Texas, western Oklahoma, Arkansas, and Louisiana; eastward to Georgia, north to Quebec, and west to Manitoba, North Dakota, Nebraska, and Kansas.

REMARKS. *Celtis* was a name given by Pliny to a sweet-fruited lotus, and *occidentalis* means "western." Vernacular names are Nettle-tree, False-elm, Bastard-elm, Beaverwood, Juniper-tree, Rim-ash, Hoop-ash, and One-berry. The tree is drought resistant and often planted for shade in the South and for shelter-belt planting. The wood is occasionally used commercially for fuel, furniture, veneer, and agricultural implements. The fruit is known to be eaten by 25 species of birds, especially the gallinaceous birds. It was also eaten by the Indians.

Common Hackberry is rather variable in size and shape of leaves and fruit, and botanists have described a number of varieties to fit these differences.

Big-leaf Common Hackberry, *C. occidentalis* var. *crassifolia* Gray, is perhaps the most common variety in east Texas. The leaves are large, very coarsely serrate, cordate at base, and rough to the touch above, and the hairy petioles are shorter than the fruit pedicels. It occurs mixed with the species, and intergrading forms appear to be rather common.

Dog Hackberry, *C. occidentalis* var. *canina* Sarg., is a variety with oblong-ovate acuminate leaves, abruptly cuneate at base, finely serrate and glabrous or hairy on veins beneath; petioles glabrous or rarely pubescent. Not known to occur in Texas, but common in Oklahoma and northward.

Small Hackberry

Celtis tenuifolia Nutt. [A, C]

FIELD IDENTIFICATION. Eastern shrub or small tree to 24 ft.

FLOWERS. In spring, small axillary, 5–6-parted; staminate in small pedunculate clusters near the base of twigs of the year, calyx 5-lobed; stamens 5, opposite the calyx-lobes, exserted, usually no ovary in staminate flowers; pistillate flowers appearing with leaves, pediceled, solitary or paired from upper axils, stamens present or absent; ovary ovoid, 1-celled, 1-ovuled, ovule single and suspended; style very short, stigmas 2, elongate, subulate, recurved, divergent.

FRUIT. Drupe September–October, subglobose, 1/5–1/3 in. in diameter, orange to brown or red, thin-fleshed, sweet; stone 1/5–1/4 in. long, subglobose, light to dark brown, seed coat somewhat granular; peduncles 1/8–2/5 in., shorter than the subtending petioles, or longer.

LEAVES. Simple, alternate, deciduous, usually broad-ovate to deltoid, apex blunt, acute or short-acuminate, base oblique and 3-nerved, mostly entire on margin (on young shoots sometimes few-toothed), blade length 3/4–4 in., width 1/2–1 3/4 in., thin and smooth, surfaces grayish green but darker above, lower surfaces more or less pubescent and veiny, petioles pubescent.

TWIGS. Slender, reddish brown, pubescent at first, later glabrous and darker brown to gray; bark often with corky ridges.

RANGE. On dry and rocky foothills. Southern to eastern Oklahoma, Arkansas, and Louisiana; eastward to northern Florida, and northward to Pennsylvania, Indiana, Kansas, and Missouri.

REMARKS. *Celtis* is the name given by Pliny to a sweet-fruited African lotus. The species name, *tenuifolia*, refers to the

thin leaves. It is listed as *C. pumila* by some authors. Vernacular names are Sugarberry, Nettleberry, and Nettle-tree.

Georgia Hackberry, *C. tenuifolia* var. *georgiana* (Small) Fern. & Schub., is a variety with leathery, pubescent, scabrous leaves. It was formerly listed as *C. georgiana* Small and *C. pumila* var. *georgiana* Sarg. It occurs in Arkansas, Oklahoma, Louisiana, Georgia, Missouri, Virginia, and District of Columbia.

Spiny Hackberry

Celtis pallida Torr. [B, C]

FIELD IDENTIFICATION. Spiny, spreading, densely branched evergreen shrub attaining a height of 18 ft.

FLOWERS. Axillary, inconspicuous, in 2-branched, 3–5-flowered cymes, pedicels about 1/12 in. long; flowers greenish white, polygamous or monoecious; corolla absent; calyx-lobes 4 or 5; stamens as many as the calyx-lobes; style absent; stigmas 2, each 2-cleft and spreading; ovary sessile, 1-celled.

FRUIT. Drupe subglobose or ovoid, yellow or orange, thin-fleshed, mealy, acid, edible, 1/5–1/3 in. in diameter; stone ovoid, oval or obovoid, reticulate, acute, about ¼ in. long and ⅜ in. wide.

LEAVES. Alternate, simple, small, 3-nerved, deep green, scabrous and puberulent, elliptic to oblong-ovate; rounded, acute or obtuse at the apex; oblique and somewhat semicordate at base; coarsely toothed on margin, or entire; blades ½–2¼ in. long, ½–1 in. wide; petioles pubescent, 1/16–3/16 in., or longer.

BARK. Mottled gray to reddish brown, rather smooth and tight, sometimes with long, stout, gray or brown spines. Bark only rough at base of very old trunks.

TWIGS. Divaricate, flexuous, spreading, smooth, gray or reddish brown, glabrous or puberulent; with stipular spines ¼–1 in., stout, straight, single or paired, often at ends of shoots; lenticels small, pale, and usually numerous.

RANGE. Central, western, and southern Texas, New Mexico, Arizona, and Mexico. In Mexico from Chihuahua to Baja California, and south to Oaxaca.

REMARKS. The genus name, *Celtis*, is the classical name for a species of lotus, and the species name, *pallida*, refers to paleness of the branches. Commonly used vernacular names in Texas and Mexico are Desert Hackberry, Chaparral, Granjeno, Granjeno Huasteco, Capul, and Garabata.

The Indians of the Southwest are reported to have ground the fruit and eaten it with fat or parched corn. It is reported that the larvae of the snout butterfly feed upon the foliage. Spiny Hackberry is also considered a good honey plant. Many birds consume it, particularly the cactus wren, cardinal, pyrrholuxia, towhee, mockingbird, thrasher, scaled quail, Gambel's quail, and green jay. The raccoon, deer, and jack rabbit eat it occasionally. The wood is used for fence posts and fuel, and the plant is of some value in erosion control.

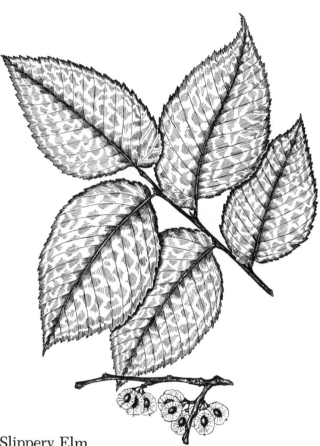

Slippery Elm

Ulmus rubra Muhl. [A, C]

FIELD IDENTIFICATION. Tree attaining a height of 75 ft, with spreading branches and a broad open head.

FLOWERS. February–April, before the leaves, born in dense fascicles on short pedicels; perfect; no petals; calyx campanulate, green, hairy; calyx-lobes 5–9, lanceolate and acute; stamens 5–9, with elongate yellow filaments and reddish purple anthers; pistil reddish, compressed, divided into a 2-celled ovary and 2 exserted, spreading, reddish purple stigmas.

FRUIT. Ripening April–June. Samara short-stalked, green, oval to orbicular, apex entire or shallowly notched, ¼–¾ in. long; seed flattened with the surrounding wing reticulate-veined; seed area reddish brown and hairy; and wing area glabrous. Minimum seed-bearing age of tree 15 years, optimum 25–125, and maximum 200 years. Good crops every 2–4 years and light crops intervening.

LEAVES. Buds densely rusty-tomentose; leaves simple, alternate, deciduous, blades 4–8 in. long, 2–3 in. wide, obovate, ovate to oblong, acuminate at apex; rounded, cordate to cuneate, and inequilateral at base; margin coarsely and sharply double-serrate; dark green and very rough above because of tiny pointed tubercles, also pubescent when young and later more glabrous; paler and soft-pubescent beneath, often with axillary hairs; petioles ⅓–½ in., stout; leaves fragrant when dry.

TWIGS. Gray, stout, roughened and densely pubescent when young, more glabrous later.

BARK. Gray to reddish brown, ridges flattened, fissures shallow, inner bark mucilaginous and fragrant.

WOOD. Reddish brown, tough, strong, heavy, hard, compact, durable, weighing 43 lb per cu ft.

RANGE. Texas, Oklahoma, Arkansas, and Louisiana; eastward to Florida, north to Maine and Quebec, and west to Ontario, Minnesota, Wisconsin, and Nebraska.

REMARKS. *Ulmus* is the ancient Latin name for elm, and the species name, *rubra*, refers to the reddish wood. The older name *U. rubra* Muhl. has precedence over the name *U. fulva* Michx., as used in most books. Vernacular names are Rock Elm, Red Elm, Sweet Elm, Indian Elm, Moose Elm, Gray Elm, and Soft Elm. The wood is used for making posts, ties, sills, boats, hubs, agricultural implements, furniture, slack cooperage, veneer, and sporting goods. In frontier days the bark was often chewed as a thirst quencher. White-tailed deer, rabbit, porcupine, and moose browse the twigs and foliage. The tree is rather short-lived and subject to insect damage. It has been cultivated since 1830.

American Elm

Ulmus americana L. [A, B, C]

FIELD IDENTIFICATION. Much-loved and famous American tree, admired for graceful vaselike shape. Attaining a height of 120 ft, but generally under 70 ft, and often buttressed at base. Known to reach an age of 300 years or more.

FLOWERS. February–April, before the leaves, in axillary, 3–4-flowered (occasionally to 12) fascicles; pedicels slender, jointed, drooping, nearly sessile or to 1 in. long; individual flowers perfect, petals absent; calyx campanulate, red to green, lobes 7–9 and short; stamens 5–8, exserted, with slender filaments and red anthers; pistil pale green, compressed, composed of a 2-celled ovary and 2 spreading inwardly stigmatic styles.

FRUIT. Ripening March–June. A samara, about ½ in. long, red to green, oval-obovate, consisting of a central flattened seed surrounded by a membraneous wing; wing reticulate-veiny, glabrous but ciliate on margin, a deep terminal incision reaching the nutlet. The minimum seed-bearing age is 15 years and the maximum 300 years. Good crops occur most years.

LEAVES. Simple, alternate, deciduous, 4–6 in. long, 2–3 in. wide, oval, obovate or oblong, acute or abruptly acuminate at apex; veins conspicuous to the serrations; somewhat cordate on one side at base and rounder or cuneate on the other side, giving an inequilateral shape; margin coarsely and doubly serrate, upper surface dark green and mostly smooth (occasionally scabrous on vigorous shoots); lower surface pubescent at first, but glabrate later; petioles 1/5–1/3 in., rather stout.

TWIGS. Slender, varying shades of brown, pubescent at first, glabrous later.

BARK. Light to dark gray, ridges flattened and scaly, fissures deep.

WOOD. Light to dark brown, sapwood whitish, coarse-grained, tough, heavy, hard, strong, weighing 40 lb per cu ft, difficult to split, durable, bends well, shrinks moderately, tends to warp and twist.

RANGE. Moist soils of bottom lands and upland flats. Texas, Oklahoma, Arkansas, and Louisiana; eastward to Georgia and Florida, northward to Newfoundland, and west to Ontario, North Dakota, Montana, and Nebraska.

REMARKS. *Ulmus* is the ancient Latin name for elm, and the species name, *americana*, refers to its native home. Vernacular names are Rock Elm, Common Elm, Soft Elm, Swamp Elm, White Elm, and Water Elm. Known to the lumber trade as White Elm and makes up the greater part of elm lumber and logs. In most cases the trade does not distinguish between the elm species. A very desirable ornamental tree for street and park planting, attaining large size and much admired for the graceful upsweep of the branches. It is sometimes used for shelter-belt planting in the prairie states, but *U. pumila* is considered superior for that purpose. The wood is used for woodenware, vehicles, baskets, flooring, veneer, furniture, cooperage, cabinets, sporting goods, stock staves, boxes, crates, framework, agricultural implements, trunks, handles, toys, car construction, shipbuilding and boatbuilding, and fuel. It is reported that the Indians used the wood for canoes and the bast fiber for ropes. The fruit is often eaten by gallinaceous birds, and the young twigs and leaves are browsed by white-tailed deer, opossum, and cottontail. In the northern part of its range it appears to be subject to the attack of the elm-leaf beetle, *Galerucella xanthomelaena*, and in some areas large numbers of trees are killed by the Dutch elm disease, caused by a fungus, *Graphium ulmi*, and by phloem necrosis, caused by a virus. American Elm is distinguished from Slippery Elm by the former having leaves less scabrous above and the samara being ciliate on the margin.

Cedar Elm

Ulmus crassifolia Nutt. [A, B, C]

FIELD IDENTIFICATION. Tree attaining a height of 90 ft, with slender, somewhat drooping branches and a narrow or

rounded crown. Twigs or branches often with lateral corky wings.

FLOWERS. Borne usually in July in small, 3–5-flowered fascicles; pedicels slender, ⅓–½ in.; calyx campanulate, hairy, red to green, 6–9-lobed, lobes hairy and acute; no petals; stamens 5–6, with slender filaments and reddish purple anthers; pistil green, flattened, pubescent, composed of a 2-celled ovary and 2 exserted spreading styles.

FRUIT. Samara borne in late summer, small, ¼–½ in. long, oval-elliptic or oblong, green, flattened, pubescent; composed of a central seed surrounded by a wing which is deeply notched at apex and ciliate on margin.

LEAVES. Simple, alternate, somewhat persistent, blades 1–2 in. long, ¾–1 in. wide, elliptic to ovate, acute or obtuse at apex, rounded or cuneate to oblique at base, doubly serrate on margin; dark green, stiff and very rough to the touch above, pubescent beneath; petiole about ⅓ in., stout, hairy.

TWIGS. Reddish brown, pubescent, often with brown, thin, lateral, corky wings. The only other Texas elm with corky wings is the Winged Elm.

BARK. Brown to reddish, or gray, ridges flattened and broken into thin, loose scales.

WOOD. Reddish brown, sapwood lighter, brittle, heavy, hard.

RANGE. Often in limestone soils. Texas, Oklahoma, Arkansas, and Louisiana; east to South Carolina, north to New York, and west to Kansas.

REMARKS. *Ulmus* is the ancient Latin name, and *crassifolia* refers to the rough, thick leaves. Vernacular names are Scrub Elm, Lime Elm, Texas Elm, Basket Elm, Red Elm, and Southern Rock Elm. It is often planted as a shade tree, but the wood is considered inferior to other elms because of its brittle and knotty character. It is sometimes used for hubs, furniture, and posts.

Winged Elm

Ulmus alata Michx. [A, B, C]

FIELD IDENTIFICATION. Tree attaining a height of 60 ft, with slender branches and a rounded or oblong crown. Often with conspicuous corky wings on the twigs and branches.

FLOWERS. Before the leaves in spring, borne in few-flowered drooping fascicles on filiform pedicels; flowers perfect, petals absent; calyx campanulate, red to yellow, the 5 lobes obovate and rounded; stamens 5, with long, slender filaments and reddish anthers; pistil green, hairy, flattened, composed of a tomentose 2-celled ovary tipped by 2 spreading styles.

FRUIT. Samara reddish or greenish, long-stipitate, ovate to elliptic or oblong, 1/4–1/3 in. long; seed solitary, flattened, ovoid; wing flat, thin, narrow, prolonged into divergent, apically incurved beaks; seed and wing hairy, especially on margin; the reddish samaras giving the tree a reddish appearance when in fruit.

LEAVES. Simple, alternate, deciduous, ovate-oblong to oblong-lanceolate, occasionally somewhat falcate, blades 1/2–3 in. long, coarsely and doubly serrate on margin, acute or acuminate at apex, wedge-shaped or subcordate at base, pale-pubescent or glabrous beneath, with axillary hairs and prominent veins; petioles about 1/3 in. long, stout, pubescent.

TWIGS. Reddish brown, slender, pubescent at first, glabrous later, often with conspicuous, opposite, thin, corky wings. The only other elms having corky wings are the Cedar Elm, September Elm, and Rock Elm.

BARK. Reddish brown to gray, ridges flat with closely appressed scales, fissures irregular and shallow.

WOOD. Brown, close-grained, compact, heavy, hard, difficult to split, weighing 46 lb per cu ft, not considered as strong as other elms.

RANGE. Texas, Oklahoma, Arkansas, and Louisiana; eastward to Florida, north to Virginia, and west through Ohio and Indiana to Kansas and Missouri.

REMARKS. *Ulmus* is the ancient Latin name, and *alata* refers to the corky wings on the twigs. Vernacular names are Cork Elm, Water Elm, Wahoo Elm, Red Elm, and Witch Elm. The Winged Elm is a favorite shade and ornamental tree. It is easily transplanted, sprouts readily from seed, is a rapid grower, and is rather free of disease and insects. The wood is generally used for the same purposes as other elms, such as tool handles, vehicle parts, and agricultural implements. Formerly the bark was used in some localities for baling twine.

Siberian Elm

Ulmus pumila L. [A, B, C]

FIELD IDENTIFICATION. Graceful cultivated shrub or small tree with slender drooping branches.

FLOWERS. March–April, appearing with or before the leaves, axillary, inconspicuous, greenish, clustered, short pediceled, perfect or rarely polygamous, petals absent; calyx campanulate, 4–5-lobed; stamens 4–5, with green to violet anthers; style 2-lobed, ovary flattened and 1-celled.

FRUIT. Samara April–May, clustered ¼–½ in. long and broad, rarely more; oval to obovate, composed of a central, dry, compressed nutlet surrounded by a wing which is thin, reticulate-veined, membranous, semitransparent, apex with a notch sometimes reaching one-third to one-half of the way to the nutlet; pedicel 1/25–1/8 in.

LEAVES. Simple, deciduous, alternate, oval to ovate or elliptic, blade length 1–2 in., width ½–1 in., margin doubly serrate, apex acute, base cuneate or somewhat asymmetrical, leathery and firm; upper surface olive green to dark green, glabrous, veins impressed; lower surface paler and glabrous, or somewhat pubescent when young or with axillary tufts of hair; turning yellow in autumn; petiole glabrous or pubescent, 1/6–1/2 in., stipules caducous.

TWIGS. Slender; when young brownish and pubescent; when older brown to gray and glabrous; bark of trunk gray to brownish.

RANGE. A native of Asia, extensively cultivated in the United States. In its typical form a small-leaved shrub or tree from Turkistan to Siberia, Mongolia, and North China.

REMARKS. The genus name, *Ulmus*, is the ancient Latin name for elm, and the species name, *pumila*, refers to its shrubby habit in some forms. Often wrongly called Chinese Elm, but that name should properly apply to *U. parvifolia* Jacq. Both the Siberian and the Chinese Elm are cultivated in the Gulf Coast states for ornament. The Siberian Elm is being extensively planted in the prairie-plains region as shelter belts, and has some use as a game cover. It is rather drought resistant and seems to be less susceptible to the Dutch elm disease, *Graphium ulmi*, than the native elm species. The wood is hard, heavy, tough, rather difficult to split, and is used in China for agricultural implements, boatbuilding, and wagon wheels. The inner bark was once made into coarse cloth.

Chinese Elm

Ulmus parvifolia Jacq. [A, B, C]

FIELD IDENTIFICATION. A cultivated, attractive, semi-evergreen tree, attaining a height of 45 ft or more, but usually smaller. The branches slender to form a broad-rounded, open crown. Bark usually smooth, thin and pale gray; young trees often marked with white blotches, or circular, white bands; older trunks developing irregular shallow fissures with thin, small scales, which exfoliate to expose an orange-red inner bark.

FLOWERS. Borne August–September in axillary clusters on short pedicels, on twigs of the preceding season; bisexual or more rarely unisexual; corolla absent; calyx campanulate; the 4–5 lobes (or sometimes more) divided below the middle; stamens as many as the calyx-lobes and opposite them, the filaments straight, long-exserted; ovary superior, 1-celled, 1-ovuled; styles 2.

FRUIT. Samara flat, oval to ovate or elliptic, with a broad, narrow, membranous wing surrounding the seed and notched at apex; from about 1/3 in. long and glabrous.

LEAVES. Simple, alternate; texture subcoriaceous; shape elliptic to ovate; apices acute to obtusish; margin mostly simply serrate; base rounded to cuneate or somewhat unequal sided; length ¾–2½ in. Upper surface glabrous or somewhat roughened with minute papilla; lower surface glabrous or with pale pilose scattered hairs, but more so on the venation; color rather lustrous, olive green to dark green above, but somewhat paler beneath; venation with 8–10 straight, lateral veins to a side, and each ending in a tooth. Stipules linear-lanceolate, narrow at the base. Petioles very short, 1/25–1/4 in. long, pale strigose-hairy.

TWIGS. Slender, gray to brown, pubescent when young, more glabrous later.

RANGE. A native of China, Korea, and Japan. Cultivated in the Gulf Coast states and occasionally escaping. In Houston, Texas, a considerable number cultivated on the grounds of the Town and Country Shopping Center on Katy Freeway.

REMARKS. The genus name, *Ulmus*, is an ancient Latin name. The species name, *parvifolia*, refers to the small leaves. Closely related species have been described by *U. sieboldii* Daveau, *U. shirasawana* Daveau, and *U. coreana* Nakai, but they differ little from *U. parvifolia*. Chinese Elm is also sometimes confused with Siberian Elm, *U. pumila* L.

Water Elm

Planera aquatica (Walt.) Gmel. [A, B, C]

FIELD IDENTIFICATION. Contorted shrub or tree to 40 ft, growing in swampy ground.

FLOWERS. Three kinds of flowers on the same tree—male,
female, and perfect. Staminate flowers fascicled, 2–5 flowered; petals none; calyx 4–5-lobed, bell-shaped, greenish
yellow, lobes ovate and obtuse; stamens 4–5, filaments filiform, exserted; pistillate flowers 1–3 together, perfect; ovary
ovoid, stalked, tubercular, 1-celled; styles 2, reflexed, stigmatic along inner side.

FRUIT. Peculiar, covered with irregular warty excrescences,
leathery, oblong-ovoid, compressed, ridged, about ⅓ in. long,
short-stalked; seed ovoid.

LEAVES. Elmlike, alternate, deciduous, blades 2–4 in. long,
½–1 in. wide, ovate or oblong-lanceolate, crenulate-serrate,
acute to obtuse at apex, cordate or oblique at base, dark
green, paler below; petioles stout, puberulent, about ¼ in.
long; stipules lanceolate, caducous.

BARK. Light reddish brown or gray, dividing into large shreddy scales.

WOOD. Soft, weak, light, close-grained, light brown, weighing 33 lb per cu ft.

RANGE. In swamps or river-bottom lands. Texas, Oklahoma, Arkansas, and Louisiana; eastward to Florida, northward to North Carolina, and west through Kentucky and Illinois to Missouri.

REMARKS. The genus name, *Planera*, is in honor of the German botanist Johann Jakob Planer (1743–1789), a professor at the University of Erfurt, and the species name, *aquatica*, refers to the swampy habitat of the tree. The peculiar little warty fruit is considered to be an important duck food in swampland areas. Squirrels also eat the fruit. The wood has no commercial importance.

Mulberry Family (Moraceae)

Common Paper Mulberry

Broussonetia papyrifera (L.) Vent. [A, B, C]

FIELD IDENTIFICATION. Small tree, rarely to 50 ft, with irregular spreading branches.

FLOWERS. Dioecious, staminate catkins peduncled, cylindric, pendulous, 2½–3½ in. long; no petals; stamens 4; calyx 4-lobed; pistillate in globose heads with a tubular perianth; ovary stipitate, stigma filiform and slender.

FRUIT. Globose, about ¾ in. across, a multiple fruit composed of many 1-seeded drupelets which are reddish orange and which protrude from the persistent calyx.

LEAVES. Alternate, deciduous, long-petiolate, blades 3–8 in. long, ovate, margin coarsely dentate and often deeply lobed; apex acuminate; base cordate or rounded; rough above, conspicuously veined and velvety-pubescent beneath; stipules ovate-lanceolate, deciduous.

TWIGS. Stout, hirsute, tomentose.

BARK. Smooth, tight, reticulate, green to yellow.

WOOD. Coarse-grained, soft, light, easily worked.

RANGE. Texas, New Mexico, Oklahoma, Arkansas, and Louisiana; eastward to Florida, and northward to Missouri and New York. A native of Asia. Cultivated and escaping to grow wild in some areas in the United States.

REMARKS. The genus, *Broussonetia*, is named in honor of

Auguste Broussonet, a French naturalist; and the species name, *papyrifera*, refers to the use of the inner bark in papermaking. The inner bark is also used for making cloth in the tree's native home of Japan and China. The famous tapa cloth of the South Pacific Islands is also made from the bark by macerating it and pounding with a wooden mallet. It is often planted for ornament in the United States, being drought resistant and a rapid grower, and sprouting freely from the root. The fruit is also eaten by a number of species of birds.

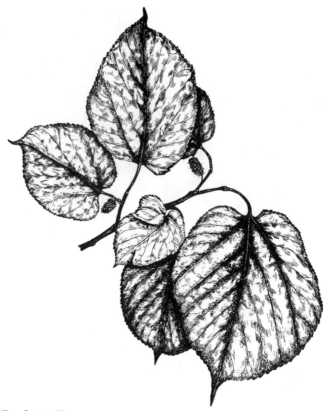

Red Mulberry

Morus rubra L. [A, B, C]

FIELD IDENTIFICATION. Handsome tree to 70 ft, with a rather broad, spreading crown.

FLOWERS. With the leaves in spring, green; petals absent; staminate spikes cylindric, 2–3 in. long; stamens 4, green; filaments flattened; calyx with 4 ovate lobes; pistillate spikes about 1 in., cylindric, sessile; calyx 4-lobed; styles 2; ovary ovoid, flat, 2-celled, 1 cell generally atrophies.

FRUIT. Ripening May–August, a cylindric syncarp ¾–1¼ in. long, resembling a blackberry, red at first, becoming purplish black, juicy, edible; achene ovoid, acute, light brown, covered by the succulent calyx. Minimum seed-bearing age of the tree 10 years, optimum 30–85 years, maximum about 125 years.

LEAVES. Simple, alternate, deciduous, 3–9 in. long, ovate or oval, or 3–7-lobed, doubly serrate, rough and glabrous above, soft pubescent beneath, very veiny, acute or acuminate at apex, cordate or truncate at base, turning yellow in autumn; petiole 1–2 in.; stipules lanceolate and hairy. The lobing of the leaves varies considerably on different trees or even on the same tree; some are only serrate, while others have numerous lobes.

BARK. Dark brown to gray, ½–¾ in. thick, divided into irregular, elongate plates separating into appressed flakes.

WOOD. Light orange, sapwood lighter, durable, close-grained, light, soft, weak, weighing about 45 lb per cu ft, used for boats, fencing, cooperage, and railroad crossties.

RANGE. Usually in rich moist soil. Does not grow well on thin, poor soil. Texas, Oklahoma, Arkansas, and Louisiana; eastward to Florida, north to Vermont, and west to Ontario, Wisconsin, Michigan, Minnesota, Nebraska, and Kansas.

REMARKS. The genus name, *Morus*, is the classical name of the mulberry, and the species name, *rubra*, a Latin word for "red," has reference to the red, immature fruit. The fibrous bark was used to make cloth by early Indians. The fruit is known to be eaten by at least 21 kinds of birds, fox squirrels, and human beings. Although the fruit is sweet, it does not seem to be very much in demand for culinary uses. For fruit-bearing purposes the trees may be planted 20–40 ft apart. Trees should not be planted next to walks because the abundant ripe fruit mashes readily underfoot. Often planted for ornament and known in cultivation since 1629.

Black Mulberry

Morus nigra L. [A, B, C]

FIELD IDENTIFICATION. Cultivated shrub or tree attaining a height of 30 ft, or occasionally larger. The trunk is short and the wide-spreading branches form a broad, rounded, or irregularly shaped crown.

FLOWERS. Staminate flowers in cylindrical spikes ⅓–1 in., longer than the peduncles; stamens 4, inserted opposite the sepals under the ovary, filaments filiform; sepals 4; pistillate spikes cylindric-oval, ⅓–¾ in., shorter than the pubescent peduncles; sepals 4, lateral ones largest, sepals enclosing the fruit at maturity and becoming succulent; ovary sessile, 1-celled, style terminal and short, stigmas 2 and ascending.

FRUIT. Syncarp dark red or black, fleshy, oval-oblong, ⅓–1 in. long, achenes included in calyx and tipped by persistent stigmas.

LEAVES. Simple, alternate, deciduous, thin, ovate to oval, blades 1½–6 in. long, apex acute or short-acuminate, margin coarsely toothed or sometimes with one or more lobes, base rounded, cordate or semitruncate, upper surface dull dark

green, usually rough and becoming glabrous, lower surface paler and sparingly pubescent on the veins to glabrous; young foliage pubescent; petioles usually shorter than the blade, one-fourth to one-half as long.

TWIGS. Young ones green to brown and pubescent, older ones darker brown to gray or glabrous.

RANGE. Old gardens, roadsides, thickets, and waste grounds. Cultivated in Texas, Louisiana, Oklahoma, and Arkansas; eastward to Florida and north to New York. A native of western Asia.

REMARKS. The genus name, *Morus*, is the classical Latin name of mulberry, and the species name, *nigra*, refers to the black color of the fruit. It is sometimes grown for fruit or for shade. Although Black Mulberry is sometimes reported as being cultivated in the Southwest, many times incorrect identifications are made because of its close resemblance to a black-fruited race of White Mulberry, *M. alba* var. *tatarica* (L.) Ser.

White Mulberry

Morus alba L. [A, B, C]

FIELD IDENTIFICATION. An introduced tree to 40 ft, and attaining a diameter of 3 ft.

FLOWERS. Staminate and pistillate catkins axillary, borne on the same tree or on different trees; staminate catkins ⅜–1 in., cylindric, slender, drooping; calyx 4-parted, lobes ovate; stamens 4, elastically expanding; pistillate catkins drooping, oblong or oval to subglobose, cylindric, ½–⅔ in. long, about ¼ in. in diameter; calyx 4-parted, lateral sepals largest, calyx greatly enlarging to envelop the achene at maturity; ovary sessile, 2-celled, 1-cell atrophies; styles 2, linear, stigmatic down the inner side.

FRUIT. Borne June–August on slender, glabrous or pubescent peduncles ¼–⅔ in. long, pendent, subglobose to oval or oblong, white to pink (rarely black), ½–¾ in. long and about ¼ in. wide, sweet; fruit a syncarp, or an aggregation of ovate, compressed achenes each covered by the succulent, thickened calyx, the whole fruit as a unit thus juicy and elongate.

LEAVES. Alternate, deciduous, ovate to oval or asymmetrical, heart-shaped, blades 2½–8 in. long, 1–4½ in. wide; margin with blunt, crenate teeth or often also 1–6-lobed, apex acute or short-acuminate; base semicordate, rounded or truncate, 3-veined; thin and smooth; upper surface olive green, lustrous and glabrous, paler and glabrous beneath; petiole ½–1½ in., shorter than the blade, slender, glabrous or slightly pubescent.

TWIGS. When young reddish brown, glabrous to slightly pubescent, when older slender, glabrous, gray.

BARK. Light to dark gray, broken into narrow furrows and irregular, often twisted, ridges.

RANGE. Escaping cultivation to roadsides, fields, and thickets. Naturalized Texas, Oklahoma, Arkansas, and Louisiana; north to Maine, and west to Minnesota and Wisconsin. Native home not positively known, either Europe or China, but most authorities cite an Asiatic origin. A cosmopolitan plant, known in nearly all parts of the world.

REMARKS. The genus name, *Morus*, is the classical Latin name, and the species name, *alba*, refers to the white fruit. It is also known under the names of Silkworm Mulberry, Russian Mulberry, Morera, and Morea. The fruit is not as juicy as the native Red Mulberry and is somewhat smaller. It also seems to vary as to sweetness, on some trees being very sweet and on others so insipid and dry as to be hardly edible. Although the fruit of the species is most commonly white or pink, some varieties produce red or black fruit. The fruit has some wildlife value, being eaten readily by a number of species of birds, opossum, and raccoon, as well as by poultry and hogs. The wood is hard and durable and is used for furniture, utensils, and boatbuilding.

Osage-orange

Maclura pomifera (Raf.) Schneid. [A, B, C]

FIELD IDENTIFICATION. Tree attaining a height of 60 ft, with a milky sap and bearing stout thorns.

FLOWERS. April–June, dioecious, green, staminate in long-peduncled axillary racemes, 1–1½ in. long; petals none; stamens 4, exserted; calyx 4-lobed; pistillate in globose dense heads about 1 in. in diameter; calyx 4-lobed, thick, enclosing the ovary; ovary ovoid, compressed, 1-celled; style filiform, long, exserted.

FRUIT. September–October, a syncarp, or aggregation of 1-seeded drupelets, globose, yellowish green, 4–5 in. in diameter; achenes surrounded by enlarged fleshy calyx; juice of fruit milky and acid.

LEAVES. Deciduous, alternate, entire, broad-ovate to ovate-lanceolate, rounded or subcordate at base, or broadly cuneate, acuminate at apex, 3–6 in. long, tomentose at first, lustrous later, yellow in autumn, petioles ½–2 in., stipules triangular, small, early deciduous.

BARK. Brown to orange, deeply furrowed, ridges rounded and interlacing.

WOOD. Bright orange or yellow, heavy, hard, durable, strong, weighing 48 lb per cu ft.

RANGE. Arkansas, Oklahoma, Louisiana, Missouri, and south into Texas. Well developed in the Oklahoma Red River Valley. Also escaping cultivation throughout Eastern United States.

REMARKS. The genus name, *Maclura*, is in memory of William Maclure, an early American geologist, and the species name, *pomifera*, means "fruit-bearing." The name Bois d'Arc was given to it by the French, meaning "bow-wood," with reference to the fact that the Osage Indians made bows from the wood. Vernacular names are Hedge-apple, Horse-apple, Mock-orange, and Yellow-wood. Yellow dye was formerly made from the root bark. Also the bark of the trunk was used for tanning leather. Squirrels feed on the little achenes buried in the pulpy fruit, and black-tail deer browse the leaves. The tree was formerly much planted as windbreaks or hedgerows, and has been cultivated since 1818.

Common Fig

Ficus carica L. [A, B, C]

FIELD IDENTIFICATION. Deciduous spreading shrub or tree to 30 ft. Branches numerous, stout, glabrous, spreading or ascending, forming a rounded or flattened crown. Sap thick and milky.

FLOWERS. Borne inside a hollow pear-shaped receptacle with a narrow orifice, axillary, solitary, greenish or brown to violet, length 1½–3⅓ in., staminate flowers nearly sessile, with 2–6 sepals and 1–3 stamens; pistillate flowers short-stalked; style lateral and elongate; ovary sessile, 1-celled.

FRUIT. Synconium obovoid to ellipsoid, fleshy, achenes small, numerous, included in fruit; taste mild, sweet, mucilaginous; firm and leathery.

LEAVES. Simple, alternate, ovate to oval, usually 3–7-lobed, some leaves lobed a second time; lobes obovate or obtuse at apex and irregularly dentate, blades 4–8 in. long and about as broad, base cordate or truncate, scabrous above and below with stout, stiff hairs, venation palmate; petioles ¾–2 in., usually one-half to two-thirds as long as the blade, lightly to densely pubescent.

TWIGS. Smooth, stout, gray, pubescent at first, branches glabrous later.

RANGE. Cultivated in Texas, Oklahoma, Arkansas, and Louisiana; eastward to Florida and Tennessee, and northward along the Atlantic coastal plain as far north as New York. Not escaping cultivation readily because of frost kill. In old gardens, fields, and along roadsides. A native of western Asia. Cultivated since ancient times.

REMARKS. The genus name, *Ficus*, is the ancient Latin name. The species name, *carica*, is from Caria in Asia Minor.

Magnolia Family (Magnoliaceae)

Southern Magnolia

Magnolia grandiflora L. [A, B, C]

FIELD IDENTIFICATION. Large evergreen tree attaining a maximum height of 135 ft, but usually not over 50 ft. Possibly one of the largest trees known has been recorded from Pascagoula, Mississippi, with a trunk circumference of 13 ft 7 in., height of 52 ft, and spread of 92 ft.

FLOWERS. April–August, solitary on short pedicels, terminal, cup-shaped, 6–9 in. across; petals 6–18, rounded or obovate, white, often purple at base, arranged in a series; sepals 3, petal-like; stamens numerous, short, filaments purple; anthers linear, opening on the inner side; pistils numerous, coherent along a prolonged receptacle to form a fleshy cone, ovules 2.

FRUIT. Ripening July–October, cone ovoid to cylindric, rose-colored, fleshy, rusty-hairy, imbricate, 2–4 in., 1½–2 in. wide. Each carpel splits dorsally to expose 1 or 2 red, obovoid seeds suspended on thin threads. From 40–60 seeds per cone.

LEAVES. Very variable, alternate, simple, evergreen, coriaceous, blades 4–9 in. long, 2–3 in. wide, elliptic or oval, acute or obtuse at apex, cuneate at base, margin entire, shiny and dark green above, rusty-tomentose beneath; petioles stout, tomentose, about ¾ in.; stipules foliaceous, deciduous.

TWIGS. Green to olive, stout, hairy, or glabrous later.

BARK. Aromatic, bitter, grayish brown, breaking into small, thin scales.

WOOD. Creamy white, hard, weak, not durable, fairly heavy.

RANGE. In rich, moist soil; Texas, Oklahoma, Arkansas, and

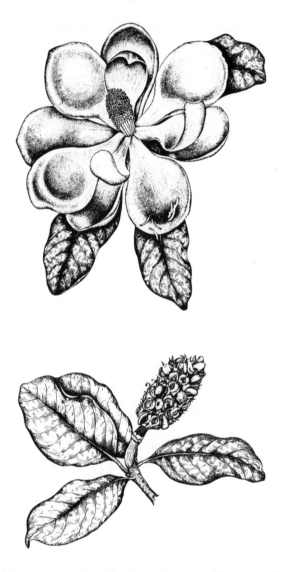

Louisiana; eastward to Florida and north to North Carolina. Cultivated for ornament as far north as Washington, D.C.

REMARKS. The genus name, *Magnolia*, is in honor of Pierre Magnol, professor of botany at Montpellier, and the species name, *grandiflora*, refers to the large flowers. Vernacular names are Bull-bay, Great Laurel Magnolia, and Loblolly Magnolia. The seeds are eaten by at least 5 species of birds and by squirrels. The wood is used for fuel, baskets, crates, woodenware, furniture, and shades. This species and others of the same genus are widely cultivated for their beautiful flowers and showy leaves, both in the United States and in Europe. It has been cultivated since 1734. Horticulturists have also developed a number of clones from the Southern Magnolia, among which are the Exmouth, Gallisson, Glorious, Goliath, Narrow-leaf, and Round-leaf.

Ashe Magnolia

Magnolia ashei Weatherby [A]

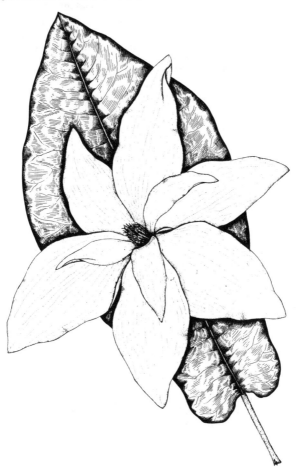

FIELD IDENTIFICATION. Mostly a shrub, but sometimes a small slender tree to 15 ft, with a broad round top. Easily recognized by the obovate to elliptic-lanceolate leaves, which are light green above and silvery white beneath, and 1–2 ft long.

FLOWERS. In spring, terminal on stout pubescent or glabrous pedicels, fragrant, creamy white, very large, solitary, perfect, cup-shaped, often 12 in. in diameter; petals 6–8, 4–6 in. long, 2–3 in. broad, elliptic to oval; anthers opening inwardly; pistils coherent to form a fleshy cone.

FRUIT. In summer, cone cylindric-ovoid, tomentose, fleshy, green to rose-colored, 2–4½ in. long, 1–2 in. broad, carpels opening on the back and discharging red seeds attached by slender threads; seeds oval, flattened, conspicuous.

LEAVES. Simple, alternate, deciduous, thin, very large, sometimes to 2 ft long and 1 ft wide; obovate-spatulate or elliptic-lanceolate; cordate-auriculate at base; acute or rounded at apex; margin wavy, entire; light green and lustrous above; silvery white glaucous beneath and somewhat pubescent along main vein.

TWIGS. Reddish brown, smooth, slender, pubescent at first, later glabrous.

BARK. Gray to reddish brown, mostly smooth or slightly roughened.

WOOD. Soft, durable, easily worked, weighing about 30 lb per cu ft.

RANGE. Only western Florida and eastern Texas. Very rare in Texas, found possibly only in 2 counties.

REMARKS. The genus name, *Magnolia*, is in honor of Pierre Magnol, professor of botany at Montpellier, and the species name, *ashei*, is in honor of William Willard Ashe, American botanist (1872–1932). This tree is very similar to the Big-leaf Magnolia, *M. macrophylla*, but the fruit is ovoid-elliptic instead of globose-ovoid, the petals are smaller (4–6 in. long), and the leaves are shorter and less pubescent below.

Pyramid Magnolia

Magnolia pyramidata Bartr. [A]

FIELD IDENTIFICATION. Slender tree attaining a height of 30 ft, with ascending branches. Recognized by the almost whorled leaves with conspicuous earlike lobes at the base.

FLOWERS. Solitary on stout, terminal peduncles, somewhat fragrant, 3½–4 in. across at maturity, perfect; petals creamy white, imbricate, oblong to lanceolate, acute or acuminate, clawed, veiny, soon drooping; sepals 3, spreading or recurved, oblong to obovate, apex short-pointed, much shorter

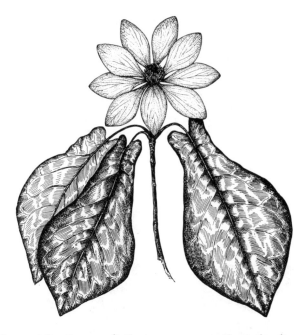

than petals; stamens distinct, numerous, 1/6–1/4 in., imbricate in many series at base of receptacle, filaments short and distinct, anthers introrse and adnate to the inner side of the filament; styles and stigmas stout, forming a head of imbricate follicles on the elongate receptacle, ovules 2 in each cavity.

FRUIT. A conelike echinate fruit composed of numerous, rose-colored follicles, apices with short, incurved, persistent beaks; oblong to ellipsoid, length 2–2½ in.; seeds 2 in each follicle, red, ovoid, pendulous on a thread.

LEAVES. Deciduous, alternate, or almost whorled terminally, oblong to spatulate, apex obtuse or acute, base contracted with 2 spreading lobes, margin entire, thin, upper surface bright green, lower surface paler, glabrous and glaucous, especially when young, blade length 5½–8½ in., width 3½–4½ in., midrib slender and yellow, veinlets reticulate; petioles green to tan or brown, ⅓–2¾ in.

TWIGS. Slender, green to reddish brown, later gray, leaf scars oval or half-round, lenticels small and pale.

BARK. Smooth, tight, gray to reddish brown.

RANGE. Low rich woods near streams. In southeastern Louisiana in Washington Parish, and rarely in east Texas; eastward to Florida and Georgia, and northward to South Carolina.

REMARKS. The genus name, *Magnolia*, is in honor of Pierre Magnol (1638–1715), professor of medicine and director of the botanical garden at Montpellier, France. The species name, *pyramidata*, refers to the pyramidal fruit. Vernacular names are Southern Cucumber-tree and Mountain Magnolia. Pyramid Magnolia is closely related to the Fraser Magnolia, *M. fraseri*, but has smaller flowers, and a shorter fruit. Fraser Magnolia is confined mostly to the Appalachian Mountains and Piedmont region, while Pyramid Magnolia is a tree of low grounds of the coastal plain area. The latter tree was first cultivated in 1825 and is occasionally grown for ornament in the United States and in Europe.

Sweet-bay Magnolia

Magnolia virginiana L. [A, B]

FIELD IDENTIFICATION. Swamp-loving shrub or tree attaining a height of 30 ft. The largest specimen ever recorded is in Cambden, South Carolina. This tree has a height of 67 ft and a circumference of 6 ft. One of the field marks for identification is the conspicuous white undersurface of the leaves.

FLOWERS. Borne on short slender pedicels, very fragrant,

depressed-globose, 2–3 in. broad; petals 8–12, elliptic, obovate or oval, obtuse; sepals 3, obtuse, shorter than petals, obovate or oblong; stamens short-filamented, numerous on a prolonged receptacle.

FRUIT. Pistils coherent to form an ellipsoidal, imbricate, fleshy, red cone 1–2 in. long; cone splitting at maturity to discharge from each carpel 1–2 red, oval seeds suspended on thin threads.

LEAVES. Scattered, alternate, simple, undulate, oblong, elliptic or oval, obtuse at apex, broad-cuneate at base, green above, white or pale glaucous beneath, blades 3–6 in. long, 1–2½ in. wide; petioles slender, smooth, about 1 in.

TWIGS. Slender, bright green, glabrous or hairy.

BARK. Pale gray to brown, smooth, aromatic, bitter.

WOOD. Pale brown, sapwood white, soft, weighing 31 lb per cu ft.

RANGE. Usually in low, wet, acid, sandy soil. Texas, Oklahoma, Arkansas, and Louisiana; eastward to Florida, northward to Pennsylvania, and in isolated stations to Massachusetts.

REMARKS. The genus name, *Magnolia*, is in honor of the botanist Pierre Magnol, and the species name is for the state of Virginia. Vernacular names are Swamp-bay, Beaver-tree, White-bay, White-laurel, Swamp Magnolia, Swamp-sassafras, and Indian-bark. This species is easily identified by the white undersurface of the leaves. Although deciduous in the North, the leaves tend to be evergreen in the South. It is reported that the flowers have been used in perfume manufacture, and the leaves as a flavoring for meats. The tree is sometimes confused with the Red Bay, *Persea borbonia*, which also has leaves used for flavoring purposes. Sweet-bay Magnolia is occasionally cultivated for ornament and is thicket forming by sprouts from the roots. The flowers are small, but have a penetrating fragrance. The wood is used for making light woodenware articles.

Tulip-tree

Liriodendron tulipifera L. [A]

FIELD IDENTIFICATION. Large, handsome tree capable of attaining a height of 100–200 ft and a diameter of 4–10 ft. Lower part of trunk generally devoid of branches, upper branches forming a small, pyramidal to oblong crown. Trunks notable for columnar grandeur and straight, limbless uniformity.

FLOWERS. April–May, conspicuous, on green and glabrous peduncles 1–2½ in.; perfect, 3–4 in. across, cup-shaped;

petals 6, erect, yellowish green, orange-banded at base, obovate to elliptic or oblong, apex rounded or truncate, 1½–
2½ in.; sepals 3, greenish and thinly glaucous, elliptic to
spatulate or ovate, rounded or truncate at apex, spreading or
reflexed; stamens numerous, long, conspicuous; anthers
linear, 1–1¼ in., as long as the filaments or longer; pistils
flat, narrow, scalelike, imbricate into a spindle-shaped cone,
stigmas short and recurved above.

FRUIT. A samara-bearing cone, ripening September–
November, composed of closely imbricate, woody, brown,
dry indehiscent carpels, about 3 in. long; seeds 1–2 (1 seed
often abortive), testa thin and leathery.

LEAVES. Simple, alternate, deciduous, 4–6 in. long and broad,
apex deeply notched, with 2 large acute lobes on each side
of notch; lateral notches separating one large upper lobe
and a smaller lower lobe, base of leaf truncate or cordate or
sometimes rounded; upper surface dark green, glabrous,
shiny; lower surface pale, glabrous, and somewhat glaucous,
turning yellow in autumn; petioles 1–6 in., slender, glabrous;
stipules persistent, foliaceous on young shoots.

TWIGS. When young reddish brown to greenish, shiny,
smooth, glabrous, sometimes glaucous-purple; leaf scars

rather large, semi-orbicular; older twigs slender, smooth, mottled gray, brittle.

BARK. At first gray, thin, tight, later gray to brown with rounded ridges and deep, confluent furrows.

WOOD. Growth rings distinct, heartwood variable in color, generally yellow, tan, or brown, sometimes with shaded mixtures of green, blue, or black; sapwood creamy white; straight-grained, light, soft, fairly stiff, moderately brittle, easily worked, split resistant, seasons well, except under decay conditions, takes glue readily, paint and varnish absorption good, takes a high polish, shrinkage considerable, nail-holding ability rather low, weighs about 26 lb per cu ft. The wood of Tulip-tree has a wide variety of uses including veneer, boxes, crates, plywood, pulp, hat blocks, furniture, cabinetwork, millwork, musical instruments, toys, novelties, cigar boxes, barrel bungs, and others.

RANGE. Seldom in pure stands, but mixed with a variety of trees. In rich, moist soil, Louisiana and Arkansas; eastward to Florida, and north to Massachusetts, Vermont, Rhode Island, Michigan, Wisconsin, and Ontario. Most abundant on mountain slopes west of the Blue Ridge.

REMARKS. The genus name, *Liriodendron*, means "lily-tree," and the species name, *tulipifera*, may be translated "tulip-bearing." Other vernacular names in use are Yellow-poplar, Yellow Wood, White Wood, Tulip-poplar, Saddleleaf, Canoe Wood, Cucumber-tree, Blue-poplar, White-poplar, Lynn-tree, Saddle-tree, and Hickory-poplar. The use of the name "Poplar" is misleading, because the tree is not related to the genus *Populus*, which contains the cottonwood trees.

The plant is known to be eaten by at least 10 species of birds, including the bobwhite quail, and also by red squirrel, white-tailed deer, and cottontail. The birds and squirrels eat the seed, and the deer and rabbit browse the leaves.

Custard-apple Family (Annonaceae)

Common Pawpaw

Asimina triloba (L.) Dunal [A, C]

FIELD IDENTIFICATION. Spreading shrub or broad-crowned tree attaining a height of 40 ft.

FLOWERS. Axillary, solitary, perfect, on stout rusty-hairy pedicels, 1–2 in. across, appearing with or before the leaves; petals 6, purplish green, veiny, the 3 outer ovate-obovate or orbicular, larger than the 3-pointed, erect, glandular inner ones; stamens many, short; pistils few to many; style in-

wardly stigmatic; ovary 1-celled, ovules numerous; calyx of 3 ovate, acuminate, pale green sepals, much smaller than petals.

FRUIT. Bananalike, borne singly, or in oblique clusters of 2–4, oblong-cylindric, often falcate, apex and base pointed or rounded, 2–7 in. long, 1–2½ in. thick, green when young, brown or black when mature; pulp sweet, white or yellow, aromatic, edible; seeds several, dark brown, large, bony, rounded, flat, horizontal, about 1 in. long and ½ in. broad.

LEAVES. Deciduous, alternate, simple, oblong-obovate abruptly pointed or acute at apex, obtuse or cuneate at base, entire, thin, rusty-pubescent when young, globous later, blades 4–11 in. long, 2–6 in. broad, odorous when bruised; petioles ⅓–1 in., stout.

TWIGS. Slender, olive brown, often blotched, smooth, rougher when older, and often with warty excrescences.

BARK. Dark brown, thin, smooth, later with shallow fissures.

WOOD. Pale yellow, coarse-grained, soft, weak, weighing 24 lb per cu ft.

RANGE. Rich soil of bottom lands. East Texas, Arkansas, and

Louisiana; eastward to Florida, and north to New York, Michigan, and Nebraska.

REMARKS. The genus name, *Asimina*, is from the early French name *Asiminier*, which in turn was derived from the Indian *Arsimin*. The species name, *triloba*, refers to the petals, which are in sets of 3. Vernacular names are Fetid-shrub and Custard-apple. Pawpaw fruit falls to the ground in autumn and must be stored until ripe. It may be baked into pies, made into dessert, or eaten raw with cream as a breakfast food. When eaten raw it is cloyingly sweet with a custardlike flavor. Seemingly a taste for it must be cultivated because some consider it nauseating. The food value is largely carbohydrate. The fruit varies greatly in size and flavor. Some are large, yellow fleshed, highly flavored, and early ripening. Others are white fleshed, mildly flavored, and late ripening. Handling the fruit is known to produce a skin rash on some people. The rough bark is sometimes used as a rope substitute. Birds are fond of the fruit, and it is also eaten by gray fox, opossum, raccoon, and squirrel. The seeds of the Pawpaw contain an alkaloid, asiminine, which is reported to have emetic properties. The bark was once used as a medicine and contains the alkaloid analobine.

Small-flower Pawpaw

Asimina parviflora (Michx.) Dunal [A, C]

FIELD IDENTIFICATION. Irregular, straggling shrub to 12 ft.

FLOWERS. Imbricate in the bud, solitary, small, inconspicuous, green to dark purple; pedicels very short, 1/16–1/5 in., with reddish brown tomentum; sepals 3, broadly oval or ovate, 1/5–1/4 in., green or yellowish, hairy; corolla about ⅝ in. wide or less, composed of 6 petals (3 spreading and 3 erect), outer 3 petals reddish brown or purple, oblong to ovate, apex obtuse or rounded, ⅛–⅜ in., densely puberulent; inner 3 petals erect, recurved at apex, shorter than the outer 3, about ⅛ in., reddish brown, puberulent; stamens numerous, crowded on a somewhat convex receptacle; pistils protruding from the mass of stamens, few or many, ovaries 1-celled.

FRUIT. August–September, berry solitary or 2–4 together, oblong, ellipsoid, or oval, often asymmetrical, sparingly pubescent; immature fruit greenish yellow, and mature turning black, ¾–2 in. long, pulpy, edible, but cloyingly insipid; seeds several, bony, turgid.

LEAVES. Leaves simple, alternate, deciduous, heavy-scented, thin, pinnate-veined, shape variable, oblong to elliptic or obovate, mostly broadest above the middle, apex acute or short-acuminate, base narrowed; thin, dull green and glabrous above, lower side with more or less reddish brown

tomentum, especially on the vein; blade length 2¼–6¾ in.; petioles 1/16–1/2 in., with densely reddish brown tomentum.

TWIGS. Young twigs with dense reddish brown tomentum; older twigs smooth, glabrous, gray to reddish brown, strong-scented.

RANGE. In rich, moist soil, often along streams. In eastern Texas in Hardin, Newton, Jasper, Montgomery, and Orange counties; eastward through Louisiana to Florida, and northward to North Carolina.

REMARKS. The genus name, *Asimina*, is from an old French name, *Asiminier*, and the species name, *parviflora*, refers to the small flowers. Vernacular names are Small-fruited Pawpaw, Small Custard-apple, and Custard-banana. The fruit is considered to have the same nutritive value, weight for weight, as the banana. The bark was at one time used in domestic medicine as a bitter.

Laurel Family (Lauraceae)

Camphor-tree

Cinnamomum camphora Nees & Eberm. [A, B, C]

FIELD IDENTIFICATION. Handsome cultivated tree to 40 ft, and 2 ft in diameter, evergreen, dense, stout, round-topped.

FLOWERS. Borne in axillary, slender-peduncled, green and glabrous panicles 1¾–3 in.; individual flower pedicels ⅛–¼ in.; glabrous; petals absent; perianth-tube short, segments 5–6, early deciduous to leave a truncate cup-shaped receptacle about ¼ in. long which is rugose, glabrous, and granular; stamens in 2–4 dissimilar groups, some rows gland-appendaged and some abortive; ovary 1-celled, with a slender style and minute stigma.

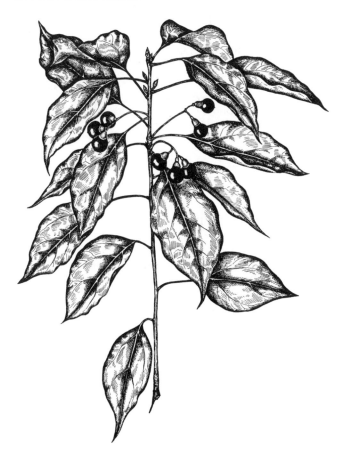

FRUIT. Drupe solitary or a few together on the ends of the long, slender peduncles, globose, black, lustrous, fleshy, ¼–⅓ in. in diameter; seed solitary, globose, black, ridged around the center.

LEAVES. Persistent, essentially alternate but often opposite, elliptic to ovate, apex acute to acuminate, base acute, blade length 1¼–4½ in., width ¾–1½ in., margin entire and somewhat wavy on the plane surface, upper surface dark green, lustrous, and glabrous, veins yellowish green, lower surface paler and lightly glaucous, aromatic when bruised; petioles essentially glabrous, ¾–1½ in.

TWIGS. Slender, elongate, green, and glabrous.

BARK. On young branches smooth, green to reddish brown or gray, on old trunks light to dark gray, broken into deep fissures and flattened, confluent, wider ridges.

RANGE. A native of Japan, China, and Malaya. Planted as an ornamental in Texas, Oklahoma, Arkansas, and Louisiana; east to Florida. Sometimes escaping cultivation. Often planted on the streets of Houston, Texas. Does well in cultivation in southern California.

REMARKS. The genus name, *Cinnamomum*, is the ancient Greek name, and the species name, *camphora*, refers to the camphorous aromatic resin which the tree contains. The wood yields the camphor of commerce. The camphor is obtained by passing a current of steam through the chips, and the volatilized camphor is then condensed into crystals and oil. Later the crystals and oil are separated by filtration under pressure. About 30 lb of chips is required for 1 lb of camphor.

Common Spice-bush

Lindera benzoin (L.) Blume [A]

FIELD IDENTIFICATION. Stout, glabrous, aromatic shrub of damp woods. Attaining a height of 20 ft, with usually several stems from the base.

FLOWERS. Appearing before the leaves, polygamodioecious, yellow, fragrant, ¼–⅓ in. broad, in lateral, almost sessile, dense, umbellike clusters of 3–6 flowers; involucre of 4 deciduous scales; petals absent; sepals 6, thin, obovate to elliptic, apex obtuse to retuse or truncate; staminate flowers with 9 stamens (in 3 series), some filaments glandular at base, anthers introrse, 2-celled and 2-valved; pistillate flowers with 12–18 rudimentary stamens in 2 forms (glandular and glandless); ovary globose, style slender and columnar.

FRUIT. Ripening August–September, drupes solitary or in

small clusters on pedicels 1/12–1/5 in., orbicular to obovoid, elongate, about 2/5 in. long, red, fleshy, spicy; 1-seeded, seeds light brown, speckled darker brown.

LEAVES. Leaf buds scaly, leaves simple, alternate, deciduous, obovate to oval or elliptic, apex acute or short-acuminate, base acute or acuminate, margin entire, thin, bright green above, glaucous, beneath glabrous, more rarely pubescent, blade length 2–4¾ in., width 1–2½ in.; petioles 3/16–3/4 in. Twigs often with 2 leaf sizes, much smaller ones sometimes at base of larger ones.

TWIGS. Slender, glabrous, smooth, brittle, bark with corky lenticels, spicy to the taste.

RANGE. Sandy or peaty soils in low woods or swamps. Central Texas, Oklahoma, Arkansas, and Louisiana; eastward to Florida, north to Maine, and west to Ontario, Michigan, and Kansas.

Hairy Common Spice-bush

REMARKS. The genus name, *Lindera*, is for John Linder, a Swedish physician (1676–1723). The species name, *benzoin*, denotes its similarity, in odor, to the true balsamic resin of *Styrax benzoin*, an Asiatic tree. Vernacular names are Benjamin-bush, Spice-wood, Fever-bush, Snap-bush, and Wild Allspice. There are also a few varieties of Common Spice-bush, such as the Hairy Common Spice-bush, *L. benzoin* var. *pubescens* (Palm. & Steyerm.) Rehd., which has pubescent and ciliate leaves and petioles. Some authorities list the Common Spice-bush under the scientific name of *Benzoin aestivale* (L.) Nees.

The leaves, twigs, bark, and fruit contain an aromatic oil which was made into a fragrant tea by the pioneers. The bark is aromatic, tonic, astringent, stimulant, and pleasant to chew. A substitute for allspice was once made from the dry, powdered drupes. Twenty-four species of birds are known to feed upon the fruit; also rabbit and white-tailed deer nibble the leaves.

Red Bay

Persea borbonia (L.) Spreng. [A, B, C]

FIELD IDENTIFICATION. An evergreen tree to 70 ft, with a
trunk diameter of 1–3 ft. The stout erect branches form a
dense symmetrical head.

FLOWERS. Small, borne in few several-flowered axillary
panicles; peduncles pubescent to glabrous, ½–2 in., often
reddish because of pubescence; corolla absent; calyx bell-
shaped, pale yellow, 6-parted, in 2 series; outer series broadly
ovate and puberulous; inner series oblong-lanceolate, acute,
hairy; stamens 12, in 3–4 series, anthers opening by uplifted
valves (anthers of 3 stamens turned down, others introrse);
filaments flattened; pistil sessile, ovary 1-celled, style slender,
stigma disklike.

FRUIT. Drupe about ½ in. long, globose or obovoid, lustrous,
bright blue to black; seed solitary, ovoid, flesh thin and dry.

LEAVES. Simple, alternate, persistent, aromatic, elliptic-
oblong, margin entire (more rarely remotely serrate), apex
acute or acuminate, base wedge-shaped, bright green, lustrous above, glaucous beneath, 3–4 in. long, 1–1½ in. broad,

thickened, veins rather obscure; petiole ½–1 in. long, stout, grooved above, rigid, reddish brown; leaf scars circular, bundle scar solitary.

TWIGS. Slender, angled, gray- or brown-hairy, dark green at first, later light brown.

BARK. Reddish brown to grayish brown, fissures deep, ridges broad and scaly, ¼–¾ in. thick.

WOOD. Reddish brown, sapwood lighter, close-grained, fairly hard and strong, weighing about 40 lb per cu ft.

RANGE. Rich sandy soils of river-bottom lands or swamps, usually near the coast. Texas, Oklahoma, Arkansas, and Louisiana; eastward to Florida, and northward to eastern Virginia.

REMARKS. The genus name, *Persea*, is the ancient Greek name for an unidentified Egyptian tree. The species name, *borbonia*, is the old generic name of *Persea*. Vernacular names are Sweet Bay, Florida-mahogany, Tiss-wood, Laurel-tree, and Isabella-wood. The fruit is eaten by at least two species of birds. Soups and meats are often flavored with the leaves. The wood is used for furniture, boatbuilding, interior finish, and cabinetmaking. The tree is worth cultivation for its evergreen leaves and ornamental fruit. It is sometimes confused with Sweet-bay Magnolia, *Magnolia virginiana* L.

A tree closely related to the Red Bay is the Swamp Bay, *P. palustris* (Raf.) Sarg. It is chiefly characterized as having the petioles, peduncles, and flower parts more pubescent than in Red Bay. Some have considered the differences as slight and reduced it to a form of Red Bay, *P. borbonia* forma *pubescens* (Pursh) Fern.

Also a plant known as Shore Bay, *P. littoralis* Small, found on coastal dunes from Rockport, Texas, eastward to Florida, shows little difference when compared to the Red Bay. The fruit averages slightly larger and the plant somewhat more shrubby in habit, but many intergrading forms are found. It should be relegated to the status of a synonym of the Red Bay.

Also, a plant known as Silk Bay, *P. humilis* Nash, may be considered as a synonym of Red Bay, as far as Texas material is concerned.

Therefore, for the purposes of this field guide, the Red Bay, *P. borbonia* (L.) Spreng., appears to be the common species of the Gulf Coast region from Texas to Florida, with minor variations.

Common Sassafras

Sassafras albidum (Nutt.) Nees [A, B, C]

FIELD IDENTIFICATION. Tree attaining a height of 90 ft, with a flattened oblong crown, and short, crooked branches.

FLOWERS. March–April, dioecious, axillary, in racemes about 2 in. long; calyx yellowish green, of 6 spreading sepals; corolla absent; stamens in 3 sets of 3 each, the inner set glandular at the base; anthers 4-celled, with flattened, elongate filaments; pistillate flowers with an erect columnar style and depressed stigma, also 6 sterile stamens.

FRUIT. Drupaceous, blue, lustrous, ½ in. long, oblong or spherical, borne on a thickened red pedicel, pulpy; stone solitary, light brown, dispersed chiefly by birds.

LEAVES. Alternate, simple, deciduous, thin, aromatic, blades 3–5 in. long, ovate or elliptic, entire on the margin, or divided into 2–3 mitten-shaped lobes, lobes acute or obtuse; cuneate at base, bright green above, glabrous and glaucous beneath, often hairy on the veins; petioles about 1 in.

TWIGS. Yellowish green, mucilaginous, pubescent at first, turning glabrous and orange-red later.

BARK. Reddish brown to gray, aromatic, irregularly broken into broad flat ridges.

WOOD. Orange-colored, aromatic, durable, close-grained, soft, weak, brittle, weighing 31 lb per cu ft.

RANGE. Texas, Oklahoma, Arkansas, and Louisiana; eastward to Florida, north to Maine, and west to Ontario, Michigan, and Iowa.

REMARKS. The genus name, *Sassafras*, is a popular one

derived from the word *salsafras*, which was given by early
French settlers, with reference to its medicinal properties;
and the species name, *albidum*, refers to a light-colored
condition of the wood. Other commonly used vernacular
names are Ague-tree, Cinnamon-wood, Smelling-stick,
Saloop, and Gumbo-file. The tree is long-lived and rather
free of diseases. The fruit is known to be eaten by 28 species
of birds, and the leaves browsed by woodchuck, white-tailed
deer, marsh rabbit, and black bear. The wood is used for
posts, rails, buckets, cabinets, and interior finish.

Silky Sassafras, *S. albidum* var. *molle* (Raf.) Fern., is a
variety with buds and twigs pubescent, leaves glaucescent
and silky pubescent beneath, at least while young. Texas to
Florida; north to Ontario and Michigan. In Texas west to
the Brazos River.

Witch Hazel Family (Hamamelidaceae)

Vernal Witch Hazel

Hamamelis vernalis Sarg. [A]

FIELD IDENTIFICATION. Shrub attaining a height of 9 ft, and
often sending up sprouts from the base. Differs from the
Common Witch Hazel in that the flowers are produced in
winter or early spring.

FLOWERS. Borne January–April, fragrant, sessile or short-
peduncled, solitary or clustered; calyx 4-lobed, lobes dark red
within; bractlets 2–3 at base of the calyx; petals 4, ⅜–⅝
in. long, yellow or reddish at base, in some forms all red,
long, narrow; stamens usually 8, very short, alternate with
the petals, 4 perfect and anther-bearing, the remainder imperfect; styles 2, short.

FRUIT. Capsule woody, dehiscent from a 2-beaked apex, 2-
coated, the inner and outer coat separating; seeds 1–2, large
and bony, discharged elastically; calyx large and persistent.

LEAVES. Simple, alternate, deciduous, blade length 2–4¾
in., obovate to elliptic or oval, apex rounded to obtuse, base
cuneate to rounded, margin sinuate-wavy; upper surface dull
green, with veins impressed; lower surface paler green,
sometimes glaucous or somewhat hairy, veins straight and
prominent beneath. Some forms with rather permanent
stellate pubescence.

TWIGS. Rather stout, light brown to reddish brown or gray,
densely stellate-tomentose, later smooth and glabrous, light
or dark gray.

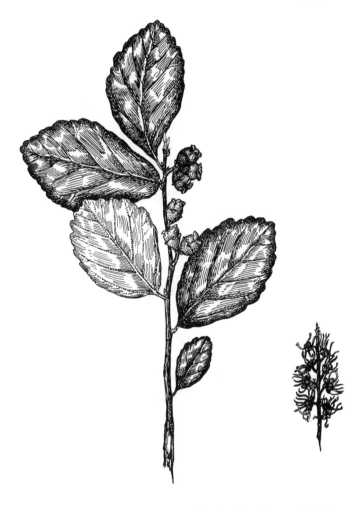

RANGE. Rocky shores and stream banks. East Texas, Louisiana, Alabama, Oklahoma, Arkansas, and Missouri.

REMARKS. The genus name, *Hamamelis*, is from the Greek words *hama* ("at the same time") and *melon* ("apple"), possibly because of the presence of both fruit and flower simultaneously. The species name, *vernalis* ("spring"), refers to its early-blooming habit, from midwinter to spring. It is also known as Ozark Witch Hazel.

Two varieties have been segregated. The Red-petal Vernal Witch Hazel, *H. vernalis* forma *carnea* Rehd., has the petals inside of calyx, and stamens dark red. The Woolly-leaf Vernal Witch Hazel, *H. vernalis* forma *tomentella* Rehd., has leaves densely hairy on the lower surface.

Common Witch Hazel

Hamamelis virginiana L. [A, B, C]

FIELD IDENTIFICATION. Tall shrub or tree to 30 ft.

FLOWERS. In axillary or terminal perfect clusters, bright
yellow, petals 4, crisped; sepals 4, recurved, brown to yellow
within, subtended by 2 or 3 bracts; stamens 8, awl-shaped, 4
normal and 4 staminodial; styles 2, awl-shaped, stigma very
small; ovary formed of 2 basally coherent 1-celled carpels.

FRUIT. Capsule woody, about ½ in. long, 2-beaked, 2-coated,
surmounted by the 2 styles, dehiscent to discharge forcibly
2 oblong, bony, shiny, black seeds; calyx large and persistent.

LEAVES. Alternate, simple, deciduous, oval or obovate, wavy-
toothed, straight-veined, acuminate or broadly acute at apex,
oblique at base, usually glabrous above, somewhat pubescent
beneath, blade 6 in. long and 3 in. broad on the average, or

on older branches much smaller; stipules lanceolate, deciduous; petioles 1/5–3/5 in.

TWIGS. Slender, zigzag, reddish or orange, hairy or glabrous; lenticels pale, small; buds brownish, hairy, about ½ in. long; leaf scars lunate.

BARK. Brown, thin, smooth when immature, and scaly when mature.

WOOD. Reddish brown, hard, close-grained, sapwood almost white, weighing 43 lb per cu ft.

RANGE. Usually in rich moist, sandy soil in semishade. Texas, Oklahoma, Arkansas, and Louisiana; eastward to Florida, and north to Ontario and Nova Scotia.

REMARKS. The genus name, *Hamamelis*, is from the Greek words *hama* ("at the same time") and *melon* ("apple"), possibly because of the presence of both fruit and flower simultaneously; and the species name, *virginiana*, refers to the state of Virginia. The common name was applied because of the hazellike straight veins of the leaves. Vernacular names are Winter Bloom, Spotted-alder, Tobacco-wood, Pistacio, Snappy Hazel, and Witch-elm.

Witch Hazel flowers are conspicuous because they bloom in the autumn when the leaves are about to be shed. The mechanically forcible discharging of the seeds is another unusual feature. In superstitious lore the twigs are used as divining rods to locate water or mineral deposits. The rods are held in the palm in a certain manner and will presumably turn and point toward the earth at the desired spot. Medicinal extracts, lotions, and salves are prepared from the leaves, twigs, and bark, mostly by distillation process. The distillate contains tannic acid, and is used to lessen inflammation, stop bleeding, and check secretions of the mucous membranes. The remedial qualities of the drugs are probably overestimated. The fruit and young twigs are eaten by at least 5 species of birds, cottontail, white-tailed deer, and beaver. It is reported that the Indians prepared a tea from the leaves. Seemingly, it is gaining in popularity as an ornamental plant in the United States and in Europe. It was introduced into cultivation in 1736.

American Sweetgum

Liquidambar styraciflua L. [A, B, C]

FIELD IDENTIFICATION. Large tree, attaining a height of 150 ft, with palmately lobed, serrate, alternate leaves. The branches and twigs are corky-winged, or wingless on some trees.

FLOWERS. March–May, monoecious, very small, greenish; perianth none; staminate flowers in terminal, erect, tomen-

tose racemes 2–3 in. long; stamens numerous, set among
tiny scales, filaments slender and short; pistillate flowers in
axillary, globose, long-peduncled, drooping heads; styles 2,
inwardly stigmatic, sterile stamens 4.

FRUIT. September–November, persistent, globular, spinose,
lustrous, 1–1½ in. in diameter, long-peduncled, resulting
from the aggregation of the many 2-celled ovaries which are
tipped by the 2-beaked or hornlike styles; ovules many, but
maturing only 1–2 flat-winged seeds, the rest abortive, light
brown; good seed crops every three years, light years in
between.

LEAVES. Simple, alternate, deciduous, petioled, broader than
long, blades 3–9 in. wide, with 3–7 acuminate lobes; lobes
oblong-triangular, glandular-serrate; slightly cordate or
truncate at base; glabrous and glossy above, pubescent along
the veins beneath, aromatic when bruised; petioles 2–4¾
in., slender, stipules falling away early.

TWIGS. At first with rusty red tomentum, later glabrous and
with wide corky wings, or some trees without wings.

BARK. Very rough, deeply furrowed, ridges rounded, brown
to gray.

WOOD. Fine-grained, fairly hard, not strong, heartwood reddish brown, takes a high polish, sapwood white or pinkish,
weighing about 37 lb per cu ft.

RANGE. Usually in low bottom-land woods. In east Texas,
Oklahoma, Arkansas, and Louisiana; eastward to Florida,
north to New York and Connecticut, and west to Illinois and
Missouri; also in mountains of Mexico.

REMARKS. The genus name, *Liquidambar*, refers to the amber-
colored liquid sap, and the species name, *styraciflua*, is from

styraci ("storax") and *flua* ("fluidus"). Vernacular names are White Gum, Alligator-tree, Opossum-tree, Red Gum, Bilsted, Satin-walnut, Gum-wood, California Red Gum, and Star-leaf Gum. Medicinally the tree is known as "copalm balsam," and the resinous gum is used extensively in Mexico and Europe, especially as a substitute for storax. Various ointments and syrups are prepared from it and are used in the treatment of dysentery and diarrhea. The gum is sometimes chewed by children. It is also used as a perfuming agent in soap, and as an adhesive. It is reported as excellent for healing wounds. The reddish brown wood is used for flooring, furniture, veneers, woodenware, general construction, boxes, crossties, barrels, sewing machines, cabinets, molding, vehicle parts, conveyors, musical instruments, tobacco boxes, and other articles. At least 25 species of birds are known to feed upon the fruit, as well as the gray squirrel and Eastern chipmunk. The autumn foliage is conspicuous because of its beautiful color variations of red and yellow. It has been cultivated since 1681 and is highly ornamental. It is rapid growing, long-lived, and relatively free from insects and disease damage. Perhaps it could be used more extensively in reforestation projects because of its rapid growth in cut-over lands.

Sycamore Family (Platanaceae)

American Plane-tree (Sycamore)

Platanus occidentalis L. [A, B, C]

FIELD IDENTIFICATION. Tree attaining a height of 170 ft, with reddish brown bark which scales off to expose the white, smooth, new bark.

FLOWERS. April–May, monoecious, the separate heads globose and peduncled; staminate head red, with 3–8 short-filamented stamens accompanied by tiny, club-shaped scales; pistillate heads solitary, green at first, brown when mature, composed of angular ovaries set among tiny scales; ovary linear, 1-celled; style elongate, threadlike; carpels mingled with staminodia.

FRUIT. Ripe September–October, borne on peduncles 3–6 in. long, usually solitary, persistent, globose, 1–1½ in. in diameter, light brown; achenes numerous, obovoid, small, leathery, obtuse at the apex, hairy at base, 1-seeded.

LEAVES. Simple, alternate, deciduous, thin, broadly ovate, 4–12 in. across; margin usually set with 5 short, sinuate, acuminate lobes with large teeth between; truncate or heart-

shaped at the base; bright green above, paler and densely pubescent along the veins beneath; stipules sheathing, conspicuous, toothed, 1–1½ in.; petiole stout, woolly, shorter than the blade, 3–5 in.

TWIGS. Slender, shiny, tomentose at first, glabrous later, orange-brown to gray.

BARK. Reddish brown, scaling off in thin plates to expose the conspicuous white, or greenish, new bark.

WOOD. Light brown, rather weak, close-grained, hard, weighing 33 lbs per cu ft, difficult to work.

RANGE. In rich bottom-land soils, mostly along streams. Texas, Oklahoma, Arkansas, and Louisiana; east to Florida, and north to Maine, Minnesota, Nebraska, and Ontario.

REMARKS. The genus name, *Platanus*, is the classical name of the Plane-tree, and the species name, *occidentalis*, means "western." Vernacular names are Buttonwood, Buttonball-tree, and Water-beech. The wood is used for crates, interior

Smooth American Plane-tree

finishing, furniture, cooperage, rollers, butcher blocks, and tobacco boxes. It attains the largest size of any deciduous tree in the United States and is often planted for ornament. It is slow growing but long-lived, and old trees are often hollow with decay. It was first cultivated in 1640. The seeds are eaten by a number of species of birds and sometimes by muskrat.

Smooth American Plane-tree, *P. occidentalis* var. *glabrata* (Fern.) Sarg. is a variety with less numerous and more angular teeth to the leaves. It occurs in Texas on limestone soils from the Colorado River westward to the Devils River and the Rio Grande. Also in Coahuila and Nuevo León, Mexico.

Rose Family (Rosaceae)

Genus *Crataegus*

THE CRATAEGUS PROBLEM

The genus *Crataegus* with its numerous variations and hybrids represents a very difficult taxonomic complex. One of the difficulties appears to be in the separation of the so-called successful hybrid misfits from the normal, well-distributed, sexual, diploid species. To make the matter more complicated, many of the nonhybrid good species cannot be determined with certainty by any one set of parts or characters. It is evident that too many species have been described. Most of the 1,100 specific names given during the last 25 years were applied by the authors C. S. Sargent, W. W. Ashe, and C. D. Beadle. Many of these have been, and more probably will be, reduced to synonymy as a better knowledge of the group is achieved.

Faced with the very difficult problem of choosing the tree and shrub species of the southwestern United States, the author has turned to Dr. Ernest J. Palmer of Webb City, Missouri, for advice. Dr. Palmer is the leading authority on this group and has done much to clarify many problems concerning its species. He has studied the group closely for more than thirty years and has contributed a monographic treatment in the 1950 edition of *Gray's Manual of Botany* by M. L. Fernald. Dr. Palmer has graciously provided a list of those southwestern species which he considers to be valid and also has contributed a key to both the series and the species.

Using these keys and list as a basis of approach, the author has carefully reviewed all of the original descriptions of Palmer, Sargent, Ashe, and Beadle. This was supplemented by inspection of all of the type material available at the Missouri Botanical Garden, the New York Botanical Garden, the Smithsonian Institution, and the Arnold Arboretum. Although five years were spent in the study of this complex group, the author makes no claim to having clarified all the problems concerning the southwestern species. The last word has certainly not been said, and the material presented is only broadly interpreted. Changes and corrections will undoubtedly have to be made when the species become better known.

The key is in two parts: a Key to the Series of *Crataegus* and a Key to the Species under the Series. In the Key to the Series, the characters of the series are outlined in contrasting pairs of statements or, occasionally, groups of three contrasting statements. Always choose the statement which most closely describes the plant you have to identify. For example, first compare the two statements designated as (a). If the first (a) is the one which seems to apply to the plant in question, then choose between the two (b) characters. It will be noted that the first (b) requires a further choice between (c) and (c), whereas the second (b) leads to the number and name of a series. Whenever a sequence of choices leads to the name of a series, turn to the Key to the Species under the Series and proceed in the same manner.

The reader will note that both the series and the species sections of the following keys refer to all of the species of *Crataegus* in Texas and adjacent states. However, only the east Texas species are marked A, B, or C, in the species key.

KEY TO THE SERIES OF *Crataegus*

(a) Veins of the leaves running to the sinuses as well as to the points of the lobes
  (b) Leaves thin but firm, early deciduous; fruit 1/8–1/5 in. thick; nutlets 3–5; native species
    (c) Leaves mostly 1¼–1⅞ in. wide, ovate or deltoid in outline; flowers opening in May; fruit with deciduous calyx exposing tips of nutlets . . . .
    . . . . 1. **Cordatae** Beadle
    (c) Leaves mostly ⅝–1½ in. wide, narrowly obovate to deltoid in outline; flowers opening in March or April; fruit with persistent calyx . . . .
    . . . . 2. **Microcarpae** Loud.
  (b) Leaves thick, persistent until late in the season; fruit ⅜–¼ in. thick; introduced species . . . .
  . . . . 3. **Oxyacanthae** Loud.
(a) Veins of the leaves running only to the points of the lobes
  (d) Fruit red or yellow or remaining green at maturity; thorns usually long and slender, to 1¾–2½ in. long, or rarely thornless
    (e) Flowers single or 2–5 in simple clusters; stamens 20–25
      (f) Leaves mostly 1⅜–2½ in. long; petioles slender, ⅜–⅝ in. long; sepals not foliaceous, entire or serrate; fruit ½–¾ in. thick, becoming mellow or succulent, edible; arborescent shrubs or small trees in wet or swampy ground . . . .
      . . . . 5. **Aestivales** Sarg.
      (f) Leaves mostly ⅝–1¼ in. long; petioles stout, 1/8–1/5 in. long; sepals foliaceous, pectinate or deeply glandular-serrate; fruit ⅜–⅞ in. thick, remaining firm or hard, scarcely edible; slender shrubs 1½–6 ft tall, in dry or sandy ground . . .
      . . . . 6. **Parvifoliae** Loud.
    (e) Flowers more numerous, usually 5–20 in simple or compound cymes or corymbs; stamens 5–20
      (g) Flowers opening in late March through April according to latitude; nutlets plane on ventral surfaces
        (h) Foliage and inflorescence glandular, usually conspicuously so
          (i) Leaves mostly narrowly obovate or spatulate,

broadest above the middle except at the ends
of branchlets where sometimes broadly oval
or suborbicular; fruit red or orange-red, becoming mellow; arborescent shrubs or small
trees.................... 7. **Flavae** Loud.

(i) Leaves mostly ovate, oblong-ovate, or rhombic
in outline, broadest at or below the middle,
gradually or abruptly narrowed at base, usually lobed, especially at the ends of branchlets; fruit bronze-green or dull red, remaining
firm or hard; shrubs usually less than 9 ft
tall.................. 8. **Intricatae** Sarg.

(h) Foliage and inflorescence eglandular, or if
slightly glandular, the glands small and soon
deciduous

(j) Leaves mostly narrowly obovate, cuneate or
oblong-obovate, unlobed or very obscurely
lobed except at the ends of branchlets,
where sometimes broadly obovate to oval
or suborbicular

(k) Leaves thick or firm, glossy above in most
species; fruit remaining hard and often green
at maturity; nutlets 1–3 (or rarely 2–5 in
a few species) ..... 10. **Crus-galli** Loud.

(k) Leaves thin to firm, not coriaceous, dull
green above; fruit becoming soft or mellow; nutlets usually 3–5

(l) Leaves relatively thin, the veins obscure,
mostly 1¾–2½ in. long, quite variable
in shape, often oblong-obovate or rhombic, unlobed or slightly lobed except at
the ends of branchlets where broadly
oval or ovate and more deeply lobed;
fruit 1/4–7/16 in. thick; bark thin, exfoliating from orange-brown inner bark
.... 9. **Virides** Beadle

(l) Leaves firm, more uniform in shape,
mostly oblong-obovate, unlobed or with
small shallow lobes above the middle;
veins distinctly impressed above, mostly
1¼–2 in. long; fruit usually ⅜–⅝ in.
thick; bark gray, thick, slightly scaly or
ridged........... 11. **Punctatae** Loud.

(j) Leaves mostly oblong-ovate to rhombic, or
broadly ovate to suborbicular at the ends of
branchlets, all sharply lobed; New Mexico
.... 12. **Rotundifoliae** Egglest.

(j) Leaves mostly ovate or deltoid in outline,
broadest below the middle, often rounded,
tuncate, or subcordate at base; Arkansas
and eastward, except some species in 16
and 19

(m) Sepals entire or serrate, not pectinate or
deeply glandular-serrate; filaments as long
or nearly as long as the petals; nutlets 3–

5, usually less than 5

(n) Leaves thin, glabrous except for short pilose hairs above while young; stamens about 10; fruit less than 7/16 in. thick, becoming succulent..............
.... 13. **Tenuifoliae** Sarg.

(n) Leaves firm or thick; fruit usually 7/16 in. or more thick, remaining firm or hard

(o) Young leaves scabrate with sparse hairs above, becoming glabrous; fruiting calyx small and sessile......
.... 14. **Silvicolae** Beadle

(o) Young leaves glabrous above, glabrous or rarely pubescent beneath; fruiting calyx elevated and usually prominent
.... 15. **Pruinosae** Sarg.

(m) Sepals conspicuously glandular-serrate or pectinate; filaments distinctly shorter than the petals; nutlets usually 5

(p) Foliage and inflorescence pubescent; flowers ¾–⅞ in. wide; fruit pubescent at least while young, ripening in August or early September.... 16. **Molles** Sarg.

(p) Foliage and inflorescence glabrous; flowers ¾–1 in. wide; fruit glabrous, ripening in October.............
.... 17. **Dilatatae** Sarg.

(d) Fruit blue or black at maturity; thorns short and stout, usually less than ¾ in. long

(q) Leaves mostly abruptly pointed or rounded at the apex, lustrous above; fruit blue at maturity (except in rare form), glaucous; eastern Texas and eastward
.... 4. **Brevispinae** Beadle

(q) Leaves mostly acute or acuminate at the apex, dull green above; fruit turning from purple to black, lustrous but not glaucous; New Mexico and westward................ 18. **Douglasianae** Egglest.

(q) Flowers opening late, April or May according to latitude; nutlets pitted on ventral surfaces......
.... 19. **Macracanthae** Loud.

KEY TO THE SPECIES UNDER THE SERIES

1. **Cordatae** (only one species in this area)...........
..............................1. *C. phaenopyrum*

2. **Microcarpae**

a. Leaves mostly broadly ovate in outline, often as broad or broader than long, deeply incised, rounded to cordate at base; anthers red; fruit oblong...............
.......................2. *C. marshallii* [A, B, C]

a. Leaves mostly narrowly obovate or spatulate, unlobed or nearly so except at the ends of branchlets, cuneate or attenuate at base; anthers pale yellow; fruit subglobose..................3. *C. spathulata* [A, B, C]

3. **Oxyacanthae** (only one species in this area)........
.................................4. *C. monogyna*
4. **Brevispinae** (only one species in this area)........
......................5. *C. brachyacantha* [A, B, C]
5. **Aestivales**
  a. Pubescence on the under surface of the leaves rusty
    brown, mainly along the veins; fruit ripening in May
    ....6. *C. opaca* (typical) [A, B]
  a. Pubescence on the under surface of the leaves gray,
    mainly in the axils of the veins; fruit ripening in June
    ....6a. *C. opaca* var. *dormanae* [A, B, C]
6. **Parvifoliae** (only one species in this area)........
.................................7. *C. uniflora* [A]
7. **Flavae** (only one species in this area)...........
.................................8. *C. pearsonii* [A]
8. **Intricatae**
  a. Foliage and inflorescence glabrous or essentially so
    b. Leaves mostly 1⅝–2½ in. long, 1–2 in. wide; flowers
      ⅝–¾ in. wide
      c. Fruit remaining dry and hard; sepals glandular-
        serrate
        d. Terminal leaves often ovate and deeply lobed
          near the base; fruit remaining green or yellow-
          ish green
          e. Anthers white or pale yellow (rarely pink)
            ....9. *C. intricata* var. *straminea*
          e. Anthers pink or red (rarely white); fruit sub-
            globose or short-oblong; nutlets 2–4, usually
            2–3.....................9a. *C. neobushii*
        d. Terminal leaves usually oblong-ovate or broadly
          elliptic, not deeply lobed; fruit becoming dull
          red
          f. Fruit subglobose; nutlets 3–5...........
            ....10. *C. buckleyi*
          f. Fruit obovoid or oblong; nutlets 2–5, usually
            less than 5.................11. *C. rubella*
      c. Fruit becoming mellow or juicy; sepals entire or
        finely glandular-serrate...................
        ....12. *C. padifolia* var. *incarnata*
    b. Leaves mostly 1–1⅝ in. wide; flowers ½–⅝ in. wide
      ....13. *C. pagensis*
  a. Foliage and inflorescence pubescent, at least while
    young; young leaves and inflorescence sparsely pilose,
    becoming glabrous or nearly so; stamens about 20;
    anthers red; fruit usually less than 7/16 in. thick,
    glabrous
    g. Leaves mostly 1⅝–2 in. long, 1¼–1⅝ in. wide;
      flowers mostly 6–12 in corymb; fruit subglobose,
      about 7/16 in. thick, orange-colored; arborescent
      shrub or small tree..............16. *C. harveyana*
    g. Leaves mostly ¾–1⅝ in. long and wide; flowers
      mostly 3–8 in corymb; fruit oblong or pyriform,
      about ⅓ in. thick, dull red; widely branching shrub
      3–6 ft tall....................14. *C. ouachitensis*

a. Foliage and inflorescence pubescent throughout the
season; stamens about 10; anthers cream-white or pale
yellow; fruit pubescent while young..............
..........................15. *C. biltmoreana*

9. Virides
a. Mature leaves and inflorescence glabrous or essentially
so (except in variety of no. 17)
b. Leaves firm but comparatively thin at maturity, dull
green above; nutlets normally 5
c. Leaves variable in shape, mostly oblong-ovate or
oblong-elliptic, glabrous (except in variety); anthers pale yellow or rarely pink.............
......................17. *C. viridis* [A, B, C]
c. Leaves more uniform in shape, mostly ovate or
oblong-ovate, pubescent above as they unfold, soon
glabrous; anthers pink....22. *C. sutherlandensis*
b. Leaves thick or subcoriaceous at maturity, glossy
above, nutlets 3–5
d. Leaves mostly 2–2¾ in. long; terminal leaves
broadly ovate and sharply lobed; fruit 1/4–7/16
in. thick........................18. *C. nitida*
d. Leaves mostly 1⅝–2½ in. long; terminal leaves
broadly ovate to suborbicular; fruit about ⅓ in.
thick......23. *C. glabriuscula* forma *desertorum*
a. Foliage and inflorescence conspicuously pubescent
while young, the leaves more or less pubescent throughout the season
e. Mature leaves comparatively thin; flowers mostly
8–15 in corymb; fruit subglobose
f. Leaves pubescent beneath throughout the season;
flowers ½–⅝ in. wide....................
...............*C. viridis* var. *velutina* [A, B, C]
f. Leaves strongly pubescent while young, becoming
nearly glabrous; flowers about ¾ in. wide......
......................19. *C. anamesa* [A, B]
e. Mature leaves thick or subcoriaceous, pubescent
while young, becoming glabrous and glossy above
and slightly hairy along the veins beneath
g. Flowers ¾ in. or more wide, mostly 10–20 in
corymb; sepals narrowly lanceolate, long-acuminate................20. *C. stenosepala* [A, B, C]
g. Flowers ⅝–¾ in. wide, mostly 5–15 in corymb;
sepals lanceolate or deltoid-lanceolate, broad based
h. Leaves mostly 1¼–1¾ in. long; fruit subglobose
or ovoid, orange-red, becoming mellow......
....................21. *C. poliophylla* [A, B]
h. Leaves mostly 1–1¼ in. long; fruit subglobose,
dull red, remaining hard and dry...........
..........................24. *C. amicalis*

10. Crus-galli
a. Foliage and inflorescence glabrous or essentially so,
except in no. 30 and in var. of no. 32, in which the
young leaves are more or less pubescent
b. Mature leaves thick or subcoriaceous and glossy
above (except sometimes in shade)

c. Leaves mostly obovate or spathulate, distinctly
   longer than broad, broadest above the middle, except sometimes at the ends of branchlets
   d. Serration of the leaves sharp with acute teeth;
      fruit usually 1/3–1/2 in. thick; nutlets 1–3, usu-
      ally 1 or 2
      e. Terminal shoot leaves unlobed or rarely very
         obscurely lobed; flowers 7/16–5/8 in. wide;
         stamens about 10 (except in var. *leptophylla*)
         . . . . 25. *C. crus-galli* [A, B, c]
      e. Terminal shoot leaves often slightly lobed;
         flowers about 3/4 in. wide; nutlets usually 2
         . . . . 26. *C. bushii* [A]
   d. Serration of the leaves shallow or crenate; fruit
      1/4–2/5 in. thick; nutlets usually 2 . . . .
      . . . . 34 and 34a. *C. pyracanthoides* vars. [A]
c. Leaves broader, mostly broadly obovate, oblong-
   obovate or oval, only slightly longer than broad
   or often as broad as long at the ends of shoots
   f. Young leaves quite glabrous; terminal shoot
      leaves usually broadly ovate to suborbicular
      g. Flowers 1/2–5/8 in. wide; fruit 7/16 in. or less
         thick; nutlets usually 3; terminal leaves broad-
         ly ovate or oblong-ovate, sometimes slightly
         lobed toward the base. . . . . 27. *C. palmeri*
      g. Flowers 5/8–3/4 in. wide; fruit 7/16–1/2 in.
         thick (or smaller in varieties); terminal leaves
         broadly oval or suborbicular, often with sev-
         eral small shallow lobes. . . 29. *C. reverchonii*
      g. Flowers about 1/2 in. wide; corymbs glabrous;
         stamens 10, anthers red or pink; fruit ellip-
         soidal; leaves oblong. . . . .
         . . . . 29a. *C. cherokeensis* [A]
   f. Young leaves sometimes slightly villous, soon
      glabrous (except in var. of no. 32 where they
      are permanently pubescent)
      h. Leaves mostly obovate or oblong-obovate;
         terminal leaves incisely lobed; flowers usual-
         ly 8–15 in lax corymbs
         i. Leaves sharply and deeply serrate; terminal
            shoot leaves mostly oval with 2–3 pairs of
            small shallow lobes; stamens about 10;
            fruit 7/16–1/2 in. thick, dull red; nutlets
            2–3. . . . . 32. *C. regalis*
         i. Leaves with sharp but shallow serrations;
            terminal leaves mostly elliptic, sometimes
            slightly lobed toward the apex; flowers
            about 3/4 in. wide; stamens about 10; fruit
            about 7/16 in. thick, bright orange or
            orange-red; nutlets usually 3 . . . .
            . . . . 30. *C. mohrii*
      h. Terminal shoot leaves broad-obovate to ellip-
         tic, glabrous at maturity, unlobed but deeply
         and irregularly serrate; flowers mostly 5–6 in

compact corymbs; stamens 20, anthers pink
...................36. *C. sublobulata* [A]

h. Terminal shoot leaves ovate to oval or obovate,
pale villose below at maturity............
...................36a. *C. warneri* [A]

b. Mature leaves comparatively thin, not subcoriaceous,
yellowish green, slightly lustrous but not glossy above

j. Leaves mostly elliptic or oblong-obovate, longer
than wide except sometimes at the ends of shoots,
the veins obscure; fruit subglobose or slightly
obovoid, dull red at maturity.....28. *C. acutifolia*

j. Leaves mostly broadly obovate or rhombic, nearly
or sometimes quite as broad as long, the veins
slightly impressed above; fruit oblong, green or
yellowish flushed with red at maturity.........
...................33. *C. sabineana* [A]

a. Foliage and inflorescence pubescent while young and
usually throughout the season

k. Leaves mostly obovate or oblong-obovate, broadest
above the middle except sometimes at the ends of
shoots

l. Fruit 7/16 in. or less thick, remaining dry and
hard

m. Flowers 7/16–5/8 in. wide; fruit red or orange
at maturity, not lustrous

n. Flowers mostly 4–5 in compact corymbs; stamens about 20; anthers pale yellow......
...................38. *C. berberifolia* [A]

n. Flowers mostly 8–12 in loose corymbs; stamens about 10; anthers usually pink, rarely
white............39. *C. engelmannii* [A, C]

l. Fruit ½–¾ in. thick, becoming mellow or succulent; flowers 5/8–¾ in. wide..............
...................31. *C. palliata*

k. Leaves broader, mostly oblong-obovate, oval or elliptic, usually broadest about the middle

a. Leaves pubescent beneath throughout the season;
flowers flattish, not noticeably cup-shaped

o. Leaves mostly broadly obovate or oval, those at the
ends of shoots similar but larger and relatively broader; sepals entire or minutely serrate; anthers yellow

p. Flowers about 5/8 in. wide; stamens about 20; fruit
subglobose or short-oblong.......40. *C. subpilosa*

p. Flowers about ¾ in. wide; stamens about 10; fruit
ovoid..............32a. *C. regalis* var. *paradoxa*

o. Leaves mostly rhombic or oval, those at the ends of
shoots broadly oval to suborbicular; sepals conspicuously glandular-serrate; anthers pink or red.....
...................41. *C. traceyi*

a. Leaves slightly pubescent on both sides while young,
becoming glabrous at maturity; flowers cup-shaped
...................30. *C. mohrii*

11. **Punctatae**

a. Leaves mostly obovate or oblong-obovate, or at the

ends of shoots elliptic or oval; flowers 5–12 in villose corymbs

  b. Flowers mostly 5–8 in corymbs; usually less than ¾ in. wide; stamens 10–20, usually 10–15; anthers white or pale yellow.............42. *C. collina*

  b. Flowers mostly 8–12 in corymbs, usually ¾ in. or more wide; stamens about 20; anthers pink or rose ....44. *C. verruculosa*

a. Leaves mostly broadly oval or ovate; flowers mostly 8–15 in glabrous corymbs.............43. *C. fastosa*

a. Leaves oval to obovate, acute or acuminate at apex; fruit often rather longer than broad, bright canary yellow; flowers in broad 7–8 flowered, slightly villose corymbs...................43a. *C. brazoria* [A, B]

12. Rotundifoliae

a. Leaves elliptic, oval or suborbicular, usually slightly lobed, more or less pubescent while young; fruit about 7/16 in. thick, dark red or rarely dull yellow at maturity ....45. *C. chrysocarpa*

a. Leaves mostly ovate or obovate, glabrous; fruit about ⅓ in. thick, orange-red or reddish orange at maturity ....46. *C. erythropoda*

13. Tenuifoliae (only one species in this area)........ ....47. *C. macrosperma*

14. Silvicolae (only one species in this area)........... ....48. *C. iracunda* var. *silvicola*

15. Pruinosae

a. Flowers ½–¾ in. wide; fruit 7/16–5/8 in. thick with prominent elevated calyx

  b. Leaves of flowering spurs mostly 1–1¾ in. wide; terminal shoot leaves larger, ovate or deltoid, sharply lobed

    c. Leaves mostly abruptly narrowed or rounded at the base; fruit usually pruinose............. ....49. *C. pruinosa*

    c. Leaves mostly rounded, truncate or subcordate at base; fruit not pruinose

  b. Leaves of flowering spurs mostly 1–1⅜ in. wide, the terminal lobe often conspicuously elongate especially at the ends of shoots...........51. *C. gattingeri*

    d. Leaves with shallow or obscure lobes, mostly rounded or abruptly narrowed at base; fruit with a narrow slightly elevated calyx............ ....51a. *C. disjuncta*

  b. Leaves of flowering spurs mostly 1⅜–1¾ in. wide; terminal shoot leaves sometimes as broad as long or broader, the terminal lobe not conspicuously elongate

    e. Leaves glabrous or esentially so from the first... ....50. *C. mackenzii*

    e. Leaves short villose above while young, and pubescent along the veins beneath throughout the season............50a. *C. mackenzii* var. *aspera*

a. Flowers ¾–1 in. wide; fruit ⅝–¾ in. thick, subglobose or depressed-globose, often wider than long, with a broad, slightly elevated, calyx.......53. *C. platycarpa*

16. **Molles**
  a. Leaves of flowering spurs mostly oval or ovate, rounded
     at base; terminal shoot leaves broadly ovate, often trun-
     cate or subcordate at base
    b. Fruit bright red at maturity
      c. Leaves longer than broad except rarely at the ends
         of shoots
        d. Mature leaves firm but comparatively thin;
           flowers numerous, to 15–20 in corymb
          e. Fruit ripening in August or September; flesh
             succulent and edible; nutlets 4–5, usually 5
             . . . . .54. *C. mollis* [A, B, C]
          e. Fruit ripening in October; flesh dry and
             mealy; nutlets 3–5 . . . . .57. *C. limaria*
        d. Mature leaves thick or subcoriaceous; flowers
           mostly 5–12 in corymb
          f. Leaves bluish green; flowers mostly 5–12 in
             compound corymbs; stamens about 20 . . . . . .
             . . . . .60. *C. lanuginosa*
          f. Leaves dull yellowish green; flowers mostly
             5–8 in simple corymbs . . . .
             . . . . .64. *C. greggiana*
      c. Leaves often as broad as long, comparatively
         small; terminal shoot leaves sometimes broader
         than long . . . . .62. *C. brachyphylla* [A]
    b. Fruit bright yellow at maturity . . . .
       . . . . .63. *C. viburnifolia* [B, C]
  a. Leaves of flowering spurs mostly elliptic or oblong-
     ovate, noticeably longer than broad, gradually or
     abruptly narrowed at base; terminal shoot leaves
     broader, usually rounded or rarely truncate at base;
     fruit red at maturity; sepals glandular-serrate
    b. Stamens 10 or less; nutlets 3–5 . . . . .56. *C. noelensis*
    b. Stamens about 20; nutlets 4–5, usually 5, except in
       no. 58
      c. Mature leaves thick; sepals foliaceous, deeply
         glandular-serrate; anthers large, dark red; fruit
         with thick mellow flesh, edible . . . .
         . . . . .55. *C. texana* [A, B, C]
      c. Mature leaves relatively thin; sepals not foliaceous,
         more or less glandular-serrate; fruit with thin dry
         or mealy flesh, scarcely edible
        d. Anthers white or pale yellow; sepals laciniately
           glandular-serrate; nutlets 3–5 . . . .
           . . . . .58. *C. invisa* [A]
        d. Anthers pink or rose, or sometimes white in
           no. 59; nutlets 4–5, usually 5
          e. Flowers about 1 in. wide; sepals glandular-
             serrate; fruit bright red or crimson and lus-
             trous at maturity . . . . .59. *C. dispessa*
          e. Flowers about ¾ in. wide; sepals sparingly
             and irregularly glandular-serrate; fruit dull
             dark red at maturity . . . .
             . . . . .61. *C. dallasiana* [A, C]

Parsley Hawthorn

Crataegus marshallii Egglest.—Series Microcarpae (2) [A, B, C]

FIELD IDENTIFICATION. Shrub or small tree attaining a height of 20 ft, with smooth gray bark and spreading crooked branches.

FLOWERS. Borne in villose corymbs of 3–12; petals 5, white, spreading, rounded, inserted on the disk margin; calyx 5-lobed, lobes lanceolate, acuminate, often glandular-serrate; stamens about 20, with red anthers; styles 1–3; nearly the whole of the inflorescence white-pubescent.

FRUIT. Pome oblong or ovoid, about ⅓ in. long, bright red, shiny, slightly pubescent; flesh thin, yellow, edible; nutlets 1–3 usually 2, smooth, rounded.

LEAVES. Simple, alternate, deciduous, ovate to orbicular, ¾–1½ in. long; acute at the apex; truncate, cuneate, or subcordate at base; incised into 5–7 deep clefts and serrate on the margin; pubescent on both faces when young, when older more glabrous above but hairy along veins beneath; petioles 1–2 in., slender, tomentose.

TWIGS. Brown to gray, pubescent when young, smooth later, crooked; bearing stout, straight, brown, scattered spines 1–2 in. long.

BARK. Gray to brown, smooth, scaling off in large thin plates to expose reddish brown inner bark.

WOOD. Reddish brown, heavy, hard, strong, weighing 46 lb per cu ft, of no particular commercial value.

RANGE. Texas to Florida; north to Oklahoma, Arkansas, Missouri, and Virginia.

REMARKS. *Crataegus* is a Greek word meaning "strong," in reference to the tough wood, and the species name, *marshallii* is in honor of the botanist Humphrey Marshall. Parsley Haw could be more extensively cultivated for its beautiful foliage, white flowers, and scarlet fruit.

Little-hip Hawthorn

Crataegus spathulata Michx.—Series Microcarpae (2) [A, B, C]

FIELD IDENTIFICATION. Shrub or small tree to 25 ft, with a broad open head and bearing sparse straight spines.

FLOWERS. March–May, borne in glabrous, many-flowered corymbs; individual flowers about ½ in. in diameter on slender pedicels; petals 5, white, rounded, spreading, inserted on the margin of the disk; stamens about 20. Calyx-tube obconic, glabrous, with 5 lobes; lobes deltoid, entire, minutely glandular at apex.

FRUIT. Pome ripe in October, globose or nearly so, bright red, ¼ in. or less in diameter, tipped with the persistent

reflexed calyx-lobes; flesh dry, thin, and mealy; nutlets 3–5, slightly ridged or smooth on back.

LEAVES. Simple, alternate, deciduous; spatulate to oblanceolate, sometimes 3–5-lobed at the apex; crenate-serrate on the margin, the cuneate base entire and tapering to a winged petiole; apex acute or rounded; hairy when young on both sides, at maturity becoming firm, glabrous, shiny and dark green above, and glabrous or villose on the veins beneath; 1–2 in. long, 1–1½ in. wide; terminal leaves with stipules stalked, foliaceous, falcate, serrate, and to ½ in. wide.

TWIGS. Reddish brown, glabrous, crooked, armed or unarmed; spines sparse, slender, more or less straight, brown, 1–1½ in. long.

BARK. Light brown to gray, smooth, flaking off.

WOOD. Reddish brown, heavy, hard, strong, weighing 45 lb per cu ft, not large enough for commercial use.

RANGE. Oklahoma, Arkansas, and eastern Texas; eastward to Florida and northward to South Carolina and Virginia.

REMARKS. *Crataegus* is a Greek word meaning "strong," in reference to its tough wood, and the species name, *spathulata*, refers to the spathe- or spoon-shaped leaves.

Blueberry Hawthorn

Crataegus brachyacantha Engelm. & Sarg.—
Series Brevispinae (4) [A, B, C]

FIELD IDENTIFICATION. Beautiful round-topped tree attaining a height of 40 ft, armed with short curved spines.

FLOWERS. Borne in many-flowered glabrous corymbs; flowers about ⅓ in. across, white at first and orange with age; petals 5, borne on the edge of the disk, rounded, spreading; stamens 15–20, anthers yellow; styles 3–5; calyx-tube obconic, glabrous, 5-lobed; lobes triangular to lanceolate, gland-tipped, entire.

FRUIT. Ripe pomes borne a few in a cluster on erect pedicels in August; depressed, subglobose or obovoid, bright blue or black and glaucous, ⅓–½ in. long, flesh thin; nutlets 3–5, round at apex, acute at base, rounded or with 2 slight grooves on the back, about ¼ in. long, light brown.

LEAVES. Simple, alternate, deciduous, those on vigorous shoots often quite distinct from those on slow-growing spurs, oblong-obovate or oblong-lanceolate or ovate-rhombic, leathery; acute or obtuse at apex; cuneate to truncate or cordate at the base; crenate-serrate on margins and lobed on some; when lobed usually 3-lobed with the middle lobe longest and somewhat shallowly cleft again, or only serrate; dark green, glabrous and lustrous above; paler, and glabrous or pubescent beneath, ¾–3½ in. long, about ½–2 in. wide; petiole ½–¾ in., slender, sometimes winged; stipules foliaceous, ovate-triangular, asymmetrical, broader than long, elongate and acuminate pointed on one side, the other side shortened and coarsely toothed also across the apex, to 1 in. long.

TWIGS. Green and minutely pubescent at first, glabrous and reddish brown to gray later; spines short, ⅓–⅔ in. long, stout, usually curved but some straight, gray to brown.

BARK. Smooth and gray on young trunks, on old trunks gray to brown and divided into narrow flattened ridges and shallow furrows, loosening with age into thin scales to expose reddish brown inner bark.

WOOD. Hard, strong, heavy, not large enough to be commercially usable.

RANGE. Margins of streams and swamps, Texas and Louisiana; east to Georgia and north to Arkansas. In Texas west to the Trinity River. Locally abundant between Hull and Saratoga, Texas.

REMARKS. *Crataegus* is from an ancient Greek word and means strength in reference to the tough wood, and the species name, *brachyacantha*, refers to the short thorns. The French gave the tree the name of Pomette Bleu in reference to the blue fruit, which is unusual for a hawthorn.

May Hawthorn

Crataegus opaca Hook. & Arn.—Series Aestivales (5) [A, B]

FIELD IDENTIFICATION. Shrub or small tree up to 30 ft, with slender erect branches and a rounded head.

FLOWERS. Borne before the leaves in February or March, in 2–5-flowered glabrous corymbs; corolla about ¾ in. across; petals 5, white, spreading, rounded, inserted on the margin of the disk; stamens about 20 with rose-purple anthers; styles 3–5; calyx-tube obconic, glabrous, 5-lobed; the calyx-lobes triangular, acute and gland-tipped, entire or serrulate on margin, often reddish-colored.

FRUIT. Pome borne in May, large, ½–¾ in. across, red, dotted, fragrant, globose, somewhat depressed, calyx persistent; flesh juicy, sweet-acid; nutlets 3–5, rounded.

LEAVES. Simple, alternate, deciduous, oblong to obovate or elliptic, acute or rounded at the apex, cuneate at the base, margin crenate-serrate or often 3-lobed, 1–2½ in. long, ½–1⅓ in. wide; dark green and usually glabrous above; lower surface clothed with dense rusty brown pubescence, especially on the veins; petioles slender, rusty-pubescent.

TWIGS. Brown to gray, hairy at first, glabrous later; unarmed, or bearing stout, straight, brown spines ½–1 in.

BARK. Dark reddish brown, deeply fissured into persistent scales.

WOOD. Heavy, hard, strong, not large enough for commercial use.

RANGE. The species is found in wet soil in Texas, Arkansas, Louisiana, and north to South Carolina.

REMARKS. *Crataegus* is from an ancient Greek word meaning "strength," in reference to the wood, and the species name, *opaca*, refers to the dull fruit. It was formerly listed under the name of *C. aestivalis* (Walt.) Torr. & Gray, but this name now applies to another species. Also known as the Riverflat Hawthorn. This is the famous May Haw of the South, from which preserves are made. The large size and acid character of the pomes make it particularly desirable for that purpose.

One-flower Hawthorn

Crataegus uniflora Muenchh.—Series Parvifoliae (6) [A]

FIELD IDENTIFICATION. Slender shrub 3–12 ft, with crooked, thorny branchlets. Usually with a solitary flower or fruit.

FLOWERS. Opening in May, pedicels short, tomentose, single, or rarely 2–3 together; corolla ⅜–⅝ in. wide, petals 5, white, rounded, deciduous; calyx-lobes 5, foliaceous, lanceolate, pectinate-laciniate or deeply glandular-serrate; stamens 20 or more, filaments filiform; anthers small, oblong, white or pale yellow; styles 5–7.

FRUIT. Pome maturing in October, calyx persistent on the fruit with prominent reflexed lobes, fruit body ⅜–½ in. thick, pubescent, subglobose or slightly pyriform, greenish yellow to dull red, flesh firm, dry and mealy; nutlets 3–5 (usually 5), about ⅓ in. long, grooved dorsally, bony.

LEAVES. Simple, alternate, deciduous, subcoriaceous, apex obtuse to rounded or acute, base cuneate, margin sharply or crenately serrate, unlobed or sometimes obscurely lobed above the middle, leaf varying in shape from obovate to spatulate or cuneate, sometimes oblong or elliptic, upper leaf surface dark green and lustrous, with scattered hairs to glabrous; lower leaf surface pubescent, especially along the veins which run to the points of the marginal teeth; petioles very short or leaf almost sessile, pubescent.

TWIGS. Slender, stiffened, when young reddish brown to gray and densely pubescent, when older gray and glabrous; spines slender, straight or slightly curved, gray to black, ½–2¼ in. long; bark of trunks gray or dark brown.

RANGE. In woods or on sandy or rocky banks. Eastern Texas; eastward to Florida and Georgia, northward to Pennsylvania and New York, and westward to the Ozark region of Arkansas and Missouri.

REMARKS. The genus name, *Crataegus*, refers to the Greek word for hard wood. The species name, *uniflora*, means "one-flowered." It is also known as the Dwarf Thorn.

Pearson Hawthorn

Crataegus pearsonii Ashe—Series Flavae (7) [A]

FIELD IDENTIFICATION. Small spreading tree to 15 ft, with rough bark and crooked recurved branches.

FLOWERS. Borne in simple, or compound, 3–5-flowered corymbs; pedicels white-hairy, ½–1 in.; corolla 4/5–1 in. wide; petals 5, white, oval to obovate, narrowed into a short claw; calyx more or less hairy at first; sepals 5, about ¼ in. long, oblong-linear, acuminate, serrulate, glandular; stamens 20, anthers yellow.

FRUIT. Early deciduous, on peduncles ½–¾ in. long, sub-globose, ⅓–½ in. in diameter, bright red, flesh soft, juicy, acid; seeds 3–5, about ⅓ in. long, dorsally rounded, ventral side straight.

LEAVES. Of 2 types, smaller leaves spatulate to obovate or cuneate, apex rounded or abruptly acute, base gradually narrowed or cuneate, singly or doubly toothed on margin, teeth often glandular and glands often extending down on petiole which is ¼–⅔ in.; leaf surfaces glabrous at maturity above, or slightly puberulous beneath; leaves of young vigorous shoots often larger and almost oval, to 2¼ in. long and wide, apex rounded or abruptly acute, margin doubly serrate or some with short acute lobes as well as serrations above the middle, base almost rounded in some or abruptly narrowed, base of blade slightly decurrent on the petiole; petiole ¼–½ in., shorter in proportion to the blade than the

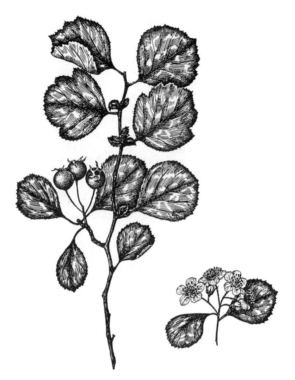

smaller leaves, black glands on petiole as well as on teeth; veins impressed above and surface glabrous, lower surface with veins more prominent and mostly ending in the teeth, glabrous or slightly pubescent when mature.

TWIGS. Slender, light to dark gray or brown, mostly glabrous.

RANGE. Low sandy soil in Louisiana, Mississippi, and southeast Texas.

REMARKS. The genus name, *Crataegus*, is the classical Greek name of the hawthorn. The species name, *pearsonii*, honors the botanist Gilbert Pearson. A synonym is *C. florens* Beadle.

Green Hawthorn

Crataegus viridis L.—Series Virides (9) [A, B, C]

FIELD IDENTIFICATION. Tree attaining a height of 35 ft and forming a broad rounded crown. The trunk is often fluted, and the twigs are sparsely spined, or not at all.

FLOWERS. Opening March–April. Borne in many-flowered, glabrous corymbs; individual flowers on slender pedicels,

about ¾ in. in diameter; petals 5, rounded, spreading, inserted on the disk margin in the calyx-throat; stamens 15–20, anthers yellow; styles 2–5, hairy at the base; calyx-tube obconic, glabrous, with lobes entire, lanceolate, glabrous or puberulent, or pubescent to villose in some varieties.

FRUIT. Pome globose or depressed-globose, in drooping clusters, red to orange and often glaucous (sometimes remaining greenish), 1/6–1/4 in. in diameter; calyx-lobes 5, small, often dropping away early from the fruit; nutlets 4–5, obscurely ridged or grooved on the back, 1/6–1/8 in. long.

LEAVES. Simple, alternate, deciduous, ovate-oblong, acute to acuminate or rarely obtuse at the apex, cuneate or rounded at the base; serrate to doubly serrate and often shallowly lobed toward the apex, teeth usually few or none at the cuneate base; dark green and shiny above and becoming glabrous later, paler beneath with axillary tufts of white hairs, blades ¾–3½ in. long, ½–2 in. wide; petiole slender and glabrous.

TWIGS. Gray or reddish, with or without spines; spines when present slender, pale, sharp, ¼–1 in.

BARK. Gray to reddish brown, shedding in small scales.

WOOD. Reddish brown, heavy, hard, tough, weighing about

40 lb per cu ft, not large enough to be commercially valuable.

RANGE. The species is known from Texas in the eastern and upper coastal regions; Louisiana, Arkansas, and eastern Oklahoma; eastward to Florida, northward to southeastern Virginia, and westward to southwestern Indiana, Kansas, and Missouri.

REMARKS. The genus name, *Crataegus*, is from an ancient Greek word meaning "strength," in reference to the tough wood, and the species name, *viridis*, means "green." Vernacular names are Green Thorn and Southern Thorn.

Velvety Green Hawthorn

Crataegus viridis var. *velutina* (Sarg.) Palmer—Series Virides (9) [A, B, C]

FIELD IDENTIFICATION. Tree attaining a height of 20–25 ft, with a trunk 8–10 in. in diameter covered with rough, dark, scaly bark.

FLOWERS. Opening the latter part of April, borne in hairy 7–12-flowered corymbs with slender villose pedicels; calyx-tube narrowly obconic, villose, the 5 lobes gradually narrowed from a broad base, short, acute, entire, slightly villose; stamens 20, anthers yellow; styles 5; petals 5, rounded, white.

FRUIT. Borne in slender, glabrous, few-fruited clusters, fruit body subglobose, orange-red, pale-dotted, about ¼ in. in diameter; calyx prominent, with a deep narrow cavity pointed inward from the bottom, and closely appressed lobes; flesh thin, dry and mealy; nutlets 5, acute at base, rounded, dorsally ridged and grooved, about 1/6 in. long and ⅛ in. wide.

LEAVES. Simple, alternate, deciduous, blade ovate to obovate, apex acute or rounded, base entire and gradually narrowed and cuneate, margin sharply and often doubly serrate with straight glandular teeth; half-grown when the flowers open, young ones covered with short white hairs above, hoary-pubescent below, and often with tufts of white tomentum; mature ones glabrous, smooth and lustrous above, and lower surface with pale matted hairs, length 1¾ in., width 1½–2 in.; petioles slender, thickly covered at first with matted hairs, later glabrous, length ½–1 in.

TWIGS. Slender, at first hoary-tomentose and light reddish brown; later becoming marked with lenticels and pubescent to glabrous, becoming gray, bearing straight chestnut brown spines ¾–1½ in. long.

RANGE. Usually in dry sandy soils, but also on clays. In Texas in the valley of the lower Brazos River (Brazoria County). Also from eastern Texas to Louisiana, and Arkansas. In Arkansas in Hempstead and Bowie counties.

REMARKS. The genus name, *Crataegus*, refers to the strong wood, and the variety name, *velutina*, is for the velvety tomentum on young leaves.

Small-leaf Green Hawthorn

Crataegus viridis forma *abbreviata* (Sarg.) Palmer—Series Virides (9) [A, B]

FIELD IDENTIFICATION. Shrub or small tree to 18 ft, with a slender trunk.

FLOWERS. Opening in April, corymbs slightly villose, compact, 10–15-flowered; petals 5, white, rounded; calyx-tube broad-obconic, slightly villose, the 5 sepals short, entire, often slightly villose or externally glabrous, villose within; stamens 20, anthers yellow, styles 4–5.

FRUIT. Maturing in October, in lax drooping clusters with slightly villose or glabrous pedicels, subglobose, dark red, ¼–⅓ in. in diameter, flesh thin and succulent, calyx little enlarged, with a deep cavity in the bottom; nutlets 4–5, rounded at the ends, broader at apex than at base, slightly grooved dorsally, 1/8–1/6 in. long.

LEAVES. Simple, alternate, deciduous, at first with short white hairs and dense tomentum below, expanding when the flowers open and then glabrous or slightly hairy along the midrib, or with a few axillary tufts below, yellowish green, thin, ovate to obovate, elliptic or suborbicular, apex acute or rounded and abruptly short-pointed, base narrowed and cuneate or rounded, margin often glandular-serrate, usually only above the middle, and often slightly divided usually toward the apex into short acute lobes, blade length 1–1⅓ in., ¾–1 in. wide; petiole slender, slightly villose-pubescent early in the season, soon becoming glabrous; leaves on young shoots broad-ovate to semiorbicular or elliptic, apex rounded or acuminate, base rounded or cuneate, often laterally lobed, 1½–2 in. long and broad.

TWIGS. Slightly villose at first, later glabrous and orange-brown, eventually gray to brown; unarmed, or with spines slender, straight, 1–1¾ in.

RANGE. Low woods on the Brazos River, near Brazoria, Brazos County, Texas.

REMARKS. The genus name, *Crataegus*, is the ancient name referring to the hard wood. The species name, *viridis*, means "green," and the form name, *abbreviata*, is for the short leaf.

Coast Hawthorn

Crataegus anamesa Sarg.—Series Virides (9) [A, B]

FIELD IDENTIFICATION. Shrub 12–15 ft, with trunks covered with gray slightly scaly bark. Branches erect, smooth, dark gray.

FLOWERS. Appearing at the end of March or early in April, ¾–1 in. in diameter, in compact mostly 10–15-flowered densely villose corymbs crowded on the branches; petals 5, white, rounded; calyx-tube narrow-obconic, glabrous except for occasional short white hairs, the lobes gradually narrowed from the base, entire or rarely minute-dentate, glabrous on the outer surface, villose on the inner surface, mostly deciduous from the ripe fruit; stamens 20, anthers pale yellow; styles 4 or 5.

FRUIT. Ripening early in October, on nearly glabrous pedicels, in few-fruited drooping clusters, subglobose to short-oblong or slightly obovoid, dark red, 1/3–2/5 in. in diameter, the calyx little enlarged, with a deep narrow cavity directed inward from the apex; nutlets 4 or 5, narrowed and rounded at the ends, only slightly grooved on the back, about 1/5 in. long, the dark narrow hypostyle extending to below the middle.

LEAVES. Elliptic to broad-ovate or slightly obovate, acute at apex, gradually or abruptly narrowed and cuneate at base, finely serrate with short broad teeth, and often slightly divided above the middle into broad rounded lobes; tinged with red as they unfold, and villose above and thickly covered below with matted white hairs. Not more than half-grown when the flowers open, and then glabrous or nearly glabrous above, sparingly villose and conspicuous below by the broad snow-white to dark gray band; apparently spineless. White hairs along the lower part of the midrib, and at maturity subcoriaceous, nearly glabrous, dark green and lustrous on the upper surface, pale on the lower surface, 1¼–2 in. long or wide; petioles slender, densely villose early in the season, becoming glabrous, ⅝–¾ in. long; leaves on vigorous shoots broad-ovate, rounded or acute at apex, rounded or broad-cuneate at base, finely serrate, slightly lobed with short broad lobes, to ¼ in. long and wide, their petioles stout, slightly wing-margined at apex, often furnished with occasional glands, 1–1⅓ in. in length.

TWIGS. Slightly zigzag, young ones densely white-hairy, later glabrous and reddish brown to dark gray, usually spineless, or occasionally a few spines.

RANGE. Fort Bend County, Texas.

REMARKS. The genus name, *Crataegus*, is the classical name of the hawthorn. The species name, *anamesa*, means "middle" or "intermediate" and refers to the fruit size. The size of the fruit of this species is intermediate between that of typical *C. viridis* L. and that of a small group of species with fruit ⅝–¾ in. in diameter of which *C. nitida* Sargent is the best known. Although much more pubescent, this Texas shrub resembles in the shape of its leaves another of the large-fruited Virides species, *C. atrorubens* Ashe of East St. Louis, Illinois. *C. anamesa* has also been listed under the name of *C. antiplasta* Sargent.

Narrow-sepal Hawthorn

Crataegus stenosepala Sarg.—Series Virides (9) [A, B, C]

FIELD IDENTIFICATION. Shrub or small tree 12–15 ft, with stems forming large thickets, and covered with dark slightly scaly bark.

FLOWERS. Opening toward the end of March, ¾ in. in diameter, in wide loose 10–20-flowered, slightly villose corymbs; petals 5, white, rounded; calyx-tube broad-obconic, sparingly covered with long white ridged hairs, the lobes gradually narrowed from the base, slender, long-acuminate, minutely and irregularly serrate, glandular ciliate, glabrous on the outer surface, obscurely ciliate on the inner surface, ¼–⅓ in. long; stamens 20, anthers pale yellow; styles 5.

FRUIT. Ripening early in October, ellipsoidal to slightly obovoid, on slender glabrous pedicels in drooping clusters, orange-red, ¼–⅓ in. long, 1/5–1/4 in. thick, with thin dry flesh, the calyx with a distinct tube, spreading lobes and a deep narrow cavity pointed in from the apex; nutlets 4 or 5, rounded at base, acute at apex, only slightly grooved on the back, ¼–⅓ in. long and 1/8–1/6 in. wide, the pale broad hypostyle extending to the middle.

LEAVES. Elliptic to oblong-elliptic or obovate, acute or acuminate at apex, gradually narrowed and cuneate at base, sharply and coarsely serrate above the middle with straight teeth, and often divided toward the apex into short lobes; when they unfold deeply tinged with red and slightly pubescent, nearly half-grown when the flowers open and then roughened above by short white hairs and conspicuous below by the thick snow-white pubescence along the midrib and on the petioles, the villose primary veins, and the axillary clusters of white hairs; and at maturity glabrous, yellowish green and lustrous on the upper surface, paler on the lower surface, blades 1½–2¼ in. long and 5/8–1 1/4 in. wide with a thin midrib and slender primary veins impressed above; petioles ¼–⅓ in. in length; leaves on vigorous shoots oblong-obovate, thicker, acuminate, cuneate at base, more coarsely serrate, more deeply lobed, and to 2¾ in. in length and 1½ in. wide.

TWIGS. Slender, slightly zigzag, white-hairy at first, becoming glabrous; at first reddish brown, later ashy gray and glabrous; spines numerous, nearly straight, slender, ¾–1⅔ in. long.

RANGE. Specimens collected by E. J. Palmer in Fort Bend County, Texas. Type specimen deposited in the herbarium of the Missouri Botanical Garden.

REMARKS. The genus name, *Crataegus*, is the classical name of the hawthorn, and the species name, *stenosepala*, refers to the remarkably long slender calyx-lobes. The leaves also are conspicuous when the tree flowers, owing to the broad band of snow white tomentum covering the under side of the lower half of the midrib. *C. stenosepala* is sometimes listed under the name of *C. antemima* Sargent.

Rosemary Hawthorn

Crataegus poliophylla Sarg.—Series Virides (9) [A, B]

FIELD IDENTIFICATION. Tree occasionally 12–15 ft, with a trunk 3–4 in. in diameter, covered with dark rough bark, smooth ashy gray branches.

FLOWERS. Opening late in March or early in April, about ⅝ in. in diameter, in wide lax 7–15-flowered densely villose corymbs; calyx-tube broad-obconic, villose, the lobes short, gradually narrowed from the base, glandular-serrate or nearly entire, glabrous on the outer surface, slightly villose on the inner surface; stamens 20, anthers yellow; styles 4–5; petioles 5, white, rounded.

FRUIT. Ripening late in September, in pendent clusters, globose to short-oblong or ovoid, orange-red, ¼–⅓ in. in diameter, the calyx prominent, with a short tube, reflexed lobes and a wide shallow cavity at the apex; nutlets 4 or 5, rounded at apex, gradually narrowed at base, slightly grooved on the back, 1/8–1/6 in. long, 1/12–1/8 in. wide, the narrow hypostyle extending to the middle.

LEAVES. Oblong-obovate to elliptic, acute to acuminate at apex, gradually narrowed and cuneate at base, finely double-serrate above the middle with straight teeth and usually irregularly divided toward the apex into short acute lobes; thickly covered when they unfold with white hairs longer

and more abundant on the lower than on the upper surface, nearly glabrous above when the flowers open and more or less pubescent below, and at maturity subcoriaceous, glabrous, yellowish green and lustrous on the upper surface, paler on the lower surface, blades 1¼–1½ in. long and 1–1¼ in. wide, with a prominent midrib and slender veins deeply impressed above; on leading shoots to 2½ in. long and 1¾ in. wide; petioles slender, deeply grooved, narrowly wing-margined toward the apex, densely villose-pubescent early in the season, becoming glabrous, ⅝–¾ in. long.

TWIGS. Slender, thickly covered early in the season with long matted white hairs, becoming glabrous and ashy gray, and armed with slender straight spines ⅝–1 in. in length.

RANGE. Rare and local, Brazoria and Ft. Bend counties, Texas. Usually in thickets in drained soil.

REMARKS. The genus name, *Crataegus*, is the classical name of the hawthorn, and the species name, *poliophylla*, is from the "rosemarylike," or gray and woolly leaves.

Cock's-spur Hawthorn

Crataegus crus-galli L.—Series **Crus-galli** (10) [A, B, C]

FIELD IDENTIFICATION. Shrub or tree to 30 ft, and 6–12 in. in diameter. The branches are stout, rigid, horizontal or drooping, forming a round-topped or broadly depressed crown.

FLOWERS. Opening May–June after the leaves, in lax, many-flowered, glabrous corymbs; pedicels slender and glabrous, corolla 1/2–3/5 in. broad, petals 5, white, reflexed after anthesis; calyx-tube narrow and obconic, glabrous, sepals 5, 1/8–1/5 in. long, linear-lanceolate, entire or glandular-serrate; stamens 10, anthers pink or white; styles 2, hairy at the base.

FRUIT. Maturing in October, persistent over winter, short-oblong to subglobose or ovoid (occasionally slightly 5-angled), dull red, 1/3–1/2 in. long, with a terminal depression, flesh thin and dry; nutlets 2 (rarely 1 or 3), ridged dorsally, ends rounded, about 1/4 in. long.

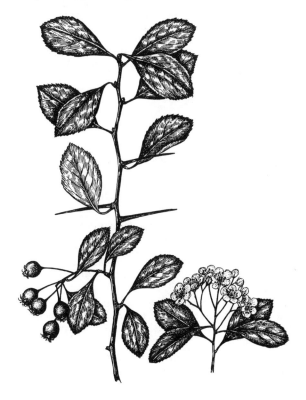

LEAVES. Simple, alternate, deciduous, thick and leathery at maturity, mostly obovate to oblanceolate, apex obtuse to rounded or acute, base gradually cuneate, margin sharply and minutely toothed above the middle, teeth often glandular; upper surface dark green and lustrous, lower surface paler and reticulate-veined, blade length 3/5–4 in., width ½–1⅓ in., turning yellow, orange, or red in the fall; petiole ½–¾ in. long, stout, winged above; leaves on young shoots often longer and apex acute or acuminate.

TWIGS. Stout, reddish brown to gray, glabrous, armed with sharp, straight or slightly curved spines 2–8 in. long, sometimes with lateral spines; bark of trunk dark brown to gray, breaking into small scales with irregular, moderately deep fissures.

WOOD. Heavy, hard, fine-grained, suitable for tool handles.

RANGE. Fence rows, woods, and thickets. The species and varieties are widespread. East Texas, Oklahoma, Arkansas, and Louisiana; east to Georgia, north to Michigan, Kansas, and southern Quebec, and west to Ontario.

REMARKS. The genus name, *Crataegus*, is the classical Greek name for hawthorn. The species name, *crus-galli*, refers to the long thorns which resemble the spurs of a fowl. Cock's-spur Hawthorn is very desirable for cultivation because of the rounded crown, shiny leaves, and conspicuous flowers. It is perhaps the most widely planted hawthorn in the United States and Europe.

Bush's Hawthorn

Crataegus bushii Sarg.—Series Crus-galli (10) [A]

FIELD IDENTIFICATION. Large shrub or tree to 25 ft, 10 in. in trunk diameter. The spreading branches forming a rounded crown.

FLOWERS. April–May, borne in broad, many-flowered, slender-pediceled, glabrous corymbs; corolla ¾–1 in. across; petals 5, white, oval, veiny; calyx-tube broadly obconic, sepals 5, 1/6–1/5 in. long, glabrous, linear-lanceolate, entire or obscurely toothed; stamens 20, anthers large and pink; styles 2–3, basally hairy.

FRUIT. Maturing October–November, clusters drooping and few-fruited, short-oblong, green to reddish, length 1/3–2/5 in., sepals often deciduous; flesh thin, firm, dry; nutlets 2–3, about ¼ in. long.

LEAVES. Simple, alternate or clustered, deciduous, obovate or sometimes oval or elliptic, apex rounded to obtuse or acute, base cuneate or abruptly contracted, margin coarsely serrate above the middle, surfaces white-hairy at first, later firm and leathery, upper surface shiny, dark green and glabrous,

lower surface paler and usually with scattered white hairs on the veins and midrib, veinlets reticulate, blade length 1¼–1½ in., width ½–1½ in.; petioles 1/5–3/5 in., white-hairy, or with age less so, somewhat winged by the gradually narrowed leaf bases; leaves on vigorous shoots usually somewhat larger and tending to be more elliptic.

TWIGS. Slender, elongate, nearly straight, essentially glabrous, chestnut brown at first, gray later, spineless, or spines 1½–1¾ in. long, straight, brown, lustrous, some spines bearing reduced leaves; bark or trunk dark brown or grayish brown with irregular fissures and breaking into small scales.

RANGE. In Texas near Marshall, Harrison County; in Louisiana in Winn Parish, Calcasieu Parish, and Natchitoches Parish. Specimen examined from type tree, collected by B. F. Bush, No. 1368, Fulton, Arkansas, April 16, 1902. Deposited in the New York Botanical Garden Herbarium.

REMARKS. The genus name, *Crataegus*, is the classical Greek name for hawthorn. The species name, *bushii*, is in honor of its discoverer, Benjamin Franklin Bush (1858–1937), botanist of Missouri. A synonym is *C. triumphalis* Sarg.

Pyracantha Hawthorn

Crataegus pyracanthoides Beadle—Series **Crus-galli** (10) [A]

FIELD IDENTIFICATION. Shrub or small tree 6–15 ft, the trunk or main stems clothed with ashy gray or brownish, either smooth or scaly, bark.

FLOWERS. Open early in April when the leaves are almost fully grown, produced in compound, glabrous, many-flowered corymbs; pedicels and hypanthium glabrous; petals 5, white, rounded, spreading; sepals 1–1½ in. long, entire or remotely serrate, spreading or reflexed after anthesis; stamens 7–12, the anthers purplish; styles 2–3.

FRUIT. Ripens in September, globose or nearly so, 1/5–1/3 in. in diameter, bright red at maturity; nutlets mostly 2, 1/5–1/4 in. long, the ventral surface nearly plane; hypostyle about half the length of the nutlet.

LEAVES. Obovate, oblanceolate or elliptic, the blades 5/8–2 in. long, 1/3–1⅓ in. wide, glabrous, acute or rounded at the apex, cuneate at the base, the margins serrate above the middle; they are glabrous, or when young a few bear weak hairs along the midrib on the upper surface, bright green and lustrous above, pale green beneath, eventually firm or subcoriaceous in texture, fading to tones of yellow, orange, and brown; petioles 1/12–2/5 in. long, margined.

TWIGS. Slender, brown to gray, armed with chestnut brown or gray spines 5/8–1 1/2 in. long.

RANGE. Louisiana, Alabama, and northern Florida; to Virginia and up the Mississippi Valley to Missouri and Indiana.

REMARKS. The genus name, *Crataegus*, is the classical name of the hawthorn. The species name, *pyracanthoides*, refers to the pyracanthalike fruit. Also known as Montgomery Hawthorn.

Unique Pyracantha Hawthorn

Crataegus pyracanthoides var. *uniqua* (Sarg.) Palmer—Series Crus-galli (10) [A]

FIELD IDENTIFICATION. Slender tree to 20 ft, with wide-spreading branches forming a flat head.

FLOWERS. Opening in April, in 5–8-flowered, glabrous corymbs, pedicels slender; calyx-tube narrowly obconic, the 5 lobes short, broad and acuminate, margin entire or slightly dentate, somewhat hairy within, later reflexed; stamens 20, anthers white; styles 2–3.

FRUIT. Ripening in October, on slender drooping pedicels, short-oblong, rounded at the ends, dull red, ⅜–½ in. long and about ⅓ in. thick; calyx conspicuous with a deep wide cavity broad in the bottom; sepals 5, reflexed, appressed, slightly hairy within, persistent; flesh thin, dry, hard; nutlets 2 or 3, broad and rounded at the base, keeled on the back with a high wide-grooved ridge, ¼–⅓ in. long and about 1/8–1/6 in. wide; hypostyle conspicuous and broad, extending to below the middle of the nutlet.

LEAVES. About half-grown when the flowers open, simple, alternate, deciduous, oblong-obovate, apex acute or occasionally rounded, base gradually narrowed or cuneate; teeth on margin straight, incurved and glandular, usually above the middle, length ¾–1¾ in., width ⅜–¾ in., on vigorous shoots broadly obovate, acute or rounded at base, more closely serrate, 2–2½ in. long and 1–1⅓ in. wide; surfaces when young glabrous except along the veins; at maturity glabrous, thin but firm, upper surface dark green and shiny, paler beneath, midrib and veins rather slender.

TWIGS. Slender, slightly divaricate, yellow to orange or reddish brown, armed or unarmed, spines straight or slightly curved, shiny brown, ⅜–¾ in.

RANGE. In southwestern Arkansas, eastern Texas, and northwestern Louisiana. This tree is found in Texas in low rich woods near Marshall, Harrison County; Louisiana at the marble quarry near Winnfield, Winn Parish.

REMARKS. The genus name, *Crataegus*, is the classical name of the hawthorn. The variety name, *uniqua*, means "unique." This hawthorn has been variously described under the synonyms of *C. uniqua* Sarg., *C. arioclada* Sarg., and *C. cocksii* Sarg.

Cherokee Hawthorn

Crataegus cherokeensis Sarg.—Series Crus-galli (10) [A]

FIELD IDENTIFICATION. Small tree with slightly scaly bark.

FLOWERS. Opening early in April, 2/5–1/2 in. in diameter, on slender glabrous pedicels, in 5–7-flowered globose glabrous corymbs; petals 5, white, rounded, calyx-tube narrow-obconic, glabrous, the lobes slender, gradually narrowed from the base, long acuminate, entire or slightly and irregularly toothed above the middle, glabrous; stamens 10, anthers red; styles 1–3, usually 2.

FRUIT. Ripening late in September, ellipsoidal, dull orange-red, 2/5 in. long, about ¼ in. thick, the persistent calyx sessile or raised on a short tube; nutlets narrowed and rounded at the ends, only slightly ridged on the back, ¼–⅓ in. long, 1/8–1/5 in. wide, the narrow hypostyle extending to below the middle.

LEAVES. Oblong-obovate, apex rounded or acute, gradually narrowed and cuneate at base, finely, often doubly, serrate, usually only to the middle with acute teeth thickened at apex, glabrous with the exception of a few hairs on the upper side of the midrib early in the season, thin, dark green and lustrous above, paler below, blades 1½–1¾ in. long, ⅜–¾ in. wide, with a slender midrib and thin obscure primary veins, on vigorous leading shoots usually acute at apex, often acutely lobed above the middle, 1½–2 in. long, 1½–1¾ in. wide; petioles slender, often wing-margined nearly to the base, glabrous, on vigorous shoots 1/5–1/2 in. long.

TWIGS. Slender, glabrous, often zigzag, reddish brown to orange-brown at first, later dark grayish brown; spines numerous, straight, slender, 1–1½ in. long.

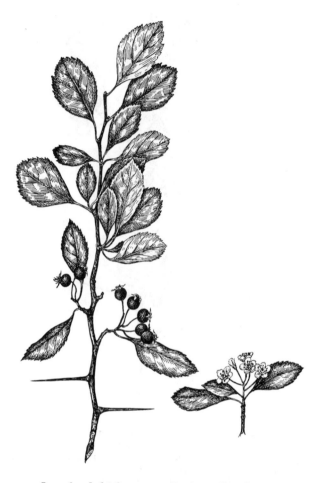

RANGE. In upland thickets, near Larissa, Cherokee County, Texas.

REMARKS. The genus name, *Crataegus*, is the classical Greek name of hawthorn. The species name, *cherokeensis*, refers to its being in Cherokee County, Texas.

San Augustine Hawthorn

Crataegus sublobulata Sarg.—Series Crus-galli (10) [A]

FIELD IDENTIFICATION. A round-topped tree 24–30 ft high, with a short trunk covered with soft, corky, slightly ridged bark, the branches wide-spreading.

FLOWERS. Opening late in March and early in April, about
⅝ in. in diameter, on slender glabrous pedicels in compact
5–6-flowered corymbs; petals 5, white, rounded; calyx-tube
narrow-obconic, glabrous, the lobes slender, acuminate,
entire or furnished above the middle with occasional slender
teeth, glabrous on the outer surface, sparingly villose-
pubescent on the inner surface; stamens 20, anthers pink;
styles 2–5.

FRUIT. Mature August–September, short-oblong to subglobose or rarely to obovoid, orange-red, 1/3–2/5 in. long and
about ¼ in. broad; nutlets usually broader at apex than at
base, prominently ridged on the back, 1/5–1/6 in. long and
1/8–1/5 in. wide, the broad hypostyle extending to below
the middle and often nearly to the base.

LEAVES. Broad-obovate to elliptic, acute or rounded at apex,
abruptly or gradually narrowed and cuneate at base, coarsely, deeply, and irregularly serrate with acuminate teeth, and
often sublobulate with acuminate lobules, tinged with red
and covered above with short white hairs, deciduous before
the flowers open except from the upper side of the midrib,

glabrous at maturity, thick, dark green and lustrous on the upper surface, paler on the lower surface, 1¼–1½ in. long, 1–1⅓ in. wide with a stout midrib and prominent primary veins, or on vigorous shoots often 1½–2 in. long and 1⅓ in. wide; petioles stout, wing-margined often nearly to the middle, grooved and villose-pubescent on the upper side, ⅜–⅝ in. long.

TWIGS. Slender, slightly zigzag, when young reddish brown, later gray to brown and glabrous; spines numerous, slender, straight, lustrous, chestnut brown to grayish brown, ½–1½ in. long.

RANGE. Known from borders of woods near San Augustine, San Augustine County, Texas.

REMARKS. The genus name, *Crataegus*, is the classical Greek name of hawthorn. The species name, *sublobulata*, refers to the deep nearly lobelike leaf serrations, unusual in plants of the Crus-galli group. It is well distinguished from *C. bushii* Sargent (the species of southern Arkansas, western Louisiana, and eastern Texas, with 20 stamens and rose-colored anthers) by the shape of the leaves.

Warner Hawthorn

Crataegus warneri Sarg.—Series Crus-galli (10) [A]

FIELD IDENTIFICATION. Shrub or tree to 24 ft, with dark bark scaly near the base. The erect branches form a narrow head.

FLOWERS. Opening from the 10th to the middle of April, ⅜–⅝ in. in diameter, on stout densely villose pedicels in compact many-flowered villose corymbs; petals 5, white, spreading; calyx-tube narrowly obconic, thickly covered with matted pale hairs, the lobes narrowed from a broad base, slender, acuminate, glandular-serrate, slightly villose on the outer surface, puberulous on the inner surface; stamens 10, anthers reddish purple; styles 2, rarely 3.

FRUIT. Ripening in September, on slightly villose pedicels; ellipsoidal to subglobose, orange-red, about ⅓ in. long, the calyx little enlarged with a short tube and a wide shallow cavity in the bottom, and with spreading, often deciduous, lobes; nutlets 2 or 3, rounded at the ends, ridged on the back with a broad deeply grooved ridge, 1/6 in. long and about ⅛ in. wide, the narrow hypostyle extending to the middle.

LEAVES. Ovate to oval or obovate, rounded or acute and short-pointed at apex, gradually or abruptly narrowed and cuneate at base, and coarsely serrate above the middle with straight gland-tipped teeth, nearly full-grown when the flowers open, and then covered above with short white hairs and villose below along the midrib and primary veins; at maturity thin, dark green and glabrous or occasionally still

villose on the midrib above, pale and still villose below along
the slender midrib and primary veins, 1¼–2 in. long and
1–1½ in. wide; petioles stout, wing-margined to the base,
densely villose at maturity, 1/5–1/3 in. in length; leaves on
vigorous shoots broad-ovate to semiorbicular, short-pointed
at the rounded or acute apex, rounded and gradually narrowed below into a broad wing extending nearly to the base
of the short petiole, more coarsely serrate, subcoriaceous,
roughened above, 1¾–2⅓ in. long and broad, with a stout
midrib and primary veins villose below.

TWIGS. Slender, pale hairy, reddish brown, glabrous with
maturity; spines stout or slender, chestnut brown, 1–2 in.
long.

RANGE. In Texas at Huntsville in Walker County, near
Larissa in Cherokee County, and near Palestine in Anderson
County.

REMARKS. The genus name, *Crataegus*, is the classical name
for the hawthorn, and the species name, *warneri*, honors
S. R. Warner, professor of botany.

Sabine Hawthorn

Crataegus sabineana Ashe—Series Crus-galli (10) [A]

FIELD IDENTIFICATION. Tree 12–30 ft.

FLOWERS. Borne in few-flowered corymbs, petals 5, white, rounded; stamens 10–20, stigmas usually 3.

FRUIT. Corymbs simple, 3–5-fruited, glabrous, pedicels slender, 1–2 in. long; fruit body oblong, 1/2–3/5 in. long, base narrowed, greenish yellow with a red cheek; flesh thin and green; calyx-lobes 5, reflexed, linear, apex acuminate, margin sharply serrate, later brown and deciduous, cavity conical and shallow.

LEAVES. Simple, alternate, deciduous, broadly obovate or rhombic, apex acute, base cuneate, margin coarsely and sharply serrate, blade length 1–1¾ in.; petioles 1/12–1/8 in. long, winged at the blade base.

TWIGS. Stout, glabrous, tan to reddish.

RANGE. Eastern Texas and western Louisiana.

REMARKS. The genus name, *Crataegus*, is the classical name, and the species name, *sabineana*, is from the Sabine River.

Marshall Hawthorn

Crataegus berberifolia var. *edita* (Sarg.) Palmer—Series Crus-galli (10) [A]

FIELD IDENTIFICATION. Tree attaining a height of 35 ft and a diameter of ¾–1 ft. The stout branches ascending or spreading to form a rounded crown.

FLOWERS. Usually opening in April, corymbs narrow, few-flowered, compound, pedicels ½–¾ in., villose; petals 5, rounded, corolla when open ½–⅔ in. across; calyx-tube narrowly obconic, glabrous or somewhat hairy toward the base, sepals 5, linear-lanceolate, green to reddish, entire or obscurely glandular-toothed, glabrous or puberulous; stamens 20, anthers purplish; styles 2–3.

FRUIT. Maturing October–November, clusters drooping and few-fruited, pedicels about ½ in. long, somewhat hairy or glabrous, fruit body short-oblong, greenish red, ¼–⅓ in. long, sepals deciduous or semipersistent; flesh green, dry, thin; nutlets 2 or 3 with broad low ridges, about ¼ in. long, hypostyle 1/6–1/5 in. long.

LEAVES. Simple, alternate or somewhat clustered, deciduous, oblong-obovate or oval to elliptic, apex acute or rounded, base cuneate, margin singly or doubly serrate (on younger shoots sometimes lobed and larger), dark green and lustrous, glabrous or slightly roughened, paler and scabrate

beneath with some persistent pubescence along the midrib, blade length 1¼–2 in., width ½–1 in.; petiole ⅓–½ in., stout, white-hairy at first, sparsely pubescent to glabrous later.

TWIGS. Slender, rather straight, brown at first to gray later, white-hairy at first but eventually glabrous; spines slender, straight, chestnut brown to gray, ¾–2 in. long; trunk with dark scaly bark.

RANGE. Swampy woods near Shreveport, Louisiana; Marshall, Texas; and Camden, Arkansas. The specimen examined was collected by B. F. Bush, Oct. 9, 1901, at Marshall, Texas, sheet No. 1009. Deposited in the New York Botanical Garden Herbarium.

REMARKS. The genus name, *Crataegus*, is the classical Greek name for the hawthorn. The species name, *berberifolia*, is for the barberrylike leaves, and the variety name, *edita*, means "standing out" or "elevated."

Engelmann Hawthorn

Crataegus engelmannii Sarg.—Series Crus-galli (10) [A, C]

FIELD IDENTIFICATION. Tree 15–20 ft, with a diameter of 5–6 in. Branches usually wide-spreading and usually horizontal, forming a low flat-topped or rounded head.

FLOWERS. April–May, flowers white, 5-petaled, about ¾ in. in diameter, in wide 8–12-flowered, slender-branched cymes thickly coated with long pale hairs; bracts about ½ in. long, linear-lanceolate, tomentose or villous; calyx tomentose, villous, or nearly glabrous, the lobes narrow, acuminate, entire, glabrous on the outer surface, and usually more or less pubescent on the inner surface, reflexed after anthesis, often deciduous before the ripening of the fruit; stamens 10; filaments slender; anthers small, rose-colored; styles two or three.

FRUIT. Ripening early in November, globose, about ⅓ in. in diameter, bright orange-red with a yellow cheek and thin dry green flesh; tube of the calyx prominent, the cavity broad in proportion to the size of the fruit, shallow, nutlets

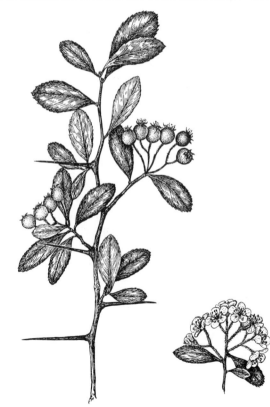

2 or 3, thick, prominently ribbed on the back with high rounded ridges, ¼ in. long.

LEAVES. Simple, alternate, deciduous, broadly obovate or rarely elliptic, apex rounded or short-pointed, gradually narrowed below into short glandular pilose petioles, coarsely glandular-serrate with incurved teeth usually only above the middle and generally only at the apex, coriaceous, dark green, lustrous and roughened on the upper surface with short rigid pale hairs, pale on the lower surface, pilose above and below on the slender midribs and on the thin obscure primary veins and veinlets, 1–1½ in. long, ½–1 in. broad; stipules linear-lanceolate, light red, ⅓ in. long, caducous.

TWIGS. Slightly zigzag, marked with large scattered white lenticels, at first clothed with pale hairs, becoming nearly glabrous and reddish brown during the first season, and lighter colored and gray or gray tinged with red during their second year, and armed with remote slender straight or slightly curved chestnut brown spines 1½–2½ in. long.

RANGE. Dry hillsides and slopes of limestone soil. East and north-central Texas, Oklahoma, Kansas, Missouri, Arkansas, Tennessee, Kentucky, Alabama, Mississippi, and Illinois.

REMARKS. The genus name, *Crataegus*, is the classical name of the hawthorn. The species name, *engelmannii*, honors George Engelmann (1809–1884), a German-born American physician and botanist of St. Louis, Missouri, who first collected it.

Brazoria Hawthorn

Crataegus brazoria Sarg.—Series Punctatae (11) [A, B]

FIELD IDENTIFICATION. Tree to 25 ft and 6–10 in. in diameter, the branches ascending to form a rounded crown.

FLOWERS. Opening in March, in hairy 7–9-flowered corymbs, pedicels slender, bearing white 5-petaled corollas; calyx-tube obconic, pale-hairy; lobes 5, oblong to linear, acuminate, margin entire or glandular-serrate, hairy externally and within; stamens 20, anthers red; styles 5, basally hairy.

FRUIT. Maturing September–October, corymbs lax and few-fruited, subglobose to short-oblong, yellow, some pale-dotted, length ⅓–½ in., flesh yellow and thin; nutlets 5, about ¼ in. long, dorsally rounded and grooved.

LEAVES. Simple, alternate, deciduous, oval to obovate, apex acute or acuminate, base cuneate or gradually narrowed, margin glandular-serrate except near the base, young leaves reddish and pale-hairy; older leaves dark green, shining and glabrous, lower surface paler, blade length 2–2½ in., width 1¼–1½ in.; leaves on young shoots usually larger, broad-

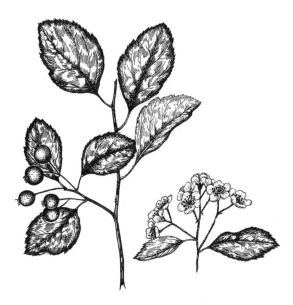

ovate to oblong, base rounded or broadly cuneate; petioles ⅓–¾ in., tomentose at first, glabrous later.

TWIGS. When young pale-hairy and reddish brown, later puberulous or almost glabrous, reddish brown to gray, unarmed, or with a few slender gray spines.

RANGE. Bottom lands of the Brazos River, Brazoria and Matagorda counties in Texas.

REMARKS. The genus name, *Crataegus*, is the classical name for the hawthorn. The species name, *brazoria*, is given for the town of Brazoria, Texas.

Downy Hawthorn

Crataegus mollis (Torr. & Gray) Scheele—Series Molles (16) [A, B, C]

FIELD IDENTIFICATION. Tree attaining a height of 40 ft and a diameter of 12–18 in., branches stout and spreading to form a round-topped crown.

FLOWERS. Opening April–May, corymbs many-flowered and broad, pedicels densely hairy; bracts and bractlets conspicuous; corolla white, 5-petaled, about 1 in. across; calyx-tube narrowly obconic, densely tomentose, lobes 5, linear to lanceolate, apex acuminate, margin serrate and red-glandular, externally villose, tomentose within; stamens 20,

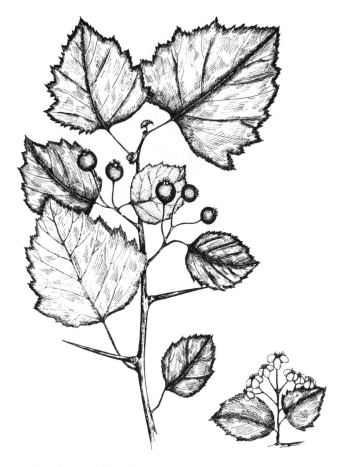

anthers large, light yellow; styles 4–5, basally hoary-tomentose.

FRUIT. Maturing in September, corymbs hairy, few-fruited, drooping, subglobose or short-oblong, terminally rounded, somewhat pubescent, scarlet, some dark dotted, ⅔–1 in. in diameter; flesh yellow, dry, mealy; nutlets 4–5, light brown, dorsally rounded and lightly ridged, about ¼ in. long; fruiting calyx-lobes deciduous when fruit half grown, at first erect, incurved, and hairy.

LEAVES. Simple, alternate, deciduous, broad-ovate, apex acute, base rounded or cordate, margin doubly serrate, and also with 4–5 lateral acute or rounded lobes on each side; mature leaves with upper surfaces dark yellowish green; lower surface paler and pubescent, particularly along the midrib, lateral veins 4–5 pairs, length and width of blades 3–4 in.; leaves on young shoots larger, lobes and basal sinus deeper; petioles ½–1¼ in. long, stout, densely hairy at first, later pubescent, some with minute dark glands.

TWIGS. Stout, densely white-villose at first, when older becoming glabrous, gray, bearing stout, shiny, chestnut brown spines 1–2 in. long.

RANGE. In rich bottom lands. In Texas in Dallas, Grayson, and Lamar counties, and Oklahoma; east to Alabama, north to Ontario, and west to Minnesota and South Dakota.

REMARKS. The genus name, *Crataegus*, is the classical name for hawthorn, and the species name, *mollis*, refers to the soft-hairy foliage. Downy Hawthorn has also been listed in the literature under the names of *C. arkansanum* Sarg., *C. lasiantha* Sarg., and *C. gravida* Beadle. Vernacular names in use are Red Haw and Downy Thorn.

Short-leaf Hawthorn

Crataegus brachyphylla Sarg.—Series Molles (16) [A]

FIELD IDENTIFICATION. Tree 18–21 ft, with a trunk 2–7 in. in diameter, the slender spreading branches forming an often irregular head.

FLOWERS. About ⅝ in. in diameter, petals 5, white, rounded, appearing in the early part of April when the leaves are more than half grown, in small compact 5–8-flowered corymbs, densely covered, like the slender pedicels and narrow obconic calyx-tube, with long matted snow-white hairs; calyx-lobes narrow, long-acuminate, laciniately glandular-serrate, thickly covered with white hairs; stamens 20, anthers deep rose-colored.

FRUIT. Ripening early in September, on slightly villose pedicels, in erect clusters, subglobose, dull dark red, 2/5–1/2 in. in diameter, with thin flesh, the calyx little enlarged, with a deep narrow cavity pointed inward; nutlets usually 3, acute at base, rounded at the broader apex, only slightly ridged on the back, ¼–⅓ in. long and 1/8–1/6 in. wide, the broad hypostyle extending to the middle.

LEAVES. Broad-ovate, acute or rounded at apex, truncate or rounded at the wide base, coarsely, often doubly, serrate, with straight acuminate teeth, covered when they unfold with short hairs; below with long white matted hairs persistent during the season; at maturity thin, yellowish green and glabrous on the upper surface, blades 2–2¾ in. long and 2–2⅓ in. wide, with a slender midrib and primary veins; petioles slender, thickly covered with matted white hairs early in the season, becoming glabrous or nearly glabrous before autumn, ¾–1¼ in.; leaves on vigorous shoots rounded at apex, cordate at the broad base, slightly and irregularly lobed laterally, coarsely double-serrate and to 2¼–3 in. long and wide, with petioles ⅔–1¼ in. long.

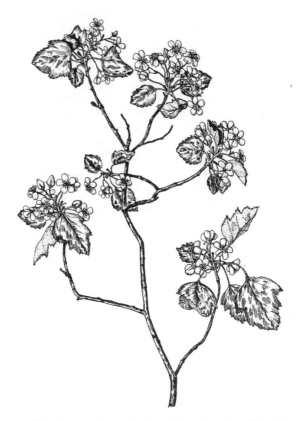

TWIGS. Slender, nearly straight, at first densely white-hairy, later reddish brown to gray and shiny; spineless, or some twigs armed with occasional straight or slightly curved spines 1¼–1½ in. long.

RANGE. Dry gravelly ridges or woods. Near Fulton, Hempstead County, Arkansas. Reported also from eastern Texas.

REMARKS. The genus name, *Crataegus*, is the classical name of the hawthorn. The species name, *brachyphylla*, means "short-leaf."

Viburnum Hawthorn

Crataegus viburnifolia Sarg.—Series Molles (16) [B, C]

FIELD IDENTIFICATION. Tree attaining a height of 35 ft and a diameter of 12 in. The large spreading or ascending branches shaped into an irregular crown.

FLOWERS. Opening in March, corymbs 5–12-flowered, spreading, on slender, densely tomentose pedicels; corolla white, 5-petaled, about ¾ in. across; bracts and bractlets large, leaflike, lanceolate to spatulate, obscurely serrate terminally; calyx-tube narrowly obconic, densely white-hairy, 5-lobed, lobes long-acuminate, margin laciniately glandular-serrate, moderately villose externally, inwardly densely villose; stamens 20; anthers white; styles 4 or 5.

FRUIT. Maturing in October, corymbs lax and few-fruited with somewhat hairy or semiglabrous pedicels, bright yellow, subglobose, ⅔–¾ in. in diameter; flesh yellow and soft; nutlets 4 or 5, ends rounded, dorsally ridged and grooved, length about ¼ in.

LEAVES. Simple, alternate, deciduous, elliptic to ovate or oval, apex acute to rounded, base cuneate or concave, margin doubly serrate with glandular teeth, entire toward the base, some leaves with a few short acute lobes; young leaves white-hairy above and densely hoary-tomentose beneath; mature blades 2½–3½ in. long, 2–2½ in. wide, leathery, upper surface dark green, shiny, and roughened, lower surface paler and hairy; petioles densely tomentose at first, later almost glabrous, 2/5–1 1/2 in. long.

TWIGS. Unarmed or with a few stout gray spines, hoary-tomentose at first, brown to gray, shiny and glabrous finally.

RANGE. In low wet woods, bottom lands of the Brazos River in Texas. Near Brazoria, Columbia, Sweeney, and Wharton, Texas. Specimens examined at the Missouri Botanical Garden Herbarium: B. F. Bush, No. 1219, common in woods at Columbia, Texas; E. J. Palmer, No. 4984, low woods, Colorado River, Wharton County, Texas; E. J. Palmer, No. 6636, low woods, Wharton County, Texas.

REMARKS. The genus name, *Crataegus*, is the classical name for hawthorn, and the species name, *viburnifolia*, refers to the *Viburnum*-like leaves.

Texas Hawthorn

Crataegus texana Buckl.—Series Molles (16) [A, B, C]

FIELD IDENTIFICATION. Shrub or broad, round-topped tree attaining a height of 30 ft.

FLOWERS. Borne in many-flowered hairy corymbs; pedicels and hypanthium villose; bracts villose; petals 5, oblong-obovate and acute, white, rounded, spreading, attached to the disk margin; perianth about ¾ in. in diameter; calyx-tube obconic with 5 lobes; lobes acuminate, villose, glandular-serrate; stamens 20, with red anthers; styles 5, surrounded by tomentum at base.

FRUIT. Ripening in October in drooping clusters; peduncles tomentose or glabrous; pome large, ½–1 in. long, bright red, dotted, obovate or short-oblong, rounded at the ends, with persistent pubescence, but glabrous at maturity; calyx persistent and enlarged; flesh soft, yellow, sweet, edible; nutlets 5, ¼–⅓ in. long, smooth or slightly grooved.

LEAVES. Simple, alternate, deciduous, ovate, blades 3–4 in. long, 2½–3 in. wide; apex acute or rounded; base truncate or cuneate; rarely subcordate, margins glandular serrate and incisely lobed into 8–10 divisions; dark green, shiny and mostly glabrous above; paler and pubescent beneath, especially along the veins; petioles stout, grooved, ½–¾ in. long, tomentose at first but almost glabrous later.

TWIGS. Green and hairy at first, reddish brown to gray and more glabrous later; spines lustrous brown, shiny, thin, almost straight, some 2 in. long; some trees with no thorns.

BARK. Scaly, reddish brown to gray.

WOOD. Tough, hard, heavy, not large enough to be commercially valuable.

RANGE. The Texas coast region, west to the Navidad River. In Jackson, Victoria, Gonzales, Bexar, Matagorda, Hardin, Galveston, Harris, and Jefferson counties.

REMARKS. The genus name, *Crataegus*, is an ancient Greek word meaning "strong," with reference to the tough wood, and the species name, *texana*, refers to the state of Texas as the habitat of the tree.

Turkey Hawthorn

Crataegus invisa Sarg.—Series Molles (16) [A]

FIELD IDENTIFICATION. Tree attaining a height of 30 ft and a tall trunk 8–10 in. in diameter. Branches stout and spreading into a wide, open irregular crown.

FLOWERS. Opening in March, corymbs 6–12-flowered, broad, pedicels densely white-hairy; corolla white, 5-petaled, about ¾ in. across; calyx-tube densely white-hairy, lobes 5, apex acuminate, margin laciniately glandular-serrate, externally hairy, less so within; stamens 20, anthers white; styles 3–5, basally white-hairy.

FRUIT. Maturing in October, corymbs few-fruited, spreading or erect on pubescent or semiglabrous pedicels, body short-oblong, terminally puberulent, red to orange, often pale-dotted, about ½ in. in diameter; flesh yellow, scant, dry; nutlets 3–5, rounded at the ends, faintly grooved dorsally, 1/5–1/4 in. long; calyx on mature fruit green or reddish, mostly hairy.

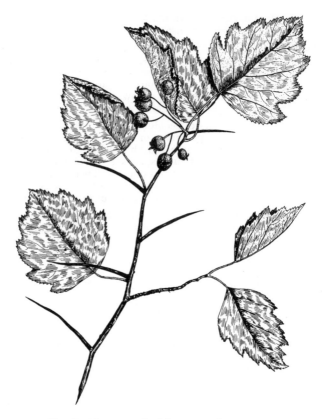

LEAVES. Simple, alternate, deciduous, oval to ovate, apex acute or acuminate, base cuneate or rounded, coarsely serrate or some with shallow acuminate or acute lobes above, blades 2½–3 in. long, 2–2½ in. wide; young leaves densely villose above at first; lower surface with long white hairs; mature leaves thin, yellowish green, roughened and shiny above, lower surface hairy; leaves on young shoots larger, broad-ovate, apex acuminate, base broadly cuneate, margins more coarsely and deeply toothed and lobed; petioles 1½–2 in. long, very villose at first, later much less so.

TWIGS. Stout, at first densely tomentose, gray to brown, later somewhat pubescent to glabrous, dark gray, spineless, or with scattered, slender, straight, brown spines 1–1¼ in. long. Bark on older branches and trunk dark brown, broken into small, tight scales.

RANGE. In woods of bottom lands; in Arkansas in Hempstead County, Oklahoma in Choctaw County, and Texas in San Augustine County.

REMARKS. The genus name, *Crataegus*, is the classical name for hawthorn. The species name, *invisa*, meaning "hateful" or "hostile," is not of certain application, but perhaps refers to the dreaded or hated thorns. It has also been listed in the literature under the names of *C. limaria* Sarg. and *C. berlandieri* Sarg.

Dallas Hawthorn

Crataegus dallasiana Sarg.—Series Molles (16) [A, C]

FIELD IDENTIFICATION. Tree attaining a height of 25 ft and a diameter of 4–10 in. The branches ascending or erect to produce an irregularly shaped crown.

FLOWERS. Opening in April, corymbs many-flowered with slender, very hairy pedicels; corolla white, 5-petaled, each about ⅝ in. across; calyx-tube densely hairy; lobes 5, hairy, long-acuminate, margin with a few glandular serrations; stamens 20, anthers pink; styles 5.

FRUIT. Maturing in July, corymbs few-fruited, pedicels pubescent and mostly erect, shape of fruit globose, dark red, ⅜–½ in. in diameter; nutlets 5, ends acute, body flattened, dorsally grooved, or ridged, 1/4–5/16 in. long; calyx persistent, conspicuous, lobes spreading and green or reddish.

LEAVES. Simple, alternate, deciduous, blades 1¾–2½ in. long, 1¼–1½ in. wide, oblong to ovate, apex acuminate or rounded, base cuneate to concave, margin doubly serrate except at base, sometimes shallowly lobed above; young leaves densely villose and tomentose; at maturity yellowish green, upper surface shiny and glabrous, lower surface paler and pubescent along the veins; petioles ¼–⅔ in. long, slender, tomentose at first but glabrous later, somewhat winged toward the blade.

TWIGS. Slender, rather divaricate, at first densely tomentose and reddish brown, later gray and shiny, bearing slender spines 1¼–2¼ in. long.

RANGE. Northeastern Texas and adjacent Oklahoma.

REMARKS. The genus name, *Crataegus*, is the classical name, and the species name, *dallasiana*, is for Dallas County, Texas, where it occurs along bottom-land streams.

Pear Hawthorn

Crataegus calpodendron (Ehrh.) Medic.—
Series Macracanthae (19) [A]

FIELD IDENTIFICATION. Shrub or small tree attaining a height of 15–18 ft, the scaly branches thorny or thornless.

FLOWERS. In many-flowered villose or tomentose corymbs; petals 5, white, rounded, corolla ⅜–⅝ in. wide when spread; stamens about 20, anthers pink or rarely white; calyx-tube pubescent, the 5 lobes glandular-serrate or pectinate.

FRUIT. Oblong or obovoid, occasionally subglobose, about ⅓ in. thick, at first pubescent, later glabrous, bright red or orange-red; flesh thin, sweet, and succulent; nutlets 2–3, deeply pitted on the inner surface.

LEAVES. Simple, alternate, deciduous, blade oblong-elliptic or rhombic, margin coarsely serrate, except near the base, often with 3–5 pairs of irregular lateral lobes above the middle (sometimes lobed only on the vegetative shoots), young leaves short-villous above; when mature, pubescent beneath, dull yellowish green, firm, veins impressed above; petioles stout, ⅜–⅝ in. long, sometimes wing-margined nearly to the base.

TWIGS. Young ones tomentose, reddish brown, later glabrous and gray, bark on old trunks and limbs furrowed and thick; spineless, or spines ½–2 in. long, stout, slender, sharp, straight or slightly curved.

RANGE. The species and its varieties occur in open woods and thickets, often along small rocky streams. East Texas and Arkansas; east to Georgia, north to New York and Ontario, and west to Minnesota.

REMARKS. The genus name, *Crataegus*, refers to the hard wood of some species. The species name, *calpodendron*, means "urn-tree" and refers to the shape of the fruit.

Carolina Cherry-laurel

Prunus caroliniana (Mill.) Ait. [A, B, C]

FIELD IDENTIFICATION. Evergreen tree attaining a height of 40 ft, with alternate, leathery, entire or toothed leaves.

FLOWERS. In short, axillary racemes; flowers perfect, white, pedicels about ½ in. long with acuminate bracts; calyx-tube narrow-obconic, 5-lobed; lobes suborbicular, reflexed, deciduous; petals 5, white, boat-shaped, erect, smaller than the sepals; stamens numerous, exserted, orange, longer than the petals; filaments distinct; ovary sessile, small, 1-celled; style simple and slender; stigma club-shaped; ovules 2.

FRUIT. Drupe conic-ovoid or oval, abruptly pointed, black, lustrous, persistent; about ½ in. long, skin thick, flesh thin and dry, not edible; seed ovoid, acute, rounded at base, about ½ in. long, dorsal groove prominent.

LEAVES. Alternate, simple, persistent, coriaceous, shiny, margin entire or a few with remote spine-tipped teeth, oblong-lanceolate, apex acute or acuminate, mucronate, base

wedge-shaped, glabrous and dark green above, paler beneath, 2–4½ in. long, ¾–1½ in. wide, aromatic when crushed, taste bitter because of prussic acid; petioles stout, about ⅓ in. long; stipules lanceolate.

TWIGS. Slender, glabrous, green to red or grayish brown.

BARK. Gray, thin, smooth, or later irregularly roughened, marked with blotches.

WOOD. Reddish brown, hard, heavy, strong, close-grained.

RANGE. In Texas, extending from the valley of the Guadalupe River, eastward through eastern Texas and Louisiana to Florida, northward to the Carolinas.

REMARKS. The genus name, *Prunus*, is the classical name. The species name, *caroliniana*, refers to the Carolina region. Vernacular names are Wild Peach, Cherry-laurel, Carolina Cherry, and Mock-orange. The leaves contain prussic acid which is injurious to livestock. A number of birds feed on the seeds. The tree is widely cultivated as a popular ornamental and can be trained into hedges.

Black Cherry

Prunus serotina Ehrh. [A, B, C]

FIELD IDENTIFICATION. Tree to 100 ft, with oval-oblong or lanceolate leaves which are finely callous-serrate on the margin.

FLOWERS. March–June, racemes in spring with immature but nearly expanded leaves; individual flowers white, about ¼ in. in diameter, borne on slender pedicels; petals 5, obovate; stamens numerous, in 3 ranks; stigmas flattened; calyx-tube saucer-shaped, the lobes short, ovate-oblong, acute.

FRUIT. Ripening June–October, drupe borne in racemes, thin-skinned, black when mature, juicy, bitter-sweet, ⅓–½ in. in diameter; stone oblong-ovoid, about ⅓ in. long. The commercial seed-bearing age is about 10 years, with 25 to 75 as the most prolific and 100 as the maximum. Good crops are borne almost annually.

Escarpment Black Cherry

LEAVES. Simple, alternate, finely callous-serrate, apex acuminate, base cuneate, oval-oblong, or oblong-lanceolate, firm, dark green and lustrous above, glabrous or hairy on midrib beneath, blades 2–6 in. long, 1–2 in. broad, with one or more red glands at base, tasting of hydrocyanic acid.

BARK. Reddish brown, gray or white, striped horizontally with gray to black lenticels, smooth when young, broken into small plates later, bitter to the taste.

WOOD. Rich reddish brown, sapwood whitish or light brown, heavy, moderately hard, strong, bends well, shock resistance high, works well, finishes smoothly, glues well, seasons well, shrinks moderately, moderately free from checking and warping, weighing about 36 lb per cu ft, taking a beautiful polish.

RANGE. Texas, Oklahoma, Arkansas, and Louisiana; eastward to Florida, north to Nova Scotia, west to North Dakota, Nebraska, and Kansas, and southward in Mexico.

REMARKS. *Prunus* is the ancient classical name, and the species name, *serotina*, means "late-flowering." It is also known under the vernacular names of Mountain Black Cherry and Rum Cherry. The bark is used medicinally as a cough remedy. The fruit is used as a basic flavoring extract, and is also eaten raw by man. It is eaten by a wide variety of wildlife, including 33 birds, raccoon, opossum, squirrel, bear, and rabbit. The foliage is considered to be poisonous to livestock. The wood is used for furniture, cabinetmaking, printer's blocks, veneer, patterns, panels, interior trim, handles, woodenware, toys, and scientific instruments. The tree has been cultivated for ornament since 1629.

Escarpment Black Cherry, *P. serotina* var. *eximia* (Small) Little, has flowers 35–60 on the rachis, pedicels 1/8–1/5 in. (or 1/6–1/4 in. in fruit); the 5 petals 1/10–1/6 in. long or wide; calyx segments 1/25–1/15 in. long; drupe about 3/8 in. across; leaves 2–3½ in. long, 1¼–1¾ in. wide, margin with 4–6 teeth every 3/8 in., surfaces glabrous or some with axillary red tufts of hairs; petioles 5/8–3/4 in. (to 1¼ in. sometimes). In Texas in the valley of the Colorado River, in San Saba and Burnet counties; south to Comal and Medina counties; west to the south fork of the Llano River in Kimble County and to the west fork of the Nueces River in Kinney County.

Common Choke Cherry

Prunus virginiana L. [A, B, C]

FIELD IDENTIFICATION. Large shrub or small tree to 30 ft, with erect or horizontal branches.

FLOWERS. April–July, in short, dense, cylindric racemes 3–6 in. long; flowers ¼–⅓ in. in diameter, borne on slender, glabrous pedicels from the axils of early-deciduous bracts; corolla small, white, 5-merous; petals rounded, short-clawed; filaments glabrous; style thick, short, with orbicular stigmas; calyx-tube 5-lobed, lobes short, obtuse at apex, glandular-laciniate on the margin.

FRUIT. Ripening July–September, cherry ¼–⅓ in. thick, globose, lustrous, dark red, scarlet, or nearly black; skin thick, flesh juicy, acidulous and astringent, barely edible; stone oblong-ovoid, one suture ridged, the other suture acute. Good crops are borne almost annually.

LEAVES. Alternate, simple, deciduous, thin, blades ¾–4 in. long, ½–2 in. wide, oval to oblong or obovate, abruptly acuminate or acute at the apex, rounded to cuneate or somewhat cordate at the base, sharply serrate on the margin, dark green and lustrous above, paler on the lower surface, sometimes pubescent on veins, turning yellow in autumn, strong odor when crushed; petioles slender, ½–1 in., 2 glands at the apex.

TWIGS. Reddish brown to orange-brown, glabrous, slender, leticels pale.

BARK. Dark gray to brown or blackish; old trees somewhat irregularly fissured into small scales with paler excrescences, smoother and tighter when young, inner bark ill-scented.

WOOD. Light brown, sapwood lighter, close-grained, moderately strong, hard, heavy, weighing 36 lb per cu ft.

RANGE. The species and its varieties rather widespread. Texas, New Mexico, Oklahoma, Arkansas, and Louisiana; eastward to Georgia, northward to Maine and Newfoundland, and west to British Columbia, Washington, Oregon, and California.

REMARKS. The genus name, *Prunus*, is the classical name, and the species name, *virginiana*, refers to the state of Virginia. Vernacular names are Wild Black Cherry, Cabinet Cherry, Rum Cherry, Whiskey Cherry, Black Chokeberry, California Chokeberry, Eastern Chokeberry, Eastern Choke Cherry, Western Choke Cherry, and Caupulin. The tree is sometimes planted for ornament and for erosion control. It has been in cultivation since 1724. It has a tendency to form thickets of considerable extent from root sprouts. The fruit is used to make jellies and jams and is eaten by at least 40 species of birds and browsed by black bear and cottontail. The bark is sometimes used as a flavoring agent in cough syrup.

Oklahoma Plum

Prunus gracilis Engelm. & Gray [A, C]

FIELD IDENTIFICATION. Straggling thicket-forming shrub 1–15 ft.

FLOWERS. Opening in March, usually before the leaves, borne in sessile lateral umbels, 2–4 in a cluster; pedicels slender, pubescent 1/3–2/5 in. long; corolla 1/4–1/3 in. broad; petals 5, white, rounded, imbricate, spreading, inserted in the throat of the hypanthium; stamens numerous, inserted with the petals, filaments filiform and distinct; ovary sessile, 1-celled, ovules 2 and side by side, pendulous; style simple and terminal; calyx with 5 imbricate sepals which are spreading, deciduous, ovate to ovate-lanceolate, obtuse to acute, entire or denticulate, and finely pubescent.

FRUIT. Drupe maturing June–August, subglobose or ovoid to somewhat pointed at the ends, to ⅝ in. in diameter, usually red with a slight bloom, pulpy; stone oval, indehiscent, obtuse at ends, bony, nearly smooth, slightly flattened; seed with membranous testa.

LEAVES. Simple, alternate or fascicled, deciduous, length 1–2 in., elliptic to oval or ovate, margin finely and sharply serrate with appressed teeth, apex acute or obtuse, base gradually narrowed, thickish, upper surface slightly pubescent to glabrous when mature, lower surface reticulate-veined and densely pubescent; winter buds with imbricate scales; petioles short, pubescent, glandless.

TWIGS. Slender, slightly divaricate, soft-pubescent, reddish brown, later gray and glabrous.

RANGE. On dry sandy soils in the sun. North Texas, Oklahoma, and western Arkansas, to Tennessee and Kansas.

REMARKS. The genus name, *Prunus*, is the ancient Latin name, and the species name, *gracilis*, refers to the slender branches. The plant was introduced into cultivation in 1916. It is susceptible to black-knot fungus disease on the limbs and twigs. The fruit is edible but not of particularly good quality. Also known as the Sour Plum.

Chickasaw Plum

Prunus angustifolia Marsh. [A, B, C]

FIELD IDENTIFICATION. Twiggy shrub forming dense thickets, or a short-trunked, irregularly branched tree to 25 ft.

FLOWERS. March–April, in lateral 2–4-flowered umbels borne before the leaves on slender, glabrous pedicels ¼–½ in.; corolla white, about ⅓ in. across; petals 5, obovate, rounded at apex, somewhat clawed at base; calyx-tube campanulate, glabrous, 5-lobed; lobes ovate, obtuse, ciliate, pubescent within; stamens usually 15–20, filaments free with oval anthers; ovary 1-celled.

FRUIT. May–July, drupe globose, ½–¾ in. in diameter, red or yellow, yellow-dotted, lustrous, little bloom if any, skin thin with juicy, edible, subacid flesh; stone ovoid to oblong, about ½ in. long, rounded, somewhat grooved on the dorsal suture, rugose and turgid.

LEAVES. Alternate, simple, deciduous, 1–2 in. long, ⅓–⅔ in. wide, lanceolate or oblong-lanceolate, acuminate to acute and apiculate at the apex, rounded or broadly cuneate at the base, troughlike, glabrous and lustrous green above, paler and glabrous or pubescent beneath, sharply serrate with small glandular teeth; petioles slender, glabrous or puberulous, ¼–½ in. long, glandless or with 2 red glands near the apex.

TWIGS. Reddish brown, lustrous, hairy at first but glabrous later, slender, zigzag, often with spinescent spurlike lateral divisions; lenticels horizontal, orange-colored.

BARK. Reddish brown to dark gray, scales thin and appressed; lenticels horizontal and prominent.

WOOD. Reddish brown, sapwood lighter, rather soft, not strong, fairly heavy, weighing 43 lb per cu ft.

RANGE. Thought to be originally native in Texas and Oklahoma but now rather rare in a wild state. Arkansas and Louisiana; eastward to Florida, northward to New Jersey, and west to Illinois.

REMARKS. The genus name, *Prunus*, is the classical name for the European plum, and the species name, *angustifolia*, refers to the narrow foliage. Often called Mountain Cherry in some localities. Seldom found in a wild state but most often around dwellings. It is sometimes used in shelter-belt planting.

Flatwoods Plum

Prunus umbellata Ell. [A, B, C]

FIELD IDENTIFICATION. Shrub or small twiggy, flat-topped tree rarely over 20 ft.

FLOWERS. In 2–4-flowered umbels; individual flowers white, ½–¾ in. broad, borne on slender glabrous pedicels about ½ in. long; petals 5, rounded, clawed at base; stamens 15–20, filaments slender; ovary 1-celled; calyx obconic, glabrous or puberulent, 5-parted; sepals ovate, obtuse or acute at the apex, puberulent on the exterior, pubescent within.

FRUIT. Drupes on stems ½–1 in. long, about ½ in. in diameter, globose, no basal depression, usually dark purple with a bloom, sometimes red or yellow, skin tough; stone oval or subglobose, about ½ in. long, acute at ends, slightly roughened, ridged on the ventral suture and grooved on the dorsal.

LEAVES. Alternate, simple, deciduous, blades hardly over 2½ in. long, oblong, lanceolate, or occasionally oval, obtuse or acute at apex, rounded, cordate, or broadly cuneate at base, glandular-serrulate on margin, glabrous above, pubescent beneath along the midrib, firm; petiole 1/5–1/3 in. long, glabrous or pubescent.

TWIGS. Slender, spurlike, dark, reddish brown, lustrous, pubescent at first but later glabrous, more or less thorny.

BARK. Dark brown, scales small, persistent, appressed.

WOOD. Reddish brown, lighter sapwood, close-grained, heavy, hard.

RANGE. Usually in sandy soil; Texas, southern Arkansas, and Louisiana; eastward to Florida and northward on the coastal plain to southern North Carolina.

REMARKS. The genus name is the classical name for a plum of Europe, and the species name, *umbellata*, refers to the umbellate flower clusters. Some of the vernacular names are Hog Plum, Sloe, and Black Sloe. The fruit is used in considerable quantities for jellies and preserves.

Wild-goose Plum

Prunus munsoniana Wight & Hedrick [A, B, C]

FIELD IDENTIFICATION. Thicket-forming shrub or small round-topped tree to 25 ft.

FLOWERS. In 2–4-flowered corymbs; pedicels slender, glabrous, ⅔–1 in., bearing flowers 1/2–3/5 in. in diameter; calyx-tube obconic, with 5 sepals which are ovate-oblong, acute or obtuse, glandular on the margin, glabrous or pubescent; petals about ¼ in. long, white, oblong-obovate, abruptly contracted into a short claw, entire or somewhat erose; stamens usually 15–20, filaments with oval anthers; ovary 1-celled, with 2 ovules, style terminal.

FRUIT. Drupe globose to oval, about ¾ in. long, red or yellow, white-dotted, bloom light, skin thin, flesh yellow and juicy; stone oval, pointed at the apex, truncate at the base, grooved on the sutures, roughened.

LEAVES. Alternate, simple, deciduous, blades 2½–4 in. long, ¾–1¼ in. wide, lanceolate to oblong-lanceolate, acute or acuminate at the apex, cuneate or rounded at the base, finely glandular-serrate on the margin, bright lustrous green above, sparingly pubescent, especially along the veins beneath; petioles slender, glabrous or pubescent, biglandular at the apex.

TWIGS. Reddish brown, shiny, glabrous; lenticels pale and numerous.

BARK. Reddish or chestnut brown, thin, smooth.

RANGE. Texas, Oklahoma, Arkansas, and Louisiana; north to Kansas, Kentucky, and Illinois.

REMARKS. The genus name, *Prunus*, is the classical name of a European plum, and the species name, *munsoniana*, refers to T. V. Munson (1823–1913), American botanist. The tree is grown both for ornament and for its fruit.

Mexican Plum

Prunus mexicana Wats. [A, B, C]

FIELD IDENTIFICATION. Shrub or small tree to 25 ft, with an irregular open crown.

FLOWERS. White, ¾–1 in. in diameter, borne on slender glabrous pedicels in 2–4-flowered umbels; petals 5, ovate-oblong, rounded, narrowed into a claw, entire or crenulate, pubescent, much longer than the calyx-lobes; stamens 15–20; style elongate, ovary 1-celled; calyx-tube obconic, puberulous on the exterior, tomentose within, 5-lobed; lobes ovate to oblong, entire or serrate, ciliate and glandular on the margin, about as long as the tube.

FRUIT. Drupe subglobose to short-oblong, dark purplish red with a bloom, 1¼–1⅓ in. in diameter; flesh juicy, of varying palatability; stone ovoid to oval, dorsal edge ridged, ventral edge grooved, smooth, turgid.

LEAVES. Alternate, simple, deciduous, thickish, blades 1¾–3½ in. long, 1–2 in. wide, ovate to elliptic or obovate; abruptly acuminate at the apex; cuneate or rounded at the base; singly or doubly serrate with apiculate teeth; upper surface yellowish green, glabrous, shiny, hairy below especially on the veins; prominently reticulate-veined both above and below; petioles stout, pubescent, hardly over 3/5 in. long, glandular at the apex.

TWIGS. Slender, stiff, glabrous, or pubescent early, shiny, grayish brown.

BARK. Gray to black, exfoliating in platelike scales when young, when older rough and deeply furrowed.

RANGE. Texas, Louisiana, Arkansas, and Oklahoma; north to Missouri, Tennessee, and Kentucky, and southward into northeastern Mexico.

REMARKS. The genus name, *Prunus*, is the ancient classical name for a plum of Europe, and the species name, *mexicana*, refers to this species' southwestern distribution. It is sometimes known as Big-tree Plum, because of the fact that it is treelike and does not sucker to form thickets. It is rather drought resistant and has been used as a grafting stock.

Hortulan Plum

Prunus hortulana Bailey [A, C]

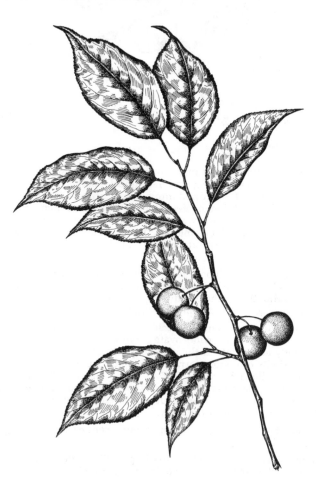

FIELD IDENTIFICATION. Many-stemmed shrub or small tree to 30 ft, with a broad round-topped crown.

FLOWERS. Maturing late March–early May. Borne in 2–3-flowered umbels on slender, puberulous or glabrous pedicels 1/5–1/2 in. long; flower white, ⅔–1 in. in diameter; petals 5, oval-oblong, rounded at the apex, long-clawed, entire or erose; stamens numerous; ovary short; calyx-tube obconic, glabrous, 5-lobed; lobes glabrous, oblong-ovate, acute or obtuse, glandular-ciliate, pubescent, about as long as the tube.

FRUIT. Maturing August–October. Drupe globose to ellipsoid, ¾–1 in. long, red or yellow-red, white-dotted, lustrous, little or no bloom, thin-skinned; stone turgid, reticulate, ⅔–¾ in. long, rounded or short-pointed at the apex, rounded or truncate at the base, grooved on the dorsal suture.

LEAVES. Alternate, simple, deciduous, blades 4–6 in. long, 1–1½ in. wide, oblong-obovate to oblong-oval, acuminate at the apex, cuneate or rounded at the base; upper surface glabrous, dark green, lustrous; lower surface glabrous or slightly pubescent; finely glandular-serrate on the margin; petiole slender, orange-colored, 1–1½ in. long, glandular.

TWIGS. Dark reddish brown, stout, rigid, glabrous, or pubescent, occasionally somewhat spinescent.

BARK. Dark or light brown, exfoliating into large thin plates.

RANGE. Texas, Oklahoma, Arkansas, and Louisiana; northward to Missouri, Iowa, Kansas, Kentucky, and Tennessee.

REMARKS. The genus name, *Prunus*, is the ancient Latin name, and the species name, *hortulana*, means "of gardens" and refers to its value in horticulture.

Peach

Prunus persica Batsch [A, B, C]

FIELD IDENTIFICATION. Tree attaining a height of 24 ft, with a rounded crown and spreading branches.

FLOWERS. Usually expanding before the leaves March–May, subsessile, solitary or 2 together, fragrant, perfect, 1–2 in. across; petals 5, pink, spreading, rounded; calyx with the 5 sepals externally pubescent; stamens 20–30, filaments usually colored like the petals, exserted, slender, distinct; ovary tomentulose, 1-celled and sessile, the 2 ovules pendulous; pistil solitary with a simple terminal style.

FRUIT. Drupe maturing July–October, subglobose, grooved on one side, velvety-tomentose, 2–3⅓ in. in diameter, fleshy, separating in halves at the sutures; stone elliptic to ovoid-elliptic, usually pointed at distal end, deeply pitted and fur-

rowed, very hard; fruit of escaped trees usually harder and smaller.

LEAVES. Numerous, conduplicate in the bud, almond-scented, impregnated with prussic acid, simple, alternate, some appearing clustered, elliptic-lanceolate to oblong-lanceolate, broadest at the middle or slightly above the middle, 3–6 in. long, apex long-acuminate, base varying from acute to acuminate or broad-cuneate, margin serrate or serrulate, surfaces glabrous and lustrous, bright green, thin; petioles glandular, ⅜–⅝ in.

RANGE. A native of China but extensively cultivated from Texas eastward to Florida and northward to New York and southern Ontario. Sometimes escaped from cultivation in the southeastern United States.

REMARKS. The genus name, *Prunus*, is the classical Latin name of a plum of Europe. The species name, *persica*, means "Persian" and is also an old generic name for peach. The genus name of *Amygdalus* L. is used by some authors.

Common Pear

Pyrus communis L. [A, B, C]

FIELD IDENTIFICATION. Tree generally pyramidal and upright, living to an old age. Attaining a height of 75 ft and 2–3 ft in diameter. The branches are stiff, upright, and sometimes thorny.

FLOWERS. March–May, with or before the leaves; cymes simple, terminal, 4–12-flowered, borne on short twigs of the preceding year; pedicels ½–2 in., pubescent at first, glabrous later; corolla white or pink, 1–2 in. broad, 5-petaled, petals broad-oblong, rounded, short-clawed; stamens numerous, exserted; anthers yellow, small, 2-celled, sacs longitudinally dehiscent; styles 5, distinct to the base, stigma small, ovules 2 in each cavity, cavities as many as the styles; disk cushion-like; calyx urn-shaped, the 5 acute lobes about as long as the tube.

FRUIT. Ripening July–October, pome pear-shaped, tapering to the base, in the wild form about 2 in. long, much longer in cultivated forms, yellow to reddish, flesh with abundant grit cells; seeds small, smooth, brown to black, endosperm none, cotyledons fleshy, the pome consisting of the thickened calyx-tube and receptacle enclosing the carpels.

LEAVES. Simple, alternate, deciduous, usually on short lateral spurs, ovate to elliptic or obovate, margin finely serrate to entire, apex acute or acuminate, sometimes abruptly so, base usually rounded, blade length 1½–4 in., young leaves downy and ciliate, mature leaves lustrous, dark green to olive green above, lower surface paler, both sides glabrous or nearly so; petioles 1¼–3 in., as long as the blades or longer.

TWIGS. Somewhat pubescent at first, glabrous later, reddish brown to gray or black.

WOOD. Reddish brown, hard, fine-grained, 51 lb per cu ft.

RANGE. Common Pear is a native of Europe and Asia and escapes cultivation in some areas in the Southwest and elsewhere in North America. It is often cultivated in Texas, Oklahoma, Arkansas, and Louisiana.

REMARKS. The genus name, *Pyrus*, is the classical name for the pear tree, and the species name, *communis*, means "common." The tree is sometimes used for shelter-belt planting and for wildlife food.

Southern Crab-apple

Pyrus angustifolia Ait. [A]

FIELD IDENTIFICATION. Usually a small tree with rigid, thorny branches forming a broad open head. More rarely larger, and to 35 ft, with a diameter of 10 in.

FLOWERS. In simple, terminal, 3–5-flowered cymes, very fragrant; pedicels ¾–1 in. long, slender, puberulous at first, glabrous later; flowers perfect, about 1 in. in diameter; petals 5, obovate to oblong, clawed at base, about ¼ in. wide, white to pink; stamens shorter than the petals, about 20 in 3 series; ovary 5-celled, carpels leathery, styles 5, united and hairy below; calyx 5-lobed, lobes about as long as the tube, glabrous externally, tomentose within.

FRUIT. Pome depressed-globose, ¾–1 in. in diameter, often broader than long, waxy, pale yellowish green, fragrant, flesh acid and sour.

LEAVES. Simple, alternate, deciduous, or persistent southward, blade length 1–3 in., width ½–2 in., elliptic to oblong on flower spurs and crenately serrate (on young shoots oval

to obovate and with lobes as well as serrations), apex obtuse
to acute or rounded and often apiculate, base narrowed and
cuneate, firm and leathery, dull green, hairy when young,
but glabrous with age, midrib sometimes remaining pubescent; petiole slender, about ¾–1 in., green to reddish, villose
at first, glabrous later; stipules linear, about ⅓ in. long,
reddish.

TWIGS. Stout, smooth, light brown to reddish brown, pubescent at first, older twigs glabrous, lenticels scattered, orange-
colored; buds small, about 1/16 in. long, dark brown, obtuse,
the 4 outer scales imbricate and pubescent; leaf scars very
narrow, bundle scars 3, pith homogeneous.

BARK. Dark reddish brown to gray, fissures rather deep,
ridges narrow, separating into small, platelike scales.

WOOD. Heartwood reddish brown, sapwood yellow, close-
grained, hard, heavy, weighing about 43 lb per cu ft.

RANGE. Woods, thickets, riverbanks. In Oklahoma, Arkansas,
and Louisiana; eastward to Florida, northward into Illinois,
and west to Missouri and Kansas.

REMARKS. The genus name, *Pyrus*, is the classical name for the pear tree, and the species name, *angustifolia*, refers to the narrow leaves. Also known under the vernacular names of Narrow-leaf Crab-apple and Wild Crab-apple. The wood of Southern Crab-apple is used for levers, tools, and small woodenware objects. The acid, sour fruit is made into preserves and cider. It is eaten by many species of birds and animals, including the bobwhite quail, blue jay, cardinal, ruffed grouse, prairie chicken, skunk, opossum, raccoon, cottontail, and red and gray fox.

Prairie Crab-apple

Pyrus ioensis (Wood) Bailey [A, C]

FIELD IDENTIFICATION. Tree attaining a height of 28 ft and a trunk diameter of 18 in., the numerous rigid, crooked branches forming a rounded spreading crown.

FLOWERS. Borne April–June, fragrant, in 2–5-flowered clusters on very hairy pedicels 1–1½ in.; calyx-lobes 5, lanceolate-acuminate, longer than the tube, densely white-tomentose; petals 5, white or pink, about ½ in. wide, obovate, base narrowed into a slender claw; stamens numerous, shorter than the petals; styles 5, joined below and white-hairy.

FRUIT. Maturing September–October, peduncles ¾–1½ in. long, globose, somewhat depressed, apical and basal depressions shallow, greenish to yellow, sometimes with minute, yellow dots, surface waxy and greasy to the touch, length ¾–1¼ in., width ¾–1½ in., flesh sour and astringent.

LEAVES. Simple, alternate or clustered, deciduous, length and width variable on weak and vigorous shoots, blades 1½–5 in. long, ¾–4 in. wide, elliptic to oblong or obovate-oblong, apex acute or obtuse to rounded, base cuneate or rounded, margin singly or doubly crenate-serrate, or on some deeply lobed as well; at maturity coriaceous, dark green, lustrous and glabrous above, lower surface varying from almost glabrous to densely white-tomentose, turning yellow in autumn; petioles slender, at first with hoary-white tomentum, becoming pubescent or glabrous later.

TWIGS. Reddish brown to gray, densely tomentose at first but with age less so, finally glabrous, lenticels small and pale; twigs often set with numerous short lateral shoots bearing thorns terminally; winter buds small, obtuse, pubescent.

BARK. Reddish brown to dark gray, about ⅓ in. thick, scales small, narrow, persistent.

RANGE. In Texas, Oklahoma, Arkansas, and Louisiana; eastward to Alabama and north to Minnesota.

REMARKS. The genus name, *Pyrus*, is the classical name for the pear tree, and the species name, *ioensis*, refers to the state of Iowa where it was first described. Other vernacular names are Iowa Crab, Prairie Crab, and Western Crab-apple. The flesh of this crab-apple is sour and inedible, but is sometimes used for making vinegar. It has been cultivated for ornament since 1885. It is of considerable value as food for wildlife, the fruit known to be eaten by at least 20 species of birds and mammals, including bobwhite quail, ruffed grouse, ring-necked pheasant, gray and red fox, skunk, opossum, raccoon, cottontail, woodchuck, red squirrel, and fox squirrel.

Red Chokeberry

Pyrus arbutifolia (L.) L. f. [A]

FIELD IDENTIFICATION. Deciduous, swamp-loving shrub to
12 ft. Sometimes the young shoots overtop the compound
flower clusters.

FLOWERS. Borne March–May, in terminal compound cymes
¾–2½ in. wide; axillary branches short, persistently villous,
9–20-flowered, sometimes overtopped by the sterile shoots;
flowers small, white to pink, ⅓–½ in. broad; calyx urn-
shaped, sepals 5, ovate to triangular, apex acute to obtuse,
usually glandular, tomentose; petals 5, 1/6–1/4 in. long,
spreading, obovate to oval, concave, apex rounded, base
short-clawed; stamens numerous (about 20), exserted, filaments shorter than the petals, anthers reddish or purplish;
ovary woolly above, styles 5 and united at base, persistent.

FRUIT. Pome ripening September–October, globose or short pear-shaped, 1/6–1/4 in. in diameter, conspicuously bright red at maturity, hairy at first, glabrous later, long persistent, carpels leathery; seeds 1–5, some usually abortive.

LEAVES. Convolute in the bud, simple, alternate, deciduous, oval to elliptic or oblong to obovate; apex obtuse or acute to short-acuminate and apiculate; base cuneate or narrowed; margin serrulate-crenulate, the teeth rounded, incurved, and glandular, blade 1–3 in. long; upper surface usually glabrous, midrib sometimes glandular; lower surface densely gray-tomentose; petioles 1/8–2/5 in., semiglabrous to tomentose; stipules narrow, early deciduous. Leaves turning red in autumn.

TWIGS. Brown to gray, persistently tomentose-hairy, older glabrate.

RANGE. Wet woods and swamps. East Texas, Oklahoma, Arkansas, and Louisiana; eastward to Florida, northward to Nova Scotia, and west to Minnesota.

REMARKS. The genus name, *Pyrus*, is the classical name of the pear tree. The species name, *arbutifolia*, refers to the *Arbutus*-like leaves. Also known under the vernacular names of Choke-pear and Dogberry. The fruit is a valuable wildlife food in fall and winter, being eaten by at least 13 species of birds, including bobwhite quail, ruffed grouse, ring-necked pheasant, and cedar waxwing. It has been cultivated since 1700. Red Chokeberry is somewhat subject to blight and borer attacks, withstands city smoke, and the leaves are tardily deciduous. It could be more extensively cultivated for its attractive flowers, brilliant fruit, and colorful autumn leaves.

Shadblow Service-berry

Amelanchier arborea (Michx. f.) Fern. [A]

FIELD IDENTIFICATION. Slender shrub or small round-topped tree seldom over 25 ft.

FLOWERS. March–May, racemes 3–7 in. long, rather dense, erect or nodding, silky-hairy, fragrant, 6–12-flowered; calyx 5-cleft, campanulate, glabrous or hairy, sepals triangular-ovate; petals 5, white, elliptic to obovate, 1/2–1 in. long; stamens about 20; ovary 5-celled, terminating in 2–5 styles with broad stigmas.

FRUIT. June–July, on long pedicels, subglobose, 1/4–1/2 in. in diameter, dry, reddish purple, tasteless or sweetish; seeds small and numerous (4–10, some abortive), usually dispersed by birds and animals.

LEAVES. Alternate, simple, deciduous, oval to oblong or obo-vate, acute or acuminate at the apex, rounded or cordate at the base, sharply and finely serrate on the margin, glabrous or nearly so above, paler and pubescent beneath or finally glabrous, blades 2–5 in. long, 1–2 in. wide; petioles 1½–2 in., slender, hairy at first but glabrous later.

TWIGS. Reddish brown to black, slender, rather crooked, somewhat hairy when young but glabrous later; lenticels numerous and pale.

BARK. Gray to black, thin, smooth, in age becoming shallowly fissured with scaly longitudinal ridges.

WOOD. Brown, close-grained, hard, strong, tough, elastic, weighing 49 lbs per cu ft.

RANGE. Oklahoma, Arkansas, Louisiana, and northeast Tex-as; eastward to Florida and northward to Quebec, Ontario, and Newfoundland.

REMARKS. The genus name, *Amelanchier*, is derived from the French name of a European species. The species name, *arborea*, refers to the treelike character of this species. Vernacular names are Boxwood, Billberry, June-plum, Indian-cherry, Swamp Shadbush, Indian-pear, Juice-pear, Sugar-pear, Plum-pear, and Berry-pear. It is occasionally cultivated in gardens for the showy white flowers. Dwarf plants are often found growing in sterile ground. The berries may be eaten uncooked or made into pies. Shadblow Serviceberry is a valuable wildlife plant, its fruit being eaten by at least 35 species of birds and its foliage browsed by cottontail and white-tailed deer. The wood is sometimes used for making handles.

Narrow-leaf Firethorn

Pyracantha angustifolia (Franch.) Schneid. [A, B, C]

FIELD IDENTIFICATION. Cultivated half-evergreen shrub with diffusely spreading, irregular, spiny branches, or sometimes a tree to 20 ft. Occasionally almost prostrate in form.

FLOWERS. April–May, corymbs axillary, pubescent, many-flowered, ½–3 in. broad; calyx 5-lobed, lobes short, about 1/16 in. long, broadly obtuse to acute, white-hairy; margins thin and whitened, glandular or glandless, ciliate; corolla about ⅜ in. across, white, 5-petaled; petals spreading, suborbicular, narrowed to a broad base; stamens exserted, numerous, spreading, filaments white, anthers yellow; carpels 5, spreading, free on the ventral side, on the dorsal side partially connate with the calyx-tube.

FRUIT. Pomes persistent in the winter, numerous, red to orange, 1/5–3/8 in. across, depressed-globose, fleshy, calyx remnants persistent; seeds 5, about ⅛ in. long, black, lustrous, 2 surfaces plane, dorsal surface rounded, one end rounded, the other abruptly apiculate-pointed.

LEAVES. Simple, alternate, or somewhat clustered on short, lateral, spinescent branches, half-evergreen, leathery, oval-oblong to oblanceolate, apex obtuse to rounded or notched, base cuneate, margin entire, length ½–1¾ in.; upper surface dark green, shiny, apparently smooth (but often with scattered, white, cobwebby hairs under magnification); lower surface much paler, glabrous, or with a few white hairs along the main vein, obscurely reticulate-veined; petioles 1/16–1/4 in., pubescent to glabrous; stipules minute, caducous; buds small and pubescent.

TWIGS. Green to grayish with dense fine pubescence; secondary twigs almost at right angles, and usually short and spiniferous; spines straight, ⅛–½ in. long, often pubescent at the base with apex reddish brown and more glabrous.

RANGE. Cultivated in gardens in Texas, Louisiana, Arkansas, Oklahoma, and elsewhere, sometimes escaping. Hardy as far north as Massachusetts. A native of southwest China.

REMARKS. The genus name, *Pyracantha*, is from the Greek words *pyr* ("fire") and *akanthos* ("thorn"), alluding to the bright red fruit. The species name, *angustifolia*, refers to the narrow leaves. The plant is often cultivated for ornament. Robin and cedar waxwing, as well as other birds, eagerly devour the fruit. Other closely related species, such as the Scarlet Firethorn, *P. coccinea* Roem., with crenate more glabrous leaves, are also cultivated extensively.

Loquat

Eriobotrya japonica Lindl. [A, B, C]

FIELD IDENTIFICATION. Evergreen tree often planted for ornament in the warmer parts of the United States. Persistent in abandoned gardens for many years. Attains a height of 25 ft, with an open but rather rounded crown.

FLOWERS. August–November, fragrant, borne in terminal woolly panicles 4–7½ in. long, buds with conspicuously rusty-woolly tomentum, flowers about ½ in. across; calyx-lobes 5, ⅛–¼ in. long, acute, densely rusty-woolly; petals 5, white, oval to suborbicular, short-clawed; stamens 20; styles 2–5, connate below, ovary inferior, 2–5-celled, cells 2-ovuled.

FRUIT. In spring, pome edible, small, pear-shaped or spherical, yellow 1½–3 in. long, endocarp thin; seeds large, ovoid, solitary or a few.

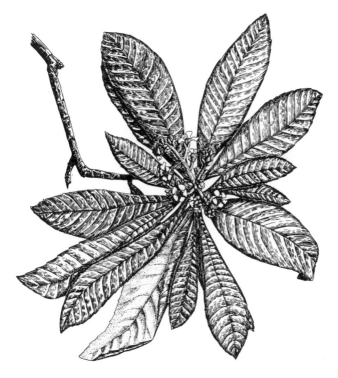

LEAVES. Simple, alternate, sessile or very short-petioled, crowded terminally and whorled to give a rosettelike appearance, rather stiff and firm, large and ornamental, 4–12 in. long, oval to oblong or obovate, margin with remote slender teeth but entire toward the base; upper surface with veins deeply impressed, dark green, lustrous, at maturity glabrous; lower surface much paler and densely feltlike with rusty tomentum.

TWIGS. Stout, green to brown, densely woolly-tomentose, when older brown to dark gray and glabrous; leaf scars large, half-round, bundle scars 3.

RANGE. A native of China and Japan, much planted for ornament in Texas, Louisiana, and other Gulf states. Grown as a pot plant in the North.

REMARKS. The genus name, *Eriobotrya*, is the Greek word for "woolly cluster," referring to the hairy panicles. The species name, *japonica*, is for Japan, its original home. It is also known as Japanese-plum and China-plum. The fruit may be eaten raw or prepared as jelly, jam, pies, and preserves. It has an agreeable acid flavor.

Legume Family (Leguminosae)

Subfamily Mimosoideae

Ebony Ape's-earring

Pithecellobium flexicaule (Benth.) Coult. [B]

FIELD IDENTIFICATION. Spiny, evergreen shrub or tree. Sometimes attaining a height of 40 ft, and forming a rounded spreading head with a trunk to 3 ft in diameter.

FLOWERS. June–August, borne in fascicled spikes, perfect, fragrant; peduncles ⅓–⅔ in. long, stout, pubescent; flower spikes ⅔–1½ in. long, cylindric, dense or interrupted; corolla about ⅛ in. long, much longer than the calyx, puberulous externally, 5-lobed, lobes longer than the tube; stamens numerous, long-exserted, filaments united below; calyx campanulate, 5-lobed, about 1/25 in. long; ovary glabrous, sessile.

FRUIT. Legume 4–6 in. long, 1–1¼ in. wide, dark brown to black, straight or somewhat curved, oblique at base, rounded or short-pointed at apex, narrowly oblong, flattened, thick, stout, woody, very hard, persistent for a year or more, valves very tardily dehiscent; seeds transverse in the legume and separated by thin tissue, bean-shaped, reddish brown, about ½ in. long and ¼ in. wide, seed coat thick and crustaceous.

LEAVES. Persistent, alternate, or clustered at the nodes, twice-pinnately compound, 1½–2 in. long and 2–3 in. broad, composed of 1–3 pairs of pinnae with the lower pair shortest; leaflets 3–5 pairs per pinna, obliquely elliptic, oval or obovate, obtuse or rounded at the apex, base unequal-sided, 1/5–1/2 in. long; thin or semicoriaceous; upper surface dark green, glabrous and lustrous; lower surface paler and finely reticulate-veined; petiolules almost absent or very short; petioles ⅓–1 in. long, puberulous, often glandular at the middle or apex.

TWIGS. Conspicuously flexuous, stout, green to reddish brown and pubescent at first, later becoming light gray and glabrous; spines usually in pairs at the nodes, persistent, straight or nearly so, ¼–½ in. long, brown to black or gray.

WOOD. Dark red to purple or brown, sapwood yellow, close-grained, very durable, hard, heavy, specific gravity 1.04.

RANGE. Texas and Mexico. In Texas from the shores of Matagorda Bay to the lower Rio Grande area. Abundant in Cameron County. Commonly planted on the streets of Brownsville, Texas. In Mexico in the states of Tamaulipas and Nuevo León, also Baja California.

REMARKS. The genus name, *Pithecellobium*, is from the Greek ("monkey" and "earring"), alluding to the circular ear-like fruit of some species. The species name, *flexicaule*, refers to the flexuous branches. It is also known under the vernacular names of Texas Ebony, Ebano, and Ebony Blackbead. The wood is used for posts, fuel, and cabinetmaking. It is often planted as a shade tree, being ornamental in bloom, and is considered by some to be the most valuable native tree in the lower Rio Grande Valley. The seeds are eaten by the Mexican people and are boiled when green and roasted when ripe. The thick pod shells have been used as a coffee substitute.

Huajillo

Pithecellobium pallens (Benth.) Standl. [B]

FIELD IDENTIFICATION. Spiny shrub or small tree to 30 ft, occasionally 5–6 in. in diameter. Irregular or spreading with slender branches.

FLOWERS. May–August, in pubescent panicles 2–6 in. long; individual pedicels ⅓–1 in. long, pubescent, from lanceolate, acute, pubescent bracts; flowers white, in semiglobose heads, ⅔–¾ in. in diameter; calyx minute, 1/25 in. long, pubescent, 5-lobed, much shorter than the petals; corolla green, 1/16–1/8 in. long, tubular, puberulent, lobes 5, oblong-lanceolate, acute; stamens numerous, exserted, 1/2–3/5 in. long, persistent.

FRUIT. July–August, persistent, peduncles ½–2 in. long; pod glabrous or pubescent, linear-oblong, 2–5 in. long, about ½ in. wide, straight, apex abruptly acute or acuminate, stipitate, thin and somewhat membranous, sutures thickened, reticulate-veined, reddish brown, dehiscent at maturity into 2 papery valves; seeds ovoid or orbicular, about ¼ in. long, flattened, lustrous, dark brown to black, seed coat thin.

LEAVES. Pinnately compound, 3–6 in. long, usually 3–6 pairs of pinnae; leaflets 7–20 pairs, oblong-linear, straight or slightly curved, ⅛–⅓ in. long, obtuse or acute, asymmetrical at base and apex, puberulent, slightly revolute; rachis slender, 1½–3 in. long, pubescent, bearing a small, cup-shaped gland near the middle, base with 2 short, slender spines; petioles of pinnae 1–2 in. long, petiolules about 1/25 in. long or less, pubescent.

TWIGS. Green to brown or gray, striate, pubescent or glabrous later, set with pairs of short, straight, slender spines, usually ¼–½ in. long; lenticels white and minute.

BARK. Gray to reddish, smooth, thin, breaking into small, thin flakes, sometimes bearing a few spines.

WOOD. Dark reddish brown, close-grained, hard, heavy.

RANGE. Usually on alluvial soils of stream bottoms, or on the edges of water holes. Known from Cameron, Willacy, Hidalgo, and Starr counties in Texas. Also cultivated in other counties in southwest Texas. Specimens collected by the author at Brownsville, San Benito, Harlingen, and Mission. Largest and most abundant in Mexico, extending into the states of Nuevo León, Tamaulipas, Coahuila, and San Luis Potosí. The type specimen was first collected near Monterrey, Nuevo León.

REMARKS. The genus name, *Pithecellobium*, is from the Greek ("monkey" and "earring"), alluding to the circular earlike pods of some species. The species name, *pallens*, refers to the pale leaves. Some authorities list it under the name of *P. brevifolium* Benth. Vernacular names in use are Tenaza

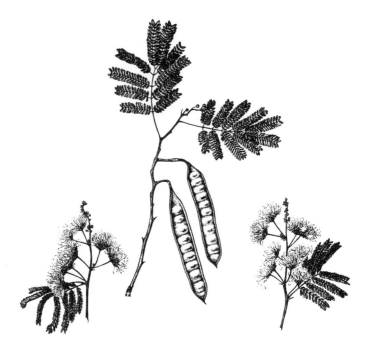

and Mimosa-bush. The flowers are good bee food, and the foliage is sometimes browsed by sheep and goats in winter. The wood is occasionally used for small woodenware articles.

Silk-tree Albizia

Albizia julibrissin (Willd.) Durazz. [A, B, C]

FIELD IDENTIFICATION. Cultivated tree attaining a height of 40 ft, with a flat top and widely spreading branches, often broader than high.

FLOWERS. May–August, on the upper ends of the branches, in axillary, tassellike, capitate clusters on slender, pubescent peduncles ½–2 in. long; heads 1½–2 in. broad, flowers perfect; stamens numerous, conspicuous, long-exserted, filamentous, 1–1½ in. long, pink distally, whitish proximally, united at base; pistils considerably longer than stamens, style white or pink, filiform, stigma minute, ovary short-stalked; corolla tubular, greenish, pubescent, ⅛–¼ in. long, 5-lobed, lobes oblong or ovate, obtuse or acute; calyx tubular, 1/12–⅛ in. long, shallowly 5-lobed, pubescent.

FRUIT. Legume on a pubescent peduncle 1–2½ in. long, oblong to linear, 5–8 in. long, ¾–1 in. wide, margin straight or wavy, apex gradually or abruptly narrowed into a long spinose point, base cuneate; valves thin, flattened, papery, yellowish brown, not separating on margin, without partitions between the seeds; seeds brown, lustrous, flattened, rounded or obtuse at the ends, about ¼ in. long, averaging 11,000 seeds per lb, one-fourth to one-third germinating.

LEAVES. Alternate, deciduous, twice-pinnately compound, 10–15 in. long; rachis green to brown, smooth or striate, pubescent, often glandular near the base; pinnae 2–6 in. long, 5–12 pairs, rachilla pubescent; leaflets 8–30 pairs per pinna, sessile or nearly so, ¼–⅜ in. long, oblong, slightly falcate, oblique; margin entire, ciliate, straighter on one side than the other; apex half-rounded and mucronulate; base truncate or rounded, attached to the rachilla on one side; main vein parallel to and close to the margin on one side; glabrous to puberulent.

TWIGS. Green to brown or gray, somewhat angular or rounded, glabrous, lenticels small but numerous.

BARK. Smooth, tight, blotched gray, sometimes brownish on young trunks or limbs.

RANGE. A native of Asia, cultivated from Washington, D.C., Philadelphia, and Indianapolis; and Maryland, south to Florida and west into Texas. Commonly planted on the streets of Houston and other Gulf Coast cities.

REMARKS. The genus, *Albizia*, was named after F. Degli Albizzi, an Italian nobleman and naturalist. The tree is often called Mimosa in the southern states. Silktree was first introduced into cultivation in 1745 and is considered a top ornamental for the South, being somewhat drouth resistant and fairly free from disease and insects. However, it has been reported that specimens in Georgia and the Carolinas have been very susceptible to the killing attacks of the root fungus *Fusorium perniciosum*. The tree does not seem to escape cultivation and reproduce readily. The seeds may furnish a limited amount of food for birds, squirrels, and other wildlife. The wood is used for cabinetmaking in its native Asiatic home.

Black-brush Acacia

Acacia rigidula Benth. [B]

FIELD IDENTIFICATION. Stiff, thorny shrub with many stems from the base, attaining a height of 15 ft. Often forming impenetrable thickets in west and southwest Texas.

FLOWERS. Heads April–May, axillary, white or light yellow, fragrant, arranged in oblong and densely flowered spikes; individual flowers small, sessile, calyx 4–5-toothed, corolla of 4–5 petals, stamens numerous, exserted, distinct.

FRUIT. Legume 2–3½ in. long, 3/16–1/4 in. wide, linear, often falcate, apex acuminate, base attenuate and stipitate, constricted between the seeds, flattened, reddish brown to black, striate and puberulent, 2-valved and dehiscent; seeds about ¼ in. long, ends rounded or obtuse, lustrous, dark green to brown, compressed.

LEAVES. Bipinnate, rachis grooved and somewhat hairy, about ⅜–1 in. long, pinnae 1–2 pairs, leaflets 2–4 pairs (or rarely 5 pairs), 1/6–1/2 in. long and ¼–⅓ in. wide, sessile or nearly so, elliptic to oblong, oblique, apex rounded and mucronate or sometimes notched, base unsymmetric, firm; surface lustrous, dark green, glabrous, nerves conspicuous.

TWIGS. Divaricate, gray to reddish, glabrous, thorns usually paired at the nodes, straight or slightly curved, slender, pale, ⅓–1 in. long.

BARK. Light to dark gray, smooth, tight.

RANGE. Widespread over Texas in areas west and southwest of the Guadalupe River. Collected by the author in Bexar, Val Verde, and Brewster counties. In Mexico in the states of Tamaulipas, Nuevo León, Chihuahua, San Luis Potosí, and Jalisco.

REMARKS. The genus name, *Acacia*, is an old word meaning "a hard, sharp point," with reference to the spinescent stipules. The species name, *rigidula*, refers to the stiff or rigid branches. Vernacular names used are Chaparro Prieto, Catclaw, and Gavia. The plant has good possibilities for use as an ornamental in dry sandy or limestone areas. It could be used also as an erosion-control plant, and the flowers are a source of honey.

This plant is sometimes listed under the name of *A. amentacea* DC. However, the latter is a closely related species of central Mexico, with a more pubescent petiole and pinnae with only 2 pairs of leaflets.

Sweet Acacia

Acacia farnesiana (L.) Willd. [A, B, C]

FIELD IDENTIFICATION. Shrub with many stems from the base, or a thorny tree to 30 ft, and 18 in. in diameter. With either a flat top in coastal specimens, or round-topped with pendulous branches.

FLOWERS. February–March, very fragrant, solitary, or 2–5 heads together on puberulous peduncles 1–1½ in. long; bracts 2, minute; heads about ⅔ in. in diameter; stamens numerous, yellow, with distinct filaments (about 20), much longer than the corolla; corolla tubular-funnelform, shallowly 5-lobed, lobes as high as broad, about 1/12 in. long; calyx about half as long as corolla-lobes, somewhat hairy; ovary short-stipitate and hairy, style filiform.

FRUIT. Legume persistent, tardily dehiscent, cylindric, oblong, thick, woody, stout, straight or curved, 2–3 in. long, ½–⅔ in. broad, short-pointed, reddish brown to purple or black, partitions thin and papery, pulp pithy; seeds in solitary compartments, transverse, ovoid, brown, shining, flattened on one side, about ¼ in. long, peduncles stout and short.

LEAVES. Pinnately compound, alternate, deciduous, 1–4 in. long; pinnae 2–8 pairs; leaflets 10–25 pairs, linear, apex acute or obtuse, or with a minute mucro, base inequilateral, length about 1/12–1/4 in., width about 1/25 in., sessile or short-petioled, bright green and glabrous or puberulent.

TWIGS. Ascending, pendulous or horizontal, slender, terete, striate, angled, glabrous or puberulent, armed with paired straight, rigid, stipular spines to 1 1/12 in. long.

WOOD. Reddish brown, sapwood paler, hard, heavy, durable, close-grained, specific gravity 0.83.

RANGE. Cultivated in tropical and semitropical regions of both hemispheres. In Texas and Louisiana; eastward to Florida, northward in New Mexico and Arizona, southward on the Texas coast through Mexico, through Central America and northern South America to the Guianas.

REMARKS. The genus name, *Acacia*, refers to the hard sharp spinescent stipules of some species. The species name, *farnesiana*, honors Cardinal Odoardo Farnese (1573–1626) of Rome. This species was the first introduced to his gardens in 1611. Our species is cultivated in France under the name of Cassie, but is usually known in Texas as Huisache; however, because of confusion with other acacias, it seems best to apply the name of Sweet Acacia. Vernacular names in the United States and Latin America are Acacia-catclaw, Honey-ball, Opopanax, Yellow-opopanax, Popinach, Hinsach, Binorama, Vinorama, Huisache (from the Nahuatl *huitzaxin*), Guisache Yondino, Guisache, Huisache de la Semilla,

Huixachin, Uisatsin, Xkantiriz, Matitas, Finisache, Bihi, Espiño, Aroma, Zubin, Zubin-ché, Gabia, Gavia, Subin, Aroma Amarilla, Espiño Blanco, Cacheto de aroma, Cuji Cimarrón, Pelá, Uña de Cabra, and Espinillo.

Sweet Acacia is commonly cultivated as a garden ornamental in tropical countries. The wood is used for many purposes, including posts, agricultural instruments, and woodenware articles. It is considered a good winter forage plant and a desirable honey plant in semiarid areas, being resistant to drought and heat. The bark and fruit are used for tanning, dying, and inkmaking. Glue from the young pods is used to mend pottery.

Berlandier Acacia

Acacia berlandieri Benth. [B]

FIELD IDENTIFICATION. Spreading shrub, with many stems from the base, or sometimes a small tree to 15 ft. The gray to white branches are thornless or nearly so.

FLOWERS. Blooming November–March, in heads on axillary, solitary or clustered, pubescent peduncles arranged in racemes; the heads white, dense, fragrant, globose, or short-spicate, ⅜ in. or more in diameter; calyx 5-lobed, pubescent, lobes valvate; corolla 5-parted, pubescent; stamens numerous, exserted, distinct, anthers small; ovary densely white-hairy.

FRUIT. Legume matures June–July, 4–6 in. long, ½–1 in. wide, linear to oblong, flat, thin, firm, straight or somewhat curved, apex obtuse or apiculate, base stipitate, margins somewhat thickened, surface whitish when young, velvety-tomentose when older, valves dehiscent; seeds 5–10, about ⅜ in. long and broad, one margin straighter than the other, compressed, dark brown, lustrous.

LEAVES. Delicate and almost fernlike in appearance, bipinnate, 4–6 in. long; pinnae 5–9 pairs (sometimes to 18 pairs); leaflets 30–50 pairs (sometimes to 90 pairs); leaflets 1/6–1/4 in. long, linear to oblong, oblique, acute, prominently nerved, at first tomentose but more glabrate later; petiolar gland sessile; stipules small, early deciduous.

TWIGS. Gray to white, tomentose when young, when older glabrous, unarmed or prickly.

BARK. Gray, on older stems with shallow fissures and broad, flat ridges.

RANGE. In sandy or limestone soils from the Nueces River valley westward and southward into Mexico. Abundant along the lower Rio Grande drainage. In Mexico in the states of Nuevo León, Tamaulipas, Querétaro, and Veracruz.

REMARKS. The genus name, *Acacia*, refers to the spinescent

stipules of some species, and the species name, *berlandieri*,
is for Luis Berlandier, a Belgian botanist who explored
the United States–Mexico boundary for the Mexican govern-
ment in 1828. Vernacular names are Thornless Catclaw,
Mimosa Catclaw, Round-flowered Catclaw, Guajillo, Huajilla, and Matoral. This species is a very famous honey plant,
producing a clear, white, excellent flavored honey. The wood
is sometimes used for fuel locally or for making handles
and small woodenware articles. It is a desirable plant for
cultivation both as a specimen plant or hedge plant in the
areas suited to it. The fernlike leaves and globose white
flower heads are very attractive. It can be propagated by
seeds or by young seedlings which come up at the base of
the old plant, but these are deeprooted and hard to transplant.

Twisted Acacia

Acacia tortuosa (L.) Willd. [B]

FIELD IDENTIFICATION. Usually a spiny, spreading shrub, with numerous stems from the base. More rarely a small tree to 20 ft, and 5–6 in. in diameter, with an irregular crown.

FLOWERS. In spring, the heads borne on solitary or clustered puberulent peduncles ⅓–1 in. long; bracts 2, minute, hairy; flower heads yellow, fragrant, globose, ¼–⅜ in. in diameter; calyx minute, shorter than the corolla, 5-lobed, lobes puberulous; corolla 5-parted, puberulous; stamens numerous, exserted, distinct, twice as long as the corolla; ovary pubescent.

FRUIT. Legume 2¾–5 in. long, about ¼ in. wide, elongate, linear, almost round but slightly compressed, somewhat constricted between the seeds, dark reddish brown to black, velvety-pubescent, tardily dehiscent, somewhat pulpy; seeds in one row, about ¼ in. long, obovoid, compressed, dark reddish brown, shiny.

LEAVES. Bipinnate, rachis slender and puberulent, short-petiolate, usually less than 1¼ in. long; pinnae 2–5 pairs (usually 3–4); leaflets 10–15 pairs, each leaflet linear to oblong, somewhat curved, apex mucronulate, base subsessile, surface light green and glabrous, 1/25–1/6 in. long.

TWIGS. Reddish brown or gray, slender, somewhat angled, glabrous or pubescent; lenticels numerous and minute; spines ¼–¾ in. long, terete, puberulent to glabrous.

BARK. Dark brown to black, deeply furrowed.

RANGE. Widespread in Texas, Mexico, the West Indies, South America, and the Galápagos Islands. In Texas from the valley of the Cibolo River to Eagle Pass on the Rio Grande. In Mexico in the states of Nuevo León, Chihuahua, Durango, Hidalgo, Puebla, Colima, and San Luis Potosí.

REMARKS. The genus name, *Acacia*, means "hard-pointed" and refers to the spinescent stipules. The species name, *tortuosa*, is for the twisted branches. It is also known under the vernacular names of Huisachillo and Juisache Chino. Twisted Acacia resembles Sweet Acacia somewhat, but the legume of the former is much narrower and elongate. Twisted Acacia is closely related to and is sometimes given the name of Schaffner Acacia, *A. schaffneri* (S. Wats.) Herm.

Catclaw Acacia

Acacia greggii Gray [B]

FIELD IDENTIFICATION. Thorny, thicket-forming shrub or small tree to 30 ft, and 12 in. in diameter. The numerous slender, spreading, thorny branches are almost impenetrable.

FLOWERS. Usually April–October; spikes 1¼–2½ in. long, about ½ in. in diameter, dense, oblong, creamy yellow, fragrant, peduncle usually about one half the length of the spike, sometimes a number of spikes clustered together at the ends of the twigs; calyx green, about 1/12 in. long (half as long as the petals), obscurely 5-toothed, puberulous on the outer surface; petals 5, 1/6–1/8 in. long, greenish, yellowish, and hairy on the margins; stamens numerous, exserted, about ¼ in. long, filaments pale yellow; ovary long-stalked, hairy.

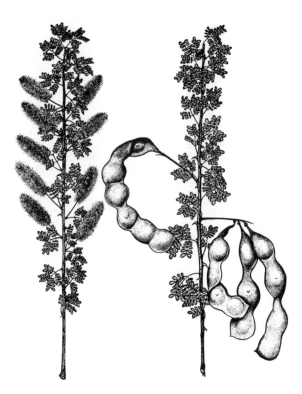

FRUIT. Persistent from July through the winter, legume 2–5½ in. long, ½–¾ in. wide, compressed, straight, curved, or often curling and contorted, constricted between the seeds, apex acute or rounded, sometimes mucronulate, base obliquely narrowed into a short stalk, margins thickened, light brown or reddish, reticulate-veined, valves thin and membranous; seeds dark brown, shiny, almost orbicular, compressed, ¼–⅓ in. long, germination about 60 percent.

LEAVES. Bipinnate, 1–3 in. long; pinnae short-stalked, 1–3 pairs, petiole with a minute brown gland near the middle; leaflets 3–7 (usually 3–5) pairs, obovate to oblong; apex rounded, obtuse or truncate, apiculate; base unequally contracted into a short petiolule; blade surface 2–3-nerved, lightly reticulate-veined, pubescent, length 1/6–1/4 in.

TWIGS. Pale brown to reddish or gray, pubescent or glabrous; spines ⅛–¼ in. long, dark brown or gray, stout, recurved, flat at base, infrastipular.

BARK. Gray to black, about ⅛ in. thick, furrowed, the surface separating into small thin scales on older trunks.

WOOD. Brown to reddish, sapwood light yellow, close-grained, hard, heavy, strong, durable.

RANGE. At altitudes of 1,000–5,000 ft, on dry gravelly mesas, sides of canyons, and banks of arroyos. In west Texas there are two more or less disjunct ranges. The more southerly of these extends southward from Bexar County to Willacy County; the other from Taylor County southwestward, with heavy concentration in the Big Bend area. Also in New Mexico, Arizona, and Colorado; north to Nevada and Utah, west to California, and south into the Mexican states of Coahuila, Chihuahua, Sonora, and Baja California.

REMARKS. The genus name, *Acacia*, means "hard-pointed" and refers to the spinescent stipules of some of the species. The species name, *greggii*, honors Josiah Gregg (1806–1850), early botanist who collected in the Southwest and northern Mexico. Vernacular names used are Devil Claws, Texas Mimosa, Paradise Flower, Gregg Acacia, Long-flowered Acacia, Huajilla, Chaparral, Gatuña, and Uña de Gato.

Catclaw Acacia often grows in almost impenetrable thickets, furnishing shelter for various birds and mammals. The seeds are eaten by scaled quail, and the leaves are nibbled by jack rabbit when other food is scarce. The wood is used for fuel, small household articles, and singletrees. Cattle browse on the young foliage when grass is scarce, but is not palatable. It apparently stands heavy grazing well and is drought resistant. The fragrant yellow flowers furnish an excellent bee food, and honey from it is of light yellow and of good flavor. The Indians of west Texas, New Mexico, and Arizona made a meal, known as "pinole," from the legumes, which was eaten in the form of mush or cakes. It is also reported that the lac insect, *Tachardia lacca* Kerr., feeds on the sap and exudes the substance from its body. This substance is used as commercial lac. However, the infestation does not appear to be abundant enough to make the gathering of the lac commercially profitable on Catclaw Acacia.

White Popinac Lead-tree

Leucaena leucocephala (Lam.) DeWit. [B]

FIELD IDENTIFICATION. Shrub or tree to 30 ft, and 4–6 in. in diameter. Branches unarmed, numerous and spreading, crown irregularly rounded, trunks short.

FLOWERS. Appearing after 3–4 years of age, borne usually on 1–3 axillary or terminal pubescent peduncles, ¾–1⅓ in. long; heads globose, dense, white or pink, ⅝–1¼ in. in diameter, the florets small, sessile, and perfect. Calyx 1/25–1/12 in. long, obconic, pubescent, teeth 5, short, minute, obtuse; petals 5, erect, distinct, linear-spatulate, 1/6–1/5 in. long or about twice as long as the calyx; stamens 10, distinct, exserted, about three times as long as the petals; ovary stipitate, pubescent, ovules numerous, style filiform, stigma minute.

FRUIT. Legume 4–9 in. long, about ⅝ in. wide, linear to oblong, obtuse to acute or abruptly pointed, base tapering, surface reddish brown, flat, finely pubescent, membranous; seeds 16–20, transverse, ovate, flattened, about ⅜ in. long, mottled-gray to black.

LEAVES. Alternate, bipinnate, 4–8 in. long, petiole 1¼–2½ in. long and glandular or glandless; pinnae 3–10 pairs; leaflets 10–20 pairs, oblique, linear-oblong or lanceolate, apex acute to obtuse, margin entire, thin, length 1/3–3/5 in., light green above, paler below.

TWIGS. Brown, slender, puberulent to glabrous, divaricate, lenticels numerous; older bark dull, reddish brown, with flattened overlapping ridges.

WOOD. Light brown, close-grained, hard, moderately heavy.

RANGE. Mostly in sandy soil of semitropical and tropical areas. Naturalized and occasionally escaping cultivation in southern Florida and the Keys. Also the lower Rio Grande Valley area of Texas in Cameron County between Brownsville and Boca Chica.

REMARKS. The genus name, *Leucaena*, is from the Greek word *leukos* ("to whiten"), which refers to the flower colors. The species name, *leucocephala*, has the same meaning ("white-head"). It is known in the American tropics under the name of Jumby-bean, Xamin, Uaxi, Guacis, Aroma Blanca, Hediondilla, and Granolino. According to legend, if horses, mules, or pigs eat the plant their hair will fall out. However, goats and cattle are said not to be affected. The seeds are made into necklaces and bracelets and are sometimes cooked and eaten with rice. It is also reported that the roots have emmenagogic and abortive properties. It is cultivated in subtropical areas and is planted as hedges in the Old World tropics.

Honey Mesquite

Prosopis glandulosa Torr. [A, B, C]

FIELD IDENTIFICATION. Thorny shrub or small tree to 30 ft, with crooked, drooping branches and a rounded crown. Trunk dividing into branches a short distance above the ground. Root system radially spreading and deep.

FLOWERS. May–September, perfect, borne in yellowish green, cylindric, axillary, pedunculate spikelike racemes; calyx bell-shaped, minute, 5-lobed, with lobes triangular; corolla greenish white, small, with 5 linear petals which are erect, pubescent within, and much longer than the calyx-tube; stamens 10, exserted, with filiform filaments and oblong anthers; ovary stipitate, pubescent; style filiform; stigma small.

FRUIT. August–September, legumes in loose clusters, 4–9 in. long, somewhat flattened, glabrous, linear, straight or curved, somewhat constricted between the seeds, indehiscent; seeds oblong, compressed, shiny, brown, set in spongy tissue.

LEAVES. Alternate, deciduous, long-petioled, bipinnately compound of 2 (rarely 3 or 4) pairs of pinnae; with 12–20 leaflets; leaflets smooth, dark green, linear, acute or obtuse at apex, about 2 in. long and ¼ in. wide.

TWIGS. Zigzag, armed with stout straight spines to 2 in. long, or sometimes spineless.

BARK. Rough, reddish brown, with shallow fissures and thick scales.

WOOD. Reddish brown, heavy, hard, durable, close-grained, sapwood yellow.

RANGE. Honey Mesquite is distributed from Kansas and New Mexico east into Oklahoma and Arkansas, and across Texas into Louisiana.

REMARKS. The genus name, *Prosopis*, is the old Greek name for the burdock. The species name, *glandulosa*, is for the glandular anther connectives of the flowers. Mesquite is often shrubby, forming thickets in dry areas and taking over grasslands rapidly. It readily sprouts from the stump, is very deep rooted, and is not easily damaged by disease or insects. The wood is used for charcoal, fuel, furniture, building blocks, crossties, and posts and is often the only wood available in regions in which it grows. Mesquite foliage and pods are eaten by livestock, and the seeds pass through the digestive tracts and grow where they fall. This fact has been responsible for much of its rapid distribution. The seeds are also considered an important wildlife food, being eaten by Gambel's quail, scaled quail, white-winged dove, rock squirrel, ground squirrel, coyote, skunk, jack rabbit, and white-tailed and mule deer. Mesquite beans played an important part in the diet of the southwestern Indian. The legumes contain as high as 30 percent sugar, and a meal known as "pinole" was prepared from them and made into bread. Fermentation of the meal also produced an intoxicating beverage. Exudation of gum from the branches and

Torrey Mesquite

trunk offers possibilities as a substitute for gum arabic and is used locally in candy. It also produces a black dye and a cement for mending pottery.

It had been considered at one time by various authors, that the species *P. juliflora* (Swartz) DC. was centered in distribution in Mexico and Central and South America. Those in the Texas area were therefore reported as *P. juliflora* var. *glandulosa* (Torr.) Cockrell, *P. juliflora* var. *velutina* (Woot.) Standl., and *P. juliflora* var. *torreyana* L. Benson. It is now interpreted (Correll and Johnston, *Manual of the Vascular Plants of Texas*, p. 783) that *P. glandulosa* Torr. is the common species of Texas, and that the only valid variety is *P. glandulosa* var. *torreyana* (L. Benson) M. C. Johnst. This variety has leaflets 2/5–1 1/5 in. long, about 5–8 times as long as broad, with 8–20 (average 10–15) pairs per pinna. Common in Trans-Pecos region. Also occurring along the Rio Grande, and then along the Gulf in the vicinity of Corpus Christi, Texas. Also in the Mexican states of Nuevo León, Coahuila, Chihuahua, and Sonora; and New Mexico and Arizona.

Nueces Mesquite

Prosopis laevigata (Willd.) M. C. Johnst. [B]

The following description follows that of Correll and Johnston, *Manual of the Vascular Plants of Texas*, p. 783:
    A small tree; pinnae usually 2 pairs per leaf; leaflets 20–27 pairs per pinna, closely set, 1/6–1/4 or to 1/3 in. long, the foliage minutely and abundantly hispidulous; pods essentially straight, nearly as thick as broad, 2¾–6 in. long. Rare in Texas, from one dilute population 3 miles southeast of Calallen, Nueces County, Coastal Bend region, spring and other times, widespread in Mexico, north to Tamaulipas, Nuevo León, and Durango; adventive in Texas.

Subfamily Caesalpinioideae

Eastern Redbud

Cercis canadensis L. [A, B, C]

FIELD IDENTIFICATION. Shrub or small tree to 40 ft, trunk usually straight, branching usually 5–9 ft from the ground, top broadly rounded or flattened. Distinctly ornamental in spring with small, clustered, rose-purple flowers covering the bare branches before the leaves.

FLOWERS. March–May, before the leaves, in clusters of 2–8, on pedicels ¼–¾ in. long; flowers 1/4–2/5 in. long, perfect, imperfectly papilionaceous, rose-purple, petals 5, standard smaller than the wings; keel petals not united, large; stamens 10, shorter than the petals; ovary pubescent, short, stipitate, style curved; calyx campanulate, 5-toothed.

FRUIT. September–October, persistent on the branches, often abundant, peduncles divaricate and reflexed, 1/3–3/5 in. long; legume 2–4 in. long, about ½ in. wide or less, tapering at both ends, flat, leathery, reddish brown, upper suture with a somewhat winged margin; valves 2, thin, reticulate-veined; seeds several, oblong, flattened, 1/6–1/5 in. long.

LEAVES. Simple, alternate, deciduous, 2–6 in. long, 1¼–6 in. broad, ovate to cordate or reniform, apex usually abruptly obtuse or acute, base cordate or subtruncate, margin entire,

palmately 7–9-veined; upper surface dull green and glabrous; lower surface paler and glabrous or somewhat hairy
along the veins, membranous at first but firm (not coriaceous) later; petioles 1¼–5 in. long, essentially glabrous,
stipules caducous.

TWIGS. Slender, glabrous, somewhat divaricate, brown to
gray, when young lustrous, when older dull.

BARK. Reddish brown to gray, thin and smooth when young,
older ones with elongate fissures separating long, narrow
plates with small scales, lenticels numerous.

WOOD. Reddish brown, sapwood yellowish, close-grained,
hard, weak, weighing 30 lb per cu ft.

RANGE. Eastern Redbud is found in rich soil along streams
or in bottom lands from central Texas, Oklahoma, Arkansas,
and Louisiana; eastward to Florida, northward to Connecticut and Ontario, and west to Michigan, Missouri, Nebraska,
and Kansas.

REMARKS. The genus name, *Cercis*, is the ancient name of
the closely related Judas-tree of Europe and Asia. According

Texas Redbud

to tradition Judas hung himself from a branch of the tree. The species name, *canadensis*, literally means "of Canada," where it is rather uncommon. Or perhaps the Linnean name refers to northeastern North America, before political boundaries were set up. The tree is a very handsome ornamental and has been in cultivation since 1641. It is reported that the acid flowers are sometimes pickled for use in salad, and in Mexico they are fried. The seeds are eaten by a number of species of birds and the foliage browsed by the white-tailed deer. Eastern Redbud also has some value as a source of honey.

Two native varieties of Redbud of Texas, Oklahoma, and Mexico are Texas Redbud, *C. canadensis* var. *texensis* (S. Wats.) Hopkins, and Mexican Redbud, *C. canadensis* var. *mexicana* (Rose) Hopkins.

Both the Texas and Mexican varieties differ from the Eastern Redbud by having conspicuously shiny and stiffly coriaceous leaves (leaves of the Eastern Redbud are dull green and not distinctly coriaceous). The leaf shapes of the species and the 2 varieties are rather similar, varying from

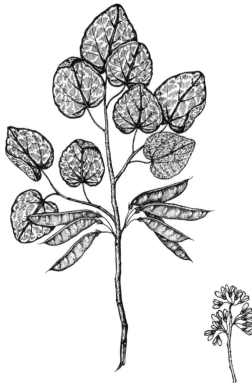

Mexican Redbud

cordate with an acute apex to reniform or rounded with the apex obtuse or emarginate.

The Texas and Mexican varieties are separated from each other on the dubious characters of the amount of hairs present on various parts. Texas Redbud has pedicels, young branchlets, and leaves glabrous or nearly so. Mexican Redbud has pedicels and young branchlets densely woolly-tomentose and leaves slightly so. These distinctions are so close that some botanists consider the Mexican Redbud to be only a hairy form of the Texas Redbud, instead of a distinct variety of the Eastern Redbud. However, since forms closely resembling *C. canadensis* var. *mexicana*, have been found in northeast Texas, it is morely likely that the latter is derived from *C. canadensis*.

Texas Redbud has been collected on limestone areas in Texas in Val Verde, Kerr, Austin, Comal, Erath, Brown, Dallas, and Hood counties. It is known in Oklahoma near Turner Falls Park in the Arbuckle Mountains, in Platt National Park at Antelope Springs, and in Mexico in Nuevo León and Tamaulipas.

Mexican Redbud has been collected on limestone areas in Texas in Brown, Dallas, Terrell, Nolan, Brewster, and Austin counties. It is the prevalent form in Trans-Pecos Texas, and occurs in Mexico in Coahuila, Nuevo León, and San Luis Potosí.

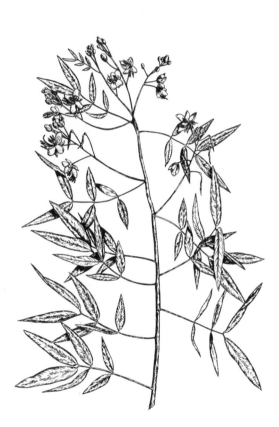

Flowering Senna

Cassia corymbosa Lam. [A, B]

FIELD IDENTIFICATION. Cultivated shrub or small tree to 12 ft, with a trunk 2–5 in. in diameter. The numerous elongate, erect or spreading branches form a rounded crown.

FLOWERS. Blooms in late summer. Borne in corymbose panicles from the leaf axils; primary peduncles glabrous, 1–2½ in. long; secondary flower-bearing pedicels to ¾ in. long; petals 5, bright yellow, nearly equal, obovate, ⅜–½ in. long; stamens 7, 3 of them long-exserted, upcurved, anthers large with oblique cuplike apices; 4 of the stamens more erect with anthers shorter; staminodia 2–3, short and flattened somewhat; style elongate, exserted, upcurved, short white-hairy; calyx of 5 sepals, green or yellowish, unequal in shape, narrowly elliptic to ovate, ¼–⅜ in. long.

FRUIT. Legume stout, thick, 1¾–6 in. long, sides convex and sutures furrowed, indehiscent.

LEAVES. Evenly pinnately compound, rachis averaging about 2 in. long, mostly glabrous; leaflets 4–6, 1–2 in. long, terminal pair longest, lanceolate to linear-elliptic or elliptic-lanceolate, apex long-acute or acuminate, base rounded and often asymmetrical, margin entire, upper surface dull green and glabrous, lower surface paler and glabrous; petiolules 1/16–1/8 in. long, glabrous or with a few sparse white hairs, or a few dark, stalked glands in the axils.

TWIGS. Young ones elongate, slender, green, glabrous; older ones brown and glabrous.

BARK. On older branches and trunk smooth, dark brown to light or dark gray, marked with numerous pale, linear, horizontal lenticels.

RANGE. A native of Argentina, cultivated in gardens in many cities along the Gulf Coast. Occasionally escaping cultivation, or persistent about abandoned gardens of eastern Texas and Louisiana; eastward to Tennessee, Georgia, and Florida.

REMARKS. The genus name, *Cassia*, is the ancient name of an aromatic plant. The species name, *corymbosa*, is for the flower arrangement. It is listed by some authors under the name of *Adipera corymbosa* Britt. & Rose. This garden shrub is gaining in popularity because of its dense foliage, bright yellow flowers, and freedom from disease.

Common Honey-locust

Gleditsia triacanthos L. [A, B, C]

FIELD IDENTIFICATION. Tree to 100 ft, with a thorny trunk and branches and a loose, open crown.

FLOWERS. May–June, perfect or imperfect, borne in axillary, dense, green racemes; racemes of the staminate flowers often clustered, pubescent, 2–5 in. long; calyx campanulate; lobes of calyx 5, elliptic-lanceolate, spreading, hairy, acute; petals 4–5, longer than calyx-lobes, erect, oval, white; stamens 10, inserted on the calyx-tube, anthers green, pistil rudimentary or absent in the staminate flower; pistillate racemes 2–3 in. long, slender, few-flowered, usually solitary; pistil tomentose, ovary almost sessile, style short, stigma oblique, ovules 2 or many; stamens much smaller and abortive in pistillate flower.

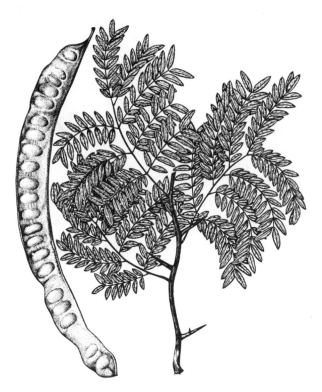

FRUIT. Ripening September–October, legume ½–1½ ft long, ½–1½ in. wide, borne on short peduncles, usually in twos or threes, dark brown, shiny, flattened, often twisted, falcate or straight, coriaceous, pulp succulent and sweetish between the seeds, occasional sterile legumes are seedless and pulpless, some trees with rather small legumes, others with large legumes, and some with a mixture of small, intermediate, and large; seeds about ⅓ in. long, oval, hard, compressed. The minimum commercial seed-bearing age is 10 years and the maximum 100 years.

LEAVES. Alternate, deciduous, once- or twice-pinnate (the twice-pinnate usually on more vigorous shoots), 5–10 in. long; pinnae 4–8 pairs; leaflets 15–30, alternate or opposite, almost sessile, ¾–2 in. long, ½–1 in. wide, oblong-lanceolate, rounded or acute at apex, cuneate or rounded or inequilateral at base, crenulate or entire on margin, dark green and lustrous above, paler and often pubescent beneath; rachis and petioles pubescent.

TWIGS. Greenish or reddish brown, lustrous, stout, armed with solitary or 3-branched thorns which are rigid, sharp, straight, shiny, purplish brown.

BARK. Grayish brown to black, on older trees with fissures

deep and narrow, separating into scaly ridges, often bearing heavy simple to multibranched thorns.

WOOD. Brown to reddish, sapwood yellowish, coarse-grained, strong in bending and end compression, stiff, highly shock resistant, tools well, splits rather easy, shrinks little, does not glue satisfactorily, rather hard, moderately durable, weighing 42 lb per cu ft.

RANGE. In moist fertile soil. Texas, Oklahoma, Arkansas, and Louisiana; eastward to Florida, northward to Pennsylvania and New York, and west to Nebraska.

REMARKS. The genus name, *Gleditsia*, is a contraction and is in honor of Johann Gottlieb Gleditsch, an eighteenth-century German botanist. The species name, *triacanthos*, refers to the commonly 3-branched thorns. Other vernacular names are Honey-shucks, Sweet Locust, Thorn-tree, Thorny Locust, Three-thorned-acacia, and Sweet-bean. It has been known in cultivation since 1700 and is often planted for ornament, particularly the thornless form. The tree has few diseases or insect pests. The wood is used for farm implements, fuel, lumber, posts, vehicles, furniture, and railroad crossties. The flowers are reported to be a good bee food, and the Indians ate the fleshy sweet pulp of the young pods, older pods turning bitter. The pods are also eaten by cattle, white-tailed deer, gray squirrel, and cottontail.

Water Locust

Gleditsia aquatica Marsh. [A, B, C]

FIELD IDENTIFICATION. Tree of deep swamps with contorted, spine-bearing branches, attaining a height of 60 ft.

FLOWERS. In May or June, perfect or imperfect, borne in slender, narrow, green, axillary racemes about 3–4 in. long; pedicels short; calyx bell-shaped, 3–5-lobed, pubescent; lobes as long as petals, narrow, acute or obtuse, somewhat pilose; petals 3–5, equal, sessile, inserted on rim of calyx-tube; stamens 3–10, distinct, exserted, filament hairy below, erect, filiform, anthers large and green, abortive and swollen in the pistillate flower; ovary nearly sessile, glabrous, rudimentary in staminate flowers, stigma smaller and oblique.

FRUIT. September–December, legume long-stipitate, oval-elliptic, oblique, brown, lustrous, thin, flat, pulpless, 1–3½ in. long; seeds 1–3, orange-brown, suborbicular, about ½ in. wide.

LEAVES. Pinnate or bipinnate, 5–10 in. long; pinnae 3–8 pairs; leaflets 5–12 pairs, ovate-oblong, obscurely crenulate or entire, rounded or emarginate at the apex, oblique at base, dark green and shining above, paler beneath, ½–1 in. long, ¼–½ in. wide; petiolules slightly hairy; petioles pubescent and grooved.

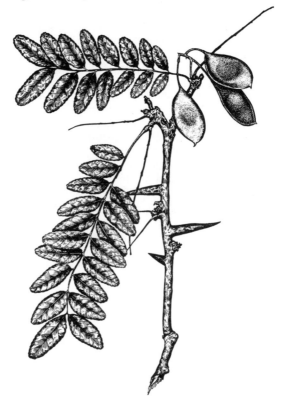

TWIGS. Gray or reddish, often with knobby spurs and corky lenticels; spines dark red and shiny, simple or compound, to 5 in. long, or spines sometimes absent.

BARK. Dull gray or reddish brown, firm, fissures narrow with small flat intervening scales, rough with small corky tubercles.

WOOD. Light reddish brown, sapwood yellow, strong, heavy, hard, close-grained, weighing 45 lb per cu ft.

RANGE. In swampland; east Texas, Oklahoma, Arkansas, and Louisiana; eastward to Florida and northward to South Carolina, Illinois, and Indiana.

REMARKS. The genus name, *Gleditsia*, is a contraction and is in honor of Johann Gottlieb Gleditsch, an eighteenth-century German botanist, and the species name, *aquatica*, refers to the plant's swampy habitat. Other vernacular names are Swamp Locust and Thorny Acacia. This tree is generally separated from Common Honey-locust, which it resembles, by its generally smaller leaves, slenderer thorns, and much smaller pulpless fruit. The wood has little commercial value except locally for posts and fuel.

A typical specimen
from Brazoria County

Texas Honey-locust

Gleditsia × *texana* Sargent (*G. triacanthos* × *G. aquatica*)
[A, B]

FIELD IDENTIFICATION. Thornless, or thorny, tree attaining
a height of 50–120 ft, with a diameter of ½–2½ ft. The
branches are erect, ascending or spreading, and the bark is
usually smooth and pale.

FLOWERS. Late in April, borne in racemes 3–4 in. long,
orange-yellow; calyx-lobes ovate, acute, villous, somewhat
shorter than the petals, stamens exserted.

FRUIT. Legume straight or falcate, compressed, with or without pulp, apex rounded or short-pointed, base broad and
abruptly rounded or pointed, thin-walled, dark chestnut
brown, puberulent, margin only slightly thickened, length

A specimen showing
a legume with straight
margins from Brazoria County

3–14 in., width ¾–1½ in.; seeds numerous, oval, flattened, dark brown, shiny, about ½ in. long or less.

LEAVES. Once- or twice-compound, puberulous, rachis slender
and puberulous to glabrous later, 12–22-foliate; leaflets
oblong-ovate, often somewhat falcate, apex rounded or acute
and apiculate, base obliquely rounded, margin obscurely
crenulate-serrate, thick and firm, upper surface dark green
and lustrous, paler on the lower surface, ½–1 in. long,
short-petiolulate.

RANGE. Besides the Brazos River area, trees which are similar have been reported from other locations in Texas. Some
have been found along the Red River near Shreveport,
Louisiana, at Yazoo City, Mississippi, and near Skelton, Gib-
son County, Indiana.

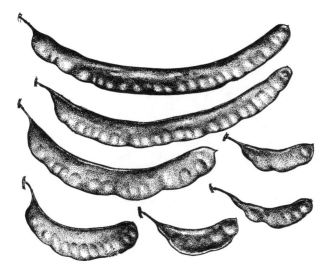

Legumes showing variation
in size and shape from
different trees in
Brazoria County

REMARKS. The genus name, *Gleditsia*, is in honor of Johann
Gottlieb Gleditsch, an eighteenth-century German botanist.
The hybrid name, *texana*, refers to its occurrence in Texas
in the bottom lands of the Brazos River.

This is a tree of rather uncertain relationship. It was first
described as a species under the name of *G. texana* Sarg.

Sargent found the grove of trees to which he gave the
name of *G. texana* growing near Brazoria in the valley of
the lower Brazos River in Texas. The author has examined
numerous specimens in the Brazoria area and has found so
many intergrades with the common Honey-locust, *G. triacanthos* L., that it is hard to determine the typical form to
which Sargent applied the name. Some trees were spineless,
and others displayed all degrees of spinescence; some bore
legumes over 1 ft long, and some only 3–5 in. long, and
some trees produced fruit both small and large. The amount
of fleshy tissue between the seeds appears to be variable
also. In fact, the great variability of the trees of the Brazoria
area is the rule rather than the exception.

Sargent later noted that some trees with these variable
characters were scattered, and some were found growing in
the vicinity of both *G. triacanthos* and *G. aquatica*. It was
therefore suggested that the variable trees might possibly be
hybrids of these two species, and the name of *G.* × *texana*
Sarg. was given by Sargent (1922).

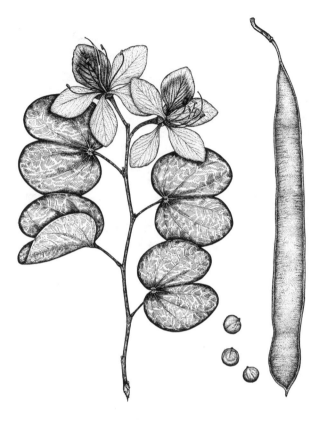

Buddhist Bauhinia

Bauhinia variegata L. [B]

FIELD IDENTIFICATION. A bush or small tree to 20 ft, with a distinct trunk, and creviced bark rough and scaly.

FLOWERS. Borne January–April in short racemes on the bare twigs and somewhat fragrant; flowers somewhat resembling orchids; 3–4 in. in diameter. Sepals ovate, large, not distinctive, tubular, ribbed, splitting open on the lower side. Petals 5, obovate, overlapping, in some with crisp and wavy edges, wider in both claw and upper section, measuring 1–1½ in. wide; color pale pink to deep magenta-pink or pinkish violet. Standard with purple-red veins; both the standard and the two upper side petals often splashed white near the base. Stamens 5–6; style long; stigma very small; ovary 1-celled.

FRUIT. Usually 12–24 in. long, straight, flat, apex acuminate; seeds round, flat, about ½ in. long.

LEAVES. Simple, in 2 alternate rows; leaf blade 3–5 in. wide, usually broader than long, cleft for a quarter to a third its length into blunt lobes; the cleft wide so that the lobes flare; apex rounded and broad; the base deeply heart-shaped with 11–13 veins, and broadened into a semicircular disk. Surfaces more or less pubescent, especially at the apex of the petiole and on the under surface. Petioles 1–2¼ in. long from slender twigs, which are glabrous or nearly so.

RANGE. A native of tropical southeast Asia and cultivated in warm regions. From central to northern Florida, and occasionally cultivated along the Gulf Coast westward to Brownsville, Texas.

REMARKS. The genus name, *Bauhinia*, honors John and Caspar Bauhin, sixteenth-century herbalists. The species name, *variegata*, refers to the multicolored petals. White Bauhinia is a variety known as *B. variegata* var. *candida* (Roxb.) Hamilton and has flowers wholly white, except for the light yellow central part of the standard petal, and in some cases of the other petals. Legume 5–7 in. long by ¾ in. wide. From southeast Asia. Cultivated at Brownsville, Texas, and in Florida.

Purple Bauhinia

Bauhinia purpurea L. [B]

FIELD IDENTIFICATION. A small nearly evergreen tree with spreading branches, and rough scaly bark. Cultivated as an ornament in the lower coastal Texas zone.

FLOWERS. Borne in rather short clusters, mostly September–December. Resembling orchids somewhat. Diameter 3–4 in.; slightly fragrant. Sepals ovate, large, not distinctive, partly united, tubular, ribbed, splitting on lower side. Petals 5, separate, with a very narrow claw, and upper part which generally measures not more than ¾ in. wide. Varying in form, but usually lanceolate-ovate and pointed, although not in the same flower, except for the standard which is the larger petal, and it is more brightly streaked than the other petals. The latter generally has a more continuous background color, such as pink, deep rose-pink, lavender, white, or yellow. There is a crimson stalk and a white splash on each side at the top of the stalk. Stamens 3–4, with pink filaments. Ovary greenish white and with a pink stalk, 1-celled; style long, deep pink.

FRUIT. Legumes reddish brown, straight, flat, apex acuminate; length to 12 in., width about 1 in. Seeds numerous, about ½ in. long, round and flattened.

LEAVES. Usually in 2 alternate rows; a little less in width than in length; cleft in blade apex one-third to one-half of the blade length, the angle at base of cleft very narrow, so that the 2 lobes flare very little and are slightly narrowed into a blunt tip. Leaf surfaces usually glabrate. Base of blade

with a semicircular disk and heart-shaped with 9–13 veins. The twigs slender.

RANGE. From tropical Asia, in India, Malaya, and southern China. In Florida grown for ornament from Vero Beach to Key West. In Texas cultivated in the Brownsville area. Rather tender and suitable for cultivation only in frost-free regions.

REMARKS. The genus name, *Bauhinia*, honors John and Caspar Bauhin, sixteenth-century herbalists. The species name, *purpurea*, refers to the basic purple color of most flowers, but there is considerable color variation. The great variety of coloring has led to the description of several so called species which really are synonyms of others or varieties. For example, *B. alba*, *B. rosea*, *B. triandra*, and *B. violacea*, belong to *B. purpurea*. The first and last have been called varieties, but no authors' names have been given to either variety. *B. triandra* is distinctive because of the rose-red flowers but is called a synonym.

Kentucky Coffee-tree

Gymnocladus dioica (L.) K. Koch [A]

FIELD IDENTIFICATION. Tree attaining a height of 100 ft with a diameter of 4 ft. Branches stout and blunt, forming a narrow, round-topped crown.

FLOWERS. Appearing May–June, after the leaves, in loosely flowered terminal racemes; staminate and pistillate racemes separate on the same tree, or on different trees; raceme of staminate flower 3–5 in. long, on stout pedicels, flowers greenish white, calyx ⅜–⅔ in. long, elongate-tubular, hairy internally and externally, 5-lobed, lobes linear-lanceolate, acuminate at apex, 1/5–1/4 in. long, shorter than the petals; petals 5, oblong, acute, equal, keeled externally, hairy on both sides, inserted on summit of calyx-tube, spreading or reflexed; stamens 10, those opposite the petals shortest, filaments filiform and hairy; anthers orange, oblong, introrse, opening lengthwise; stamens smaller and sterile in the pistillate flower, ovary rudimentary or none in the staminate flowers; pistillate raceme to 1 ft long, flowers on pedicels two to six times as long as those of the staminate flowers; ovary sessile or nearly so, superior, simple, hairy, 1-celled, 4–8-ovuled, ovules pendulous; style short, erect, oblique, lobes 2, inwardly stigmatic; pedicels of flowers from lanceolate, scarious, early deciduous bracts.

FRUIT. Legume persistent during the winter and indehiscent, on peduncles 1–2 in. long, oblong, straight or falcate, flat, thick, woody, hard, reddish brown, sometimes glaucous, 4–10 in. long, 1–2 in. wide, green to brown, pulpy between the seeds; seeds several, ovoid to obovoid, lenticular, flattened, 3/8–3/4 in. long, dark brown, bony, hard-shelled, endosperm thin.

LEAVES. Opening late in the spring, early deciduous in the fall, no terminal bud, alternate, twice-pinnately compound, 1–3 ft long, 1–2 ft wide; rachis long, slender, swollen at base; pinnae 5–13, each pinna with 7–14 leaflets which are 3/4–3 in. long, 1–1½ in. wide, ovate to oval or elliptic; apex acute or acuminate, sometimes mucronate; base cuneate, rounded or truncate; upper surface dark green and glabrous or slightly hairy on midrib, veins obscure; lower surface paler and glabrous or pubescent; petiolules about 1/25 in. long, hairy to glabrous later; stipules about 1/3 in. long, lanceolate, apex glandular-serrate; the lower pair of pinnae sometimes with single leaflets, leaflets pink to bronze-green and tomentose at first, at maturity mostly glabrous, turning yellow before falling.

TWIGS. Short, blunt, contorted, pubescent at first and reddish, later glabrous and brownish to gray; leaf scars large, conspicuous, cordate; lenticels numerous, orange-colored; pith large, salmon-colored.

BARK. Gray to brown, furrowed, roughened by small, persistent scales.

WOOD. Reddish brown, sapwood yellowish white, heavy, straight-grained, moderately strong and durable, weighing 43 lb per cu ft, taking a high polish.

RANGE. Nowhere common. In low, rich woods, mostly west of the Appalachians and north of the Gulf Coast plain. Oklahoma, Arkansas, and a few records from north Texas; east to West Virginia, north to New York and Ontario, and west to Missouri and Nebraska.

REMARKS. The genus name, *Gymnocladus*, means "naked-branched," with reference to the thick, blunt, naked branches. The species name, *dioica*, refers to the dioecious character of the flowers. Also known under the vernacular names of Chicot, Luck-bean, Coffee-nut, Kentucky-mahogany, American Coffee-tree, Nicor-tree, and Stump-tree.

The raw seeds are poisonous as they contain saponin and a toxalbumin very similar to ricin, the poisonous principle of the castor-bean plant. Roasting removes this poison, and the seeds were experimented with as a substitute for coffee in the Civil War period. The leaves are reported to be poisonous to cattle, but cases of such poisoning are infrequent. The wood is used for posts, crossties, furniture, fuel, cabinet-making, interior finish, and construction.

Jerusalem-thorn

Parkinsonia aculeata L. [A, B, C]

FIELD IDENTIFICATION. Green-barked, thorny shrub or tree to 36 ft. Branches slender, spiny, spreading, often pendulous to form a rounded head.

FLOWERS. Fragrant, borne in spring or throughout the summer especially after rains. Racemes 5–6 in. long, axillary, solitary or fascicled, pedicels ⅓–½ in. long; petals 5, imbricate in the bud, yellow, about ½ in. long, spreading, oval, clawed at the base, margin erose or entire; one petal larger than the others and bearing a gland at base, becoming red-dotted or orange with age; stamens 10, shorter than the petals, filaments distinct and hairy below, anthers yellow to reddish, opening lengthwise; ovary pubescent; calyx glabrous or nearly so, tube short, lobes oblong and reflexed, longer than the tube.

FRUIT. On pedicels ½–¾ in. long; a linear legume, 2–4 in. long, brown to orange or reddish, puberulent or glabrous, leathery, ends attenuate, constricted between the seeds, swollen portions almost terete, constrictions flattened; seeds 1–8, about ⅓ in. long, oblong, seed coat green to brown.

LEAVES. Bipinnate or rarely pinnate, petioles short, alternate or fascicled, linear, 8–16 in. long, rachis flat and winged; leaflets numerous (25–30 pairs), remote, linear to oblanceolate, about ⅓ in. long or less, inequilateral, dropping away early and leaving the persistent, flat, naked, photosynthetic rachis, petiolules slender; stipules spinescent; rachis terminating with a weak spine.

TWIGS. Somewhat divaricate, green to yellowish, puberulent to glabrous; later gray to brown or orange; spines green, brown, or black, to 1 in. long.

BARK. Thin, smooth, green, later brown to reddish with small scales on old trunks.

WOOD. Light brown to yellow, hard, heavy, close-grained, specific gravity 0.61.

RANGE. Usually in moist sandy soils, but resistant to saline

situations. In the southern half of Texas; west through New Mexico to Arizona and southward through Mexico to northern South America. Probably an escape from cultivation in California, Florida, and the West Indies.

REMARKS. The genus name, *Parkinsonia*, refers to John Parkinson, an English botanical author. The species name, *aculeata*, refers to the spines. Other vernacular names are Horsebean, Cloth-of-Gold, Crown-of-thorns, Barbados Fence Flowers, Paloverde, Lluvia de Oro, Cambrón, Espilla, Espinillo, Espinillo de España, Junco, Junco Marion, Palo de Rayo, Flor de Rayo, Yabo, Calentano, Espino Real de España, Acacia de Aguijote, Guichi-belle, Mesquite Extranjero, Guacopano, Retama de Cerda, and Retama. A grove of trees is known as a "retamal" by the Mexican people. The tree is a rapid grower and is generally free of diseases and insects. It is often grown for ornament and hedges. The wood is occasionally used as fuel and was formerly used for papermaking. An infusion of the leaves is used in tropical America as a febrifuge, for diabetes, for epilepsy, and as a sudorific and abortifacient. The leaves and pods are eaten by horses, cattle, and deer, particularly in times of stress. The Indians formerly pounded the seeds into flour to make bread. The flowers are sometimes important as a bee food.

Texas Paloverde

Cercidium texanum Gray [B]

FIELD IDENTIFICATION. Spiny, green-barked shrub or small tree to 25 ft. Usually with a short crooked or leaning trunk, or with semiprostrate lower branches.

FLOWERS. Borne in clusters or short racemes; pedicels solitary, reddish, pubescent, ¼–½ in. long; corolla yellow, of 5 imbricate petals, each about ½ in. long, ovate to elliptic, apex acute to obtuse or rounded, margin frilled and crisped. One petal abruptly contracted into a long claw at base and red-spotted; stamens 10, filaments distinct, red, glabrous; anthers yellow, opening lengthwise; pistils equaling or slightly exceeding the stamens, filiform, hairy; calyx valvate, sepals 5, linear to oblong, puberulent to pubescent, reflexed.

FRUIT. Legume 1–2½ in. long, about ¼ in. wide, flattened, apex long-apiculate, margin straight or somewhat constricted between the seeds; surfaces light brown, at first finely hairy but later glabrate; seeds usually 1–4, about ¼ in. long, dark brown, shiny, flattened, short-oblong, ends rounded.

LEAVES. Early deciduous, leaving bare twigs and branches;

leaves twice-pinnately compound, ½–¾ in. long; petiole puberulent, about ¼ in. long; leaflets 1–3 pairs (usually 1–2 per pinna); blades very short petioluled or sessile, short-oblong or narrowly obovate, somewhat broader toward the rounded apex, ⅛–¼ in. long, grayish green with closely appressed pubescence.

TWIGS. Grayish green or dark green, zigzag, very thorny, smooth, finely grooved, densely appressed pubescent, later more glabrous; spines white to green or pale brown, straight or slightly recurved, sharp, pubescent or glabrous, ¼–½ in. long.

BARK. Thin, smooth, light or dark green.

RANGE. Usually on limestone soils of flats or gentle slopes. Abundant in the vicinity of Brackettville, Del Rio, and Langtry, Texas. In Mexico in Nuevo León, Tamaulipas, and Coahuila.

REMARKS. The genus name, *Cercidium*, is from the Greek *kerkidion* ("a weaver's comb"), to which the fruit has a fancied resemblance. The species name, *texanum*, is for the state of Texas.

Texas Paloverde is closely related to Border Paloverde, *C. macrum* I. M. Johnst. Generally Texas Paloverde has fewer pinnae on an average and a hairy ovary, but intermediate forms between the two are found where the ranges overlap in the lower Rio Grande area.

Paradise Poinciana

Caesalpinia pulcherrima (L.) Swartz [B]

FIELD IDENTIFICATION. An attractive tropical shrub or irregularly branched small tree to 15 ft. The large beautiful flowers have 5 petals which are red, orange, yellow, or mottled.

FLOWERS. In upright racemes 5–20 in. long, pedicels ⅓–3 in. long and glabrous; sepals 5, about ⅗ in. long, imbricate, petaloid, oblong to oblanceolate, apex rounded, much shorter than the petals (one sepal larger than the others, concave and overlapping the others in the bud); corolla of 5 unequal petals ¾–1¼ in. long, the standard petal generally the longest with a revolute, almost tubular claw, the other petals with shorter claws, blades flabellate, margin erose and crisped, variously colored red, orange, yellow, or blotched; stamens 10, long-exserted, up-curved, filaments filiform, red, distinct, about 1 ⅗ in. long, anthers opening lengthwise; style long-exserted, filiform, stigma minute.

FRUIT. Legume 3–5 in. long, ½–¾ in. wide, broadly linear, greatly flattened, one margin straight, the other margin slightly undulate, base inequilateral, apex abruptly one-sided

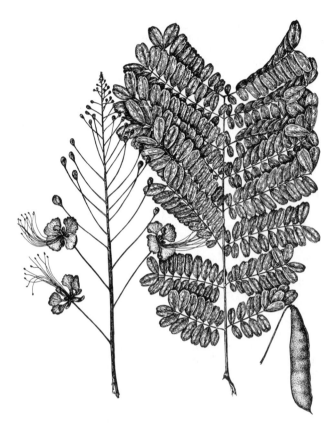

into an apiculate point, surface dark brown or black when mature; seeds 5–9, flattened, impressed on the flattened surface of the legume; peduncle 2–3 in. long, glabrous.

LEAVES. Spreading, bipinnate, 8–15 in. long, rachis green and glabrous or brownish, pinnae 3–9 pairs, each about 3½–6 in. long; leaflets 7–12 pairs per pinna, oblong to elliptic or cuneate, apex rounded or slightly notched with a minute mucro, base rounded and inequilateral, length 3/5–1 in., width 1/5–1/2 in., upper surface light green, glabrous, veins obscure; lower surface paler green, glabrous, delicately reticulate-veined; petiolules 1/25–1/16 in. long, glabrous or slightly puberulent.

TWIGS. Green, becoming dark brown or black with age, glabrate to slightly glaucous, finely grooved.

RANGE. In sandy soils, widely distributed and naturalized in tropical areas. In Texas in the lower Rio Grande area. Often planted in gardens in Brownsville, Texas, sometimes escaping cultivation to grow on the edges of old resacas. Also in southern Florida, southern California, and Mexico; southward to West Indies and continental tropical America.

REMARKS. The genus name, *Caesalpinia*, is in honor of Andreas Caesalpinus, chief physician to Pope Clement VIII. The species name, *pulcherrima*, means "very beautiful." Other vernacular names are Barbados-flower, Barbados-Pride, Flame-tree, and Dwarf Poinciana.

A variety with yellow flowers is known as *C. pulcherrima* var. *flava* Hort. The Paradise Poinciana is a popular plant in gardens in frostless areas. It is usually grown from seeds or, occasionally, greenwood cuttings.

Subfamily Papilionoideae

Texas Sophora

Sophora affinis Torr. & Gray [B]

FIELD IDENTIFICATION. A shrub or small tree to 25 ft, with spreading branches and a rounded head.

FLOWERS. In June, arranged in simple axillary racemes 2–6 in. long; pedicels slender, finely tomentose, about ½ in. long, subtended by small deciduous bracts; corolla bonnet-shaped, about ½ in. long, pink to white, somewhat fragrant; petals short-clawed, standard large, nearly orbicular, somewhat notched, reflexed, ⅜–⅝ in. long; wing and keel petals ovate to oblong and auriculate at base; stamens 10; ovary hairy and stipitate, stigma capitate; calyx campanulate, short, about ¼ in. long, abruptly narrowed at the base, obscurely 5-toothed with teeth triangular to ovate, somewhat pubescent.

FRUIT. Fruiting peduncle 2–4 in. long; legume ½–3½ in. long, abruptly constricted between the seeds, terete, black, often hairy, especially on the strictures, coriaceous, indehiscent, tipped with the prolonged style remnants, flesh thin, persistent; seeds 1–8 (mostly 4–8), ovoid or oval, seed coat brown. Constrictions between the seeds give the pod a bead-like appearance.

LEAVES. Alternate, odd-pinnately compound, deciduous; rachis lightly tomentose, 3–9 in. long, leaflets 9–19 (usually 13–15); leaflets elliptical or oval, margin entire; apex obtuse, acute, retuse and mucronulate; base rounded or cuneate, contracted into short stout petiolules 1/8–1/16 in. long; upper surface dark green to yellowish green, lustrous, glabrous or slightly hairy; lower surface slightly paler and pubescent; thin and soft; ¾–1½ in. long, about ½ in. wide; young leaves hoary-pubescent.

TWIGS. Slender, green to brown or streaked with lighter brown, nearly glabrous or puberulent, somewhat divaricate, somewhat swollen at the nodes.

BARK. Gray to reddish brown, broken into small, thin, oblong scales.

WOOD. Light red, sapwood yellow, heavy, strong, and hard.

RANGE. Usually on limestone soils of northwestern Louisiana and southwestern Oklahoma, down through central Texas. Occurs at Dallas, Kerrville, Austin, and San Antonio, Texas. Often in small groves on hillsides or along streams.

REMARKS. The genus name, *Sophora*, is from the Arabic word *Sophero*, which was applied to some tree of the same family, and the species name, *affinis*, means "related to." Another vernacular name is Eve's Necklace. The plant could be more extensively cultivated for ornament.

Mescal-bean Sophora

Sophora secundiflora (Ortega) Lag. [B]

FIELD IDENTIFICATION. Evergreen shrub, or sometimes a tree to 35 ft, with a narrow top, upright branches and velvety twigs.

FLOWERS. With the young leaves March–April; racemes densely flowered, terminal, 2–4¾ in. long, showy, violet, fragrant; pedicels 1/4–2/5 in. long, subtended by subulate bracts about ½ in. long; calyx campanulate, 1/3–2/5 in. long, oblique, the 2 upper teeth almost united throughout, the lower 3 teeth triangular to ovate; corolla bonnet-shaped, violet; standard petal erect, broad, suborbicular to ovate, crisped, notched, 3/5–2/3 in. long, somewhat spotted at the base within; wing and keel petals oblong to obovate; stamens 10; ovary white-hairy.

FRUIT. Pod in September, on pedicels 1/4–1 in. long, woody, hard, oblong, terete, densely brown-pubescent, somewhat constricted between the seeds, apex abruptly prolonged by persistent style remnants, indehiscent, 1–5 in. long, about ¾ in. wide, walls about ¼ in. thick; seeds red, 1–8 (usually 3–4), about ½ in. long, globose to oblong, often flattened at one end, hard, bony; hilum small, pale and about ⅛ in. long.

LEAVES. Odd-pinnately compound, 4–6 in. long, rachis grooved above; leaflets 5–13 (usually 5–9), persistent, elliptic-oblong or oval; apex rounded or obtuse, notched, or mucronulate; base gradually narrowed; margin entire; upper surface lustrous, leathery, reticulate, dark green, hairy when young but glabrous later; lower surface paler, glabrous or puberulent; 1–2½ in. long, ½–1½ in. wide; petioles stout, puberulous, sometimes leaflets sessile or nearly so.

TWIGS. With fine velvety tomentum at first, later becoming glabrous, or nearly so, green to orange-brown.

BARK. Dark gray to black, broken into shallow fissures with narrow flattened ridges and thin scales.

WOOD. Heartwood orange to red; sapwood yellow, hard, heavy, close-grained, specific gravity about 0.98, said to yield a yellow dye, otherwise of no commercial value.

RANGE. Usually on limestone soils in central, southern, and western Texas, New Mexico, and northern Mexico. In Texas from the shores of Matagorda Bay, almost at sea level, west into the Chisos and Davis mountains to altitudes of 5,000 ft. Frequent on the limestone hills around Austin, Texas. In Mexico from Nuevo León to San Luis Potosí.

REMARKS. The genus name, *Sophora*, is from the Arabic name *Sophero*, and the species name, *secundiflora*, refers to the one-sided inflorescence. Other vernacular names are Texas Mountain-laurel, Frigolito, Frijollito, Frijolillo, Coral Bean, Big-drunk Bean, and Colorín.

Although called Mountain-laurel in Texas this plant is not a member of the Laurel family (Lauraceae). However, neither is the so-called Mountain-laurel of the Eastern states, which is *Kalmia latifolia*, a heath. The true laurel, or Poet's Laurel, *Laurus nobilis*, is a native of Asia and south Europe. American representatives of the true Laurel family native to our area are the Red Bay, *Persea borbonia*, and the Sassafras, *Sassafras albidum*.

The persistent, shiny leaves of Mescal-bean give a lustrous effect when seen in mass at a distance. The beautiful violet flowers are very fragrant, in fact offensively so to some people. A volatile liquid alkaloid, sophorine, which is identical with cytisine, exists in many species of *Sophora*, including *S. secundiflora*, *S. tomentosa*, and *S. sericea*. Other sophoras, including *S. angustifolia*, *S. alopecuroides*, and *S. pachycarpa*, contain the alkaloids matrine and sophocarpine.

The narcotic properties of the red seeds of Mescal-bean Sophora were well known to the Indians. A powder from them, in very small amounts, was mixed with the beverage mescal to produce intoxication, delirium, excitement, and finally a long sleep. The seeds are poisonous to both humans and livestock. They were frequently used as a trade article by the Indians in the form of necklaces. The red seeds of *Erythrina herbacea* were also used for this purpose, and the two plants are often confused, but *Erythrina* has 3 leaflets only, and the pod is dehiscent at maturity. Mescal-bean is rather difficult to transplant, but this can be done if sufficient calcium is in the soil. The shrub is rather slow growing.

Drummond Rattlebox

Sesbania drummondii (Rydb.) Cory [A, B]

FIELD IDENTIFICATION. A short-lived shrub of low, wet grounds to 15 ft, with many stems from the base, or sometimes a small tree to 20 ft.

FLOWERS. Racemes 2–6 in. long, shorter than the leaves, showy, loosely flowered, slender, axillary peduncles slender upper one-third to one-half flowered, the perfect bonnet-shaped flowers on slender pedicels ¼–½ in. long; standard petal larger than the others, about as broad as long, ½–¾ in. long, orbicular, notched at the apex, base clawed, yellow and streaked with red; wing petals oblong, obtuse, yellow, ½–¾ in. long; keel petals ½–¾ in. long; stamens 10, 9 united and one free; pistil with a slender style and glabrous, stalked ovary; calyx minute, campanulate, somewhat 2-lipped with 5 short, acute, apiculate lobes.

FRUIT. Pod 4-sided and 4-winged, 2½–3½ in. long, on a stipe ⅜–⅝ in. long, persistent, leathery, indehiscent, constricted somewhat between the seeds; the several seeds separated by partitions, rattling when dry.

LEAVES. Folding in the hot sun, even-pinnately compound, 5–8 in. long, leaflets 12–60 (usually 13–40); blades narrowly oblong or elliptic, ⅜–1 in. long, base cuneate, apex rounded and mucronate; upper surface dull green, glabrous, and inconspicuously veined; lower surface paler and glabrous or somewhat glaucescent beneath; petiolules about 1/16 in. long.

STEMS. When young green and smooth, when older light brown; bark tight, on older stems separating into small, thin scales.

WOOD. Green to yellowish or white, pith large, of no commercial value.

RANGE. In low wet places. Arkansas, Texas, and Louisiana; eastward to Florida and southward into Mexico.

REMARKS. The genus name, *Sesbania*, is the Latinized version of the old Adansonian name, *Sesban*, which has presumably an Arabic origin. The species name, *drummondii*, is from Thomas Drummond, an English botanist, who collected in Texas, 1833–1834. He collected extensively in the vicinity of Galveston, Texas, where the plant is abundant. Other common names for the Drummond Rattlebox are Siene Bean, Rattle-bush, Rattle Bean, Coffee Bean, and Senna. The seeds of the Drummond Rattlebox are poisonous to livestock, especially sheep and goats, and death may follow if a quantity is eaten. The symptoms are diarrhea, extreme weakness, and lethargy from one to two days after eating. It is reported that the seeds were used as a substitute for coffee during the Civil War period. However, because of their toxic properties this seems to be open to question. The extent to which this toxicity is reduced by boiling has not been determined. Until suitable studies are made, its use for human consumption seems unwise and is not recommended.

Drummond Rattlebox has some ornamental value for planting along the edges of streams or lakes. Some closely related tropical species are now being introduced into cultivation in the Gulf Coast states and seem to do well, occasionally escaping to grow wild.

Black Locust

Robinia pseudo-acacia L. [A, B]

FIELD IDENTIFICATION. Spiny tree attaining a height of 100 ft, with a trunk diameter of 30 in. Trees rapid growing, reaching maturity in 30–40 years.

FLOWERS. May–June, attractive, fragrant, in loose, pendent racemes 4–5 in. long; individual flowers perfect, bonnet-shaped, about 1 in. long; corolla white, petals 5; standard petal obcordate, rounded, a yellow blotch often on inner

surface; wing petals 2, free; keel petals incurved, obtuse, united below; stamens 10, in 2 groups, 9 united and one free, the group forming a tube; pistil superior, ovary oblong, style hairy and reflexed, stigma small; ovules numerous; calyx 5-lobed, lower lobe longest and acuminate; pedicels about ½ in. long.

FRUIT. A legume, ripe September–October; brown, flattened, oblong-linear, straight or slightly curved, 2–5 in. long, about ½ in. wide, 2-valved, persistent; peduncle short and thick; seeds 4–8, hard, flat, mottled brown, kidney-shaped, seed dispersed September–April from the persistent legume.

LEAVES. Pinnately compound, alternate, deciduous, 8–14 in. long; leaflets 7–19, each one ½–2 in. long and ½–1 in. wide, sessile or short-stalked; rounded at both ends or sometimes wedge-shaped at base; ovate-oblong or oval, entire, mature leaves bluish green and glabrous above, usually paler and glabrous except on veins beneath; young leaves silvery-hairy, mature leaves turning yellow in autumn; stipules becoming straight or slightly curved spines; leaves folding on dark days or in the evenings.

TWIGS. Stout, zigzag, brittle, greenish brown, glabrous, somewhat angular, stipules modified into sharp spines.

BARK. Gray to reddish brown, ½–1½ in. thick, rough, ridged, deeply furrowed, sometimes twisted, inner bark pale yellow, thorns paired and scattered.

WOOD. Greenish yellow or light brown, sapwood white and narrow, durable, hard, heavy, strong, stiff, close-grained, weighing about 45 lb per cu ft, is shock-resistant, shows little shrinkage, is very resistant to decay but is difficult to hand-tool.

RANGE. Prefers deep, well-drained calcareous soil, probably originally native to the high lands of the Piedmont Plateau and Appalachian Mountains. Georgia; west to Oklahoma and Arkansas and northeast to New York. In other areas probably introduced and escaped from cultivation. Not native to Texas but persistent along fence rows, abandoned fields, and old home sites. Now commonly distributed by nurserymen in the Gulf Coast states.

REMARKS. The genus name, *Robinia*, is in honor of Jean and Vespasian Robin, herbalists to Henry IV of France, and the species name, *pseudo-acacia* ("false acacia"), refers to its resemblance to an acacia. Other vernacular names are White Locust, Yellow Locust, Red Locust, Red-flowering Locust, Green Locust, Honey Locust, Silver Locust, Post Locust, Pea-flower Locust, Silver-chain, and False-acacia Locust. The wood is highly resistant to decay.

Rose-acacia Locust

Robinia hispida L. [A]

FIELD IDENTIFICATION. Shrub 3–18 ft, spreading by stoloniferous roots. Branches numerous, erect and diffuse; twigs, petioles, and rachises bristly with reddish hairs to 1/5 in. long.

FLOWERS. May–June, racemes axillary, pendent, lax and open, 3–9-flowered, pedicels ¼–½ in. long, bristly-hairy; calyx short-hispid, somewhat 2-lipped, the upper 2 somewhat united, lateral lobes broadly lanceolate and acuminate; corolla pink, bonnet-shaped, ⅔–1¼ in. long, bearing a banner petal, 2 wing petals, and 2 keel petals; standard petal about 1 in. wide, reflexed, about the same length as the wings and keel; wing petals oblong and base auricled; keel petals curved, obtuse, base with a rounded auricle; stamens diadelphous, ovary stalked and densely glandular-hairy.

FRUIT. Legume 2–3¼ in. long, linear, flattened, often termi-
nated by the persistent style, margined along the upper
suture, conspicuously and densely reddish brown hispid,
several-seeded, tardily 2-valved.

LEAVES. Odd-pinnately compound, 5–9 in. long; leaflets 7–15,
length ¾–2 in., width ⅝–1¾ in., suborbicular, ovate or
oblong, ends rounded or broadly cuneate, apex mucronate,
petiolules ⅛–¼ in. long and bristly-hairy, thin, light green
to dark green, upper surface glabrous, lower surface glabrous or with occasional scattered hairs.

TWIGS. Young ones brown and densely reddish hispid; older
ones gray to brown, striate and glabrous. The amount of
hispidum varies considerably.

RANGE. Dry slopes, woods, and thickets. Oklahoma, eastward
to Georgia and Virginia. Mostly north of the Gulf Coast
plain. Often escaping from cultivation in more northern
areas.

REMARKS. The genus name, *Robinia*, honors Jean Robin
(1550–1629) and his son, Vespasian Robin (1579–1662), who
first cultivated the locust tree in Europe. The species name,

hispida, refers to the dense bristly hairs of foliage and inflorescence.

Eastern Coral Bean

Erythrina herbacea L. [A, B]

FIELD IDENTIFICATION. Usually a shrub with many slender, spreading stems from the base, or more rarely a tree to 25 ft, with a trunk diameter of 10 in.

FLOWERS. Borne April–June in narrow, leafless spikes 8–13 in. long; individual flowers on short, slender, glabrous or pubescent pedicels 1/25–1/2 in. long; bracts linear-lanceolate, variable in size, mostly about ⅛ in. long and 1/25 in. broad, bracteoles smaller; lower flowers fading as upper ones open; calyx campanulate, chartaceous, dark red, somewhat oblique, entire or shallowly lobed, glabrous to pubescent, about ¼ in. long; corolla scarlet, showy, tubular, closed, perfect; standard narrow-oblanceolate to elliptic, falcate, apex rounded, base cuneate-clawed, slightly smaller than the keel petals, 1⅜–2¼ in. long, 1/25–3/8 in. broad; wing petals slightly longer than the calyx and larger than the keel petals; keel petals acuminate at apex, clawed at base, ¼–½ in. long and about 1/12–1/5 in. wide; stamens

10 (9 together and 1 separate), 1 3/16–1 3/4 in. long; pistil 1–1¾ in. long; ovary pubescent, stipitate, 1-celled, style solitary and subulate, incurved, naked; stigmas small, terminal; ovules numerous.

FRUIT. Legume on stout peduncles about 1 in. long, subligneous, green to dark brown or black, linear, often falcate, slightly flattened, strongly constricted between the seeds, 2–4 in. long, apex stiff-apiculate, base stipitate and about ¾ in. long; valves 2, thin, widely dehiscent to expose 5–10 (rarely 1–2) beans which are scarlet, lustrous, hard, bony, about ¼ in. long, and persistent by the basal hilum to the valve; hilum oblong, dark, about ⅛ in. long.

LEAVES. Persistent below (inflorescences usually leafless), alternate or clustered at the nodes, 6–8 in. long, with a slender petiole and rachis occasionally armed with small, flattened, recurved prickles; leaves 3-foliate, leaflets thin, entire, deltoid to hastate; base concave, cuneate or truncate, 3-nerved; apex acuminate or acute; lateral lobes broad and rounded, much shorter than the elongate, terminal lobe; dull green to yellowish green, smooth and glabrous, 2¼–3½ in. long, 1 1/12–2 1/4 in. wide; petiolules slender, glabrous or pubescent, 1/25–1/3 in. long; stipels minute, glandlike.

STEMS. Slender, terete, green to reddish brown, smooth, finely grooved, commonly bearing scattered, stout, broad, recurved thorns; older bark whitened, thick, soft, furrows vertical; herbaceous and freezing down in northern areas, tending to be woody and perennial, or arborescent, in subtropical latitudes; roots often large, thick and tuberous.

RANGE. Eastern Coral Bean is usually found in sandy soils from Texas and Louisiana to Florida, northward to North Carolina, and south in Mexico in the states of Tamaulipas, Nuevo León, and San Luis Potosí. Eastern Coral Bean is replaced in southwestern New Mexico and Arizona by Western Coral Bean, *E. flabelliformis* Kearney.

REMARKS. The genus name, *Erythrina*, refers to the color of the flowers, and the species name, *herbacea*, to the herbaceous character of the plant in temperate regions. Also known under the vernacular English, Spanish, and Indian names of Cardinal Spear, Cherokee Bean, Red Cardinalflower, Colorín, Corolillo, Patol, Pitos, Chilicote, Zampantle, Zumpantle, Tzampantle, Tzan-pan-cuohuitl, Cozquelite, Purenchegua, Pureque, Tzinacanquahuitl, Chijol, Chocolin, Pichoco, Jiquimite, Iguimite, Peonia, Chotza, Demthy, and Macayxtli.

Various species of *Erythrina* are planted in Mexico for ornament, as hedges, or for coffee or cocoa shade. The bark is said to yield a yellow dye. The beans are strung into necklaces and used by the Mexican Indians in a game called "patol." The wood of *Erythrina* is used in Mexico for carvings of miniature statues, for corks and tobacco boxes.

Eastern Coral Bean seems to assume several forms in response to climatic influences. In northern latitudes it is usually herbaceous, freezing down each year but springing up from the roots. Along the Texas coast woody stems are developed which sometimes assume the proportions of trunks in the lower Rio Grande Valley. The herbaceous form and the arborescent form seem to be similar in all other respects, but some botanists have separated the two and given the arborescent form the name of *E. arborea* (Chapm.) Small or *E. herbacea* var. *arborea* Chapm.

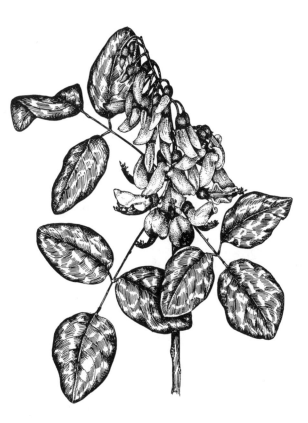

Cockspur Coral Bean

Erythrina crista-galli L. [A, B]

FIELD IDENTIFICATION. Cultivated prickly shrub, or small tree to 15 ft, with a trunk to 7 in. in diameter. The stout elongate branches form a rounded head.

FLOWERS. Borne in a large terminal panicle composed of many clusters of 1–7 flowers; pedicels ½–2 in. long, glabrous, green to reddish brown; calyx ⅜–½ in. long, reddish brown, somewhat flattened, shallowly 2-lipped, lower lip with an apiculate appendage, upper lip rounded or notched; corolla red, composed of a large standard petal and smaller wing and keel petals; standard free or nearly so, 1–2 in. long, conspicuous, erect, spreading or half-folded, oval to elliptic or obovate, apex rounded to acute; wing petals small, ¼–⅓ in. long, sometimes hidden by the calyx; keel petals 1–2 in. long, falcate, clawless, androecium included within the enveloping keels; stamens 10, exserted, 9 together and united nearly to the summit, one stamen solitary and shorter than the others; pistil slender, acuminate, falcate, flattened, reddish, barely exserted, slightly shorter than the 9 stamens, stigma minute, ovary short-stipitate.

FRUIT. Legume 3–10 in. long, cylindric; seeds varying from yellow to orange or red.

LEAVES. Alternate, 3-foliate, 6–12 in. long (including the petiole); leaflets 2–5½ in. long, blades elliptic to oval or ovate, margin entire, apex acute or obtuse, base rounded or broadly cuneate, blade often partly folded, surfaces dull green and glabrous; petioles slender, somewhat angular and finely grooved, often spiny, green to reddish brown; petiolules of terminal leaflet of 2 divisions; distal part down to the glandular stipules green, thickened, shorter than the proximal portion; petiolules of the lateral leaflets ¼–⅔ in. long, about the same length as the distal portion of the terminal petiolule.

TWIGS. Elongate, stout, usually unbranched, green to reddish brown, glabrous, angled and finely grooved; spines ¼–½ in. long, green to brown, stout, flat, straight or slightly curved, at the petiole bases or scattered.

BARK. Green on young branches, older ones tan to brown or gray with narrow fissures and rather wide flat ridges.

WOOD. Soft, light, used for corks or carvings.

RANGE. A native of Brazil, cultivated and occasionally escaping in the Gulf states. In coastal Texas and Louisiana, east to Florida.

REMARKS. The genus name, *Erythrina*, is the Greek name for red, referring to the flowers, and the species name, *crista-galli*, is the Latin for cockspur, referring to the spines of the plant. It is sometimes listed in the literature under the name of *Micropteryx crista-galli* (L.) Walp. Some of the vernacular names in use are Fireman's Cap, Common Coral-tree, Crybaby-tree, Dragon's Teeth, and Immortelle. The seeds are sometimes made into necklaces. The wood is carved into small objects. The flowers seem to vary considerably in shades of red and density of the racemes.

Rue Family (Rutaceae)

Trifoliate Orange

Citrus trifoliata L. [A, B, C]

FIELD IDENTIFICATION. Green, aromatic, spiny tree to 30 ft, with stiff, flattened branches.

FLOWERS. Borne on the bare branches of old wood in spring, axillary, subsessile, white, spreading, 1½–2 in. across, perfect; petals 5, flat, thin, oblong-obovate to spatulate, at first imbricate but later spreading, base clawed, much longer than the sepals; sepals ovate-elliptic; stamens 8–10 free; ovary pubescent, 6–8-celled, ovules in 2 rows; style stout and short.

FRUIT. Berry September–October, yellow, aromatic, densely downy, globose, 1½–2 in. across; pulp thin, acid, rather

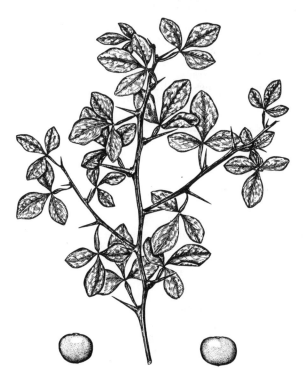

sour; seeds numerous, large, taking up the greater part of the berry, ¼–½ in. long, flattened, obovate, rounded at one end and acute at the other, white to brown, smooth, often ridged or grooved on one side.

LEAVES. Trifoliate, about 3½ in. long or less; petiole broadly winged, ⅓–1 in. long or less; leaflets 3, aromatic, elliptic, oblong, oval or obovate; margin crenate-toothed; apex obtuse, rounded or emarginate; base often cuneate or rounded (in lateral leaflets often asymmetrical); sessile or very short-petioled; terminal leaflet 1–2½ in. long, laterals usually smaller; olive green, glabrous, with pellucid dots above; lower surface paler, glabrous or puberulent along the veins.

TWIGS. Dark green, glabrous, divaricate, conspicuously flattened at the nodes to flare out into heavy, green, sharp, flattened spines ⅓–2¾ in. long.

BARK. Green or brown-streaked, smooth, often with thorns.

RANGE. Frequently planted for ornament and hedges from Texas to Florida, escaping cultivation in some areas. Hardy as far north as Washington, D.C. Native of China and Korea. Often planted for ornament in Japan.

REMARKS. The genus name, *Citrus*, is from the Greek and was given by Pliny the Elder (A.D. 23–79), a Roman naturalist. The species name, *trifoliata*, is for the trifoliate leaves. Some authors use the name of *Poncirus trifoliata* (L.) Raf. *Poncirus* is from the French word *poncire*, a kind of citrus. Some vernacular names are Bitter Orange and Limoncito. Oil from the fruit has a rancid flavor, and the pulp is aromatic.

Common Hop-tree

Ptelea trifoliata L. [A, B, C]

FIELD IDENTIFICATION. Usually a rounded shrub, but occasionally a small tree to 25 ft. Leaves divided into 3 leaflets which are very unpleasantly scented. This is an extremely variable species in both form and habit of growth, and in the size and shape of the leaflets. Numerous varieties, forms, and species have been segregated by various authors. The entire genus *Ptelea* should be revised.

FLOWERS. March–July, polygamous, in terminal cymes; flowers small, borne on slender pedicels ¼–1½ in. long; calyx-lobes 4–5, obtuse, pubescent; petals 4–5, greenish white, oblong, somewhat puberulent, exceeding the calyx-lobes; stamens 4–5, alternating with the petals, filaments hairy, anthers ovoid; pistillate flowers with a raised pistil and abortive anthers; style short, sometimes glandular-dotted, stigma 2–3-lobed, ovary puberulous.

Showing leaf variation
on the same plant

FRUIT. Ripening August–September, samaras borne in drooping clusters on slender reflexed pedicels; reticulate-veined, membranous, compressed, thin, waferlike, suborbicular or obovate, ¾–1 in. across, persistent in winter, unpleasantly scented, 2–3-celled; seeds 2–3, oblong-ovoid, acute, leathery, reddish brown, about ⅓ in. long.

LEAVES. Alternate or opposite, trifoliate; leaflets sessile or nearly so, entire or finely serrulate, ovate-oblong, acute or acuminate, wedge-shaped at base with lateral leaflets often oblique, more or less pubescent and glandular below (in *P. trifoliata* var. *mollis* densely woolly beneath), darker green and lustrous above, unpleasantly scented, 4–6 in. long, 2–4 in. wide; petiole stout, base swollen, pubescent.

TWIGS. Slender, green, yellowish or reddish brown, pubescent, unpleasantly scented when bruised.

BARK. Thin, smooth, light to dark gray or brown, numerous excrescences, bitter to the taste.

WOOD. Yellowish brown, close-grained, hard, heavy, weighing about 51 lb per cu ft.

ROOT. Taste bitter, pungent, slightly acid, aromatic.

RANGE. Common Hop-tree, with its many varieties and closely related species, is distributed over a rather wide territory, growing in various types of soil; Texas, Louisiana, Arkansas, Oklahoma, and New Mexico; eastward to Florida, westward into Arizona and California, northward into Colorado, Utah, Nebraska, Minnesota, Michigan, Illinois, and continuing on east to Ontario, New York and Quebec.

REMARKS. The genus name, *Ptelea*, is the classical name for the elm. The species name, *trifoliata*, refers to the three leaflets. Vernacular names are Three-leaf Hop-tree, Shrubby-trefoil, Swamp Dogwood, Wafer-ash, Skunk-bush, Potatochip-tree, Quinine-tree, Ague-bark, Pickaway-anise, Prairie-grub, Cola de Zorillo, and Wingseed. All parts of the plant emit a disagreeable odor. The fruit was once used as a substitute for hops in beer brewing.

Hercules-club

Zanthoxylum clava-herculis L. [A, B, C]

FIELD IDENTIFICATION. Small tree with a broad, rounded crown, easily recognized by the corky-based prickles on the trunk and branches.

FLOWERS. Dioecious, greenish white, in large terminal cymes; petals 4–5, oblong-ovate, obtuse, ⅛–¼ in. long, stamens 4–5, filaments slender and exserted, longer than the petals; pistils 2–3, styles short, with a 2-lobed stigma; calyx of 4–5 ovate or ovate-lanceolate, obtuse sepals.

FRUIT. Follicles 2–5 together, globose-obovoid, brownish, rough, pitted, apiculate, 1/6–1/4 in. long, 2-valved; seed solitary, wrinkled, black, shining, persistent outside of follicle after dehiscence.

LEAVES. Alternate, 5–15 in. long, odd-pinnately compound of 5–19 leaflets, ½–4½ in. long, subsessile, sometimes falcate, ovate or ovate-lanceolate, acute or acuminate at apex, somewhat oblique and cuneate at base, crenate-serrulate, leathery, glabrous, lustrous above and more or less hairy below, spicy and dotted with pellucid glands, bitter-aromatic, stinging the mouth when chewed; petioles somewhat spiny, stout, hairy or glabrous.

TWIGS. Brown to gray, stout, hairy at first, glabrous later, often somewhat glandular, spinescent.

WOOD. Light brown or yellow, light, soft, close-grained, weighing 31 lb per cu ft.

BARK. Light gray, thin, covered with conspicuous, conelike corky tubercles.

RANGE. Texas, Louisiana, Oklahoma, and Arkansas; eastward to Florida and northward to Virginia.

REMARKS. The genus name, *Zanthoxylum*, comes from an erroneous rendering of the Greek word *xanthos* ("yellow") plus *xylon* ("wood"); the species name, *clava-herculis*, means "club of Hercules" and refers to the trunk's thorny character. Vernacular names are Toothache, Sea Ash, Pepperwood, Prickly Yellowwood, Yellow Prickly-ash, Tongue-bush, Rabbit Gum, Wild Orange, Sting Tongue, Tear Blanket, Pillenterry, and Wait-a-bit. A number of species of birds eat the fruit.

Texas Hercules-club

Zanthoxylum hirsutum Buckl. [B]

FIELD IDENTIFICATION. Thorny shrub 3–15 ft, aromatic in all parts.

FLOWERS. Borne in early spring, dioecious, in cymes ⅓–2 in. long, 1–1½ in. wide; pedicels 1/12–1/8 in. long; sepals 5, minute, linear to subulate, acute; petals 5, greenish, elliptic, concave, about 1/12 in. long; stamens 5, exserted on filiform filaments about as long as the petals or shorter, but shorter than the anthers, wanting or rudimentary in the pistillate flowers; pistils 2–3, ovary sessile, style short, stigma entire or slightly 2-lobed.

FRUIT. Capsule borne in clusters ⅓–2 in. long on red, pubescent pedicels ¼–½ in., body of fruit subglobose, asymmetrical, glandular-dotted, apiculate, green at first, reddish brown later, about ¼ in. long, splitting into valves; seed black, shiny, obliquely ovoid, persistent to one valve.

LEAVES. Odd-pinnately compound, 1½–2½ in. long (more rarely to 4 in.); rachis red, pubescent, bearing reddish brown, straight, sharp thorns to ¼ in. long; leaflets 3–7 (usually 5), ½–1½ in. long, elliptic to oblong or oval, leathery, aromatic, glandular-dotted especially on the margin, crinkled, crenate, apex obtuse, base cuneate, lustrous above, dull beneath; lateral leaflets short-petioluled or sessile, the petiolule of the terminal leaflet longer.

TWIGS. Young ones greenish, pubescent; older ones gray and armed with stout, straight, gray or brown spines to ½ in. long.

BARK. Smooth, mottled light to dark gray; spines straight, or

slightly curved, to 1 in. long, not built up on conspicuous corky bases as in Z. *clava-herculis*.

RANGE. On sandy or gravelly soil of central west Texas. Sandy areas south of San Antonio, also between Utopia and Tarpley. Reported from Arkansas.

REMARKS. The genus name, *Zanthoxylum*, comes from an erroneous rendering of the Greek word *xanthos* ("yellow"), plus *xylon* ("wood"). The species name, *hirsutum*, refers to the hirsute twigs and leaves. It has also been listed under the names of Z. *carolinianum* var. *fruticosum* Gray and Z. *clava-herculis* L. var. *fruticosum* Gray.

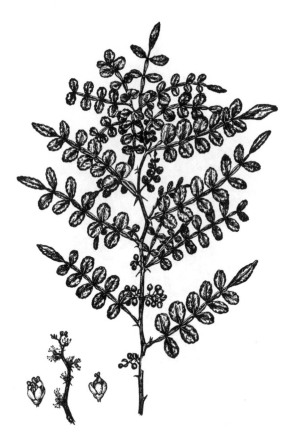

Lime Prickly-ash

Zanthoxylum fagara (L.) Sarg. [B]

FIELD IDENTIFICATION. Aromatic, thorny, evergreen shrub, or a tree to 30 ft, with a diameter of 10 in. The trunk is usually inclined, and the crown rounded or spreading with intricate branches.

FLOWERS. Borne mostly March–June on branchlets of the previous year, generally appearing after the leaves; staminate and pistillate on different trees; cymes axillary, small, cylindrical; bracts minute, ovate, obtuse, deciduous; flowers on short pedicels, small, hypogynous; sepals 4, membranous, yellowish green, triangular to ovate, acute, shorter than the petals; petals 4, yellowish green, oblong to ovate, concave, 1/12–1/8 in. long, about twice as long as the sepals; stamens 4, alternate with the petals, filaments slender and exserted; pistils 2 (rudimentary in staminate flower), style slender, stigmas capitate and obliquely spreading.

FRUIT. Ripening in September, follicle globose or obovoid, ⅛–¼ in. long, rusty brown, pitted, warty, rugose, thin-walled, splitting at maturity; seed persistently attached to the follicle lip, solitary, subglobose, black, smooth, shiny, hilum rather conspicuous, cotyledons oval and foliaceous.

LEAVES. Alternate, evergreen, odd-pinnately compound, 3–4 in. long, with 5–13 leaflets (usually 7–9) on a broadly winged rachis; leaflets opposite, ⅓–1¼ in. long, sessile or nearly so, oval to obovate, apex rounded or notched, base cuneate or rounded, margin bluntly crenulate-toothed mostly above the middle, slightly revolute, coriaceous, young leaves often bronze-green; older with upper surface bright green, shiny and glandular-punctate, lower surface somewhat paler, aromatic and bitter to taste because of pellucid glands; petiole winged and jointed.

TWIGS. Numerous, zigzag, slender, smooth, gray to brown, glabrous to puberulent, set with hooked stipular spines; buds minute, globular, dark brown, woolly; leaf scars deltoid, vascular bundles with 3 scars, pith white and not interrupted.

BARK. Gray, thin, smooth or with warty excrescences; older trunks with small, thin, appressed scales, aromatic.

WOOD. Reddish brown, sapwood yellowish, compact, hard, heavy, close-grained, specific gravity about 0.74.

RANGE. Southern Florida and southwestern and coastal Texas. Extending eastward along the Texas coast to Harris and Galveston counties. Abundant in the Texas lower Rio Grande Valley area. In Mexico in the states of Tamaulipas, Sonora, Veracruz, Yucatán, Chiapas, and Baja California.

REMARKS. The genus name, *Zanthoxylum*, comes from an erroneous rendering of the Greek word *xanthos* ("yellow"), plus *xylon* ("wood"). The species name, *fagara*, is the old generic name. Vernacular names in use in various countries are Colima, Limoncillo, Uña de Gato, Palo Mulato, Espino, Espino Rubial, Corriosa, Tomeguín, Xic-ché, and Wild Lime. It is generally known as "Colima" to the Mexican people of the Rio Grande Valley area. The plant has long been used medicinally in the Latin American countries. Various extracts of the bark and leaves are taken as a sudorific and nerve tonic. The powdered bark and leaves are used as a condiment and are also said to produce a yellow dye.

Quassia Family (Simarubaceae)

Tree-of-heaven

Ailanthus altissima (Mill.) Swingle [A, B, C]

FIELD IDENTIFICATION. Cultivated tree attaining a height of
100 ft, and a diameter of 3 ft. Handsome and rapid growing
with a symmetrical open head and stout branches.

FLOWERS. April–May, borne in clusters of 1–5 in large, loose,
terminal panicles 6–12 in.; pedicels subtended by small
bracts or none; staminate and pistillate panicles on different
plants or polygamous; flowers small, 1/5–1/3 in. across,
yellowish green; staminate flowers unpleasantly scented;
calyx regular, sepals 5, valvate in the bud, oval to oblong,
spreading, 1/8–1/6 in. long, villous near the base, inserted at
the base of the small 10-lobed disk; stamens 10 (in perfect
flowers), staminate flowers with or without a rudimentary
pistil; pistillate flowers smaller than staminate with 2 or 3
imperfect stamens or none; ovary deeply 2–5-cleft, the lobes
flat and cuneate, ovules solitary in each cavity.

FRUIT. September–October, in persistent clusters of 1–5,
samara linear-elliptic; ½–1½ in. long; flattened, thin, membranous, veiny, dry, twisted at the apex, sometimes curved,
notched on one side, brownish red, the single flattened seed
in the center, albumen thin.

LEAVES. Alternate, deciduous, odd-pinnately compound,
length 8 in.–2½ ft, rachis pubescent or glabrous, unpleasantly odorous when bruised; leaflets 11–41; petiolules ⅛–⅓
in., pubescent or glabrous, leaflets ovate to oblong or lanceolate, sometimes asymmetrical, apex acute or acuminate, base
cordate or truncate and often oblique, margin entire except
for 2–4 coarse, glandular teeth at the base, length 2–5 in.,
upper surface dull dark green, glabrous or slightly hairy,
lower surface paler and glabrous or with a few hairs on the
veins; petiole swollen at base.

TWIGS. Coarse, blunt, yellowish orange or brown, younger
ones pubescent, older ones glabrous, leaf scars large and
conspicuous, pith reddish.

BARK. Pale grayish brown, fissures shallow.

WOOD. Pale yellowish brown, medium hard, not durable,
weak, coarse, open-grained, said to make fairly good fuel,
and sometimes used in cabinet work.

RANGE. A native of China, cultivated for ornament in the
United States and sometimes escaping cultivation in our
area. Very hardy, seemingly growing well under adverse
conditions of dust, smoke, and poor soil. Often found in
waste places, trash heaps, vacant lots, cracks of pavement,
crowded against buildings, and other situations. Does best

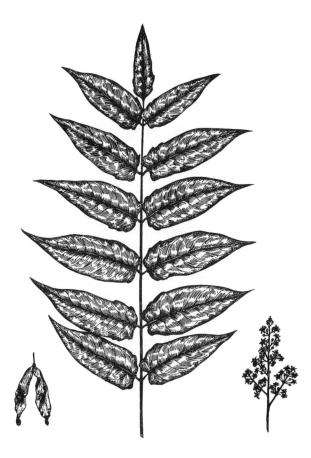

on light, moist soils. In Texas, New Mexico, Oklahoma, Arkansas, and Louisiana; east to Florida and north to Massachusetts. Also cultivated westward throughout the interior to the Pacific coast.

REMARKS. The genus name, *Ailanthus*, is from a Chinese name, *Ailanto*, meaning "tree-of-heaven" and referring to its height. The species name, *altissima*, means "very tall." Vernacular names for the tree are Copal, Tree-of-the-Gods, Chinese Sumac, Heavenward-tree, False Varnish-tree, and Devil's Walkingstick.

The tree was introduced into the United States from China by William Hamilton in 1784. It is a very rapid grower, spreads freely from suckers and by seed, is rather free of insects, but is easily storm damaged. It was once used in erosion control work in the dune areas of the Black Sea and was planted for timber in New Zealand. The seeds are known to be eaten by a number of birds, including the pine grosbeak and crossbill, and occasionally browsed by white-tailed deer. The tree is sometimes planted in China as host to a species of silkworm, *Attacus cynthia*, which produces a coarse inferior silk.

Mahogany Family (Meliaceae)

China-berry

Melia azedarach L. [A, B, C]

FIELD IDENTIFICATION. Tree to 45 ft; rounded crown; twice-compound leaves sometimes 2 ft long.

FLOWERS. March–May, panicles 4–6 in., loose, open, fragrant, showy, individual flowers about ½ in. across; sepals 5–6, lobes acute; petals 5–6, purplish, oblanceolate to narrow-oblong, obtuse; staminal tube with 10–12 stamens and sagittate anthers; ovary 5-celled, style elongate, stigma 3–6-lobed.

FRUIT. Ripening September–October, persistent, drupe ½–¾ in. in diameter, subglobose, coriaceous, fleshy, translucent, smooth, yellow, indehiscent, borne in conspicuous drooping clusters; stone ridged, seeds 3–5, smooth, black, ellipsoid, asymmetrical, acute or obtuse at ends, dispersed by birds or mammals.

LEAVES. Large, alternate, deciduous, twice-compound, to 25 in., long-petioled; leaflets numerous, ovate-elliptic, serrate or lobed, some entire, acute at apex, 1¼–2 in. long, mostly glabrous.

WOOD. Color variegated, durable, somewhat brittle.

RANGE. A native of Asia, introduced into the United States as an ornamental, and escaping to grow wild over a wide area. Texas; east to Florida, and north to Oklahoma, Arkansas, and North Carolina.

REMARKS. The genus name, *Melia*, is an old Greek name. The species name, *azedarach*, is from a Persian word meaning "noble-tree." Vernacular names are China-tree, Bead-tree, Indian-lilac, and Pride-of-India. The fruit is eaten by birds and swine, but if fermented it sometimes has a toxic effect. The fruit pulp is also used as an insect repellent and vermifuge. In some countries the hard seeds are made into rosaries. The wood was formerly used in cabinet work. China-berry grows rapidly, is rather free of insects, but cannot stand excessive droughts or much cold below zero. It is desirable as a shade tree and was formerly much planted in the South. The northern limit of hardiness is probably

Virginia. Besides the species, there occurs an umbrella-shaped variety known as the Texas Umbrella China-berry, *M. azedarach* forma *umbraculiformis* Berckm., which was reported to be found by botanists originally near San Jacinto Battlefield, Houston, Texas.

Euphorbia Family (Euphorbiaceae)

Tung-oil-tree

Aleurites fordii Hemsl. [A]

FIELD IDENTIFICATION. Tree introduced into cultivation in the Gulf states, attaining a height of 30 ft, with a rounded top and stout branches.

FLOWERS. Borne in spring, monoecious, in large conspicuous, terminal cymes; pedicels ½–5 in. long; petals 5, oblong to oblanceolate, sometimes orbicular-ovate, white, streaked with red at the base, apex rounded or more rarely truncate, length ¾–1½ in., width about ½ in.; sepals 2–3, valvate, reddish, about ¼ in. long, ovate to rounded; stamens 8–10, red, the inner row monadelphous; anthers attached terminally, splitting into 2 segments; ovary 4-celled, 1 ovule in each cell.

FRUIT. Drupe ripe in September, 1¼–3 in. in diameter, large, subglobose, smooth, seeds thick-shelled, oily, poisonous.

LEAVES. Alternate, large, ovate-cordate, margin entire or 3–5-lobed, apex acute or acuminate, base rounded or semi-

cordate, palmately-veined, upper surface dull green with fine brown hairs, lower surface paler, veins heavy, sparingly hairy or glabrous; petiole long, stout, somewhat flattened, glabrous or puberulent; 2 red, lustrous glands at the petiole apex.

BARK. Light to dark gray, smooth.

TWIGS. Stout, glabrous, dark gray to brown, somewhat swollen at the nodes and terminally; leaf scars semiorbicular or oblong, lenticels numerous.

RANGE. On dry, thin soil; drought resistant. A native of Central Asia. Grown for its oily nut in east Texas, Louisiana, Mississippi, Alabama, and Florida.

REMARKS. The genus name, *Aleurites*, is from the Greek and means "farinose" or "floury." The species name, *fordii*, is in honor of C. Ford, former superintendent of the Hongkong Botanic Garden. It is also known as China Wood-oil-tree and Candlenut-tree. This species is more hardy than other plants of the genus *Aleurites* in the Gulf Coast states area. Oil from the fruit is valuable as an ingredient of paint, varnish, soap, linoleums, etc. In Asia the oil is used as a fuel and for treating woodenware and cloth. The oil is pressed from the seeds after roasting.

Common Poinsettia

Poinsettia pulcherrima Graham [A, B, C]

FIELD IDENTIFICATION. Cultivated shrub or small tree to 24 ft, with many long stems from the base or trunk solitary. Very handsome with its brilliant red leaflike bracts in a crown below the small flowers.

FLOWERS. Unisexual, inflorescence cymose and inconspicuous, greenish yellow to reddish; involucre cuplike, 4–5-lobed, bearing a large fleshy yellow gland; 1 stamen in the staminate flower; perianth absent.

FRUIT. An exserted capsule with 3 rounded lobes, seed narrowed forward.

LEAVES. Simple, alternate, ovate-elliptic to lanceolate or panduriform, margin entire or sinuate-toothed or lobed, blade length 3–6 in., essentially glabrous at maturity; upper leaves narrower and more entire and graduating into brilliant red leaflike bracts below the flowers; stipules minute; petioles long.

STEMS. Solitary, or often many from the base, elongate, often arching, green to tan or brown.

RANGE. A native of tropical America, occurring in Mexico in Jalisco, Veracruz, and Oaxaca. Introduced in the United States and grown for ornament. Subject to freezes in the

Gulf states, but sometimes persisting in protected places. Grown as a pot plant in the North.

REMARKS. The genus name, *Poinsettia*, is in honor of Joel R. Poinsett (1779–1851), botanist of South Carolina. The species name, *pulcherrima*, refers to the beautiful bracts. This plant is known under many vernacular names in tropical America where it is native, including Flor de Fuego, Flor de Pascua, Flor de Santa Catarina, Santa Catarina, Catalina, Pano Holandés, Bandera, Bebeta, Pastora, Pastores, Pascuas, Flor de Nochebuena, and Cuitlaxochita. The stems yield a milky juice which is said to have been used by the Indians to remove hair from the skin. The bark yields a red coloring principle and the bracts a scarlet dye.

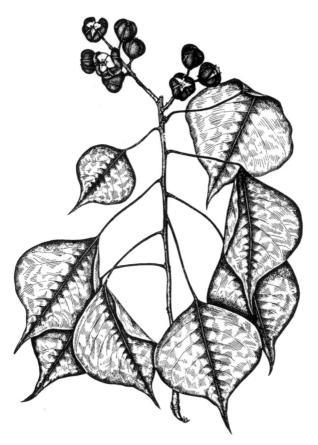

Chinese Tallow-tree

Sapium sebiferum (L.) Roxb. [A, B, C]

FIELD IDENTIFICATION. Small cultivated tree with a rounded crown, attaining a height of 30 ft.

FLOWERS. Male and female together on a yellowish green terminal spike, the pistillate below the staminate; calyx of staminate flowers 2–3-lobed, the lobes imbricate; petals absent; stamens 2–3, filaments free, anthers opening lengthwise; pistillate calyx of 2–3 sepals; ovary 1–3-celled, styles 2–3.

FRUIT. Capsule 3-lobed, lobes rounded externally and flattened against each other, ⅓–½ in. in diameter, dehiscent by the valves of the capsule falling away to expose the 3 white seeds; seed solitary, crustaceous.

LEAVES. Alternate, or rarely opposite, entire, rhombic-ovate, abruptly long-acuminate, base broadly cuneate, 1–3½ in. long, 1–3 in. broad, widest across the middle, deep green and glabrous above, paler below, turning deep red in winter; petiole slender, usually shorter than the blade, 2 glands at the apex.

TWIGS. Young twigs slender and green, older grayish brown and marked with numerous small lenticels.

BARK. Brownish gray, broken into appressed ridges, fissures shallow.

RANGE. Cultivated for ornament and sometimes escaping. Texas, Oklahoma, Arkansas, and Louisiana; eastward to Florida, along the Atlantic coast to South Carolina. A native of China.

REMARKS. The genus name, *Sapium*, was given by Pliny to a resinous pine, and the species name, *sebiferum*, refers to the vegetable tallow, or wax, of the fruit. Another vernacular name is Vegetable Tallow-tree. The milky sap is poisonous, but the tree is cultivated in China for the wax of the seed covering which is used for soap, candles, and cloth-dressing. The wax was formerly imported into the United States, but mineral waxes have almost entirely taken its place. The tree is easily propagated by seeds and cuttings and is attractive with white seeds and red leaves in the fall.

Cassava

Manihot carthaginensis (Jacq.) Muell. [A, B]

FIELD IDENTIFICATION. Large shrub or small tree to 25 ft, and 6 in. in diameter, with irregular branches forming a rounded crown; rhizomes fleshy.

FLOWERS. Axillary, solitary, or a few in short clusters; pedicels ⅓–¾ in. long; staminate and pistillate flowers borne separately; petals absent; calyx 5-parted, green with two reddish blotches on each sepal within, about ¾ in. across at anthesis; staminate with the sepals united about halfway to the base, stamens 10, slightly shorter than the sepals, the filiform filaments arising from between the lobes of a basal orange-colored disk; pistillate flowers with the 5 oblong-ovate sepals free to the base or nearly so; ovary dark green, sub-globose, smooth, immersed in a thick entire orange-colored disk; ovules 1 in each of the 3 cells; stigmas sessile, yellowish green, 3-lobed, rounded and fimbriate on margin.

FRUIT. Capsule subglobose, or slightly 3-lobed, ½–¾ in. long, pale green, smooth, glabrous, 3-celled, seeds somewhat flattened, ends obtuse or rounded, ⅜–½ in. long; peduncles stout, ½–2½ in. long, glabrous, apex with a persistent orange disk.

LEAVES. Alternate, palmately parted into 6–9 segments (rarely, more or fewer), each segment 3–8 in. long, oblanceolate,

lanceolate or narrowly elliptic, margin entire or sinuate-wavy, apex acute or acuminate, sometimes abruptly so, base gradually narrowed, upper surface dark green, glabrous and semilustrous, lower surface much paler and glabrous, venation yellowish and delicate; petiole glabrous, light green, shorter or longer than the leaf segments.

TWIGS. Young ones slender, smooth, glabrous, pale green, rather fleshy; older ones brownish and much more woody.

BARK. On trunk rather smooth, light to dark brown, marked with numerous horizontal, pale, linear to oblong lenticels.

RANGE. Cultivated in increasing amount the last few years along the Gulf Coast from Texas and Louisiana eastward to Florida. Sometimes escaping cultivation about old gardens. Also grown in southern New Mexico, Arizona, and California. A native of Venezuela, Colombia, and Brazil; also countries of Central America.

REMARKS. The genus name, *Manihot*, is the native Brazilian name. It is also known under the names of Yuguilla, Yuca de Monte, Xcache, and Cuadrado. The tree is a desirable ornamental because of the attractive segmented leaves. The seeds have emetic and purgative properties. The fleshy rhizomes are sometimes used as cassava, a starch derived after the poisonous acid is removed. However, most commercial cassava, from which tapioca is obtained, comes from the rhizomes of the closely related *M. utilissima*.

Sumac Family (Anacardiaceae)

Flame-leaf Sumac

Rhus copallina L. [A, B, C]

FIELD IDENTIFICATION. Slender-branched shrub or small tree to 25 ft.

FLOWERS. Polygamo-dioecious, about ⅛ in. across, borne in a densely pubescent, terminal thyrse about 4¾ in. long and 4 in. broad; pedicels about 1/12 in. long, pubescent; bracts very small, lanceolate, about 1/12 in. long; sepals 5, deltoid, pubescent, glandular-ciliate, 1/12–1/8 in. long, about 1/25 in. broad; stamens 5, anthers lanceolate; pistil 1, sessile, ovary pubescent, stigmas 3, styles 3; disk annular. Petals greenish white, 1/12–1/10 in. long, 1/25 in. broad, glabrous externally, a few hairs on the inner side, margin ciliate and glandular, deciduous.

FRUIT. In compact panicles, erect or drooping, persistent; drupe subglobose, flattened, red, glandular-hairy, 1/6–1/8 in. in diameter; seeds solitary, smooth.

LEAVES. Deciduous, alternate, pinnate, 5–12 in. long, rachis pubescent, broadly winged; leaflets 7–17, subsessile, inequilateral, elliptic or ovate to lanceolate, acute or acuminate at the apex, asymmetrical and obtuse, or rounded to subcuneate at the base, entire or few-toothed, lustrous, glabrous to pubescent above, hairy and glandular beneath; lateral leaflets sessile, 1–3½ in. long, ½–1¼ in. broad, terminal leaflet petiolulate or sessile.

TWIGS. Green to reddish brown, pubescent at first, glabrous later; lenticels dark.

BARK. Thick, greenish brown, excrescences circular, scales thin.

WOOD. Light brown to greenish, coarse-grained, soft, weighing 32 lb per cu ft, sometimes used for small posts.

RANGE. Moist soil in shade or sun. Texas, Oklahoma, Arkansas, and Louisiana; eastward to Georgia, northward to New Hampshire, and west to Michigan and Missouri.

REMARKS. The genus name, *Rhus*, is the ancient Latin name, and the species name, *copallina*, means "copal gum." Vernacular names for this plant are Mountain Sumac, Smooth Sumac, Black Sumac, Shining Sumac, Dwarf Sumac, Upland Sumac, and Winged Sumac.

The bark and leaves contain tannin and are used in the tanning industry. The crushed acrid fruit of this and other species was added to drinking water by the Indians to make it more palatable.

According to stomach records, the fruit has been eaten by at least 20 species of birds, and white-tailed deer occasional-

ly browse it. It is propagated by seed. It is conspicuous in fall because of the brilliant red leaves.

Flame-leaf Sumac is generally replaced in central Texas by the Prairie Flame-leaf Sumac, *R. copallina* L. var. *lanceo-*

lata Gray, which has narrower and more falcate leaves, larger clusters of fruit, and a more treelike rounded form. It is thought that the two may hybridize in their overlapping areas.

White Flame-leaf Sumac, *R. copallina* var. *leucantha* (Jacq.) DC., is a variety with white flowers found near New Braunfels, Texas.

A variety with 5–13 broader oblong to narrow-ovate leaflets has been described from Oklahoma, Texas, Arkansas, and Louisiana as *R. copallina* L. var. *latifolia* Engl., but other authors have relegated it to the status of a synonym of the species.

Staghorn Sumac

Rhus typhina Torner [A]

FIELD IDENTIFICATION. An irregularly branched, stout shrub with a rounded or flat-topped head, forming thickets by root suckers. The upright contorted branches are conspicuously velvety-hairy. Sometimes in favorable locations becoming a tree with a short, inclined trunk, a height to 40 ft, and a diameter of 3–14 in.

FLOWERS. Usually June–July, but opening gradually. Borne in dense, dioecious, terminal, greenish yellow panicles. Staminate panicles longest, usually maturing before the pistillate, and 7–12 in. long and 4–6 in. broad; panicles with acuminate bracts ½–2 in. long and early deciduous; individual flower pedicels slender with bracts 1/25–1/12 in. long, acute, hairy; petals 5, imbricated in the bud, inserted under the edge of the red, flattened disk, 1/12–1/8 in. long, linear to elliptic or oblanceolate, finally reflexed in the staminate flower, in the pistillate flower remaining erect and slightly hooded at the apex; calyx small, sepals 5, 1/25–1/12 in. long, deltoid to lanceolate, acuminate or acute, hairy beneath, ciliate; stamens 5, exserted in the staminate flowers, abortive in the pistillate flowers, filaments slender with large, orange-colored anthers 1/25–1/12 in. long; pistil ovoid, hairy; styles 3, with 3 short, fleshy capitate stigmas.

FRUIT. Ripening June–September, persistent during the winter, in dense, terminal, conical panicles 6–8 in. long and 2–4 in. wide; drupes 1/6–1/8 in. long and broad, depressed-globose, clothed with long, velvety, crimson hairs; flesh thin and dry, acrid to the taste; seed green to pale brown, somewhat oblique, slightly flattened, smooth, bony, no albumen.

LEAVES. Alternate, deciduous, odd-pinnately compound, 5–24 in. long; rachis green to reddish, with soft velvety hairs, segments ¼–⅝ in. long; petiole stout, 2¼–4 in. long, hairy, enlarged at base; leaflets 9–31, opposite or subopposite, middle pairs largest, laterals sessile or nearly so, terminal long-petiolulate, elliptic to lanceolate or ovate, sometimes

falcate, apex acute or acuminate, base rounded or semi-cordate and slightly unequal, margin remotely serrate and subrevolute (lanciniate in some varieties), length 1½–6 in., width ⅓–1¾ in., thin, veins conspicuous, upper surface light to dark green and dull to semilustrous with a few hairs or glabrous, lower surface whitish, and hairy on the veins, in fall turning brilliant shades of red, yellow, and orange.

TWIGS. Stout, brittle, brown to orange; younger with soft, brown to black, long, velvety hairs; older twigs glabrous; lenticels numerous, conspicuous, orange-brown; buds tan, conic, brown-hairy; leaf scars horseshoe-shaped, bundle scars in clusters of 3; pith round, orange-brown; sap sticky, milky, turning black on exposure.

BARK. Dark brown to gray, on young trees smooth, on older ones dark brown and separating into small squarish scales; lenticels elongate and horizontal, bark rich in tannin.

WOOD. Orange to yellow, streaked with green or brown, sap-wood whitish, light, brittle, soft, coarse-grained, weighing 27 lb per cu ft.

RANGE. Roadsides, thickets, old fields, hillsides, and dry or gravelly slopes, to 2,000 feet. Not definitely known in a wild state in our area, but cultivated in Louisiana. Native from Mississippi eastward to Florida, abundant northward through the Appalachian Mountains and throughout the eastern states to Quebec, westward to Ontario, Minnesota, and Iowa.

REMARKS. The genus name, *Rhus*, is the ancient Greek and Latin name of Sicilian Sumac, *R. coriaria* L. The species name, *typhina*, refers to the hairy cattail-like twigs. Vernacular names are Hairy Sumac, Velvet Sumac, American Sumac, Virginia Sumac, and Vinegar-tree. The name Staghorn Sumac refers to the forked velvety twigs, which resemble a stag's young antlers. The wood is rarely used for cabinets or for small articles. The young hollow stems were formerly used for maple sap taps. In frontier times ink was made by boiling the leaves. The root, bark, and leaves are rich in tannin. The crushed acid fruits, steeped in water, make a cooling drink which was much used by the Indians. The seeds are known to be eaten by 94 species of birds, including mourning dove, bobwhite quail, ringnecked pheasant, and ruffed grouse; also by skunk, white-tailed deer, cottontail, moose, and opossum. The plant often reproduces by root suckers and hence is resistant to grazing. It is sometimes planted for erosion control and for ornament and has been cultivated since 1629.

Smooth Sumac

Rhus glabra L. [A, B, C]

FIELD IDENTIFICATION. Thicket-forming shrub or small tree attaining a height of 20 ft. Leaves pinnate, bearing 11–31 elliptic or lanceolate, sharply serrate leaflets.

FLOWERS. June–August, in a terminal thyrse, 5–9 in. long; bracts narrowly lanceolate, about 1/25 in. long; calyx of 5 lanceolate sepals, each about 1/12 in. long; petals 5, white, spreading, lanceolate, 1/6 in. long or less; stamens 5; pistil 1, ovary 1-seeded, stigmas 3.

FRUIT. Ripening September–October, drupe subglobose, about 1/6 in. long, covered with short, red-velvety hairs; 1-seeded, stone smooth, seed dispersed by birds and mammals.

LEAVES. Alternate, pinnately compound, 11–31 leaflets which are elliptic, lanceolate, oblong or ovate, acuminate at the apex; rounded, subcordate, cuneate or oblique at the base, sharply serrate, usually dark green above, lighter to conspicuously white beneath; lateral ones sessile or almost so, 2½–4¾ in. long, ½–1¼ in. broad; terminal one sessile or petiolulate, 2–3¾ in. long, ½–1½ in. broad.

WOOD. Orange, soft, brittle.

RANGE. In moist, rich soil. Texas, New Mexico, Oklahoma,

Arkansas, and Louisiana; eastward to Florida, northward to Quebec, and westward to British Columbia, Washington, Oregon, Utah, Colorado, and Missouri.

REMARKS. The genus name, *Rhus*, is the ancient Latin name, and the species name, *glabra*, refers to the plant's smoothness. Vernacular names are Scarlet Sumac, Red Sumac, White Sumac, Shoe-make, Vinegar-tree, Senhalanac, Pennsylvania Sumac, Upland Sumac, and Sleek Sumac. The leaves are reported to have been mixed with tobacco and smoked. The twigs, leaves, and roots contain tannin and were used for staining and dyeing. Smooth Sumac is now used extensively for ornament. Its red clusters of fruit and long graceful leaves which turn brilliant colors in the autumn are its attractive features. It should be more extensively cultivated for ornament. Records show that the date of earliest cultivation was 1620. It is occasionally planted for erosion control and used for shelter-belt planting in the prairie states. Thirty-two species of birds are known to feed on it. Wild turkey, bobwhite, cottontail, and white-tailed deer eat it eagerly.

Poison Sumac

Toxicodendron vernix (L.) Kuntze [A]

FIELD IDENTIFICATION. Poisonous shrub or small tree to 25 ft, with pinnate leaves bearing 7–13 obovate, oblong-ovate, or oval leaflets.

FLOWERS. Polygamous, borne in axillary panicles 3–8 in. long; bracts lanceolate, 1/25 in. long or less; sepals 5, acute, about 1/25 in. long; petals 5, green, linear to oblanceolate, 1/12–1/8 in. long; stamens 5, filaments 1/25–1/12 in. long, anthers orange; styles short, stigmas 3, ovary glabrous.

FRUIT. Drupe subglobose, flattened, greenish white or gray, glabrous, 1/16–1/4 in. broad; seed flattened, striate, bony.

LEAVES. Alternate, deciduous, pinnate, 5–15 in. long; leaflets 7–13, obovate, oblong-ovate or oval, apex short-acuminate, base cuneate or rounded, entire, smooth and shining above, more or less pubescent beneath, 2½–4 in. long, 1–2 in. wide; lateral leaflets with short petiolules; petiolule of terminal leaflet longer; petioles stout and reddish.

TWIGS. Brown to orange, stout, glabrous, lenticels small and numerous.

WOOD. Yellowish brown, soft, tough, coarse-grained, weighing 27 lb per cu ft.

BARK. Gray to brown, thin, smooth, lenticels horizontal.

RANGE. In eastern Texas and Louisiana; eastward to Florida and northward to Minnesota, Ontario, New York, and Rhode Island.

REMARKS. The genus name, *Toxicodendron*, is from the ancient Greek and means "poison tree." The species name, *vernix*, means "varnish," erroneously referring to the Japanese Lacquer-tree. All parts of the plant are poisonous and produce an intense skin irritation known as "Rhus dermatitis." The tincture of *Rhus*, or *Toxicodendron*, has been used by homeopathic practitioners in the treatment of subacute and chronic rheumatism. However, beneficial results of such treatment are in doubt. It is considered to be even more poisonous than Poison-ivy and Poison-oak. Vernacular names for the plant are Poison Elder, Poison Dogwood, Swamp Sumac, Poison-wood, and Poison-tree. It was formerly listed under the scientific name of *Rhus vernix* L., but it is sufficiently different to be placed in the genus *Toxicodendron*. The sap is used to make a high-grade varnish, and concoctions of the leaves have been used medicinally by the Indians. Fifteen species of birds and the cottontail feed upon it. Poison-ivy and Poison-oak are close kin to Poison Sumac, but they are vines or low shrubs and have only 3 coarsely toothed leaflets instead of 7–13 entire leaflets.

Titi Family (Cyrillaceae)

American Cyrilla

Cyrilla racemiflora L. [A, C]

FIELD IDENTIFICATION. Swamp-loving shrub or small tree to 30 ft, with a short trunk and spreading irregular branches.

FLOWERS. In spring, racemes axillary, slender, erect or nodding, 4–6 in.; individual flowers on pedicels 1/12–1/6 in., small, white, fragrant, perfect, regular; petals 5, lanceolate-oblong, acute, about ⅛ in. long, with nectar glands at base; stamens 5, alternate with the petals, anthers oval; ovary sessile, ovoid, style short and thick with a 2-lobed spreading stigma; calyx minute, of 5 sepals which are ovate-lanceolate, acute, about 1/12 in.

FRUIT. Capsule in late summer, small, about 1/16–1/8 in. long, ovoid-conical, yellowish brown, dry, remnants of the style at apex, persistent, indehiscent, 2-celled with 2 seeds in each cell; seeds minute, dry, light brown.

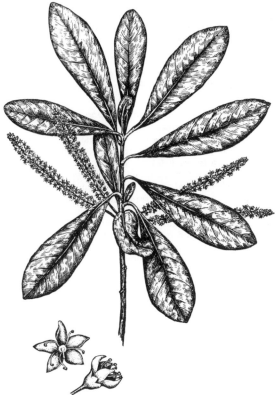

LEAVES. Alternate, often clustered at the twig tips, petioles ⅛–1 in., half-evergreen, entire on margin, oblong-obovate to elliptic, obtuse or acute at apex, cuneate at base, dark green and lustrous above, paler and reticulate-veined beneath, 2–4 in. long, ¼–1 in. wide.

TWIGS. Slender, smooth, shiny, brown to gray.

BARK. Thin, close, pale reddish brown or gray, scales small and thin, lower bark spongy.

WOOD. Reddish brown, close-grained, heavy, hard, not strong.

RANGE. In swamps on the Atlantic and Gulf coastal plains from eastern Texas eastward to Florida, and north to Virginia. Also in the West Indies, Mexico, and South America.

REMARKS. The genus name, *Cyrilla*, is in honor of Cyrillo Dominico, professor of medicine at Naples (1734–1799), and the species name, *racemiflora*, refers to the racemose flowers. Vernacular names are Black Titi, Burnwood Bark, Leatherwood, and He-huckleberry. The wood has no commercial value, but the flowers are considered good bee food. The spongy lower bark is reported to have been used formerly as a styptic. The leaves are apparently deciduous earlier and turn various brilliant colors in the autumn in the northern part of the plant's range, but in the South they remain more green and persistent. American Cyrilla is occasionally cultivated for its attractive leaves and slender white racemes of flowers. It can be propagated by seeds and cuttings.

Small-leaf Cyrilla, *C. racemiflora* var. *parvifolia* Raf., is a variety with smaller leaves and racemes and grows from Florida to Louisiana.

Holly Family (Aquifoliaceae)

Yaupon Holly

Ilex vomitoria Ait. [A, B, C]

FIELD IDENTIFICATION. An evergreen, thicket-forming shrub with many stems from the base, or a tree to 25 ft, and a diameter of 12 in. The crown is low, dense, and rounded.

FLOWERS. April–May on branchlets of the previous year, solitary or fascicled in the leaf axils, polygamo-dioecious, pedicels slender, 1/25–1/6 in. long; staminate glabrous, 2–3-flowered; pistillate puberulent, 1–2-flowered; calyx-lobes 4–5, glabrous, ovate or rounded, obtuse, about 1/25 in. long; corolla white, petals 4–5, united at base, elliptic-oblong, 1/12–1/8 in. long, about 1/12 in. wide; stamens 4–5, almost as long as the petals, anthers oblong and cordate; staminodia of the pistillate flowers shorter than the petals; ovary ovoid, 1/25–1/12 in. long, 1–4-celled, stigma flattened and capitate.

FRUIT. Often in abundance, drupe shiny red, semitranslucent, subglobose, about ¼ in. long, often crowned by the persistent stigma, nutlets usually 4, to 1/6 in. long, obtuse, prominently ribbed.

LEAVES. Evergreen, simple, alternate, elliptic-oblong to oval, margin crenate and teeth minutely mucronulate, apex obtuse or rounded and sometimes minutely emarginate and mucronulate, base obtuse or rounded, thick and coriaceous; upper surface dark lustrous green and glabrous, veins obscure; lower surface paler, glabrous, or with a few hairs on veins; petioles 1/25–1/4 in. long, grooved, glabrous or puberulent. Leaves vary considerably in size and shape on different plants.

TWIGS. Gray to brown, terete, stout, rigid, crooked, short, glabrous or puberulent; winter buds minute, obtuse, scales brown.

BARK. Averaging 1/16–1/8 in. thick, brownish to mottled gray or almost black, tight, smooth except for lenticels, or on old trunks eventually breaking into thin, small scales.

WOOD. White, heavy, hard, strong, close-grained, weighing about 46 lb per cu ft, sometimes used for turnery, inlay work, or woodenware.

RANGE. Low moist woods, mostly near the coast. Texas, Oklahoma, Arkansas, and Louisiana. Evidently reaching its largest size in the east Texas bottom lands. Eastward to Florida and northward to Virginia.

REMARKS. The genus name, *Ilex*, is the ancient name for the Holly Oak, and the species name, *vomitoria*, refers to its use as a medicine. Local names in use are Cassena, Cassine, Cassio-berry-bush, Evergreen Cassena, Yapon, Yopan, You-pon, Emetic Holly, Evergreen Holly, South-sea-tea, Carolina-tea, Appalachian-tea, Yopon del Indio, Chocolate del Indio, Indian Blackdrink, Christmas-berry.

The fruit is known to be eaten by at least 7 species of

birds. In regions where it grows it is often used as a holiday decoration. Although yellow-fruited plants have been given variety names from time to time, they do not apparently reproduce true to color and are therefore to be regarded only as unstable forms.

American Holly

Ilex opaca Ait. [A, B, C]

FIELD IDENTIFICATION. An evergreen tree to 70 ft, with short, crooked branches and a rounded or pyramidal crown.

FLOWERS. April–June, in short-stalked, axillary, cymose clusters; polygamo-dioecious, staminate in 3–9-flowered cymes, small, white, petals 4–6; stamens 4–6, alternating with the petals; pistillate flowers solitary or 2–3 together; ovary 4–8-celled, style short with broad stigmas; pistil rudimentary in the staminate flowers; calyx 4–6-lobed, lobes acute, ciliate; peduncles with 2 bracts.

FRUIT. Maturing November–December, spherical or ellipsoid, mostly red, more rarely yellow or orange, ¼–½ in. long, nutlets prominently ribbed.

LEAVES. Variable in shape, size, and spines, simple, alternate, persistent, ovate to oblong or oval, flattened, keeled or twisted, stiff and coriaceous, margins wavy, set with sharp, stiff, flat or divaricate spines, sometimes spineless; apex acute, spinose; base cuneate or rounded; upper surface dark to light green, lustrous or dull, paler and glabrous to somewhat puberulous beneath, length 2–4 in., width 1–1½ in.; petioles short, stout, grooved, sometimes puberulent; stipules minute, deltoid, acute.

TWIGS. Stout, green to light brown or gray, glabrous or puberulous.

BARK. Light or dark gray, often roughened by small protuberances.

WOOD. White or brownish, tough, close-grained, shock resistance high, works with tools well, shrinks considerably, checks or warps badly unless properly seasoned, not durable under exposure, rather heavy, specific gravity when dry about 0.61. It is used for cabinets, interior finish, novelties, handles, fixtures, and scientific instruments.

RANGE. Texas, Oklahoma, Arkansas, and Louisiana; eastward to Florida, north to Massachusetts and New York, and westward through Pennsylvania, Ohio, Indiana, and Illinois to Missouri.

REMARKS. The genus name, *Ilex*, is the old name for Holly Oak, and the species name, *opaca*, refers to the dull green leaf. Vernacular names are Yule Holly, Christmas Holly, and White Holly. The foliage and fruit are often used for holiday decorations and are sometimes browsed by cattle. At least 18 species of birds eat the fruit.

Dahoon Holly

Ilex cassine L. [A]

FIELD IDENTIFICATION. An evergreen, red-fruited holly, forming a shrub with slender, ascending branches, or a tree to 25 ft, with a diameter of 12–18 in. Usually with a low broad, rounded crown.

FLOWERS. Flowers polygamo-dioecious, usually on new growth in umbellike clusters, numerous, small, white; on hairy peduncles to 1 in. long with acute, scarious bractlets, pedicels to ¼ in., mostly 2–9-flowered in the staminate, corolla 1/6–1/5 in. broad; petals 4–6 (usually 4), obovate to elliptic, apex obtuse, united at base, about 1/10 in. long; calyx glabrous, 1/15–1/12 in. in diameter, lobes 4–6 (usually 4), ovate-triangular, margin ciliate-erose, apex acute or acuminate; stamens shorter than the petals, as many as the petals and alternate with them, filaments distinct; pistillate umbels usually 3-flowered, ovary superior, style very short;

staminodia in pistillate flowers shorter than the petals, anthers small and abortive; ovary in pistillate flowers conical, about 1/12 in. long, 4-celled, stigma capitate.

FRUIT. Ripening September–March, often abundant, persistent until the following spring, globose, 1/5–1/4 in. in diameter, bright to dull red or yellow, flesh yellow and mealy, solitary or in clusters of twos or threes; nutlets 4, bony, pale brown, prominently few-ribbed on the back and sides, base rounded, apex acute, length about 1/6 in.

LEAVES. Evergreen, leathery, flat, simple, alternate, blade length 1⅓–4 in., width ½–1½ in., oblanceolate to oblong-obovate; apex acute to obtuse and mucronate to rarely rounded or occasionally emarginate; base gradually narrowed or cuneate; margin entire and revolute, or remotely and sharply toothed above the middle; upper surface at maturity dark green, glabrous, or a few hairs along the impressed midrib; lower surface paler and glabrous or slightly hairy, primary veins slender and conspicuous; petioles to ½ in., stout, thickened at base, canaliculate, glabrate or sparingly hairy.

TWIGS. Slender, pale, and rather densely pubescent the first 2 or 3 years, later dark brown and glabrous with scattered lenticels; winter buds very small, acute, pubescent; leaf scars crescent-shaped, bundle scar solitary, pith smooth and continuous.

BARK. Thin, gray and smooth at first, darker later and roughened by lenticels.

WOOD. Pale brown, close-grained, light, soft, not strong, weighing 30 lb to the cu ft, easily worked.

RANGE. Swamplands, in sandy, acid soil, often in pine barrens. Louisiana; eastward to Florida and Georgia, and north to Virginia. Probably erroneously recorded from Texas.

REMARKS. The genus name, *Ilex*, is the ancient name for a European oak, and the species name, *cassine*, is from the Indian name, *Cassena*, which name was applied by them to a drink prepared from the Yaupon, *I. vomitoria*. Although the leaves of *I. cassine* were sometimes mixed with those of *I. vomitoria*, the former contains no caffeine. Vernacular names in use are Christmas-berry, Yaupon, and Hendersonwood. The fruit is eaten by about 10 species of birds and by the raccoon. The berries are much used during the Christmas season, and the plant has been cultivated since 1726. It is growing in demand as an ornamental plant.

Myrtle Dahoon Holly

Ilex myrtifolia Walt. [A]

FIELD IDENTIFICATION. An evergreen, red-fruited holly. Sometimes a small shrub with numerous crooked rigid stems, or a small tree to 23 ft, and a diameter of 10 in. Crown generally broad and compact.

FLOWERS. In May, borne on the new growth in simple or compound, short-peduncled cymes; staminate and pistillate on different trees or on the same tree; flowers numerous, small, inconspicuous; staminate cymes 3–9-flowered, corolla about 1/5 in. wide, petals usually 4, white, oblong-elliptic, united at base; stamens generally as many as the petals, alternate with them, filaments distinct and shorter than the petals; style of staminate flower reduced in size or abortive; calyx glabrous, 1/25–1/15 in. wide, lobes ovate-triangular; pistillate flowers 1–3 on a peduncle, ovary about 1/12 in. long, superior, 4-celled, style very short, stigma capitate, stamens usually reduced in size, in pistillate flower the pistil larger.

FRUIT. Maturing in late fall, persistent over winter, globose, about ¼ in. in diameter, red to orange or yellow, flesh thin and yellow; nutlets 4, ribbed; pedicels of fruit about 1/5 in.

LEAVES. Crowded, evergreen, simple, alternate, leathery and rigid, average length of blades ⅜–1½ in., width 1/5–1/3 in. (some plants with leaves to 2¾ in. long and 1¼ in. broad),

apex acute to obtuse, mucronate-spined, base obtuse to acute or rounded, margin entire and revolute, occasionally serrate toward the apex with a few minute spinescent teeth, linear to lanceolate or oblong; upper surface dark green and glabrous or puberulent along the midrib; lower surface paler and glabrous or slightly puberulent, midrib conspicuous, primary veins generally obscure; petioles puberulent, usually less than ⅛ in. long, but sometimes to ½ in.

TWIGS. Slender, rigid, smooth, pale, puberulent at first, glabrate later.

BARK. Pale gray or almost white, roughened by warty protuberances.

RANGE. On the coastal plain, wet acid soil around cypress ponds and swamps, and in pine barrens. Probably erroneously recorded from Texas, except occasionally in cultivation. Louisiana; eastward to Florida and northward to North Carolina.

REMARKS. The genus name, *Ilex*, is the classical name for a European oak, and the species name, *myrtifolia*, refers to the small, myrtlelike leaves. Common names are Small-leaf Dahoon, Myrtle Holly, and Cypress Holly. Myrtle Dahoon Holly leaves contain no caffeine.

Inkberry Holly

Ilex glabra (L.) Gray [A]

FIELD IDENTIFICATION. Shrub to 12 ft, much-branched, evergreen, thicket-forming as a result of underground stolons.

FLOWERS. February–July, polygamo-dioecious, axillary, solitary or a few together on new growth; staminate flowers of 3 or more together on puberulent pedicels 1/25–1/5 in.; pistillate flowers often solitary or 2–3 together, pedicels shorter than those of the staminate flowers; corolla 1/5–1/4 in. wide; petals 5–8, white, deciduous, united below, broadly elliptic or suborbicular, apex obtuse or rounded; about ⅛ in. long; stamens 4–6, shorter than petals, filaments erect and subulate, anthers introrse, 2-celled, opening longitudinally (stamens of pistillate flower usually abortive); ovary superior, free, about 1/12 in. long, 2–6-celled, stigma discoid, elevated (ovary in staminate flowers usually abortive).

FRUIT. Maturing in late autumn, persistent, solitary or 2–3 together, black, globose, 1/5–1/3 in. in diameter, stigma persistent; nutlets crustaceous, 5–8, each 1-seeded, about 1/6 in. long, black, flat.

LEAVES. Crowded, evergreen, simple, alternate, blade length ⅝–2⅓ in., width ¼–1¼ in., oblanceolate to obovate or elliptic to oval, apex obtuse to rounded and mucronulate, base acute or cuneate, margin entire or with 1–3 blunt low teeth on each side toward the apex, flat and coriaceous; upper surface lustrous dark green and glabrous, veins obscure; lower surface pale and punctate, semiglabrous or midvein puberulent; petioles 1/12–2/5 in., finely puberulent.

TWIGS. Slender, upright, terete or angled, young ones green and finely puberulent, older ones gray to black and glabrous.

RANGE. Generally near the coast in sandy, acid bogs of pinelands or prairies. Louisiana; eastward to Florida and Georgia and northward to Massachusetts. Most abundant in Florida.

REMARKS. The genus name, *Ilex*, is the ancient name for the Holly Oak, *Quercus ilex*, of Europe. The species name, *gla-*

bra, refers to the smooth glabrous leaves. The vernacular names are Gallberry, because of the bitter taste, and Inkberry, which refers to the black fruit. Also known as Appalachian Tea, Canadian Winterberry, Evergreen Winterberry, and Dye-leaves. Inkberry is considered to be a good source of honey. The fruit is eaten by at least 15 species of birds, including bobwhite quail and wild turkey, and the leaves are browsed by marsh rabbit. The plant contains no caffeine.

Tall Inkberry Holly

Ilex coriacea (Pursh) Chapm. [A]

FIELD IDENTIFICATION. Mostly an evergreen shrub, but sometimes a small tree to 15 ft.

FLOWERS. Polygamo-dioecious, solitary or clustered; staminate corolla about ¼ in. wide; petals 4–9, united below, white, oblong-elliptic, erose on the margin; stamens 4–6,

almost as long as petals, anthers opening lengthwise, staminodia about one-half as long as petals; calyx smooth with
triangular and acute lobes; pistillate flowers inclined to be
solitary, pedicel puberulent; pistil with a depressed ovary,
thick short style, and discoid stigma.

FRUIT. Drupe globose, black, lustrous, ¼–⅓ in. long, tipped
by the persistent stigma; nutlets 4–9, compressed, smooth,
about 1/6 in. long.

LEAVES. Alternate, simple, evergreen, dark, shining, stiff,
obovate, oblanceolate or elliptic, acute or short-acuminate
and spinescent at the apex, rounded or acute at the base;
entire on margin or with a few spinescent teeth; upper surface dark green and glabrous; punctate or sometimes glaucous, glabrous or puberulent beneath; petioles short and
puberulent, about ¼ in., pubescent.

TWIGS. Slender, elongate, green to gray, glabrous or puberulent, lenticels numerous, small, round.

BARK. Mottled gray or brown, smooth and tight.

RANGE. In acid, sandy, low woods. Eastern Texas, eastward to Florida. In Texas in Hardin, Jasper, Newton, and Montgomery counties, and possibly others.

REMARKS. The genus name, *Ilex*, is the ancient name of the Holly Oak, and the species name, *coriacea*, refers to the thick, leathery leaves. Vernacular names are Shining Inkberry, Large Gallberry, Baygall-bush.

Georgia Holly

Ilex longipes Chapm. [A]

FIELD IDENTIFICATION. Wide-spreading shrub or tree to 23 ft. Distinguished by elongate peduncles of the fruit. Leaves deciduous, or semipersistent southward.

FLOWERS. Inflorescences axillary, staminate and pistillate usually on different trees; staminate flowers solitary or fascicled; pistillate flowers usually solitary; pedicels ⅓–1¼ in., slender and glabrous, bearing small, 4-parted flowers; calyx about 1/12 in. in diameter, smooth, lobes of calyx triangular, acute at apex, denticulate on the margin; petals united below, elliptic; stamens about as long as the petals, but staminodia somewhat shorter; normal pistillate ovary ovoid, 4-celled, hardly over ⅛ in. long, stigma capitate.

FRUIT. Drupe red, globose, lustrous, 1/3–2/5 in. long, borne on a stalk ⅓–1¼ in.; nutlets 4, inconspicuously ribbed and striate.

LEAVES. Alternate, simple, persistent, thickish, blades ⅔–2½ in. long, ⅓–1⅓ in. wide, elliptic to elliptic-obovate or oval, acute or obtuse at the apex, minutely mucronulate, cuneate at the base; crenate-serrate on the margin, teeth often with minute bristles; glabrous and dark green above, paler beneath; petioles slender, ⅛–½ in. long, pubescent.

TWIGS. Slender, glabrous, round, green at first, gray with maturity.

RANGE. In low sandy woods. Eastern Texas in Newton, Jasper, Trinity, and San Jacinto counties, and possibly others; eastward to Florida and northward to North Carolina and Tennessee.

REMARKS. The genus name, *Ilex*, is the ancient classical name, and the species name, *longipes*, refers to the long-stemmed drupes, which are a conspicuous feature. Other names in common use are Chapman's Holly, Long-stem Holly, and Yaupon Holly. The plant has no economic importance other than the decorative value of the fruit.

Downy Georgia Holly, *I. longipes* var. *hirsuta* Lundell, has shorter fruiting pedicels, denser and coarser indument, and smaller leaves. Known from Harris, Madison, Newton, Polk, San Jacinto, Trinity, and Walker counties in Texas.

Carolina Holly

Ilex ambigua (Michx.) Chapm. [A]

FIELD IDENTIFICATION. Commonly a shrub, but sometimes a tree to 18 ft, with irregular branches and a rounded crown.

FLOWERS. In spring, borne in axillary inflorescences, staminate and pistillate usually on different trees, staminate usually fascicled but pistillate mostly solitary; pedicels smooth, slender, 1/25–1/6 in.; calyx smooth 1/25–1/12 in. in diameter, 4–5 lobed; lobes ovate, apiculate at the apex, somewhat hairy on the margin; corolla small, white, 4–5-parted; petals elliptic, ciliolate, hardly over ⅛ in. long, and longer than the stamens and staminodia; ovary ovoid, 4–5-celled, hardly over ⅛ in. long with a capitate stigma.

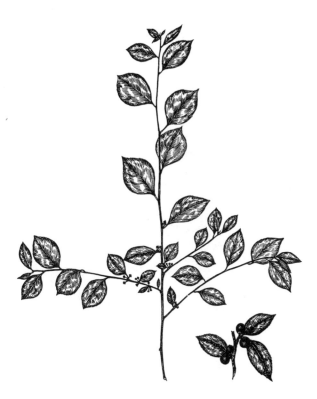

FRUIT. Drupe in late summer on very short pedicels, dark red, translucent, subglobose, hardly over ⅛–¼ in. long; nutlets 4–5, brown, striate, mostly less than 1/5 in. long.

LEAVES. Alternate, simple, deciduous, thin, oval-ovate or elliptic-lanceolate, acute or acuminate at the apex, rounded or cuneate at the base, crenate-serrulate on the margin but the lower third often entire, ¾–3 in. long; mostly glabrous above and below, but sometimes with pubescence along the veins; petioles slender, often pubescent, ⅓–½ in.

TWIGS. Rather slender, smooth, brown to purple, with prominent lenticels.

BARK. Dark brown, sometimes black, lustrous, smooth, flaking later.

RANGE. In low sandy woods; eastern Texas, Louisiana, Arkansas, and Oklahoma; eastward to Florida and northward to North Carolina.

REMARKS. The genus name, *Ilex*, is the ancient classical name, and the species name, *ambigua*, refers to its vague similarity to other species. Vernacular names are Sand Holly and Possum Holly.

Possum-haw Holly

Ilex decidua Walt. [A, B, C]

FIELD IDENTIFICATION. Usually a shrub with a spreading open crown, but sometimes a tree to 30 ft, with an inclined trunk to 10 in. in diameter.

FLOWERS. Borne March–May with the leaves, polygamo-dioecious, solitary or fascicled, borne on slender pedicels; pedicels of staminate flowers to ½ in. long, that of the pistillate flower generally shorter than the staminate; petals 4–6, white, united at the base, oblong to elliptic, 1/8–1/6 in. long; calyx-lobes 4–6, lobes ovate to triangular, acute or obtuse, entire to denticulate, sometimes ciliolate; stamens 4–6, anthers oblong and cordate, fertile stamens as long as the petals or shorter; staminodia of pistillate flowers shorter than the petals; ovary ovoid, about 1/12 in. long, 4-celled, stigma large, capitate and sessile.

FRUIT. Ripe in early autumn, persistent on branches most of the winter after leaves are shed, drupe globose or depressed-globose, orange-red, 1/4–1/3 in. in diameter, solitary or 2–3 together; nutlets usually 4, crustaceous, ovate or lunate, longitudinally ribbed, up to 1/5 in. long.

LEAVES. Simple, deciduous, alternate or often fascicled on short lateral spurs, obovate to spatulate or oblong, margin crenate-serrate with gland-tipped teeth; apex acute to obtuse, rounded or emarginate; base cuneate or attenuate, membranous at first but firm later; upper surface dark green and glabrous or with a few hairs, main vein impressed; lower surface paler and glabrous or pubescent on ribs, blade length 2–3 in., width 1/2–1 1/2 in.; petiole slender, grooved, glabrous to densely puberulent, length 1/12–1/2 in.; stipules filiform, deciduous.

TWIGS. Elongate, slender, often with many short spurlike lateral twigs, light to dark gray, glabrous or puberulent, lightly lenticellate, leaf scars lunate, buds small and obtuse.

BARK. Smooth, thin, mottled gray to brown, sometimes with numerous warty protuberances.

WOOD. White, close-grained, weighing 46 lb per cu ft, of no commercial value.

RANGE. In rich, moist soil, usually along streams or in swamps. Texas, Louisiana, Oklahoma, and Arkansas; eastward to Florida, and northward to Tennessee, Kentucky, Indiana, Illinois, Kansas, and Missouri.

REMARKS. The genus name, *Ilex*, is the ancient name of the Holly Oak, and the species name, *decidua*, refers to the autumn-shed leaves. Local names are Deciduous Holly, Meadow Holly, Prairie Holly, Welk Holly, Bearberry, and Winterberry. It is occasionally planted for ornament and is attractive in winter because of the persistent orange-red drupes. It is sometimes mistaken for a hawthorn in fruit, and possums are fond of it, hence the name, Possum-haw. At least 9 species of birds are known to feed upon the fruit, including the bobwhite quail.

Common Winterberry Holly

Ilex verticillata (L.) Gray [A]

FIELD IDENTIFICATION. Deciduous, red-fruited holly forming a shrub or small rounded tree to 25 ft.

FLOWERS. Borne May–June, pedicels 2-bracted, shorter than

the subtending petioles, staminate and pistillate pedicels
about equal in length; flowers small, inconspicuous, dioecious or polygamo-dioecious; staminate in short peduncled
cymes of 2–10 flowers; staminate corolla about ¼ in. across;
petals 4–8, imbricate in bud, greenish white, oblong or
rounded, apex obtuse, margin entire or minutely erose,
united at base; stamens usually the same number as the
petals and alternate with them, shorter than the petals and
adnate to them at base; filaments distinct and erect, anthers
introrse and longitudinally dehiscent; pistil usually reduced
in size in the staminate flower; pistillate flowers 1–3 in a
cluster, about ¼ in. across, pistil enlarged, compound, stigma broad and nearly sessile, stamens smaller and abortive;

calyx-lobes imbricate, usually the same number as the petals, ovate-triangular, apex obtuse or acute, calyx about 1/10 in. wide in the staminate flower.

FRUIT. Ripening September–October, persistent in winter, nearly sessile, globose, ¼–⅓ in. in diameter, lustrous red to orange or yellow; nutlets usually 3 to 6, testa membranous, lunate, bony, smooth dorsally, embryo minute, albumen fleshy.

LEAVES. Simple, alternate, deciduous, texture varying from thin to firm-coriaceous, generally about twice as long as wide, length of blade 1½–4 in., width ⅔–2 in., ovate to elliptic or lance-oblong, margins sharply serrate, with short appressed teeth, apex acuminate or acute, base acute to cuneate or less often rounded, upper surface glabrous or nearly so; lower surface usually pubescent and strongly veined, rarely completely glabrous; petiole 1/5–2/5 in. long, channeled above, pubescent to glabrate. Leaves turning black in autumn.

TWIGS. Gray to reddish brown, smooth at first but usually roughened by warty lenticels later, glabrous or slightly pubescent.

RANGE. Common Winterberry has a very wide distribution. It can stand lower temperatures than any other native American holly. In swamps and wet woods. Reported from southeastern Louisiana and Arkansas; eastward to Georgia and Florida, northward to Connecticut and Massachusetts, and westward to Michigan and Minnesota.

REMARKS. The genus name, *Ilex*, is the classical name for a European oak, and the species name, *verticillata*, refers to the axillary clusters of flowers. Also known under the vernacular names of Striped Alder, False Alder, Black Alder, Fever-bush, and Virginia Winterberry. The fruit is valuable as a wildlife food, being eaten by at least 20 species of birds including bobwhite quail, ruffed grouse, sharp-tailed grouse, and ring-necked pheasant. The bright red fruit is also used for winter dry bouquets. It is more persistent on the branches in the southern parts of its distribution. Common Winterberry is the most popular of the red-fruited, deciduous hollies. It has been cultivated since 1736, and is used for ornamental planting in moist places. It is rather free of insects and disease.

Mountain Winterberry Holly

Ilex montana Torr. & Gray [A]

FIELD IDENTIFICATION. Low spreading shrub or tree to 40 ft, and a trunk diameter of 10–12 in. Crown narrow and pyramidal.

FLOWERS. Dioecious or polygamous, borne usually in June when leaves are half-grown, on slender pedicels ⅛–⅓ (sometimes ½) in., staminate clustered, pistillate mostly solitary, crowded on lateral spurlike branchlets of the previous year, or solitary on branchlets of the current year; staminate calyx 1/8–1/6 in. wide, sepals 4–6 (mostly 4), triangular, acute, glabrous, ciliate; staminate corolla 1/6–1/5 in. wide; petals 4–6, white, obovate, apex obtuse; stamens as many as the petals, with shorter, distinct filaments; ovary superior, stigma broad and flat; staminate flowers with abortive pistils, and pistillate flowers with reduced stamens.

FRUIT. Ripening September–November, fruit somewhat larger than most hollies, ⅓–½ in. in diameter, globose, scarlet to orange-red or rarely yellow; nutlets about ¼ in. long, prominently ribbed on the back and sides; peduncles 1/12–1/4 in., generally shorter than the petioles.

LEAVES. Simple, alternate, deciduous, membranous, ovate to oblong-lanceolate, apex acuminate or acute, base cuneate or rounded, margin sharply serrate with minute, glandular incurved teeth, length 2–6 in., width ½–2½ in.; upper surfaces dark green, and glabrous or slightly hairy along the prominently impressed arcuate veins; lower surface paler and glabrous or slightly pubescent; leaves early deciduous, turning yellow in autumn; petioles slender, ⅓–¾ in.

TWIGS. Slender, more or less zigzag, reddish brown at first, gray later, glabrous; winter buds ovoid to subglobose, about ⅛ in. long, scales brown, keeled, apiculate.

BARK. Light brown to gray, about 1/16 in. thick, roughened by numerous lenticels.

WOOD. Creamy white, close-grained, hard, heavy, and strong.

RANGE. Usually on well-drained, wooded mountain slopes. In Louisiana recorded from West Feliciana and Winn parishes. Eastward to Florida and Georgia, northward to Tennessee, Pennsylvania, and New York, most often along the Appalachian Mountains.

REMARKS. The genus name, *Ilex*, is the ancient name for a European oak, and the species name, *montana*, refers to its mountain habitat. Also known by the vernacular names of Large-leaf Holly, Mountain Holly, and Hulver Holly. The leaves are sometimes browsed by white-tailed deer, and the fruit eaten by a number of species of birds. It has been in cultivation since 1870.

Staff-tree Family (Celastraceae)

Eastern Wahoo

Euonymus atropurpureus Jacq. [A, B, C]

FIELD IDENTIFICATION. Usually a shrub, but sometimes a small tree to 25 ft, with spreading branches and an irregular crown.

FLOWERS. May–July, borne in 7–15-flowered, axillary, trichotomous cymes; peduncles slender, 1–2 in. long, with individual perfect flowers about ½ in. wide; petals 4, purple, obovate, undulate or obscurely toothed, borne on the edge of a 4-angled disk; stamens 4, short, with 2-celled purple anthers; ovary 4-celled, style short, stigma depressed.

FRUIT. September–October, capsule deeply 3–4-lobed, smooth, about ½ in. across, persistent on long peduncles; valves purple or red, splitting open to expose brown seeds about ¼ in. long enclosed by a scarlet seed coat.

LEAVES. Opposite, petioled, deciduous, 2–5 in. long, 1–2 in. wide, ovate-elliptic, acuminate or acute at the apex, acute or cuneate at the base, finely crenate-serrate on the margin, bright green above, pale and puberulent beneath; petioles ½–1 in. long.

TWIGS. Slender, somewhat 4-angled, purplish green to brownish later; lenticels pale and prominent.

BARK. Smooth, thin, gray, with minute scales.

WOOD. Almost white, or tinged with yellow or orange, close-grained, heavy, hard, tough, weighing 41 lb per cu ft.

RANGE. Eastern Texas and Arkansas; east to northern Alabama, north to New York, and west to Ontario, Montana, Nebraska, and Kansas.

REMARKS. The genus name, *Euonymus*, is a translation of an ancient Greek term meaning "true name," and the species name, *atropurpureus*, refers to the purple flowers and fruit. Vernacular names are Spindle-tree, Burning-bush, Bleeding-heart, Arrowwood, Indian-arrow, Bitter-oak, and Strawberry-tree. The tree is sometimes used as an ornament because of its beautiful scarlet fruit in autumn, although it is subject to scale and fungus diseases. It is known to be purgative to livestock. The seeds are eaten by a number of species of birds.

Gutta-percha

Maytenus texana Lundell [B]

FIELD IDENTIFICATION. Creeping evergreen shrub or a small crooked tree rarely over 20 ft.

FLOWERS. Axillary, solitary or fascicled, peduncles 1/16–1/8 in. long, hardly over 3/16 in. across; petals 5, green to white, triangular, apex obtuse or acute; stamens 5, alternate with the petals, borne under the margin of a 5-angled viscid disk, shorter than the petals, filaments about 1/25 in. long, anthers ovoid-cordate; pistil thick, short, immersed in the disk; stigmas 3–4, sessile or nearly so, ovary 3–4-celled; calyx of 5 persistent sepals, apex obtuse or rounded, reddish, shorter than the petals.

FRUIT. Ripening in November in Texas, capsules on short axillary peduncles 1/16–1/8 in. long, ovoid to ellipsoid, ⅜–½ in. long and about ¼ in. broad, abruptly mucronulate at apex, base abruptly narrowed, 3–4-angled; dehiscent into 2–4 thin, elliptic to oval, recurved valves at maturity; seeds 2–4, bony, white to brown, ellipsoid to oblong, apices acute; dorsal face rounded, ventral face plane, about 3/16 in. long, covered with a conspicuous, red, loose, fleshy aril, calyx-lobes 4–5, minute, acute, about 1/25 in. long, pointed downward.

LEAVES. Alternate, simple, persistent, stiff, leathery, oval to oblong or elliptic, ¾–1¾ in. long, ½–1 in. wide; apex rounded, obtuse, or notched; base rounded to cuneate; margin entire or undulate; surfaces dull grayish green and glabrous with obscure veins; petioles stout, short, mostly less than ¼ in. long; stipules very small, caducous.

TWIGS. Slender, gray, glabrous, or when younger slightly puberulent, obscurely striate, sometimes prostrate, runner-like, and rooting at the nodes, or erect on larger plants.

BARK. Mottled gray to brown, smooth, thin, rougher on old bark near the base of the trunk.

RANGE. On clay mounds or sandy bluffs. At Boca Chica near the mouth of the Rio Grande below Brownsville, Texas. Also in Nueces County from King (Laureles) Ranch and southeast of Ricardo. In Mexico south into Sonora, Puebla, and Yucatán. Also in Baja California and Florida.

REMARKS. The genus name, *Maytenus*, is the name for a Chilean species, and the species name, *texana*, refers to its presence in Texas. It has also been listed under the names of *Maytenus phyllanthoides* Benth. var. *ovalifolia* Loes and *Maytenus phyllanthoides* Benth. It is also known under the vernacular names of Leather-leaf, Mangle, Mangle Dulce, Mangle aguabola. The wood is sometimes used for fuel in tropical America, but in Texas the plant is usually only a low spreading or prostrate shrub.

Maple Family (Aceraceae)

Red Maple

Acer rubrum L. [A]

FIELD IDENTIFICATION. Beautiful tree attaining a height of 100 ft, with a narrow, rounded crown.

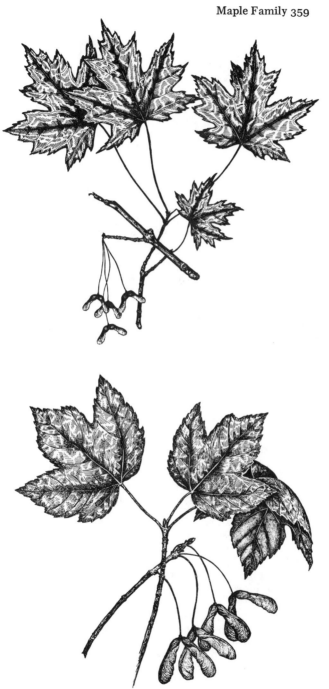

Drummond Red Maple

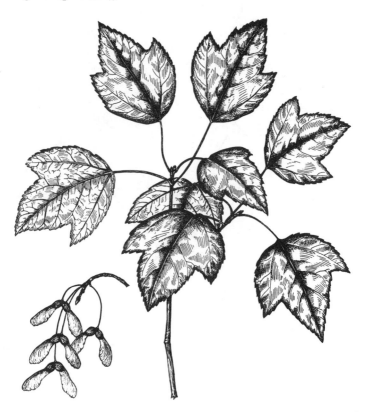

Trident Red Maple

FLOWERS. Borne in early spring before the leaves, in staminate and pistillate axillary fascicles on the same tree, or on different trees, red to yellowish green; petals 5, same length as the calyx-lobes, linear-oblong; stamens 5–8, anthers red; pistil short, ovary glabrous; styles 2, stout and spreading; calyx campanulate, 5-lobed.

FRUIT. Ripening March–June, borne on slender, drooping pedicels 2–4 in.; composed of a pair of winged, red, yellowish green or brown, flattened samaras, with a seed at the base; wings spreading, ½–1 in. long.

LEAVES. Opposite, simple, deciduous, blades ovate to oval, 2–6 in. long, 3–5-lobed; lobes acuminate or acute, irregularly serrate, sinuses angular; base truncate or somewhat cordate; bright green and glabrous above, whitish beneath; turning beautiful shades of yellow, orange, or red in autumn; petioles slender, 2–4 in., green to red.

TWIGS. Slender, glabrous, reddish, lenticels pale.

BARK. Light gray and smooth at first, becoming darker, furrowed and flaky on old trunks.

WOOD. Light reddish brown, close-grained, hard, heavy, weak, weighing 38 lb per cu ft.

RANGE. In Texas, Oklahoma, Arkansas, and Louisiana; eastward to Florida, northward to Newfoundland, and west to Ontario, Minnesota, Wisconsin, and Missouri.

REMARKS. The genus name, *Acer*, is the ancient Celt name, and the species name, *rubrum*, may refer to the red flowers, fruit, or autumn leaves. Vernacular names are Scarlet Maple, Shoe-peg Maple, Swamp Maple, Soft Maple, and Hard Maple. The wood is used for furniture, turnery, fuel, gunstocks, and woodenware. The seeds are eaten by squirrel and chipmunk, and the foliage browsed by cottontail and white-tailed deer.

Red Maple is subject to considerable variation, and some of the more constant varieties are as follows:

Drummond Red Maple, *A. rubrum* var. *drummondii* (Hook & Arn.) Sarg., is perhaps more common in east Texas than the species, with 3–5-lobed leaves which are generally broader than long, woolly white-hairy beneath, and the scarlet fruit is somewhat larger than in the species.

Trident Red Maple, *A. rubrum* var. *tridens* Wood, has smaller 3-lobed leaves, obovate, narrowed and rounded, and sparingly toothed or entire below the 3 short lobes; dark green above, white-tomentose beneath; flowers often yellowish green.

Pale-flower Red Maple, *A. rubrum* var. *pallidiflorum* Pax, has yellow flowers. A number of horticultural clones, which reproduce asexually, have been developed. The most popular are the Column (*columnare*), Dwarf (*globosum*), and Schlesinger (*schlesingeri*).

Sugar Maple

Acer saccharum Marsh. [A]

FIELD IDENTIFICATION. Large, broad, round-topped tree attaining a height of 100 ft, and a diameter of 2½ ft.

FLOWERS. Borne March–May, polygamous, pedicels slender, hairy, ¾–3 in. long, together forming a greenish yellow corymb; petals absent; calyx campanulate, 5-lobed, lobes obtuse and hairy; stamens 7–8, filaments slender and glabrous in the staminate flower, and shorter in the pistillate; ovary pale green, hairy, with 2 long-exserted stigmas.

FRUIT. Ripening September–October, borne in clusters; samara double, reddish brown, 1–1½ in. long, winged; wings ¼–½ in. wide, flat, thin, parallel or angle of divergence exceeding 45°; seeds at the samara base smooth, red,

about ¼ in. long, easily wind-borne because of the attached wing, good seed crops every 3–7 years.

LEAVES. Simple, opposite, deciduous, blades 3–6 in. long and as wide, usually 5-lobed, but occasionally 3-lobed; lobes entire or irregularly toothed or lobed, apex acuminate; base cordate, rounded, or truncate; upper surface at maturity dark green, paler and whitish to glaucous beneath; leaf turning beautiful shades of yellow, orange, or red in autumn; petioles slender, glabrous, 1½–3 in.

TWIGS. Slender, lustrous, glabrous, green at first, reddish brown later; lenticels conspicuous, pale, oblong; buds conical, reddish brown, 1/8–1/5 in. long.

BARK. Light gray to brown, smooth when young, on older trees darker and fissured with irregular scaly plates.

WOOD. Reddish brown, sapwood white, close-grained, straight- or curly-grained, hard, strong, tough, stiff, odorless, strong in bending and endwise compression, shock resistance high, tools well, stays smooth under abrasion, takes a high polish, stains well, holds nails well, fair in gluing, dries easily, shrinks moderately, not durable when exposed to decay conditions.

RANGE. Almost the entire eastern half of the United States; west to east Texas, Arkansas, Oklahoma, Louisiana, Kansas, Nebraska, North Dakota, and South Dakota. In Canada in Manitoba, Ontario, Quebec, New Brunswick, and Newfoundland.

REMARKS. The genus name, *Acer*, is the ancient name of a maple of Europe, and the species name, *saccharum*, refers to the sugar content of the sap. Vernacular names are Hard Maple, Black Maple, and Sweet Maple. This tree is considered by many to be the most valuable hardwood tree in America. The wood is used for furniture, shoe lasts, turnery, pegs, shipbuilding, fuel, crossties, veneer, athletic equipment, musical instruments, boxes, woodenware, handles, shuttles, toys, and general millwork. Individual trees produce the bird's-eye and curly grains used in furniture. The wood is also rich in potash, and the sap is a source of the sucrose-rich maple sugar which is produced mostly in the northern states and Canada. It is usually not refined but owes its flavor to impurities in the crude product.

Florida Sugar Maple

Acer barbatum Michx. [A]

FIELD IDENTIFICATION. Tree over 50 ft, with small spreading branches and rounded crown.

FLOWERS. Polygamo-dioecious, borne on long puberulent pedicels in yellowish green corymbs; petals none; stamens 7–8, exserted; ovary 2-lobed, 2-celled; styles 2, inwardly stigmatic; calyx campanulate, 5-lobed, lobes puberulent.

FRUIT. Two green to reddish winged samaras joined at the seeded base and divergent-winged toward the apices, hairy at first but becoming glabrous later, hardly over ¾ in. long, flattened; seed solitary, lustrous, green.

LEAVES. Opposite, simple, deciduous, blades 1½–3 in. long, 3–5-lobed; lobes short, acute or obtuse, entire, or lobes very coarsely toothed, truncate or subcordate or rounded at the base; dark green and shiny above, glaucous and pubescent beneath, turning red to yellow in autumn; petiole 1½–3 in., pubescent at first, glabrous later.

TWIGS. Slender, light reddish brown, glabrous.

BARK. Whitish, close, smooth when young, becoming darker and shallow-fissured later.

WOOD. Hard, strong, light, light reddish brown, individual trees sometimes found with a curly grain which makes the bird's-eye maple of commerce.

RANGE. Moist rich soil; Texas, Oklahoma, Arkansas, and Louisiana; east to Florida and north to Missouri and Virginia.

REMARKS. The genus name, *Acer*, is from the Celt, and means "hard," in reference to the wood. The species name, *barbatum*, meaning "bearded," is from the beard in the flower.

The wood of Florida Sugar Maple is used for furniture, flooring, and shoe lasts. It is also widely known as a source of maple sugar and syrup. The average tree produces 3–4 lb of sugar, and it takes about 15 quarts of sap for 1 lb of sugar. The early settlers were taught the process of maple-sugar making by the Indians. The seasons are apparently not distinct enough for a proper sap flow from southern trees. The method of propagating by seed is similar to that of northern Sugar Maple.

It appears likely that this tree is really only a southern variety of the Northern Sugar Maple, *A. saccharum* Marsh. (*A. saccharophorum* K. Koch), instead of a distinct species. In fact, at one time it did hold the rank of a variety. It appears that the principal differences are the smaller size of the Florida Sugar Maple tree, the smaller leaves with short acute lobes, the smaller samaras, and a more whitish bark.

However, these characters are not always constant, and many intergrades are found between the typical Florida Sugar Maple and the Northern Sugar Maple in east Texas.

Some botanists list Florida Sugar Maple under the scientific name of *A. floridanum* (Chapm.) Pax, but it is now shown that the name *A. barbatum* Michx. has preference.

Silver Maple

Acer saccharinum L. [A]

FIELD IDENTIFICATION. Tree to 100 ft, with a rounded crown and slender spreading branches.

FLOWERS. Before the leaves in spring, from imbricate involucres in sessile, or short-stalked, axillary clusters, greenish yellow, polygamo-dioecious; no petals; stamens 3–7, exserted; filaments slender with red anthers; pistil short, with a pubescent ovary and 2 spreading stigmatic styles; calyx obscurely 5-lobed, narrower in the staminate than in the pistillate flower, greenish yellow, pubescent.

FRUIT. Ripe when the leaves are almost mature, and pendent on slender pedicels, composed of 2 samaras with nutlets at the base and thin, widely divergent wings; samaras rather large, 1½–2 in. long, hairy at first but glabrous later, flattened, reddish brown or green, wrinkled, thin, falcate, dispersed April–June, good seed crops nearly every year.

LEAVES. Opposite, simple, deciduous, blades 6–7 in. long, borne on red, drooping petioles about 4 in., truncate or somewhat cordate at the base, 5-lobed; lobes deep, narrow, acuminate, variously toothed and cut, sinuses acute or rounded; upper surface pale green, lower surface silvery white, turning yellow in autumn.

TWIGS. Slender, brittle, shiny, reddish brown.

BARK. At first smooth and gray, later breaking into loose flakes.

WOOD. Pale brown, close-grained, somewhat brittle, even-textured, moderately strong, easily worked, decaying rapidly on exposure, weighing 32 lb per cu ft.

RANGE. East Texas, Oklahoma, Arkansas, and Louisiana; eastward to Florida, north to New Brunswick, and west to Ontario, the Dakotas, Nebraska, and Kansas.

REMARKS. *Acer* is the ancient Celt name, and the species name, *saccharinum*, refers to the sweet sap. Vernacular names are White Maple, Soft Maple, River Maple, Creek Maple, and Swamp Maple. The tree is brittle and subject to wind damage. It is also rather susceptible to insect and fungus diseases. Although short-lived it is a rapid grower and is often planted for ornament and occasionally for shelter-belt planting and stream-bank protection. Sugar is made from the sap occasionally, and the wood is made into flooring and furniture and used for fuel. The fruit is eaten by a number of species of birds and by squirrel and chipmunk.

Box-elder Maple

Acer negundo L. [A, B, C]

FIELD IDENTIFICATION. Tree attaining a height of 75 ft, with a broad rounded crown.

FLOWERS. March–May, dioecious, small, greenish, drooping, on slender stalks; staminate in fascicles 1–2 in. long; no petals; stamens 4–6, exserted, filaments hairy with linear anthers; calyx campanulate, hairy, 5-lobed; pistillate flowers in narrow racemes; ovary pubescent, style separating into 2 elongate, stigmatic lobes; calyx of pistillate flower narrowly 5-lobed.

FRUIT. Ripening August–October, borne in early summer in

drooping clusters 6–8 in. long; samara double, greenish, minutely pubescent or glabrous, 1–2 in. long; wings divergent to about 90°, straight or falcate, thin and reticulate; seeds at base of wings, solitary, smooth, reddish brown, about ½ in. long.

LEAVES. Deciduous, opposite, 6–15 in. long, odd-pinnately compound of 3–7 (sometimes 9) leaflets; leaflets short-stalked, 2–4 in. long, 1½–3 in. wide, ovate-elliptic or oval-obovate; margin irregularly serrate or lobed, mostly above the middle; acute or acuminate at apex; rounded, cuneate or cordate at the base, sometimes unsymmetrical; light green, glabrous or slightly pubescent above, paler and pubescent beneath, especially in axils of veins; petioles glabrous.

TWIGS. Slender, smooth, shiny, green to purplish green.

BARK. Young bark green, smooth, thin, later pale gray to brown, divided into narrow rounded ridges with short scales and shallow fissures.

WOOD. Whitish, light, soft, not strong, close-grained, weighing 27 lb per cu ft.

RANGE. Texas, Oklahoma, Arkansas, and Louisiana; eastward to Florida, northward to New Brunswick, and west to Ontario, Michigan, Minnesota, and Nebraska.

REMARKS. The genus name, *Acer*, is from an old Celt word, and the application of the species name, *negundo*, is obscure. The synonyms *Negundo aceroides* Moench and *Rulac negundo* (L.) A. S. Hitchcock are also used by some writers. Vernacular names are Maple-ash, Ashleaf Maple, Water-ash, Sugar Maple, Red River Maple, Black Maple, and Manitoba Maple. The tree is easily transplanted when young, grows rapidly, is short-lived, and is easily damaged by rot, insects, storm, and fire. It is widely planted as a quick-growing ornamental tree and has been extensively used in shelter-belt planting in the prairie states. The wood is used for paper pulp, cooperage, woodenware, interior finish, and cheap furniture. The seeds are eaten by many species of birds and squirrels. It is occasionally tapped for its sugary sap, which is inferior to that of Sugar Maple.

Buckeye Family (Hippocastanaceae)

Texas Buckeye

Aesculus arguta Buckl. [A, C]

FIELD IDENTIFICATION. Usually a shrub, but under favorable conditions a tree to 35 ft. The branches are stout and the crown is rounded to oblong.

FLOWERS. Inflorescence a dense, yellow panicle, borne after the leaves, 4–8 in. long, 2–3½ in. broad, primary peduncle of panicle densely brown-tomentose, secondary racemes ¾–½ in. long, 3–15-flowered, tomentose; individual flower pedicels ⅛–¼ in., densely tomentose; calyx campanulate, 1/5–1/4 in. long, brown-tomentose, 4–5-lobed above, lobes imbricate in the bud, lobes unequal, apices obtuse to rounded or truncate; petals 4, pale yellow, some reddish at the base, ⅓–¾ in. long, upright, parallel, clawed, thin, deciduous, densely hairy, margin ciliate; upper pair oval to broadly oblong; lateral pair elongate, oblong to spatulate, long-clawed, apex rounded to truncate or notched; disk hypogynous, annular, depressed; stamens 7–8, inserted on the disk, long-exserted, upcurved, unequal, filiform, hairy, longer than the petals; anthers yellow, ellipsoid, introrse, 2-celled, opening longitudinally; style 1, slender, elongate, curved; stigma terminal and entire; ovary 3-celled, sessile, cells often 1-ovuled by abortion.

FRUIT. Maturing May–June, peduncles stout, hairy at first, glabrate later; capsule ¾–1¾ in. in diameter, subglobose to obovoid or asymmetrically lobed, armed with stout warts or prickles or occasionally smooth, light brown, dehiscent into 2–3 valves at maturity; seeds usually solitary and rounded, if 2, usually flattened by pressure, coriaceous, smooth, lustrous, brown, ⅝–¾ in. in diameter.

LEAVES. Deciduous, opposite, palmately compound of 7–9 leaflets (often 7), sessile or nearly so, narrowly elliptic to lanceolate, or more rarely obovate, apex long-acuminate (less often broader and abruptly acuminate), base attenuate

to narrowly cuneate, margin finely serrate or occasionally incised above the middle, blade length 2½–5 in., width ½–2 in.; upper surface olive green, lustrous, a few fine hairs mostly along the veins; lower surface paler and more pubescent; petioles slender, 3–5 in., grooved, woolly-hairy.

BARK. Gray to black; fissures narrow, short and irregular; ridges broken into small short, rough scales.

TWIGS. Tough, stout, terete, the young ones green and glabrous to somewhat hairy, the older ones gray to reddish brown, lenticels small; leaf scars lunate or horseshoe-shaped, fibrovascular marks 3–6.

RANGE. Texas Buckeye is found on limestone or granite soils in the Edwards Plateau area of Texas, north to southern Oklahoma, and in Missouri.

REMARKS. The genus name, *Aesculus*, is the old name for a European mast-bearing tree, and the species name, *arguta*, means "sharp-toothed," perhaps referring to the foliage. Texas Buckeye is closely related to Ohio Buckeye, *A. glabra* Willd., and at one time was listed as a variety of it under the name of *A. glabra* var. *arguta* (Buckl.) Robinson. Although listed only as a shrub in most literature, Texas Buckeye becomes a tree to 35 ft and 18 in. in diameter on the Texas Edwards Plateau. The leaves and flower parts of Texas Buckeye appear to be only lightly pubescent on some specimens and heavily tomentose on others.

Ohio Buckeye

Aesculus glabra Willd. [A, C]

FIELD IDENTIFICATION. Tree attaining a height of 75 ft and a diameter of 2 ft. The branches are rather thick, and the crown broad and rounded.

FLOWERS. March–May, panicles terminal, narrow, loose, pubescent, 4–8 in. long, 2–3 in. wide; the pedicels 4–6-flowered; flowers yellowish green, ½–¾ in. long, petals 4, parallel, almost equal in length, proximal ends clawed and often hairy at the base; the lateral pair broad-ovate or oblong; the upper pair much narrower, oblong-spatulate, yellow (occasionally red-striped); stamens usually 7 or 8, long-exserted, filaments curved upward and pubescent, anthers orange-colored; ovary pubescent and prickly; calyx campanulate, 4–5-lobed above.

FRUIT. Capsule ripening September–October, on stout pedicels ½–1 in., irregularly subglobose or obovoid, capsule ¾–2¼ in. long, pale brown, leathery, roughened by warty tubercules and prickles, valves thick, 3-celled and 3-seeded, but often by abortion 1-celled and 1-seeded; seeds 1–1½ in.

wide, lustrous brown, sometimes depressed, hilum scar large, round, and pale; cotyledons thick and fleshy.

LEAVES. Opposite, on petioles 4–6 in., palmately compound of 5 leaflets (or more in the varieties); leaflets sessile or nearly so, 4–6 in. long, 1½–2½ in. broad, elliptic to oblong or oval to obovate, apex mostly acuminate, base cuneate, margin finely serrate, upper surface glabrous, lower surface paler and glabrous to pubescent on the veins, turning yellow in the autumn, fetid when crushed.

TWIGS. Reddish brown to gray, pubescent at first but glabrous later, lenticels orange-colored, bud scales keeled and apiculate.

BARK. Young bark dark brown and smoother, older gray and broken into plates roughened by small, numerous scales, odor fetid (almost white in *A. glabra* var. *leucodermis* Sarg.).

WOOD. Whitish, fine-grained, weighing 28 lb per cu ft, weak in bending and endwise compression, durability low, shock resistance low, shrinks moderately, hand tools easily, but machining properties rather low.

RANGE. In moist, rich soil of woodlands or riverbanks. Oklahoma, Arkansas, northern Mississippi, northern Alabama, and northeastern Texas; eastward to West Virginia, north to Pennsylvania, and west to Michigan, Iowa, and Kansas.

REMARKS. The genus name, *Aesculus*, is the ancient name for a European mast-bearing tree. The species name, *glabra*, refers to the smooth leaves. Other local names are Fetid Buckeye, Stinking Buckeye, and American Horse-chestnut. The tree is sometimes planted for ornament in the eastern United States and in Europe. It has been in cultivation since 1809. It is short-lived; the young shoots are poisonous to cattle; and hogs are poisoned by the seed. The wood is used for fuel, paper pulp, artificial limbs, splints, woodenware, boxes, crates, toys, furniture, veneer for trunks, drawing boards, and occasionally for lumber.

Red Buckeye

Aesculus pavia L. [A, B, C]

FIELD IDENTIFICATION. Shrub with an inclined stem, or more rarely a tree attaining a height of 28 ft and a diameter of 10 in. The crown is usually dense and the branches short, crooked, and ascending.

FLOWERS. March–May, panicles narrow to ovoid, erect, pubescent, 4–8 in. long; 1–numerous-flowered, pedicels slender, ¼–½ in.; flowers red, ¾–1½ in. long; calyx tubular, ⅜–⅝ in. long, dark red, tube about five times as long as the rounded lobes; petals 4, red, connivent, ⅝–1 in. long, oblong to obovate, apex rounded, base narrowed into a

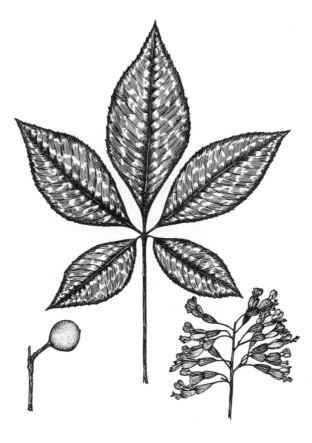

claw, limbs of the 2 superior petals shorter than the 2 lateral pairs; stamens about equaling the longest petals, exserted, usually 8 in number, filaments filiform and villous below; ovary sessile, villous, 3-celled (or by abortion fewer), style slender.

FRUIT. Capsule 1–2 in. in diameter, subglobose or obovoid, light brown, smooth but finely pitted, dehiscent into 2–3 valves; seeds 1–3, rounded, or flattened by pressure against each other, lustrous, light to dark brown, about 1 in. in diameter.

LEAVES. Deciduous, opposite, palmately compound of 5 leaflets (rarely, 3 or 7), leaflets oblong to elliptic or oval to obovate, apex acute to short-acuminate, base gradually narrowed, margin coarsely serrate, leaflet length 3–6 in., width 1–1½ in., firm; upper surface lustrous, dark green, glabrous except a few hairs on the veins; lower surface paler, almost glabrous to densely tomentose; petiole nearly glabrous or with varying degrees of hairiness, red, 3–7 in.

Yellow Buckeye

BARK. Gray to brown, smooth on young branches, on old trunks roughened into short plates which flake off in small, thin scales.

TWIGS. Green to gray or brown, crooked, stout, smooth; lenticels pale brown to orange; leaf scars large and conspicuous, with 3 fibrovascular bundles.

RANGE. Mostly along streams of the coastal plains. East and central Texas to the Edwards Plateau, Oklahoma, and Arkansas; eastward through Louisiana to Florida, north to southern Illinois, and west to southeast Missouri.

REMARKS. The genus name, *Aesculus*, is the ancient name for an old mast-bearing tree, and the species name, *pavia*, honors Peter Paaw (d. 1617) of Leyden. Some vernacular names in use for the plant are Scarlet Buckeye, Woolly Buckeye, Firecracker-plant, and Fish-poisonbush. It is reported that the powdered bark is used in domestic medicine for toothache and ulcers, the roots are used for washing clothes, and the crushed fruit is used for fish poison.

At one time the common east Texas Buckeye (*A. pavia* L.) and the Woolly Buckeye (*A. discolor* Pursh, *A. discolor* var. *mollis* [Raf.] Sarg., *A. discolor* var. *flavescens* Sarg. and *A. austrina* Small) of the Edwards Plateau area of central

Texas were considered as separate species. However, they have now been combined under the name of *Aesculus pavia* L. Also, a yellow-flowered variation of the Edwards Plateau has been relegated to the position of a variety as *A. pavia* var. *flavescens* (Sarg.) Correll. It occurs mostly on the Edwards Plateau of Edwards and Kinney counties, especially near San Marcos, New Braunfels, Boerne, Comfort, and Kerrville.

On the edges of contact of the yellow and red forms, plants with yellow flowers deeply tinged or marked with red are found (see Correll and Johnston, *Manual of the Vascular Plants of Texas*, p. 1005).

Soapberry Family (Sapindaceae)

Western Soapberry

Sapindus saponaria L. var. *drummondii* (H. & A.) L. Benson [A, B, C]

FIELD IDENTIFICATION. Tree attaining a height of 50 ft, with a diameter of 1–2 ft. The branches are usually erect to form a rounded crown.

FLOWERS. May–June, in large, showy panicles 5–10 in. long and 5–6 in. wide; perianth about 1/25 in. across; petals 4–5, obovate, rounded, white; sepals 4–5, acute, concave, ciliate on margin, shorter than the petals; stamens usually 8, inserted on the disk; style single, slender, with a 2–4-lobed stigma; ovary 3-lobed and 3-celled, each cell containing 1 ovule.

FRUIT. September–October, globular, fleshy, from white to yellowish or blackish, translucent, persistent and shriveled; seed 1, obovoid, dark brown, the other 2 seeds seeming to atrophy.

LEAVES. Short-petiolate, deciduous, alternate, 5–18 in. long, abruptly pinnate; leaflets 4–11 pairs, 1½-4 in. long, ½–¾ in. wide, falcate, lanceolate, acuminate at the apex, asymmetrical at base, veiny, yellowish green, glabrous above, soft pubescent or glabrous beneath.

BARK. Gray to reddish, divided into narrow plates that break into small reddish scales.

TWIGS. Yellowish green to gray, pubescent to glabrous, lenticels small.

WOOD. Light brown or yellowish, close-grained, hard, strong, weighing 51 lb per cu ft.

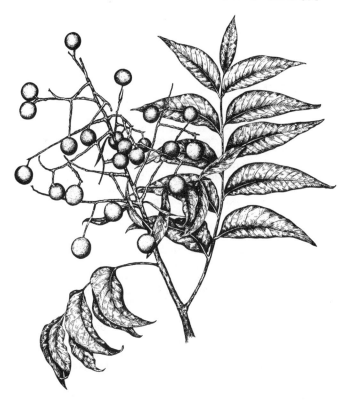

RANGE. In moist soils along streams; Texas, New Mexico, Arizona, Oklahoma, and Arkansas; eastward into Louisiana, north to Missouri and Kansas, and south into Mexico.

REMARKS. The genus name, *Sapindus*, is from *sapo* ("soap") and *Indus* ("Indies"), referring to the fact that some of the West Indian species are used for soap. The variety name, *drummondii*, is in honor of the botanist Thomas Drummond. Vernacular names are Amole de Bolita, Tehuistle, Palo Blanco, Jaboncillo, Wild China-tree, and Indian Soap-plant.

The fruit of this tree, and related species, contains the poisonous substance saponin, which produces a good lather in water. It is used in Mexico as a laundry soap. The fruit is also used medicinally as a remedy for renal disorders, rheumatism, and fevers. Buttons and necklaces are made from the seeds. The wood is of little value except for making baskets and frames and as fuel. Soapberry makes a desirable shade tree and could be more extensively planted for orna-ment. It has been cultivated since 1900 and is sometimes used for shelter-belt planting.

Mexican-buckeye

Ungnadia speciosa Endl. [B, C]

FIELD IDENTIFICATION. Western shrub or tree to 30 ft, and
10 in. in trunk diameter. Branches small and upright to
spreading with an irregularly shaped crown.

FLOWERS. Borne in pubescent fascicles in spring, appearing
with the leaves, or just before them; polygamous and
irregular, about 1 in. across, fragrant; petals usually 4 or
occasionally 5, rose-colored, deciduous, obovate, erect,
clawed, margin crenulate, somewhat tomentose, with a tuft
of fleshy hairs; disk 1-sided, oblique, tongue-shaped, connate with the ovary base; calyx campanulate, 5-lobed, lobes
oblong-lanceolate; stamens 7–10, unequal, exserted, inserted
on edge of disk, filaments filiform and pink, anthers oblong
and red; ovary ovoid, stipitate, hairy, 3-celled, rudimentary
in the staminate flower, ovules 2; style subulate, elongate,
filiform, slightly upcurved; stigma terminal, minute.

FRUIT. Capsule stipitate, broad-ovoid, crowned by the style
remnants, about 2 in. broad, leathery, roughened, reddish
brown, 3-celled and 3-valved, dehiscent in October while
still on the trees, but hardly opening wide enough to release
the large seeds; seeds usually solitary because of the abortion of the others, about ½ in. in diameter, round, smooth,
shining, black or brown, hilum scar broad.

LEAVES. Odd-pinnately compound, alternate, deciduous, 5–
12 in. long, leaflets 5–7 (rarely, 3), ovate to lanceolate, apex
acuminate, base rounded or cuneate, margin crenate-serrate,
3–5 in. long, 1½–2 in. wide, rather leathery, upper surface
dark green, lustrous and glabrous, lower surface paler and
pubescent to glabrous; petiole 2–6 in.; petiolule of terminal
leaflet ¼–1 in.; lateral leaflets sessile or very short-
petioluled.

TWIGS. Buds imbricate, ovate to almost globose, leaf scars
large and obcordate, twigs slender, terete, brown to orange
and pubescent at first, later reddish brown and glabrous.

BARK. Mottled gray to brown, thin, tight, smooth, broken
into shallow fissures on old trunks.

WOOD. Reddish brown, sapwood lighter, brittle, soft, close-
grained.

RANGE. Usually in limestone soils of stream banks, moist
canyons, or on bluffs. In Texas, New Mexico, and Mexico.
In Texas of greatest abundance west of the Brazos River. A
few trees found as far east as Harris County, Texas. In
Mexico in the states of Nuevo León, Coahuila, and Chihuahua.

REMARKS. The genus name, *Ungnadia*, is in honor of Baron
Ungnad, ambassador of Emperor Rudolph II. The species
name, *speciosa*, means showy, with reference to the flowers.
Also known under the vernacular names of Monillo, Texas-
buckeye, Spanish-buckeye, New Mexican-buckeye, False-

buckeye, and Canyon-buckeye. The tree should be grown
more for ornament, being very beautiful in the spring. The
flowers resemble Redbud or Peach blossoms at a distance. It
is also a source of honey. The sweet seeds are poisonous to
human beings. Seemingly a few may be eaten with impunity,
but a number cause stomach disturbances. The leaves and
fruit may also cause some minor poisoning to livestock,
but they are seldom browsed except in times of stress. Children in west Texas sometimes use the round seeds for
marbles.

Buckthorn Family (Rhamnaceae)

Texas Colubrina

Colubrina texensis (Torr. & Gray) Gray [B]

FIELD IDENTIFICATION. Thicket-forming shrub rarely over 15 ft, with light gray divaricate twigs.

FLOWERS. April–May, borne in axillary, subsessile clusters; perfect, tomentose, greenish yellow, less than ⅓ in. across; petals 5, hooded and clawed; calyx 5-lobed, persistent on the fruit, lobes triangular-ovate; stamens 5, inserted below the disk, opposite the petals, filaments filiform; ovary 3-celled, immersed in the disk, styles 3, stigma obtuse.

FRUIT. Pedicels recurved, ¼–⅓ in. long, drupes borne at the twig nodes, ovate to subglobose, tomentose at first, later glabrous, dry, crustaceous, brown or black, about ⅓ in. in diameter, style persistent to form a beak, separating into 2–3 nutlets; seeds one in each partition, about 3/16 in. long, rounded on the back, angled on the other 2 surfaces, dark brown, shiny, smooth.

LEAVES. Simple, alternate or clustered, grayish green, blades ½–1 in. long, ovate, obovate or elliptic, densely hairy at first and glabrous later; 3-nerved, margin denticulate and ciliate; apex rounded, sometimes apiculate; base cuneate, rounded, truncate or subcordate; petioles ⅛–⅜ in. or less, hairy, reddish.

TWIGS. Slender, ashy gray, noticeably divergent, scarcely spiniferous, densely white-tomentose at first but glabrous later.

BARK. Gray, smooth, close, cracked into small, short scales later.

RANGE. Central, western, and southwestern Texas and New Mexico; Mexico in the states of Nuevo León, Coahuila, and Tamaulipas.

REMARKS. The genus name, *Colubrina*, is from *coluber* ("a serpent"), perhaps for the twisting, divaricate branches or for the sinuate grooves on the stems of some species. The species name, *texensis*, refers to the state of Texas. A vernacular name is Hog-plum. The dark brown or black drupes are persistent.

Bluewood Condalia

Condalia hookeri M. C. Johnst. [B]

FIELD IDENTIFICATION. Thicket-forming spinescent shrub or tree to 30 ft, with a diameter of 8 in. The branches are rigid and divaricate.

FLOWERS. Solitary, or 2–4 in axillary clusters, sessile, or on short pedicels about 1/16 in. long; calyx 1/16–1/8 in. broad, glabrous or nearly so; sepals 5, green, spreading, triangular, acute, persistent; disk fleshy, flat, somewhat 5-angled; petals absent; stamens 5, shorter than the sepals, incurved, inserted on the disk margin; ovary superior, 1-celled, or sometimes imperfectly 2–3-celled; styles stout and short, stigma 3-lobed.

FRUIT. Ripening at intervals during the summer, drupe black at maturity, shiny, smooth, subglobose, somewhat flattened at apex, ¼–⅓ in. in diameter, thin-skinned, fleshy, sweet, juice purple; seed solitary, ovoid to globose, flattened, acute at one end and truncate at the other, light brown, crustaceous, about ⅛ in. long.

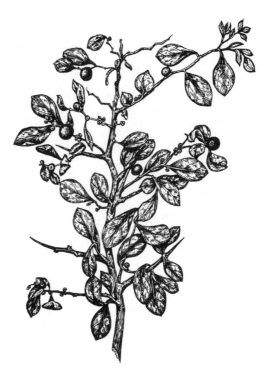

LEAVES. Alternate, or fascicled on short, spinescent branches, obovate to broadly spatulate, margin entire, apex rounded to retuse or truncate and mucronate, base attenuate or cuneate, leathery, ⅓–1½ in. long, ⅓–½ in. wide; light green and lustrous, pubescent at first, glabrous later, paler beneath, midrib prominent, subsessile or short-petioled.

TWIGS. Divaricate, ending in slender, reddish or gray thorns, green to brown or gray, finely velvety-pubescent at first but glabrous later.

BARK. Smooth, pale gray to brown or reddish on branches and young trunks. Old trunks with narrow, flat ridges, deep furrows, and breaking into small thin scales.

WOOD. Light red, sapwood yellow, close-grained, heavy, hard, dense, specific gravity 1.20.

RANGE. Dry soil, central, southern, and western Texas. On the Texas coast from Matagorda County to Cameron County, frequent along the lower Rio Grande. In central Texas in greatest abundance on the limestone plateau area and west to the Pecos River. Less common west of the Pecos and north into the Panhandle area of Texas. Also in Mexico in Nuevo León and Tamaulipas.

REMARKS. The genus name, *Condalia*, is in honor of Antonio Condal, Spanish physician of the eighteenth century, and the species name, *hookeri*, is for Joseph Dalton Hooker (1817–1911) of England. Some vernacular names are Brazil, Logwood, Purple Haw, Capulin, Capul Negro, and Chaparral. The wood yields a blue dye, and is sometimes used for fuel. The flower pollen serves as bee food, and the black fruit makes good jelly, but it is difficult to gather because of the thorns. Birds eagerly devour the fruit. The bushes often form impenetrable thickets.

A variety has been described as the Edwards Bluewood, *C. hookeri* var. *edwardsiana* (V. L. Cory) M. C. Johnst. It differs from the typical species in its longer and narrower light-colored leaves, which are spatulate instead of obovate. At the type locality the tallest shrubs were about 9 ft high, the average was about 7½ ft. The type locality was 29 airline miles northwest of Rocksprings, Edwards County, Texas, at an altitude of approximately 2,400 ft.

Lote-bush Condalia

Zizyphus obtusifolia (T. & G.) Gray [B]

FIELD IDENTIFICATION. Stiff, spiny, much-branched shrub with grayish green grooved twigs.

FLOWERS. Inconspicuous, in clustered umbels; pedicels 1/25–1/12 in. long, pubescent or villous; corolla small, green, 5-parted; petals 5, hooded and clawed, shorter than the sepals; sepals 5, triangular, acute, soft-hairy; stamens 5, inserted on the edge of the disk, opposite the petals; filaments subulate with anther sacs opening lengthwise; style partly 2-cleft with a basal 2–3-celled ovary immersed in a flattened, obscurely 5-lobed disk.

FRUIT. In June, drupe globular, 1/3–2/5 in. in diameter, black, fleshy, not palatable; stone solitary, hard, with a thin, membranous testa.

LEAVES. Alternate, green, thin, firm, glabrous or puberulent, blades ½–1¼ in. long, elliptic, ovate, or narrowly oblong; apex obtuse, acute, retuse or occasionally emarginate; margin entire to coarsely serrate; base narrowed and 3-veined; petioles one-third to one-fourth as long as the blade.

TWIGS. Divaricate, grayish green, grooved, glaucous; spines stout, straight or nearly so, green or brown, to 3 in. long.

BARK. Smooth, light or dark gray.

RANGE. Widespread in central, southern, and western Texas. At altitudes of 5,000 ft in the Chisos Mountains in Brewster County to almost sea level at the mouth of the Rio Grande in Cameron County. On the central Texas limestone plateau. Also in Arizona, New Mexico, and northern Mexico.

REMARKS. The genus name, *Zizyphus*, is from an ancient Greek name derived from the Persian *zizafun*. The species name, *obtusifolia*, is for the obtuse-pointed leaves. Other names used at one time are Z. *lycioides* Gray and *Condalia lycioides* (Gray) Weberb. Vernacular names are Texas Buckthorn, Chaparral, Chaparro Prieto, and Abrojo. The mealy drupe is edible but not tasty. It is eaten by gray fox, raccoon, and various birds. The roots are used as a soap substitute and as a treatment for sores and wounds of domestic animals.

Common Jujube

Ziziphus jujuba Lam. [A, B]

FIELD IDENTIFICATION. Tree to 50 ft, with a diameter of 10

in. The short trunk supports slender ascending branches formed into a rounded head.

FLOWERS. Borne March–May in the axils of the leaves, solitary or a few together on glabrous pedicels 1/16–3/16 in. long; flowers perfect, 1/16–1/8 in. across, yellowish green; calyx campanulate, spreading, 5-lobed, lobes ovate-triangular, acute, keeled within; petals 5, hooded, clawed, 1/25–1/12 in. long, much smaller than the sepals and alternating with them; stamens 5, as long as the petals or shorter and opposite to them; ovary 2–4-loculed, style 2-parted.

FRUIT. Ripe July–November, slender-pediceled, drupe very variable in size and shape, subglobose to oblong, ½–1 in. long, green at first, turning yellowish, reddish brown or black at maturity, pulp yellow, sweet, shriveling later, acidulous; 1–3-celled; seeds usually 2, deeply furrowed, oblong, reddish brown to gray, apices pointed, about ¾ in. long.

LEAVES. Alternate on short thickened spurlike twigs, often somewhat fascicled, ovate to oblong or lanceolate; apex obtuse; base rounded or broadly cuneate, sometimes inequilateral; margin shallowly toothed, some teeth minutely mucronulate; distinctly 3-nerved at base; upper surface dark waxy green and glabrous; lower surface paler and the 3 nerves more conspicuous, glabrous to pubescent, stipules spinescent.

TWIGS. Stout, green to gray or black, some nodes thickened, lateral branchlets thickened and leaves often fascicled on them. Spinelike stipules ⅛–¾ in. long, straight or curved.

BARK. Mottled gray or black, smooth on younger branches, on older branches and trunks roughly furrowed and peeling in loose shaggy strips.

RANGE. Grows on most soils, except very heavy clays or swampy ground. Considered to be a native of Syria. Widely distributed in the warmer parts of Europe, south Asia, Africa, and Australia. Cultivated in North America in Florida, California, and the Gulf Coast states. First introduced into America from Europe by Robert Chisholm in 1837 and planted in Beaufort, North Carolina.

REMARKS. The genus name, *Ziziphus*, is from an ancient Greek name derived from the Persian *zizafun*. The species name, *jujuba*, is the French common name, derived from the Arabic. The tree is also known as the Chinese Date. It is popular with the Chinese and as many as 400 varieties have been cultivated by them. The fruit exhibits great variety in shape, size, and color, sometimes becoming as large as a hen egg. It is processed with sugar and honey and sold in Chinese shops.

In India the wood is used for fuel and small timber, and the leaves for cattle fodder and as food for the Tasar silkworm and lac insect. In Europe it has long been used as a table dessert and dry winter sweetmeat. The Common Jujube has also been used in shelter-belt planting and for wildlife food. *Z. jujuba* var. *inermis* is a thornless variety.

Humboldt Coyotillo

Karwinskia humboldtiana (R. & S.) Zucc. [B]

FIELD IDENTIFICATION. Shrub or small tree attaining a height of 24 ft.

FLOWERS. In axillary, sessile or short-pedunculate, few-flowered cymes ⅓–½ in. long, persistent, perfect; petals 5, hooded, clawed; calyx of 5 sepals, glabrous, about ⅛ in. broad, sepals triangular, acute, keeled within; stamens 5, inserted on the edge of a disk, longer than the petals, filaments subulate; styles united except at apex, stigmas obtuse, ovary immersed by the disk and 2–3-celled.

FRUIT. In October, peduncle one-third to one-half as long as the drupe, subglobose, brown to black at maturity, apiculate, ¼–⅜ in. long; stone solitary, ovoid, smooth, grooved on one side, about ¼ in. long, poisonous.

LEAVES. Opposite or nearly so, ovate, elliptic or oblong; apex acute, obtuse or mucronate; base cuneate or rounded, ¾–1¾ in. long, ½–¾ in. wide, margin entire or undulate, dark lustrous green above, firm, glabrous or puberulent, paler

beneath, conspicuously pinnate-veined and marked with black spots and longitudinal marking on veins and young twigs; petioles slender, 1–3 in.

TWIGS. Gray to reddish brown, smooth, glabrous or puberulent; lenticels abundant, white, oval to oblong.

BARK. Gray, smooth, tight.

WOOD. Hard, strong, tough, but of no commercial value.

RANGE. Dry plains and prairies in the western and south-western parts of Texas. Abundant near the mouth of the Pecos River and near the mouth of the Rio Grande in Cameron County. In Mexico in the states of Tamaulipas, Veracruz, Yucatán, Oaxaca, and Baja California, and south into Central America.

REMARKS. The genus name, *Karwinskia*, is in honor of Wilhelm Friedrich von Karwinski, a Bavarian botanist, who collected plants in Mexico in 1826. The species name, *humboldtiana*, honors Alexander von Humboldt (1769–1859), a Prussian naturalist who explored South America and Mexico, 1799–1804.

In Mexico this plant is known under many local names, such as Tullidora, Capulincillo, Capulincillo Cimarrón, Capulín, Palo Negrito, Margarita, Cacachila, China, Cacohila Silvestre, Frutillo Negrito, Cochila, and Margarita del Cero. The oily seeds are poisonous and when eaten cause paralysis in the limbs of human beings and domestic animals. It is reported that a decoction of the leaves and roots is less poisonous and is used locally in Mexico for fevers. The plant is easily propagated by root divisions.

Carolina Buckthorn

Rhamnus caroliniana Walt. [A, B, C]

FIELD IDENTIFICATION. Shrub or small tree attaining a height of 35 ft, with a diameter of 8 in.

FLOWERS. May–June, borne solitary or 2–10 in peduncled umbels, peduncles to 2/5 in. long or often absent, pedicels 1/8–1/4 in.; flowers perfect, small, greenish yellow; petals 5, each about 1/25 in. long or broad, apex broad and notched, base acute, concave; stamens 5, included, anthers and filaments less than 1/25 in. long; style equaling the calyx-tube, stigma 3-lobed, ovary glabrous and 3-celled; calyx-tube campanulate, about 1/12 in. long, 1/8 in. wide at apex, the 5 sepals glabrous and triangular, apices acuminate.

FRUIT. Drupes August–October, persistent, sweet, spherical, 1/3–2/5 in. in diameter, red at first, at maturity black and lustrous, 3-seeded (occasionally 2–4-seeded); seeds 1/5–1/4 in. long, reddish brown, rounded almost equally at apex and base, rounded dorsally, inner side with a triangular ridge from the apex to notch at base.

LEAVES. Abundant, scattered along the branches, simple, alternate, deciduous, elliptic to broadly oblong, apex acute or acuminate, base cuneate to acute or rounded, sometimes inequilateral, margin indistinctly serrulate or subentire, rather thin, prominently parallel-veined; upper surface bright green, smooth and lustrous, pubescent to glabrous; lower surface velvety pubescent to only puberulent or gla-

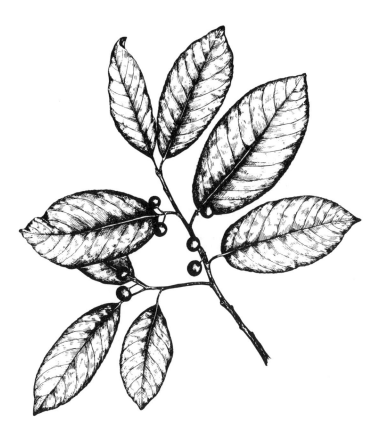

brous, length of blade 2–6 in., width 1–2 in., turning yellow in the fall; petiole slender, 2/5–3/5 in., widened at base, glabrous or pubescent.

TWIGS. Slender, young ones green to reddish, later gray; pubescent at first, glabrous later; sometimes terminating in a cluster of very small folded leaves.

BARK. Gray to brown, sometimes blotched, smoothish, furrows shallow.

WOOD. Light brown, sapwood yellow, close-grained, fairly hard, rather weak, weighing 34 lb per cu ft.

RANGE. Most often in low grounds in eastern, central, and western Texas as far west as the Pecos River, Arkansas, Oklahoma, and Louisiana; eastward to Florida, northward to North Carolina, and west to Missouri.

REMARKS. The genus name, *Rhamnus*, is from an ancient Greek word. The species name, *caroliniana*, refers to the state of South Carolina where it grows. Other vernacular names are Yellow Buckthorn, Indian-cherry, Bog-birch, Alder-leaf Buckthorn, and Polecat-tree. The fruit is eaten by several species of birds, especially the catbird. The shrub appears susceptible to the crown rust of oats. The handsome leaves and fruit make the tree a good ornamental possibility. It is apparently adjustable to both moderately acid and alkaline soil types.

Lance-leaf Buckthorn

Rhamnus lanceolata Pursh [A]

FIELD IDENTIFICATION. Small to large shrub to 9 ft, with an erect and widely branched habit.

FLOWERS. Appearing with the leaves April–May, solitary or in axillary clusters of 2–4 on pedicels 1/12–1/4 in. long, dioecious, greenish, 1/12–1/8 in. broad; petals 4–5, sub-orbicular or obcordate, concave, apex deeply notched, about half as long as the sepals, smaller in the pistillate flowers, inserted on the margin of the disk; stamens 4–5, as long as the petals, filaments short, inserted on the edge of the disk, anthers obtuse; ovary 2–4-celled, glabrous, nearly free, styles united below, bifid above (styles usually short and included in the staminate flower, longer and exserted in the pistillate); calyx-tube campanulate, about ⅛ in. broad; sepals 4–5, tri-angular-ovate, acute, about as long as the tube.

FRUIT. Ripening June–September, drupe 1/5–1/3 in. thick, obovoid to globose, black, 2-seeded; seeds 1/5–1/4 in. long, cartilaginous, deeply grooved dorsally, endosperm fleshy.

LEAVES. Appearing with the flowers, abundant, deciduous, simple, alternate, blades 1–3½ in. long, ½–1 in. wide, ellip-tic to lanceolate or oblong, rarely oval, apex acute to acumi-nate or obtuse on floral branches, base cuneate, obtuse or rounded, margin finely serrulate with incurved, glandular teeth, upper surface glabrous or nearly so, lower surface lighter green and more or less pubescent, especially pubes-cent on the 6–9 pairs of parallel, but inconspicuous, veins; petiole 1/5–2/5 in. long, pubescent to glabrous.

TWIGS. Slender, reddish brown and pubescent at first, later gray, glabrous, and smooth.

RANGE. The species is generally found in moist calcareous soils or on banks or hillsides. Eastern Texas, Arkansas, and Alabama; north to Pennsylvania and west to South Dakota, Illinois, and Missouri.

REMARKS. The genus name, *Rhamnus*, is the ancient Greek name, and the species name, *lanceolata*, refers to the lance-shaped leaves. The plant is of no great economic importance. The fruit is eaten by at least 5 species of birds. It is occasionally cultivated for ornament. The seeds are sown in the fall or stratified for spring planting, and the plant is also propagated by cuttings or grafting. Lance-leaf Buckthorn is apparently hardy as far north as Massachusetts.

Linden Family (Tiliaceae)

American Linden

Tilia americana L. [A]

FIELD IDENTIFICATION. Tree known to attain a height of 130 ft, with a diameter of 4 ft. The branches are usually small and horizontal, or drooping, forming a broad, round-topped head. The root system is wide-spreading, and root sprouts often grow at the base of the trunk.

FLOWERS. May–June, perfect, borne in loose drooping cymes with pedicels slender and glabrous, 6–15-flowered; peduncle 1½–4 in., slender and glabrous, attached to a large foliaceous bract; bract 2–5 in. long, ¾–1½ in. wide, membranous, glabrous, strongly veined, narrowly oblong, apex rounded or obtuse, base narrowed, sessile or short-stalked; sepals 5, small, ovate, acuminate, pubescent within, puberulent externally, considerably shorter than the petals; petals

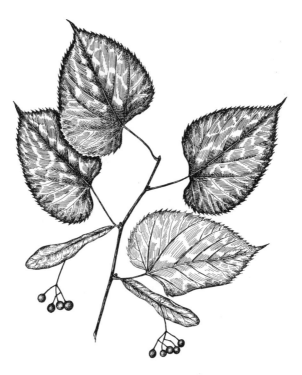

5, yellowish white, lanceolate, crenate, alternate with the sepals, a small scale alternating with each petal; stamens numerous, shorter than the petals; ovary 1, 5-celled, each cell 2-ovuled, ovules anatropous; style simple and tomentose.

FRUIT. Drupaceous, dry, persistent, globose to ovoid, apex rounded or pointed, ¼–⅓ in. long, densely brown-tomentose; 1–2-seeded.

LEAVES. Simple, alternate, deciduous, broad-ovate, apex acute or acuminate, base commonly unsymmetrical, obliquely cordate or almost truncate, margin coarsely serrate, individual teeth with slender, gland-tipped apices; thick and firm, upper surface dark green and glabrous, lower surface paler green and glabrous or some with axillary tufts of hairs, length of blades 5–6 in., width 3–4 in., prominently yellow-veined; petioles 1½–2 in. long, about one-third the length of the blade.

TWIGS. Slender, somewhat divaricate, glabrous, smooth, green to brown, gray later; lenticels numerous, oblong; winter buds dark red, ovoid, about ¼ in. long, mucilaginous; leaf scars half-elliptic, stipule scars conspicuous.

BARK. Light brown to gray, about 1 in. thick on the trunk, the deep furrows separated by narrow, flat-topped, confluent ridges which shed small thin scales.

WOOD. Light brown to reddish brown, straight-grained, rather soft, moderately weak in bending and endwise compression, low in shock resistance, works well with hand tools, finishes smoothly, holds glue, paint, and lacquer well, resistant to splitting, holds nails poorly, seasons well but shrinks considerably, low in durability, weighing 28 lb per cu ft.

RANGE. Rich, moist soil of woods and bottom lands. Northeast Texas, Oklahoma, Arkansas, Missouri, Tennessee, Kentucky, and Georgia; north to Nebraska, Kansas, North Dakota, Minnesota, Illinois, Indiana, Michigan, Pennsylvania, Maine, New Brunswick, Quebec, and Ontario.

REMARKS. *Tilia* is the classical Latin name, and the species name, *americana*, refers to its distribution. It has many vernacular names, such as Bast-tree, Lin-tree, Lime-tree, Bee-tree, Blacklime-tree, White Lind, Whitewood, Southern Lind, American Basswood, Yellow Basswood, Whistlewood, Spoonwood, Daddynuts, Monkeynuts, and Wickyup.

The American Linden has been cultivated for ornament since 1752. The tough inner bark was formerly used for mat fiber and rope by the Indians. The flowers are valuable for bee pasture, and young trees furnish wildlife cover. The fruit is known to be eaten by a number of species of birds and rodents. The wood is valuable for paper pulp, woodenware, cheap furniture, plywood, veneers, panels, cooperage, boxes and crates, casks and coffins, handles, shades, blinds, fixtures, appliances, excelsior, and millwork.

Carolina Linden

Tilia caroliniana Mill. [A, C]

FIELD IDENTIFICATION. Large tree with an irregular, rounded top.

FLOWERS. Borne on slender peduncles, pubescent, in 8–15-flowered cymes and subtended by conspicuous papery bracts; bracts linear, elliptic to obovate, cuneate at the base, rounded or acute at apex, somewhat pubescent at first, becoming glabrous later, 4–5 in. long, about 4/5 in. wide, decurrent or almost so to the peduncle base; sepals 5, shorter than petals, ovate, acuminate, ciliate, brown-pubescent on the exterior, white-hairy within; petals 5, lanceolate, acuminate, somewhat longer than sepals; stamens many, with filaments forked at apex; staminodia about as long as sepals; ovary superior, 5-celled, with a slender style and 5-lobed stigma.

FRUIT. Nutlet subglobose to ellipsoid, apiculate, tomentose, or pubescent, rather small, about 1/8 in. in diameter, 1–3-seeded.

LEAVES. Alternate, simple, deciduous, blades 2⅓–4½ in. long, 1¾–3½ in. wide, broadly ovate, abruptly acuminate,

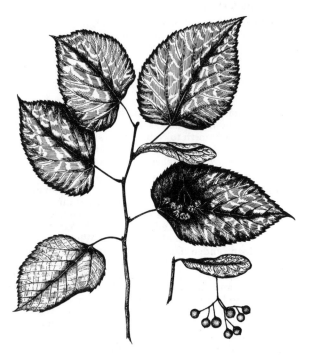

base truncate or cordate and asymmetrical; margin coarsely dentate with glandular apiculate teeth; upper surface dark green, lustrous and glabrous at maturity, lower surface thinly tomentose with brownish fascicled hairs; leaves tomentose on both sides when young; petioles stout, glabrous or slightly pubescent, 1–1½ in.

TWIGS. Slender, reddish brown, pubescent at first, glabrous later.

BARK. Gray, with shallow fissures and flat ridges.

WOOD. Light-colored, soft, light, easily worked.

RANGE. Central and eastern Texas, southwestern Arkansas, and western Louisiana; eastward to Georgia and Florida, and north to North Carolina.

REMARKS. The genus name, *Tilia*, is the classical name, and the species name, *caroliniana*, refers to the states of Carolina. Vernacular names are Basswood, Lime-tree, Whitewood, and Bee Basswood. The tree is a rapid grower and is often planted for ornament. The flowers make good honey, and the wood is used with other species for making interior finishing and woodenware.

The species has a variety known as *T. caroliniana* var. *rhoophila* Sarg., which occurs in Arkansas, Louisiana, and Texas, west to the Guadalupe River. It is distinguished by pubescent twigs and winter buds, larger leaves, and tomentose clusters of more numerous flowers.

Florida Linden

Tilia floridana Small [A, C]

FIELD IDENTIFICATION. Tree attaining a height of 40 ft, with an irregular, rounded crown.

FLOWERS. Borne on tomentose pedicels from large membranous bracts in drooping cymes; bracts decurrent on the petiole, membranous, greenish, glabrous, linear to oblong or spatulate, often falcate, rounded at the apex, 3–6 in. long, flowers in flattened cymes; sepals 5, ovate, acuminate at apex, tomentose, shorter than the petals; corolla about ¼ in. long, yellowish; petals 5, lanceolate; stamens numerous; staminodia often present, oblong-obovate, shorter than the petals; ovary broad, tomentose, 5-celled, style slender, with 5-lobed stigmas.

FRUIT. Nutlet globose or ovoid, apiculate, tomentose, about ¼ in. in diameter, usually 1–3-seeded, ripe in September.

LEAVES. Alternate, simple, deciduous, blades 3–5 in. long, 2½–3½ in. wide; broad-ovate, acuminate at apex, sometimes abruptly so; truncate, rounded, or cordate, and un-

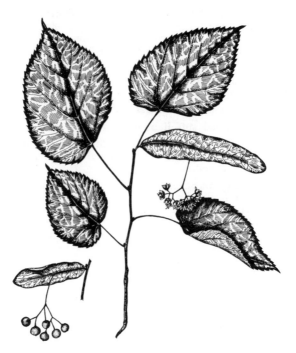

symmetrical at the base; margin coarsely serrate with apiculate teeth; at maturity dark green and glabrous above,
pale and sometimes silvery glaucous, or with axillary hairs
beneath; young leaves tomentose; petioles slender, usually
glabrous, ¾–1 in.

TWIGS. Slender, reddish brown to yellow, tomentose or glabrous.

BARK. Gray, furrows shallow, ridges flat-topped, interlacing
into small angular blocks.

WOOD. Light-colored, light, soft, easily worked.

RANGE. Central and eastern Texas, eastern Oklahoma, Arkan-
sas, and Louisiana; eastward to Florida and northward to
North Carolina and Virginia. In Mexico in Nuevo León,
Coahuila, and Chihuahua.

REMARKS. The genus name, *Tilia*, is the classical name, and
the species name, *floridana*, refers to the plant's Floridian
habitat. Other names are Bee Linden and Florida Basswood.
The tree is propagated by stratified seeds and by layering.
It is a rapid grower and sometimes is planted for ornament. The nectar is a good bee food, and the wood is used

along with other species for interior trim, wood carving, and small woodenware articles.

Mallow Family (Malvaceae)

Shrub-althea

Hibiscus syriacus L. [A, B, C]

FIELD IDENTIFICATION. Much-branched shrub or small tree 3–18 ft. Often grown for ornament and developed into a large number of horticultural forms with single and double, variously colored flowers.

FLOWERS. Showy, perfect, solitary, axillary, on peduncles of variable length; bractlets subtending the calyx usually 5–7, ⅜–¾ in. long, linear to linear-spatulate; calyx longer or shorter than the bractlets; sepals 5, triangular ovate or lanceolate, about as long as the tube; petals 5, very variable in color in the many horticultural forms, white, pink, lavender, rose, with a crimson or purplish blotch at the base, 1¾–3 in. long, rounded to obovate, margins sometimes undulate; staminal column prominent with numerous anthers below, and apex 5-parted with capitate stigmas; ovary sessile, 5-celled and loculicidally 5-valved.

FRUIT. Capsule oblong-ovoid, apex drawn tightly, ¾–1 in. long, pubescent, more or less dry, larger than the calyx.

LEAVES. Alternate, triangular to rhombic-ovate or elliptic to oval, blades 1½–4¾ in. long, margin variously crenate-toothed or notched with rounded or acutish teeth, usually more or less 3-lobed also; young leaves pubescent, when older becoming glabrous or nearly so; palmately veined with 3 veins more conspicuous; petioles generally shorter than the blades; winter buds minute. Some forms with variegated leaves are known.

BARK. Gray to brown, somewhat roughened.

RANGE. Cultivated in gardens and occasionally escaping to roadsides, thickets, and woods. Texas, Oklahoma, Arkansas, and Louisiana; eastward to Florida and northward to Missouri, Ohio, and Massachusetts. Also in coastal regions of Canada.

REMARKS. The genus name, *Hibiscus*, is the ancient name of the European Marsh-mallow, and the species name, *syriacus*, is for Syria, where it was once supposed to be native. However, more recent investigations prove it to be originally from China and India. It is also known under the vernacu-

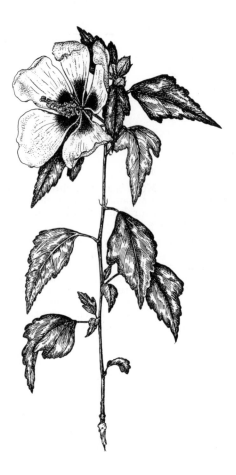

lar names of Rose-of-Sharon and Rose-mallow. It was introduced into cultivation about 1600.

Confederate-rose

Hibiscus mutabilis L. [B]

FIELD IDENTIFICATION. A cultivated, tropical or semitropical, large, many-stemmed shrub, or in favorable circumstances treelike. The twigs, pedicels, peduncles, leaves, and fruit pubescent to tomentose. The large 5-petaled flowers vary in color.

FLOWERS. Usually axillary and clustered toward the ends of the branches. Flowers bisexual, 5-merous; corolla 3–4 in. in diameter, from white to pink or red and somewhat hairy externally. Calyx-lobes 5, broad-ovate to ovate-lanceolate, tomentose; subtended by slender, tomentose bracteoles. Staminal column anther-bearing below the apex; style branches 5, slender and spreading.

FRUIT. Capsule globose, about 1 in. or so long, hairy, dry, dehiscent, dividing into 5 segments at maturity.

LEAVES. Simple, alternate, palmately veined and lobed. Shape broad-ovate to nearly round-ovate, 4–8 in. in diameter; 3–5-lobed, averaging to one-half the depth of the blade; the lobes triangular-acute or acuminate, the terminal lobe usually the longest; margins between lobes shallowly crenate-dentate; surfaces light hairy above, but pubescent or tawny-tomentose beneath; leaf petioles pubescent to tomentose.

TWIGS. Light to dark green or brown, when young tomentose, older pubescent.

RANGE. A native of China. Cultivated in gardens of the Texas Gulf Coast from Galveston to Brownsville.

REMARKS. The genus name, *Hibiscus*, is the ancient name of the European Marsh-mallow. The species name, *mutabilis*, refers to the changing colors of the flowers. Another vernacular name is Cotton-rose. A double-flowered variation is known.

Chocolate Family (Sterculiaceae)

Chinese Parasol-tree

Firmiana simplex W. F. Wight [A, B]

FIELD IDENTIFICATION. Cultivated shrub or tree to 35 ft, with a smooth green bark and a rounded crown.

FLOWERS. In a pubescent, terminal panicle 4–12 in. long; flowers monoecious, small, greenish yellow; petals absent; calyx petallike, sepals 5, valvate, colored, linear to narrowly oblong, reflexed, 1/3–2/5 in. long; stamens united in a column, bearing a head of 10–15 sessile anthers; carpels 5, nearly distinct above, each terminating into a peltate stigma, carpels 2¼–4 in. long at maturity.

FRUIT. A follicle, stipitate, leathery, carpels veiny, finely pubescent, distinct before maturity and spreading open into 5 leaflike bodies bearing 2–several seeds on their margins; seeds globular, pealike, about ¼ in. or less in diameter, albuminous; carpels rudimentary and free in the staminate flowers. A peculiar feature is the black or brown fluid which covers the fruit and is liberated when the follicle bursts.

LEAVES. Alternate, simple, blades 4–12 in. broad and long, cordate to orbicular, palmately 3–5-lobed, lobes entire and acuminate, dull green and glabrous or lightly pubescent above, lower surface glabrous to tomentulose; petiole glabrous or pubescent, usually 5–18 in. long.

TWIGS. Stout, smooth, grayish green, bark of trunk also smooth and green.

RANGE. A native of Japan and China. Cultivated in the United States and escaping to roadsides, woods, and thickets. From South Carolina to Florida and westward to Texas and California. Hardy as far north as Washington.

REMARKS. The genus name, *Firmiana*, honors Karl Joseph von Firmian (1718–1782), at one time governor of Lombardy. The species name, *simplex*, refers to the lobed but

simple leaves. It is also known as Varnish-tree, Phoenix-tree, and Bottle-tree. It is an excellent tree for lawn and shade and has been cultivated since 1757, being easily grown from seed.

A variety with creamy white, variegated leaves is known as *F. simplex* var. *variegata*. Two other species are cultivated in California.

Camellia Family (Theaceae)

Virginia Stewartia

Stewartia malacodendron L. [A]

FIELD IDENTIFICATION. Shrub with upright branching stems, or a small tree to 20 ft.

FLOWERS. Borne April–July, axillary, showy, perfect, solitary or occasionally in pairs, peduncles very short; sepals 5, im-

bricate, broad-ovate to orbicular, apex acute or obtuse, about
⅜ in. long, surface pubescent, united at base and subtended
by 1–2 bractlets; petals 5, spreading, concave, white, obovate, margin crenulate, length 1¼–2 in., somewhat silky-
pubescent, united at base; stamens numerous, in 3–4 series;
filaments purple, united at base into a short tube and hairy
below; anthers blue, introrse, versatile; style 1, compound,
stigma terminal and 5-lobed, surpassing the stamens; ovary
superior, 5-celled, ovules 2 in each cavity.

FRUIT. Capsule depressed-globose, crustaceous, ½–¾ in. in
diameter, angles very low, 5-celled, loculicidally dehiscent;
seeds lenticular, shiny, thick and crustaceous, marginless;
embryo straight.

LEAVES. Simple, alternate, deciduous, membranous, blades
2–4½ in. long, 1½–2 in. broad, oval to elliptic or ovate to
obovate, apex short-acuminate or acute, base acute, margin
finely and sharply serrate with mucronate teeth, mostly gla-

brous above, lower surface light green and pubescent; petioles 1/6–1/3 in., pubescent to glabrous.

TWIGS. Slender, light to dark brown or gray, smooth, pubescent at first, glabrous later.

RANGE. In well-drained, rich, deep soils of wooded banks or hillsides. Eastern Louisiana. Rarely found in Texas, but one colony known 15 miles northwest of Burkville on Little Cow Creek in Newton County. Eastward to Florida and northward to eastern Virginia.

REMARKS. The genus name, *Stewartia*, is in honor of John Stuart (1713–1792), Earl of Bute and patron of botany. The species name, *malacodendron*, is from the Greek *malakos* ("soft") and *dendron* ("tree"), referring to the silky pubescence. Also known under the vernacular names of Silky Camellia and Round-fruited Stewartia.

St. John's-wort Family (Hypericaceae)

Sandbush St. John's-wort

Hypericum fasciculatum Lam. [A]

FIELD IDENTIFICATION. Tall evergreen shrub, under favorable conditions treelike and 3–20 ft in height.

FLOWERS. Through the spring and summer, borne in narrow loose panicles, or some inflorescences corymbose; petals 5, convolute, obliquely apiculate, about 1/3 in. long; stamens numerous, filaments elongate; styles long; sepals 5, about equal, linear, about as long as the petals or fully half as long, 1/8–1/6 in. long, 1/15–1/25 in. wide.

FRUIT. Capsule ovoid or conic-ovoid, 1/6–1/5 in. long, styles persistent, splitting by dehiscence, incompletely 3-celled by intrusion of the placentae.

LEAVES. Numerous, simple, fascicled, a group of smaller ones clustered in the axils of the larger ones, linear-filiform, fleshy, acute at apex, sessile at base, margin entire and revolute, length 3/8–3/4 in.

TWIGS. Numerous, green to brownish, glabrous, sharply angled.

RANGE. Mostly in low, sandy, acid pinelands, often in shallow ponds where its presence indicates a hard sandy bottom. Eastern Texas, eastward through Louisiana to Florida.

REMARKS. The genus name, *Hypericum*, is from the ancient Greek word *huperikon*, which was applied to a species of

St. John's-wort. The species name, *fasciculatum*, refers to the clustered (fascicled) leaves.

Tamarisk Family (Tamaricaceae)

French Tamarisk

Tamarix gallica L. [B]

FIELD IDENTIFICATION. Shrub with contorted branches, or a tree to 30 ft, with a twisted trunk.

FLOWERS. Borne in summer on the current wood, in white or pink racemes, which are grouped to form terminal panicles of variable length; pedicels about 1/50 in. long; sepals 5, 1/25–1/12 in. long, ovate; corolla petals 5, 1/25–1/12 in. long, oblong, mostly deciduous from the mature fruit; stamens 5, filaments 1/12–1/10 in., enlarged toward the base and attached to the corners of the 5-angled disk, anthers mucronate, 2-celled; ovary 1/25–1/15 in. long, set on the disk; styles 3, about 1/50 in. long, clavate.

FRUIT. Capsule very small, 1/12–1/8 in. long, dehiscing into 3 parts; seeds numerous, minute, tufted with hairs at apex.

LEAVES. Foliage sparse, delicate, grayish green, scalelike, alternate, imbricate, 1/50–1/8 in. long, deltoid to lanceolate, acute to acuminate, entire and scarious, glabrous; bracts 1/25–1/15 in. long.

BRANCHES. Drooping and graceful, often sweeping the

African Tamarisk

ground, young ones glabrous or glaucous, reddish to gray later.

WOOD. Light-colored, close-grained, takes a high polish, often twisted or knotty.

RANGE. French Tamarisk was introduced to the United States from Europe. It now grows as an escape from cultivation from Texas eastward to Florida, westward to California, and north to Arkansas and South Carolina.

REMARKS. The genus name, *Tamarix*, is the ancient name, probably with reference to the Tamaracine people of southern Europe, where the plant grew. The species name, *gallica*, refers to a Gallic tribe who lived where the plant grew. Other names are Salt-cedar, Manna-bush, Athel, Eshel, Asul,

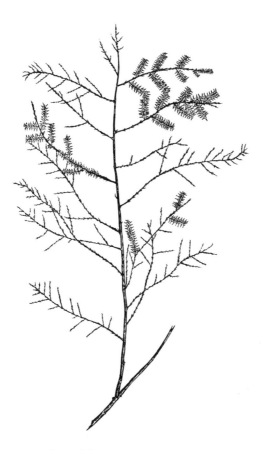

Five-stamen Tamarisk

Athul, and Atle. The low-sweeping branches make excellent wildlife cover.

African Tamarisk, *T. africana* Poir., has black to dark purple bark, sessile leaves, and flowers borne in racemes 1¼–2¾ in. long; ¼–⅓ in. broad, smaller on green branches of the current year; bracts longer than pedicels. Flowers pentamerous; sepals subentire, the outer 2 slightly keeled and longer than the inner more obtuse ones; petals 5, ovate to broadly trulliform-ovate, about 1/12–1/8 in. long in vernal flowers, ⅛ in. long or more in aestival; staminal filaments inserted on gradually tapering lobes of disk. A native of the European and Mediterranean region. Grown in California, Arizona, Texas, and South Carolina.

Five-stamen Tamarisk, *T. pentandra* Pallas, is a shrub or small tree 10–15 ft high. The branches are long, slender,

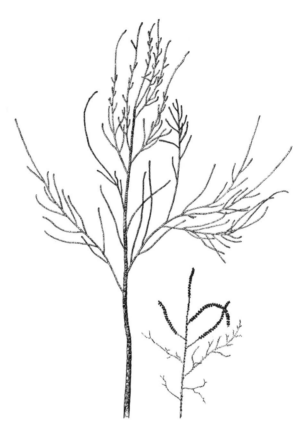

Athel Tamarisk

and plumose, the shoots purplish when young. The largest leaves 1/12–1/8 in. long, lanceolate, others very small, scale-like, crowded, rather glaucous. Flowers rosy pink, usually borne August–September, about ⅛ in. wide, in cylindrical racemes 1–2 in. long; the current season's shoots transformed into slender panicles; bearing 5 stamens. A native of southeastern Europe. First cultivated in 1880 and is late flowering. It may be pruned back hard in the winter. Also listed as *T. pallasii.*

Athel Tamarisk, *T. aphylla* Karst., may be either a bush or tree to 25 ft high. The branches are fastigiate, long, slender, cylindrical-jointed. Leaves reduced to a very short sheath minutely glandular-pitted and salt-secreting with a minute point. Flowers borne in July on more or less interrupted spikes, bisexual, nearly sessile, pink in color, about ⅛ in. broad. Also listed under the names of *T. articulata* or

Smallflower Tamarisk

T. orientalis. A native of India and Africa. Extensively cultivated in coastal Texas, Arizona, and California.

Smallflower Tamarisk, *T. parviflora* DC, has brown to
deep purple bark and may be a shrub or small tree 12–18
ft high. Branches slender and dark purple. Leaves sessile,
ovate, scalelike with hard points. Flowers in April–May,
pale pink in slender racemes about 1 in. long, and 1/8–1/5
in. broad, often on the preceding year's branches; bracts
diaphanous, longer than pedicels; sepals eroded-denticulate,
the outer 2 trulliform or ovate, acute and keeled, the inner
2 ovate and obtuse; petals usually 4, parabolic or ovate,
about 1/12 in. long; stamens 4 or sometimes more, emerging
gradually from the disk lobes. A native of southeastern
Europe. First cultivated in 1853. Introduced and widely
cultivated in the United States.

Flacourtia Family (Flacourtiaceae)

Mexican Xylosma

Xylosma blepharodes Lundell [B]

FIELD IDENTIFICATION. An evergreen shrub, or an irregularly branched spiny tree, to 20 ft.

FLOWERS. Dioecious, very small, borne in axillary fascicles on pedicels 1/12–1/5 in.; petals absent; sepals 4–5, imbricate; stamens numerous, filaments free or nearly so, surrounded by a disk; ovary superior, styles 2–3.

FRUIT. In clusters at the nodes, peduncles 1/8–3/16 in., slender; fruit body subglobose, 1/5–1/4 in. in diameter, green when immature, red later, indehiscent; seeds usually 5, 1/16–1/8 in. long, white, translucent, flattened or angled at base.

LEAVES. Variable in size and shape, simple, alternate, elliptic to oblong, ovate to obovate, coriaceous; apex obtuse to acute or acuminate; base cuneate or rounded; margin coarsely and remotely toothed, or sometimes entire, somewhat revolute; blade length 1–2½ in., width ½–1¼ in., upper surface olive green, glabrous, or pubescent along the veins; lower surface paler, glabrous or pubescent along the veins; petiole variable in length, usually short.

TWIGS. Slender, gray to brown, glabrous or pubescent, with a single, slender, straight spine arising from each node, about ¼ in.; bark smooth when immature, broken into small scales later.

RANGE. Lower Rio Grande Valley area of Texas, near Combes, Cameron County, Texas. A cultivated specimen grows in the yard of Robert Runyon, 812 St. Charles Street, Brownsville, Texas. Known in the Mexican states of Nuevo León, Veracruz, and Chiapas, and also in Guatemala. The type specimen was collected at Jalapa, Veracruz, Mexico.

REMARKS. The genus name, *Xylosma*, is from the Greek words *xylos* ("wood") and *osme* ("smell"). The species name, *blepharodes*, means "fringelike," but the reason for its application is obscure. Some authors list it as *X. flexuosa* (H. B. K.) O. Ktze. Vernacular names are Brush-holly, Manzanillo, Coronilla, and Huichichiltemel. It is reported to be a local remedy for tuberculosis in Central American countries. A number of species are known from Mexico but are not often cultivated in the United States. They can be propagated from seed or from softwood cuttings; they do best under glass, being rather tender.

Papaya Family (Caricaceae)

Papaya
Carica papaya L. [B]

FIELD IDENTIFICATION. Small, usually unbranched, milky-sapped tree 9–25 ft. The very large 7–9-lobed leaves are borne at the top of the tree only.

FLOWERS. The staminate and pistillate flowers are borne on separate trees, or more rarely both sexes are on the same

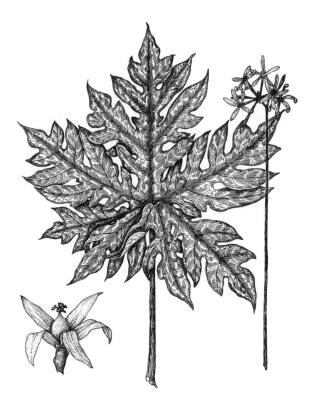

tree. Most axillary, staminate in slender, long-peduncled panicles which are 4 in. long or more; corolla about 1–1¼ in. long, salverform, yellowish white to reddish; tube slender, dilated near the top, limb 5-lobed, the segments lanceolate to elliptic or oblong, barely one-half as long as the tube; stamens 10, inserted in the corolla-throat (5 short-filamented and 5 sessile staminodia); anthers adnate to the filaments, erect, oblong-linear; calyx of staminate flowers 1/25–1/12 in. high, 5-lobed. Pistillate flowers much larger than the staminate, yellow to white, solitary, or in short-peduncled, few-flowered cymes; petals 5, distinct, linear to lanceolate, twisted, ¾–1 in. long; gynoecium a compound pistil, swollen below, style short, stigmas 5-lobed and sessile; ovules numerous, inserted in series on the 5 placentae; calyx of the pistillate flower 1/5–2/5 in. high, 5-lobed.

FRUIT. Usually November–June, but in tropical regions borne almost continually. A melonlike berry, borne near the top of the trunk on very short peduncles, usually 2–8 in. long, but rarely to 18 in. and with a weight of 20 lb, ovoid to oblong or subglobose, indehiscent with a thick rind; flesh firm, yellow or orange, taste cloyingly sweet and insipid, odor pungent; seeds numerous, subglobose, black, roughened.

LEAVES. At the top of the trunk, alternate, very large, blade 8–30 in. wide, suborbicular in outline, palmately 7–9-lobed, each lobe pinnately lobed, segments obtuse or acute, or the larger ones acuminate, upper surface dark green, lower surface paler or glaucous with prominent veins; petiole commonly as long as the blade or longer.

BARK. Green, gray, or purplish; leaf scars large and prominent.

WOOD. Exterior woody parts thin, pith large and porous, trunk often with a cavity within.

RANGE. Considered to be a native of tropical America and cultivated in the warm regions of both hemispheres. Escaped cultivation in southern Florida and the Keys. Cultivated in the lower Rio Grande area of Texas, and the fruit is often sold in the markets there.

REMARKS. The genus name, *Carica*, is from the Latin word for a dried fig, referring to the shape of the fruit. The species name, *papaya*, is thought to be from the Carib Indian name *ababai*. The *papaya* is used for food and medicine by people of the tropical and subtropical regions.

Cactus Family (Cactaceae)

Lindheimer Prickly Pear

Opuntia lindheimeri Engelm. [B]

FIELD IDENTIFICATION. A thicket-forming cactus, heavy-bodied, with a definite cylindrical trunk, erect, or much lower and prostrate. Attaining a height of 3–12 ft.

FLOWERS. April–June, numerous, shallowly bowl-shaped, usually 1 to an areole; sepals and petals numerous, intergrading, hardly distinct, yellow to orange or red, a plant usually producing only 1 shade of flowers, oval to obovate or spatulate, apices rounded or abruptly short-pointed, length ½–2½ in.; stamens numerous, much shorter than the petals; ovary inferior, 1-celled, ovules numerous on thick, fleshy stalks, placentae parietal, withered perianth crowning the ovary and later crowning the fruit; style longer than the stamens, single, thick, stigma lobes short.

FRUIT. Ripening July–September, berry very variable in size and shape, clavate to oblong or globose, length ½–2½ in., red to purple, with scattered tufts of glochids; skin thin,

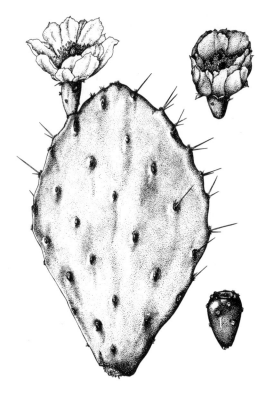

rind thick, pulp juicy; seeds very numerous, about 1/8 in. long, flattened, curved, with a thick bony aril on the edge.

LEAVES. Very small, 1/8–1/6 in. long, pointed, flattened, early deciduous.

JOINTS. Green to bluish green, orbicular or obovate, or sometimes asymmetrical, length to 11 in., flat, waxy, succulent; set with areoles 1–2⅓ in. apart, which produce dense tufts of yellow to brown barbed, minute glochids less than 3/16 in. long; larger spines 1–6, usually 1–2, one erect or semi-erect, the others generally smaller and somewhat spreading, color of spines pale yellow to almost white, sometimes brown or black at base; some joints spineless or nearly so. Some forms are known which lack spines.

RANGE. From coastal southwestern Louisiana westward in drier regions of central Texas (not in east Texas woodlands). The type specimen was collected at New Braunfels, Texas. It is common around San Antonio, Corpus Christi, and Brownsville, Texas. It is not to be confused with O. *engelmannii* of Trans-Pecos Texas.

REMARKS. The genus name, *Opuntia*, is the Latinized name for the town Opus in ancient Greece. The species name, *lind-*

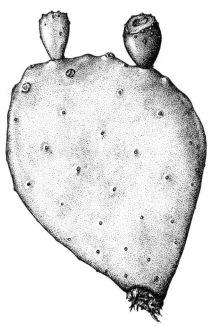

Spineless form

heimeri, is in honor of Ferdinand Lindheimer, a German-born botanist, who collected extensively in Texas in 1836 and 1842.

The plant and its relatives are known under many names in Latin-American countries, such as Nochtli, Culhua, Cancanopa, Pacal, Potzotz, Toat, Pare, Caha, Xantha, and more commonly Nopal. The fruit is known as "tuna."

The Indians and Mexican people formerly used the plant extensively for food. The fruits may be eaten raw or made into a preserve. The joints, when young and tender, are cooked and served with dressing and pepper, and are also made into candy. Syrup is made by boiling the ripe fruit and straining off the seed. The boiled and fermented juice is known as *colonche*. A thick paste made by boiling down the juice is known as *melcocha*. *Queso de tuna* (tuna cheese) is prepared from a pulp of the fruit seed. After evaporation, it is made into small cheeselike pieces. The Indians also believe that a tea made from the fruit will cure ailments caused by gallstones. Commercial alcohol has been made from the sap. The tender young joints are sometimes used as poultices to reduce inflammation. Juice of the joints is boiled with tallow in candlemaking to make the candles hard. The joints are made edible to cattle by burning off the spines. A number of animals and birds feed on the fruit. According to folk-lore, the coyote brushes the spines off the fruit with his tail before eating it.

The Nopal occupies a prominent place in the history and legend of Mexico. The Nopal and Caracara (Mexican Eagle) are the national emblems of Mexico. About 33 species of *Opuntia* are known in Texas, and about 250 species are found mostly in the southwestern United States, Mexico, and Central and South America.

Loosestrife Family (Lythraceae)

Common Crapemyrtle

Lagerstroemia indica L. [A, B, C]

FIELD IDENTIFICATION. Commonly cultivated shrub or small tree to 35 ft, with a very smooth fluted trunk.

FLOWERS. In showy, terminal panicles 2½–8 in. long, pedicels and peduncles bracted; corolla 1–1½ in. across; petals 5–7, but usually 6, purple, pink, white, red, lavender, or blue; stamens numerous, elongate, some upcurved; calyx of 5–8 sepals, shorter than the hypanthium; ovary 3–6-celled, style long and curved, stigma capitate.

FRUIT. Capsule oval-globose, about ⅓ in. long; seeds with a winged apex.

LEAVES. Opposite or alternate, deciduous, obovate-oval, entire, acute or obtuse, broad-cuneate or rounded at base, blades ½–2 in. long, subsessile, glabrous and lustrous above, paler and glabrous or pilose along veins beneath.

TWIGS. Pale, glabrous, 4-angled.

BARK. Thin, exfoliating to expose a smooth, often convoluted, pale surface.

RANGE. A native of India. Cultivated extensively in Texas, Louisiana, Oklahoma, and Arkansas; eastward to Florida, and northward to Virginia. Also cultivated in California.

REMARKS. The genus name, *Lagerstroemia*, is in honor of Magnus Lagerstroem (1696–1759), a Swedish friend of Linnaeus, and the species name, *indica*, is for India. Another vernacular name is Ladies' Streamer.

Some of the common color forms of crapemyrtle are Dwarf (*nana*), Dwarf Blue (*lavandula*), Pink, Purple (*purpurea*), Red (*magenta rubra*), and White (*alba*).

Pomegranate Family (Punicaceae)

Pomegranate

Punica granatum L. [A, B, C]

FIELD IDENTIFICATION. Cultivated, clumped shrub or tree to 25 ft. The branches erect or ascending to form an irregularly shaped crown.

FLOWERS. In simple, axillary or terminal racemes with 1–5 solitary short-peduncled flowers; flowers to 2 in. across, perfect, perigynous, showy, usually red (occasionally white or pink); calyx tubular to campanulate, later subglobose, persistent; 5–7-lobed; lobes valvate, ascending, fleshy, triangular to lanceolate, apex acute, stiffly persistent in fruit; petals 5–7, inserted on the upper part of the calyx between the lobes, imbricate, wrinkled, ⅝–1 in. long, suborbicular or obovate; stamens numerous, in several series, filaments filiform; style 1, stigma capitate; ovary inferior, embedded in the calyx-tube, comprising several compartments in 2 series, ovules numerous.

FRUIT. Berry maturing in September, pendulous, 2–4 in. in diameter, subglobose or depressed, crowned with the persistent calyx; rind thick, leathery, reddish yellow; pulp juicy, pink or red, acidulous; septa membranous, many-celled; seeds numerous, cotyledons convolute and auricled at base.

LEAVES. Simple, deciduous, alternate, opposite or clustered, blades ¾–3½ in. long, oval to oblong or elliptic to lanceolate, apex obtuse or acute, base attenuate into a short wing, margin entire, surface bright green; main vein prominent below, impressed above, other veins inconspicuous, glabrous on both surfaces; petiole ⅛–⅓ in., grooved above, green to red; winter buds with 2 pairs of outer scales.

TWIGS. Slender; younger ones green to reddish brown, somewhat striate or angular; older ones gray and more terete. Bark on older limbs and trunks gray to brown, smooth at first but eventually breaking into small, thin scales, shallowly reticulate.

WOOD. White to yellowish, hard, close-grained, specific gravity about 0.93.

RANGE. Old fields, waste places, and abandoned homesites. A native of Arabia, Iran, Bengal, China, and Japan. Hardy in the United States as far north as Washington, D.C., but does best in subtropical southern regions. Escaping cultivation in the Gulf Coast states.

REMARKS. The genus name, *Punica*, is from the Latin words for "Punic apple," and the species name, *granatum*, means "many-seeded apple." Known in the countries of Central and South America under the Spanish and Indian names of Granada de China, Granada Agria, Granado, Granada, Tzapyan, Yaga-zehi, and Yutnudidzi. The wood is sometimes used by engravers as a substitute for Boxwood (*Buxus*).

From the days of Solomon pomegranate has been used for making cooling drinks and sherbets; it is also eaten in its natural state. The astringent rind yields a black or red dye and has been used for tanning morocco leather and for ink. The fruit is sweet in the better varieties, and a spiced wine is made from the juice. The soft seeds are also eaten, sprinkled with sugar or, when dried, as a confection.

Myrtle Family (Myrtaceae)

Pineapple Guava

Feijoa sellowiana Berg. [B]

FIELD IDENTIFICATION. Cultivated shrub or small tree to 15 ft, the branches spreading to form a dense rounded head.

FLOWERS. In late spring, at the ends of branches, or axillary, solitary, 1–1½ in. in diameter, bisexual; petals 4–5, cupped, spreading, fleshy, white outside, reddish purple within; stamens numerous, long-exserted, tufted, dark red, about 1 in.

FRUIT. Maturing in early winter, berry oval to oblong, 1–2 in. long, ¾–1½ in. thick, dull green to reddish, flesh white-granular, translucent, flavor somewhat pineapplelike; fruit tipped by the irregular persistent calyx; seeds very small and numerous.

LEAVES. Opposite, or some alternate, blade 1–3 in. long, elliptic to oblong or oval, margin entire, apex rounded or obtuse, base broadly narrowed or cuneate; upper surface dark glossy green and puberulent at first to glabrous later; lower surface gray-white with soft, dense, fine tomentum; upper surface dark lustrous green; veins on the upper surface rather obscure and impressed, those of the lower surface raised and conspicuous; petiole ¼–½ in., somewhat channeled above, densely tomentose.

TWIGS. Young ones slender, densely gray-tomentose; older ones gray to reddish brown and glabrous; bark gray on older branches and trunk, separating into thin short scales to expose a reddish under surface.

RANGE. In Texas mostly grown as an ornamental shrub and seldom for fruit. Introduced into the United States in 1900. A native of Paraguay, Uruguay, and Argentina. Suitable for subtropical areas, but will stand some frost. Specimens grown on the University of Texas campus at Austin since 1936 have withstood 15° F.

REMARKS. The genus name, *Feijoa*, is in honor of J. da Silva Feijo, of San Sebastián, Spain. The species name, *sellowiana*, is for Friedrich Sello (1789–1831), German traveler in South America. *Feijoa* is closely related to *Psidium* but has seeds with albumen and stamens suberect in the bud. The fruit may be eaten raw but is usually crystallized or made into jam or jelly.

Common Guava

Psidium guajava L. [B]

FIELD IDENTIFICATION. Tropical shrub or small tree to 30 ft, with a trunk to 1 ft in diameter, the trunk often branching close to the ground.

FLOWERS. In spring, buds tomentose to glabrate, solitary, or in 2–3-flowered cymes; pedicels axillary, ¾–1½ in.; calyx tube oblong-ovate, slightly constricted above the ovary, closed before anthesis, splitting into 3–4 irregular segments 1/3–3/5 in. long, whitish and sparsely hairy within; petals 4–5, white, broadly oval to obovate, thin, delicate, 3/5–4/5 in. long, much longer than the sepals; stamens very numerous, borne on the disk, exserted, erect or spreading, about ½ in. long, anthers tan; stigma subcapitate and greenish; ovary inferior, ovules numerous in each cavity.

FRUIT. Maturing August–September, berry variously shaped, from globular to pyriform in certain varieties, crowned by the persistent calyx, ¾–4 in. long, pulp somewhat acid, flavor sweet, odor very musky; seeds numerous, rounded or flattened, yellowish, white, or pink.

LEAVES. Opposite, leathery, elliptic to oblong or oval, margin entire, apex obtuse to acute or rounded, base rounded or broadly cuneate, blade length 1½–6 in., width 1½–2½ in., at maturity glossy green above and glabrate with impressed veins, lower surface finely pubescent with veins prominent; petioles puberulent to glabrous, 1–2½ in.

TWIGS. Somewhat angled, tomentulose at first, later reddish brown to gray and glabrous; bark on young plants rather smooth, on old trees scaly.

WOOD. Brown to reddish, close-grained, hard, strong, elastic, specific gravity about 0.69, takes a good polish, durable on contact with the soil, but stems usually too small for commercial use.

RANGE. Native of tropical America and cultivated in subtropical areas in southern Texas, southern California, and Florida, where it sometimes escapes cultivation in peninsular Florida and the Keys. Also in the West Indies, Mexico, and Central and South America. Naturalized in Asia and Africa.

REMARKS. The genus name, *Psidium*, is from the Greek word *psidion* ("pomegranate"). The species name, *guajava*, is from the Spanish word *guayabo*. Other names sometimes used in tropical American countries are Gauave, Gaiaba, Gujavabaum, Guayabo de Venado, Guayaba de China, Guayaba Colorado, Guayaba Peruana, Guayaba Perulera, Guayaba de Gusano, Guabaya Manzano, Xalxocoth, Posh, Posh-keip, Enandi, Poos, Poos-cuy, and Bayaba. A grove of these trees is often known as a *guaya-bales* in Mexico. It is also given the English names of Sand-apple and Sand-plum.

Common Guava is a very widely known tropical fruit. It is grown in a number of varieties for its fruit, which is very variable in size and palatability. The raw fruit is only mediocre in flavor but is excellent when made into jelly, jam, paste, or confection. The fruit has a pronounced musky odor. The bark is used for tanning.

Ginseng Family (Araliaceae)

Devil's Walkingstick

Aralia spinosa L. [A,C]

FIELD IDENTIFICATION. Spiny, few-branched shrub, or slender, flat-topped tree to 35 ft. Recognized by very large, twice-pinnate leaves which are 3–4 ft long and 2–4 ft wide.

FLOWERS. July–August; the large terminal panicle of flowers is very conspicuous and is divided into smaller umbels of individual flowers. Pedicels light yellow; corolla white, ⅛ in. across; petals 5, ovate, acute; stamens 5, alternate with petals; ovary 5-celled or abortive, styles distinct, sepals triangular.

FRUIT. September–October, drupe black, fleshy, juice purple, diameter about ¼ in., flattened, 3–5-angled, style persistent; seed solitary, oblong, rounded at ends, flattened, crustaceous, brownish.

LEAVES. Alternate, compound, generally borne at top of trunk, blades 3–4 ft long, 2–4 ft wide, twice-pinnate; pinnae also pinnate with 5–6 pairs of lateral leaflets and a terminal leaflet; leaflets ovate, acute or acuminate, serrate or crenate, cuneate or rounded at base, dark green above, paler beneath, 1–4 in. long, tiny prickles often on midrib, yellow in autumn; petiole 18–20 in. long, clasping the base, prickly; stipules about 1 in. long, acute, ciliate.

BARK. Dark brown, fissures shallow, ridges irregular, armed with orange prickles, inner bark yellow, leaf scars abundant and conspicuous.

WOOD. Brown to yellow, weak, soft, light, close-grained.

RANGE. In rich, moist soil, edges of streams, woods and thickets. East Texas, Oklahoma, Arkansas, and Louisiana; east to Florida; north to New York, Indiana, and Iowa.

REMARKS. Origin of the genus name, *Aralia*, is from the French-Canadian *Aralie*, the name appended to the original specimens sent to Tournefort by the Quebec physician Sarrasin. The species name, *spinosa*, refers to the spiny trunk and branches. Vernacular names are Hercules Club, Angelica-tree, Prickly-ash, Prickly-elder, Pick-tree, Pigeon-tree, and Toothache-tree. The seeds are eaten by many birds and the leaves browsed by white-tailed deer. It is reported that the bark, roots, and berries are occasionally used in medicine. Shrub has high ornamental value and is often planted in Europe.

Dogwood Family (Cornaceae)

Flowering Dogwood

Cornus florida L. [A, B, C]

FIELD IDENTIFICATION. Shrub or tree to 40 ft, with a straggling, spreading crown.

FLOWERS. March–June, perfect in terminal dense clusters; corolla tiny, about ⅛ in. wide, greenish white, tubular; petals 4, linear, acute; stamens 4; true flowers subtended by 4 large white or pink, obcordate, emarginate bracts 1¼–2½ in. long; calyx 4-lobed; ovary 2-celled, with a slender style.

FRUIT. Drupes clustered, conspicuous, bright red, ovoid, lustrous, ¼–½ in. long; seeds 1–2, channeled, ovoid; calyx and style persistent; fruit ripe September–October, dispersed by birds and mammals.

LEAVES. Petioled, simple, opposite, entire, or barely and

minutely toothed, blades 3–5 in. long, 1½–2½ in. wide, oval to ovate or elliptic, acute or acuminate at the apex, somewhat cuneate at the base, often unequal at the base, shiny green and somewhat hairy above, much paler and pubescent below, heavily veined; petioles stout, grooved, about ¾ in.

TWIGS. Slender, yellowish green to reddish, pubescent to glabrous.

BARK. Grayish brown or black, broken into squarish rough checks.

WOOD. Brown or reddish, close-grained, strong, weighing 51 lb per cu ft.

RANGE. Oklahoma, Arkansas, Texas, and Louisiana; eastward to Florida, northward to Maine, and west to Minnesota and Ontario.

REMARKS. The genus name, *Cornus*, is a Latin word for "tough wood," and the species name, *florida*, refers to the showy petallike bracts. Vernacular names are Arrowwood, Boxwood, Cornelius-tree, False Box, Nature's Mistake, Florida Dogwood, and White Cornel. The wood is used for small woodenware articles, tool handles, wheel hubs, and pulleys. The fruit of dogwood is eaten by at least 28 species of birds and ranks 21 on the list of quail-food plants of the Southeast. It is preferred food for wild turkey, also much eaten by squirrels and white-tailed deer. It is reported that Indians made a dye from the roots.

Stiff Dogwood

Cornus foemina Mill. [A]

FIELD IDENTIFICATION. Shrub with stiff, upright irregular branches, or sometimes a small tree to 15 ft.

FLOWERS. Borne May–June in round-topped, rather open cymes 1¼–2½ in. broad; peduncles glabrous, 1–2¾ in.

long; flowers perfect, calyx of 4 minute sepals; petals 4, small, white, oblong, valvate in bud, spreading in anthesis; stamens 4, filaments long and slender, anthers bluish and versatile; style elongate, stigma capitate and terminal; ovary 2-celled, with 1 ovule in each cell.

FRUIT. Drupe maturing August–October, subglobose, 1/5–1/4 in. in diameter, pale blue; seed solitary, longer than broad, slightly furrowed.

LEAVES. Simple, opposite, blade lanceolate to elliptic or ovate-lanceolate, apex acuminate and often abruptly so, base narrowly to broadly cuneate or gradually tapering, blade length 1½–3½ in., one-third to one-half as wide, margin entire, green on both sides, lower surface slightly paler, glabrous or sparingly puberulent; petiole ¼–1 in., glabrous or sparingly puberulent.

TWIGS. Young ones reddish, later greenish to brown or gray; older ones gray and glabrous.

RANGE. Wet woods, bottom lands in sun or shade. East Texas, Louisiana, and Arkansas; east to Florida, north to Virginia, and west to Missouri.

REMARKS. The genus name, *Cornus*, is from the Latin word for "horn," referring to the hard wood. The species name, *foemina*, is a Latin derivation of *female*. It is also known under the names of *C. stricta* Lam. and *Svida stricta* (Lam.) Small.

Gray Dogwood

Cornus racemosa Lam. [A]

FIELD IDENTIFICATION. Thicket-forming shrub to 7 ft. Stems much-branched, ascending, divergent and irregular, smooth, and light gray to brown.

FLOWERS. May–June, borne in open, paniculate, convex cymes 1¼–2½ in. high or broad; peduncles of cymes ⅓–1½ in. long, conspicuously red, appressed-pubescent to nearly glabrous; individual flowers perfect, small, white; petals 4, valvate in the bud, 1/8–1/6 in. long, oblong and spreading or recurved; stamens 4, borne on the disk margin, filaments slender; style 1, ovule single and anatropous; calyx-tube adherent to the ovary, limb minutely 4-toothed.

FRUIT. Drupe ripening July–November on red pedicels, rather persistent, white to gray or greenish, depressed-globose, 1/5–1/3 in. high, pulpy, 1–2-seeded; stone subglobose, apex and base rounded, sometimes shallowly furrowed, about 1/6 in. long and wide, embryo nearly as large as the albumen, cotyledons large and foliaceous.

LEAVES. Opposite, oblong-lanceolate, elliptic or narrowly ovate, apex acuminate, base acute or occasionally rounded,

margin entire, blade length 1–4 in., width ½–1½ in., veins in 3–4 pairs, upper surface olive green, lower surface glaucous and glabrous or slightly appressed pubescent; petioles 1/8–3/5 in., glabrous or appressed-pubescent.

TWIGS. Older ones gray and smooth or somewhat angled, younger ones brown to red, bark bitter, pith white to brown.

RANGE. Sandy or gravelly soil, roadsides and fence rows, thickets, and riverbanks. Arkansas and Oklahoma; east to Virginia, north to Maine, and west to Ontario.

REMARKS. The genus name, *Cornus*, refers to the hard wood, and the species name, *racemosa*, is for the racemelike flowers (however, they are more cymose-paniculate in form). The shrub has also been known in the literature under the name of *C. paniculata* Gray, *C. femina* B. & B., *Svida femina* Small, and *S. foemina* Rydb.

Gray Dogwood has been cultivated for ornament since 1758. It is persistent on unfavorable sites and endures city smoke. Its fruit is known to be eaten by at least 25 species of birds, including ruffed grouse, sharp-tailed grouse, ring-necked pheasant, and bobwhite quail. The wood is hard, heavy, and durable but does not get large enough for commercial use.

Rough-leaf Dogwood

Cornus drummondii C. A. Meyer [A, B, C]

FIELD IDENTIFICATION. Irregularly branched shrub or small spreading tree.

FLOWERS. May–August, perfect, yellowish white, borne in terminal, spreading, long-peduncled cymes 1–3 in. across; peduncles 1–2 in. long, pubescent; individual pedicels ⅛–¾ in. long, branched, glabrous or pubescent; corolla 1/8–3/16 in. across, short-tubular; petals 4, spreading, oblong-lanceolate, acute; calyx-teeth 4, minute, much shorter than the hypanthium; stamens 4, exserted, filaments slender, white, longer than the pistil; style simple, slender, with a terminal somewhat capitate stigma; ovary inferior, 2-celled; annular ring viscid and reddish.

FRUIT. Ripening August–October, drupe globular, about ¼ in. in diameter, white, style persistent, flesh thin; 1–2-seeded, seeds subglobose, slightly furrowed.

LEAVES. Simple, opposite, deciduous, blades 1–5 in. long, ½–2½ in. broad, conspicuously veined, ovate to lanceolate or oblong to elliptic, apex acute or acuminate, base rounded or cuneate, margin entire, plane surface somewhat undulate; upper surface olive green and rather rough-pubescent above; lower surface paler, pubescent and veins prominent; petiole 1/5–3/4 in. long, slender, rough-pubescent, green to reddish.

TWIGS. Young ones green and pubescent, older ones reddish brown and glabrous.

BARK. On young branches and trunks rather smooth, pale gray to brown. On old trunks gray with narrow ridges and fissures, scales small.

WOOD. Pale brown, with sapwood paler, heavy, hard, strong, durable, close-grained.

RANGE. Edges of thickets, streams, and fence rows. Central, southern, and eastern Texas, Oklahoma, Arkansas, and Louisiana; east to Alabama and northward to Ontario.

REMARKS. The genus name, *Cornus*, is from *cornu* ("a horn"), in reference to the hard wood, and the species name, *drummondii*, is in honor of Thomas Drummond (1780–1835), a Scottish botanical explorer. Vernacular names are Cornel Dogwood, Small-flower Dogwood, and White Cornel. The word *dogwood* comes from the fact that a decoction of the bark of *C. sanguinea* was used in England to wash mangy dogs. Rough-leaf Dogwood was formerly listed by some authorities under the name of *C. asperifolia* Michx., but that name is no longer valid.

Rough-leaf Dogwood is sometimes used in shelter-belt planting in the prairie-plains region. It has been known in cultivation since 1836. The wood is used for small woodenware articles, especially shuttle-blocks and charcoal. The fruit is known to be eaten by at least 40 species of birds, including bobwhite quail, wild turkey, and prairie chicken.

Water Tupelo

Nyssa aquatica L. [A, B, C]

FIELD IDENTIFICATION. Large, semiaquatic tree with a conspicuously swollen base, and attaining a height of 100 ft. Male and female flowers on different trees, or sometimes on the same tree.

FLOWERS. March–April, in axillary clusters, polygamo-dioecious, appearing before or with the leaves; staminate clusters capitate; peduncles slender and hairy; bractlets linear and ciliate; petals 5–12, thick, oblong, early deciduous; calyx cuplike, obscurely 5-toothed, shorter than the petals; pistillate flowers solitary on a slender peduncle; bract-

lets 2–4, oblong, ciliate; calyx-tube exceeding the petals; style stout, reflexed, and revolute.

FRUIT. September–October, on drooping peduncles 3–4 in. long; drupe about 1 in. long, oblong-obovoid, dark purple, skin thick, pale-dotted, flesh thin; stone obovoid, compressed, rounded or pointed, brown or white, channeled with about 10 sharp longitudinal ridges.

LEAVES. Simple, alternate, deciduous, oblong-obovate or oval, apex acuminate or acute; base rounded, wedge-shaped or subcordate; margin entire or irregularly scallop-toothed, dark lustrous green above, paler beneath; glabrous above, pubescent beneath, 5–10 in. long, 2–4 in. wide; petioles about 2 in. long, stout, grooved, pubescent.

TWIGS. Dark red, stout, tomentose, pithy.

BARK. Grayish brown, thin, with longitudinal small-scaled ridges.

WOOD. Light brown to white, soft, light, tough, close-grained, weighing 32 lb per cu ft. Wood of roots very light, soft and spongy.

RANGE. In swamps of Texas, Oklahoma, Arkansas, and Louisiana; eastward to Florida and northward to Virginia, Illinois, and Missouri.

REMARKS. The genus name, *Nyssa*, means "water nymph," and the species name, *aquatica*, refers to the tree's habitat. Vernacular names are Tupelo Gum, Cotton Gum, Bay Poplar, Swamp Tupelo, Black Gum, Sour Gum, and Hornbeam. The fruit is eaten by at least 10 species of birds, and the wood is made into boxes, woodenware, and fruit crates. The wood of the light spongy roots is made into net floats and corks. The flowers have some value as a bee food.

Black Tupelo

Nyssa sylvatica Marsh. [A, B, C]

FIELD IDENTIFICATION. Tree to 100 ft, with horizontal branches. Male and female flowers on separate trees, or sometimes together.

FLOWERS. In axillary clusters April–June; polygamo-dioecious, greenish; staminate flowers in long-peduncled capitate clusters; petals small, thick, ovate or oblong, rounded, erect, early deciduous; calyx 5-lobed, disklike; stamens 5–12, exserted, and inserted on the calyx-disk below; pistillate flowers in slender-peduncled clusters of 2 or more; calyx like that of staminate flowers; bracts small but conspicuous and foliaceous; pistil 1–2-celled, style tubular, stigmas exserted.

FRUIT. Ripening September–October, drupelike, 1–3 in a cluster on long peduncles; bluish black, glaucous, about ½ in. long, ovoid, acid, bitter, flesh thin; stone solitary, ovoid to oblong, round or flattened, light brown, indistinctly 10–12-ribbed.

LEAVES. Simple, alternate, deciduous, entire, or with a few coarse remote teeth, 2–6 in. long, 1–3 in. wide; apex acute or acuminate; base cuneate or rounded; ovate or obovate to oval; thick, firm, lustrous green above, paler and hairy below; petiole about 1 in. long, villous-pubescent to glabrous.

BARK. Gray to brown or black, sometimes reddish-tinged; deeply fissured and broken into small irregularly shaped blocks.

WOOD. Tough, heavy, hard, light brown, grain close and twisted, hard to work, warping easily.

RANGE. In moist rich soils. Texas, Oklahoma, Arkansas, and

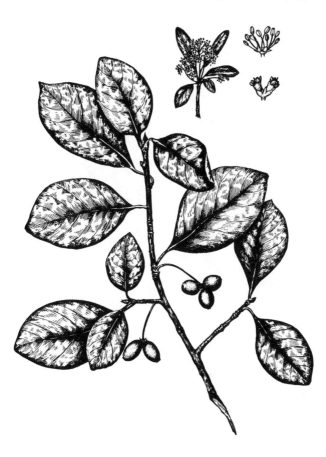

Louisiana; east to Florida, north to Maine, and west to Michigan and Wisconsin.

REMARKS. The genus name, *Nyssa*, means "water nymph," and the species name, *sylvatica*, refers to the wooded habitat. Vernacular names are Swamp-hornbeam, Yellow Gum, Snag-tree, Beetle-bung, Hornbeam, Hornpipe, Hornpine, Hornbine, Pepperridge, Bee Gum, and Sour Gum. The wood is used for veneer, plywood, railroad crossties, boxes, cooperage, pulp, woodenware, hubs, wharf piles, handles, and planing-mill products. Thirty-two species of birds eat the fruit. The foliage is browsed by black bear and white-tailed deer. The flowers serve as bee food.

A variety of Black Tupelo is Swamp Black Tupelo, *N. sylvatica* var. *biflora* (Walt.) Sarg. It closely resembles the species but has narrower obtuse leaves and drupes usually in pairs, and the seeds have ridges and ribs which are more prominent. However, trees with characters intermediate to

Swamp Black Tupelo

the species and the variety are often found, so the distinctions are not clear cut. Both trees are desirable for yard planting.

Heath Family (Ericaceae)

Farkleberry

Vaccinium arboreum Marsh. [A, B, C]

FIELD IDENTIFICATION. Stiff-branched, evergreen shrub, or small crooked tree attaining a height of 30 ft.

FLOWERS. In axillary racemes, leafy-bracted, perfect; corolla about ½ in. long, bell-shaped, pendent, 5-lobed, white or

pinkish; calyx 5-toothed; stamens 10, within the corolla, filaments hairy, anthers slender-tubed; ovary inferior, 5-celled, style filiform with a minute stigma.

FRUIT. About ⅓ in. in diameter, globose, black, shiny, sweet, mealy, dry, many-seeded, persistent, long-peduncled, ripening in winter.

LEAVES. Alternate, simple, 1–3 in. long, about 1 in. wide, oval to obovate or elliptic, entire or obscurely denticulate, mucronate and acute or rounded at apex, cuneate at base, veiny, leathery, glossy above, duller green and slightly pubescent below, deciduous in the North, persistent in the South; petioles 1/25–3/16 in. long.

TWIGS. Slender, light brown to dark brown or grayish, divergent, glabrous or puberulous.

BARK. Gray or grayish brown, thin, smooth, ridges narrow and shredding into large plates.

WOOD. Brown to reddish brown, close-grained, hard, weighing 48 lb per cu ft.

RANGE. Eastern Texas, Oklahoma, Arkansas, and Louisiana; east to Florida, northward to Virginia, and west to Missouri.

REMARKS. The genus name, *Vaccinium*, is the classical name for an Old World species, and the species name, *arboreum*, refers to the treelike habit, which is unusual for huckleberries. Vernacular names are Whortleberry, Sparkleberry, Tree Huckleberry, Gooseberry, and Winter Huckleberry. The edible fruit is eaten by a number of species of birds. The wood is used for making tool handles, and the bark for tanning leather.

He-huckleberry Lyonia

Lyonia ligustrina (L.) Britt. [A]

FIELD IDENTIFICATION. Branching shrub 3–12 ft, with more or less pubescent, entire, oblong to elliptic leaves.

FLOWERS. May–July, panicles elongate with umbellike 2–6-flowered clusters, the panicle naked (except in some varieties in which the panicles are leafy-bracted); pedicels single or clustered, 1/25–1/4 in. long, pubescent; calyx 1/8–1/6 in. broad, sepals 5, spreading, triangular-ovate, 1/25–1/12 in. long, apex acute; corolla white, subglobose to ovoid-globose, 1/8–1/5 in. long, lobes 5, short; stamens 8–12 (usually 10), included, much shorter than the corolla-tube; filaments flat, incurved, pubescent, anthers opening by 2 terminal pores; disk 8–12-lobed; style columnar, stigma truncate, ovary 4–6-celled (usually 5), ovules numerous in each cavity, pendulous.

FRUIT. Capsule dry, globose-depressed, 1/8–1/6 in. long, much longer than the persistent sepals, the 5 sutures thickened and riblike, loculicidally dehiscent into 5 valves.

LEAVES. Deciduous, alternate, firm, blades oblong to elliptic or obovate, blade length 1¼–3½ in., apex acute or abruptly acuminate, base narrowed into a petiole 1/12–1/6 in. long, margin entire or obscurely serrulate, upper surface usually glabrous, lower surface pubescent or glabrate with age.

TWIGS. Terete, spreading widely, pubescent when young, glabrous later.

RANGE. In sandy soils from Arkansas and Oklahoma eastward to Florida, and north to Quebec.

REMARKS. The genus name, *Lyonia*, is in honor of John Lyon, American botanical explorer, who died in Asheville, North Carolina, in 1818. The species name, *ligustrina*, denotes its resemblance to privet, or *Ligustrum*. Also known

under the vernacular names of Maleberry, Pepper-bush, Seedy-buckberry, White-wood, and White-alder.

Bracted He-huckleberry Lyonia, *L. ligustrina* var. *foliosi-flora* Michx., differs from the species by having panicles copiously leafy-bracted and flowers less crowded; corolla white or pinkish with sepals ovate or half-orbicular; foliage glabrous or sparingly pubescent; distinctly serrulate. Usually on the coastal plain from Florida to southern Virginia, and westward into east Texas. Intermediate forms occur between this variety and the species.

Elliott Blueberry

Vaccinium elliottii Chapm. [A]

FIELD IDENTIFICATION. Shrub 3–12 ft, sometimes in colonies. Branches numerous, slender, horizontal or ascending, often forming a crown.

FLOWERS. Usually appearing before the leaves expand, more or less fascicled, corolla cylindric to narrowly urceolate, 1/4–1/3 in. (about twice as long as thick), apex with 5 short teeth, various shades of pink; stamens 10, included, 1/6–1/5 in., filaments pubescent, anthers 2-celled, with apical pores; ovary 4–5-celled, style slender; calyx with 5 deltoid sepals.

FRUIT. Black or dark bluish, dull to lustrous or occasionally glaucous, subglobose, 1/5–1/3 in. in diameter, sometimes even greater, flavor fair to poor, seeds many.

LEAVES. Deciduous, alternate, blade 5/8–1 1/4 in. long, 1/4–5/8 in. wide, usually broadly elliptic, sometimes ovate to oval, apex acute or obtuse, base narrowed or rounded, margin entire or finely serrulate, rather thin; upper surface green, usually glabrous, but sometimes with the midrib pubescent, rather lustrous; lower surface finely pubescent to glabrous, nonglandular.

RANGE. In river-bottom lands subject to flooding, along ravines, open flatwoods, low pinelands, and thickets. Eastern Texas, Louisiana, and Arkansas; eastward to Florida, and northward to Virginia.

REMARKS. The genus name, *Vaccinium*, is from the Latin and is translated "of cows." The species name, *elliottii*, is in honor of Stephen Elliott (1771–1830), an early student of the flora of South Carolina. A vernacular name is Mayberry. *V. elliottii* is sometimes listed by authors under the name of *Cyanococcus elliottii* Small.

Sapodilla Family (Sapotaceae)

Woollybucket Bumelia

Bumelia lanuginosa (Michx.) Pers. [A, B, C]

FIELD IDENTIFICATION. Shrub or an irregularly shaped tree to 60 ft, with stiff, spinose branchlets.

FLOWERS. June–July, in small fascicles ¼–1½ in. across, pedicels hairy or subglabrous, 1/12–3/5 in. long; corolla white, petals 5, each 3-lobed, middle lobe longest, fragrant, 1/8–1/5 in. long, tube about 1/12 in. long; stamens 5, normal and fertile, also 5 sterile stamens (staminodia) which are deltoid-ovate, petaloid, and nearly equaling the corolla-tube; ovary 5-celled, hairy, style 1; calyx 5-lobed, hairy or nearly glabrous, 1/12–1/8 in. long, lobes suborbicular or ovate.

FRUIT. Berry September–October, borne on slender, drooping peduncles, subglobose or obovoid, ⅓–1 in. long, lustrous, black, fleshy; seed solitary, large, brown, rounded, scar small and nearly basal, ¼–½ in. long, no endosperm, cotyledons fleshy.

LEAVES. Alternate or clustered, often on short lateral spurs, oblong-obovate, elliptic or wedge-shaped, apex rounded or obtuse, base cuneate, margin entire, blade length 1–3 in., width ½–1 in., leathery, shiny green and smooth above, varying from rusty to white or gray-woolly beneath; petioles short, averaging about ½ in. long, tomentose.

TWIGS. Gray to reddish brown, zigzag, slender, stiff, spinose, hairy at first with gray, white, or rusty tomentum.

BARK. Dark brown or grayish, fissured and reticulate into narrow ridges with thickened scales.

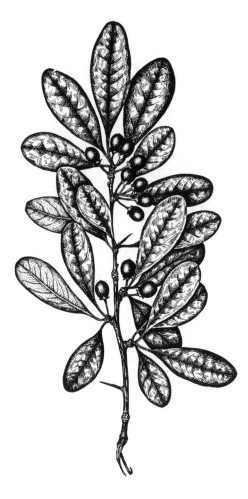

WOOD. Yellow or brown, fairly hard, close-grained, weighing about 40 lb per cu ft.

RANGE. The species occurs in east Texas, Oklahoma, Arkansas, Louisiana, eastward to Florida, north to Kansas, Missouri, Illinois, and Virginia. In central and west Texas represented by its varieties.

REMARKS. The genus name, *Bumelia*, is the ancient Greek name for the European Ash, and the species name, *lanuginosa*, refers to the woolly hairs of the leaf. Vernacular names are Woolly-buckthorn, Woolly Bumelia, Gum Elastic, Gum Bumelia, Chittamwood, False-buckthorn, and Blackhaw. The black fruit is edible, but not tasty, and produces stomach disturbances and dizziness if eaten in quantity (at least this is the experience of the author). Birds are very fond of the fruit; in fact, they get it as soon as it is barely ripe. The wood is used in small quantities for tool handles and cabinetmaking. A gum is freely exuded from wounds on the trunk and branches. The tree has been in cultivation since 1806.

Some authors have split *B. lanuginosa* into a number of varieties and forms according to color, density of hairs on the foliage, and flower parts.

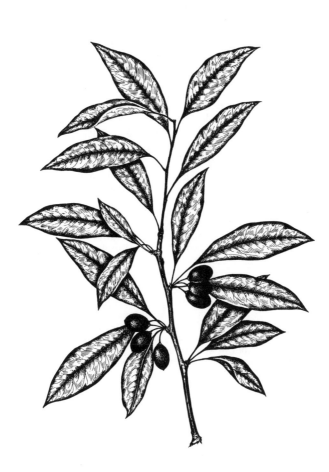

Buckthorn Bumelia

Bumelia lycioides (L.) Gaertn. [A, B]

FIELD IDENTIFICATION. Large shrub or small tree attaining

a height of 25 ft, with spreading branches usually armed with stout spines.

FLOWERS. In dense, many-flowered, axillary fascicles; pedicels glabrous, about ½ in. long; corolla white, about 1/5 in. wide, 5-lobed, lobes each 3-parted (or toothed), lanceolate; staminodia ovate, petallike, denticulate, about one-half as wide as the corolla; stamens 5, anthers sagittate; calyx 5-lobed, lobes oval or ovate; ovary 5-celled, ovoid, style thick and short.

FRUIT. Drupe oval-oblong, black, ¼–⅔ in. long, thin-skinned, pulpy, bittersweet; stone solitary, large, smooth, ovoid or obovoid, abruptly pointed at the apex, hilum large.

LEAVES. Usually clustered on short lateral spurs, except on vigorous growth, simple, alternate, deciduous, blades 2–6 in. long, ½–2 in. wide, entire on margin; acute or acuminate at apex, or rarely obtuse; base gradually tapering; bright green and glabrous above; paler, glabrous, or pubescent, and reticulate-veined beneath; petiole slender, ⅓–1 in. long, pubescent at first but glabrous later.

TWIGS. Rather stout, thick, with lateral spurlike branchlets, unarmed, or armed with stout spines, pubescent at first but later glabrous, shiny, reddish brown to gray.

BARK. Smooth, thin, reddish brown to gray, scales small and thin.

WOOD. Brown to yellow, close-grained, heavy, hard, not strong, weighing 46 lbs per cu ft.

RANGE. Eastern Texas and Arkansas, eastward to Florida, and north to Kentucky, Indiana, and Illinois. Seemingly rather rare in east Texas.

REMARKS. The genus name, *Bumelia*, is the ancient name for a kind of ash tree, and the species name, *lycioides*, applies to the *Lycium*-like fruit, which in turn is named for the country of Lycia. Vernacular names are Buckthorn, Mockorange, Ironwood, Chittamwood, and Gum Elastic. The leaves are browsed occasionally by livestock, and the fruit eaten by a number of species of birds. Various authors state that the fruit is edible, but the author has found it so bitter as to be unpalatable.

Saffron-plum Bumelia

Bumelia angustifolia Nutt. [B]

FIELD IDENTIFICATION. Spiny, divaricately branched shrub, or rarely a tree, to 27 ft, 8 in. in diameter.

FLOWERS. October–November, usually in small fascicles of 2–10 flowers on lateral, spiniferous twigs; pedicels ¼–½ in.

long, glabrous or slightly hairy; individual flowers fragrant, petals 5, 1/6–1/8 in. long, greenish white, oblong to ovate or suborbicular, concave; base bearing lateral, small, narrowly lanceolate lobes; also a set of 5 staminodia which are petal-like, elliptic to lanceolate or round-ovate, erect, erose-dentate on the margin, 1/12–1/8 in. long; stamens 5, anthers sagittate; ovary narrow-ovoid, hairy beneath but glabrous above, style 1/12–1/6 in. long, elongate; calyx glabrous and granular, 1/25–1/16 in. long, sepals in 2 series, inner series usually 3, broadly rounded, outer series 2–3, smaller, rounded to obtuse.

FRUIT. Maturing April–June on the Texas coast, borne on peduncles 1/4–1/2 in. long, glabrous or nearly so; body of fruit black, 1/4–3/4 in. long, about 1/4 in. in diameter, oblong or ellipsoid-cylindric, sometimes slightly wider distally, sometimes asymmetrical; apex of fruit truncate to rounded, with or without an apiculate style remnant; flesh thick, tough, mucilaginous, sweet; seed 3/16–1/2 in. long, elliptic to oblong, apices obtuse, acute, or rounded, somewhat flattened, seed coat white and translucent.

LEAVES. Persistent, alternate, or fascicled at nodes, variable in size, mostly less than 1 in. long, but blades on vigorous shoots sometimes to 2½ in. long, ¼–½ in. broad, oval to obovate or spatulate; margin entire; apex rounded, obtuse, truncate, or slightly notched; base gradually attenuate, cuneate, or rarely rounded; firm and leathery, finely and obscurely reticulate-veined, upper surface glabrous, dark green, and glossy; lower surface essentially glabrous or slightly puberulent when young; petioles 1/16–3/16 in. long, glabrous or pulverulent, stout.

TWIGS. Crooked, gray to brown, glabrous to slightly pubescent, laterals often short and stiff, ending in long, slender, sharp spines.

BARK. Mottled gray to brown on young stems, smooth or finely furrowed; on old trunks with gray, short, squarish, flat ridges and narrow confluent furrows.

WOOD. Brownish orange, sapwood lighter, hard, heavy, close-grained, weak, specific gravity about 0.79.

RANGE. In southern and western Texas. Often on shell mounds near the Gulf of Mexico with other chaparral growth. From Matagorda County to Cameron County. Also in peninsular Florida and the Keys. In Mexico in the states of Nuevo León, Tamaulipas, Veracruz, Oaxaca, and Chiapas. Also in Guatemala, El Salvador, Panama, Colombia, Venezuela, Cuba, and the Bahamas.

REMARKS. The genus name, *Bumelia*, is the classical name for ash tree, and the species name, *angustifolia*, refers to the narrow leaves. Some botanists refer this species under the scientific synonyms of *B. celastrina* H. B. K., *B. schottii* Britt., and *B. spiniflora* DC. Some of the vernacular names are Schott Bumelia, Antwood, Downward-plum, Bagne, Bebelamilla, Coma, Caimito, Hopuche, and Coma Resinera. The fruit is sometimes eaten in Mexico and is also used as an aphrodisiac. The heartwood is occasionally used in cabinet work.

Persimmon Family (Ebenaceae)

Common Persimmon

Diospyros virginiana L. [A, B, C]

FIELD IDENTIFICATION. Tree generally less than 40 ft, rarely reaching 70–100 ft. Habit of growth variable, usually disposed to an upright or drooping type with rounded or conical crown. Branches spreading or at right angles. Twigs self-pruning or some breaking with heavy fruit to form an irregularly shaped tree.

FLOWERS. April–June, staminate and pistillate on separate trees; pollen light and powdery, spread by wind and insects; staminate in 2–3-flowered cymes, tubular, ⅓–½ in. long, greenish yellow; stamens usually 16; pistillate solitary, sessile or short-peduncled, about ¾ in. long or less, stamens 8, some stamens abortive and some fertile; ovary 8-celled, styles 4, 2-lobed at apex; corolla fragrant, 4–5-lobed, greenish yellow, thick, lobes recurved.

FRUIT. Berry persistent, variable as to season, locality, or individual tree, some early or some late (August–February). The very early or very late fruit generally smaller than fruit which ripens about when the leaves fall, seedless fruit also generally smaller; diameter generally ¾–1½ in., shape variable from subglobose or oblate to short-oblong; calyx thick, lobes ovate and recurved; color when mature yellow to orange or dark red, often with a glaucous bloom, flesh pale and translucent, astringent and puckery to taste when green; when ripe somewhat softer and sweet with a high sugar content; 4–8-seeded, seeds large, oblong, flat, leathery, wrinkled, dark brown, about ½ in. long; some trees seedless.

LEAVES. Deciduous, simple, alternate, entire, ovate-oblong to elliptic, apex acute or acuminate, base rounded, cuneate or subcordate, blade length 2–6 in., width 1–3 in., upper surface dark green and lustrous, lower surface paler and pubescent; petiole about 1 in. long or less, glabrous or pubescent.

BARK. Brown to black, fissures deep, ridges broken into rectangular checkered sections.

WOOD. Dark brown to black, sapwood lighter, fine-grained, strong, hard.

RANGE. Thrives on almost any type of soil from sands to shales and mud bottomlands. Generally in the southeastern United States. Gulf states to Iowa and Connecticut. Seemingly the best zone is from Maryland, Virginia, and Carolinas westward through Missouri and Arkansas. In Texas west to the valley of the Colorado River.

REMARKS. The genus name, *Diospyros*, is translated "fruit-of-the-gods," and the species name, *virginiana*, refers to the state of Virginia. Vernacular names are Jove's-fruit, Winter-plum, and Possum-wood. The fruit was known and appreciated by early settlers and explorers, being mentioned in writings of De Soto in 1539, Jan de Laet in 1558, and John Smith in the seventeenth century. The wood of Persimmon is used for handles and shoe lasts, but three-fourths of the supply is made into golf clubs and shuttles. Its hardness, smoothness, and even texture make it particularly desirable for these purposes. The tree is suitable for erosion control on deeper soils because of its deep root system, but this same characteristic makes it difficult to transplant. Also, the rapid spread of a new leaf-wilt disease introduces a factor of caution before extensive plantings are made.

The fruit is eaten by at least 16 species of birds, also by the skunk, raccoon, opossum, gray and fox squirrel, and white-tailed deer. Fallen fruit is also useful in providing some forage for hogs, having a high carbohydrate content. The bark is known to have astringent medicinal properties.

Texas Persimmon

Diospyros texana Scheele [B, C]

FIELD IDENTIFICATION. An intricately branched, smooth-barked shrub or tree up to 40 ft.

FLOWERS. Dioecious, small, solitary or in few-flowered clusters; corolla urn-shaped, greenish white, pubescent, about ⅓ in. long; lobes 5, spreading, suborbicular, often notched at apex; stamens 16, included, anthers glabrous; ovary sessile, pubescent, 4–8-celled, style united with narrow stigmas; calyx-lobes 5, ovate, obtuse, spreading or reflexed, thickened, pubescent.

FRUIT. Depressed-globose, black, apiculate, pulp sweet when mature, astringent when green, about ¾–1 in. long; seeds 3–8, triangular, flattened, hard, shiny, about ⅓ in. long.

LEAVES. Persistent, alternate, leathery, entire, oblong or obovate; apex obtuse, retuse, rounded or emarginate, abruptly narrowed at base, 1–2 in. long, dark green, glabrous above or somewhat pubescent, tomentose below.

BARK. Very smooth, gray, thin layers flaking off.

WOOD. Heavy, black, compact, sapwood yellow, takes a high polish.

RANGE. In Texas and northern Mexico. In central and west Texas usually on rocky hills or the sides of ravines and canyons. Especially abundant in the Texas Edwards Plateau area. When near the coast usually on soils with lime composition because of marine shells. Probably reaching its easternmost limit in Harris County, Texas, near the coast. In Mexico in the states of Nuevo León, Coahuila, and Tamaulipas.

REMARKS. The genus name, *Diospyros*, is translated "fruit-of-the-gods," and the species name, *texana*, refers to the state of Texas. Vernacular names are Mexican Persimmon, Black Persimmon, Chapote, and Chapote Prieto. The fruit is somewhat smaller than that of the Common Persimmon but is likewise sweet and juicy at maturity and is eaten by many birds and mammals. The black juice is used to dye skins in Mexico, and the wood is used for tools and engraving blocks. It was also used in a craft now little practiced—that of ornamenting wooden objects by burning designs into them with an iron.

Sweetleaf Family (Symplocaceae)

Common Sweetleaf

Symplocos tinctoria L'Her. [A, B]

FIELD IDENTIFICATION. Semievergreen shrub or tree up to 35 ft tall and 9 in. in diameter. Branches are slender and upright, giving the tree a wide, loose-spreading appearance.

FLOWERS. Yellowish white, borne in axillary clusters, on branches of previous year, mostly March–May; scales orange-colored, ovate, acute, margin brown and ciliate; bracts 3, at base of each flower, oblong, apex obtuse or rounded, margin ciliate, one longer than others; calyx 5-lobed, oblong, sepals minute, ovate, partly united and shorter than the tube, dark green, puberulent; calyx adherent to ovary as far as sepals. Clusters of flowers 4–14, dense, sessile or short-peduncled; flower fragrant, deciduous, regular, perfect, epigynous; petals 5, obovate to spatulate, ¼–⅓ in. long, united at base; stamens numerous, conspicuously exserted, borne in clusters of 5, one cluster adhering to base of each petal, filaments slender, anthers orange-colored, 2-celled; ovary 3-celled, with 5 dark glands at apex and opposite calyx-lobes; style slender, gradually thickened toward apex and longer than corolla.

FRUIT. Drupe ripe in summer or early autumn, dry, orange-brown, about ¼–½ in. long, 1-celled; seed solitary, ovoid, pointed at ends; seed coat brown, thin, papery; calyx-lobes crowning the fruit.

LEAVES. Persistent in the South, revolute in the bud, drooping on upcurved twigs, alternate, simple, oblong to lanceo-

late or elliptic, apex acute or acuminate, base cuneate, margin obscurely and remotely serrate, or almost entire, teeth often with small, dark, caducous glands, leaf texture thickish and leathery; upper surface dark green, glabrous, and lustrous (sometimes yellowish green); lower surface paler and pubescent with arcuate veins and reticulate veinlets, blades 2–6 in. long, 1–2 in. wide, petioles ⅓–½ in. long, slightly winged, glabrous to pubescent.

TWIGS. Upcurved terminally, slender, terete, gray to reddish brown, pubescent at first, more glabrate later, lenticels scattered; leaf scars low, horizontal.

BARK. Gray to reddish, mostly smooth, but on old trunks has warty excrescences or a few narrow fissures.

WOOD. Light red to brown, sapwood almost white, close-grained, brittle, weak, soft, light, weighs about 33 lb per cu ft; no commercial value.

RANGE. Mostly on the Atlantic and Gulf Coast plain in low, rich grounds of river bottoms and bay flats. From eastern Texas, Oklahoma, Arkansas, and Louisiana, eastward to Florida and northward to Delaware.

REMARKS. The genus name, *Symplocos*, is from the Greek and refers to the united stamens. The species name, *tinctoria*, is applied because a tincture, or dye, is made from the leaves and roots. The leaves and roots are also reported to have medicinal properties. Vernacular names are Yellowwood, Wild-laurel, Florida-laurel, Dye-leaves, and Horse-sugar. The sweet leaves are greedily eaten by livestock. The seeds have also been found in the stomach of the phoebe.

Storax Family (Styracaceae)

Carolina Silver-bell

Halesia carolina L. [A, C]

FIELD IDENTIFICATION. Wide-spreading shrub or tree to 40 ft, diameter 8–18 in. Branches are spreading or erect to form a rounded or irregular crown.

FLOWERS. Borne March–May, axillary, in fascicles of 1–5; pedicels ½–¾ in. long, slender, drooping, villose; axillary bracts ovate, serrate, pubescent or semiglabrous, apex rounded, caducous; calyx obconic, 4-ribbed, glabrous to pubescent (or hoary-tomentose in var. *mollis*), adherent to ovary surface; teeth 4, small and triangular, ciliate; corolla epigynous, open campanulate, 4-lobed, narrowed below into a short tube, white, or more rarely slightly pink, about ¾ in. across; stamens 8–16, shorter than the corolla, inserted near base of tube and united into a ring, monadelphous for part of their length, filaments villose with a few white hairs, anthers linear-oblong; ovary inferior, ovules 4 in each cell, style gradually contracted into a stigmatic apex.

FRUIT. Drupe ripening in autumn, persistent, dry, bony, reddish brown at maturity, oblong to oblong-obovate, 1–2 in. long, ½–¾ in. in diameter, 4-winged; stone ellipsoid to somewhat obovoid, at base narrowed into a short stipe, at apex terminating into an elongate persistent style, ½–⅝ in. long, somewhat angled; seed solitary by abortion (sometimes 2–3), ends narrowed and rounded, dispersed by water, wind, or gravity.

LEAVES. Simple, alternate, deciduous, elliptic or oblong-obovate, apex usually acuminate, base rounded to cuneate or gradually narrowed, margin dentate; young leaves at first with upper surface densely stellate-pubescent above, lower surface with thick hoary tomentum; at maturity upper surface dark yellowish green and glabrous, lower surface pale and glabrous or slightly villose on the midrib and primary veins, blades 3–4 in. long, 1½–2 in. wide (on vigorous shoots 6–7 in.), texture thin, turning yellow in the fall; petiole slender, ¼–½ in. long, at first pubescent to tomentose but later semiglabrous.

TWIGS. Slender, terete, pithy, at first densely pubescent, later

becoming slightly pubescent to glabrous, orange-brown to reddish brown eventually; leaf scars large and obcordate; winter buds axillary, ellipsoid to ovoid, ⅛ in. long; scales thick, broad-ovate, dark red, acute, puberulous.

BARK. Reddish brown, separating into closely appressed scales, slightly ridged, about ½ in. thick.

WOOD. Heart light reddish brown, sapwood lighter colored, soft, close-grained, weighing 35.07 lb per cu ft when dry.

RANGE. In rich well-drained soils of stream banks or wooded slopes, generally where protected. Oklahoma, Arkansas, northeast Texas, and northern Louisiana; eastward to northwest Florida, northward to the Virginias, and westward to Illinois.

REMARKS. The genus name, *Halesia*, is in honor of Stephen Hales (1677–1761), English clergyman and author of *Vegetable Staticks*. The species name, *carolina*, refers to the states of Carolina where it grows. Vernacular names for the tree are Opossum-wood, Silver-bell, Snowdrop-tree, Calico-wood, Tisswood, Bell-tree, Olive-tree, and Chittim-wood. The tree is rarely attacked by insect pests but is easily storm damaged. It is very ornamental and is often cultivated in the eastern United States, California, and central Europe. It was first introduced into cultivation in 1756.

Two-wing Silver-bell

Halesia diptera Ellis [A, B, C]

FIELD IDENTIFICATION. Shrub or small tree to 30 ft, with diameter 3–12 in. Branches are slender and form a small, rounded crown.

FLOWERS. March–April, on branches of the previous year with the young leaves, borne in 2–6-flowered axillary fascicles; pedicels slender, hairy, 1½–2 in. long; flowers perfect, corolla white, drooping, broadly campanulate; tube short, about 1 in. long, nearly divided to the base into 4, spreading, oval to obovate lobes, puberulent, calyx-tube obconical, 1/8–1/6 in. long, pubescent; lobes 4, triangular, acuminate; stamens 8 or more, nearly as long as the corolla, filaments hairy; ovary 2- or rarely 4-celled, style slender, elongate, pubescent; bracts obovate, apex rounded or acute, puberulous.

FRUIT. Drupe oblong to ellipsoid, dry, flattened, 1–2 in. long, with 2 broad thin wings, the remaining angles sometimes with lesser wings, smooth, beak rather short; stone solitary, about ¾ in. long, ellipsoid, ridged, acuminate at both ends.

LEAVES. Buds obtuse, leaves simple, alternate, deciduous, ovate to oval or elliptic to obovate; apex rounded or acute to acuminate, sometimes abruptly so; base rounded or cuneate, margin with remote teeth, blades 3–4 in. long, 2–3 in. wide, upper surface light green and glabrous to pubescent, lower surface paler and soft-pubescent, veins pale and conspicuous; petioles ½–¾ in. long, light green, pubescent, slender.

TWIGS. Slender, gray to brown, lustrous; leaf scars cordate, large, raised; buds ovoid, obtuse, hairy; pith chambered.

BARK. Reddish brown to gray, fissures irregular; flakes small, thin, tight.

WOOD. Light brown, sapwood lighter, close-grained, light, soft, brittle, of little commercial value.

RANGE. In sandy, moist soil along streams or in bottomlands. Texas eastward to Florida. Evidently a Gulf Coast plain species, but extending north into Arkansas, Oklahoma, Tennessee, and South Carolina.

REMARKS. The genus name, *Halesia*, is in honor of Stephen Hales, an English clergyman (1677–1761). The species name, *diptera*, refers to the 2-winged fruit. Vernacular names are Snowdrop-tree, Snow-bell, and Cowlicks. The tree is not subject to insect damage and, being easily damaged by storms, prefers a sheltered growing site. Gray and fox squirrels sometimes eat the fruit. Silver-bell flowers are attractive but unfortunately the tree is generally irregular in shape. It has been cultivated since 1758 and is occasionally grown in Europe.

American Snow-bell

Styrax americanum Lam. [A, B]

FIELD IDENTIFICATION. Widely branched shrub attaining a height of 3–9 ft.

FLOWERS. Borne May–June, fragrant, on short, lateral, leafy branchlets; racemes axillary, short, subtended by small leafy

bracts; flowers solitary or 2–7; pedicels drooping, 1/12–3/5 in. long, when young slightly glandular-pubescent, when older glabrous; calyx greenish, truncate, 1/8–1/6 in. high, lower half adherent to the ovary; lobes 5, small, broadly triangular, sometimes glandular, usually glabrous (pubescent in var. *pulverulentum*); corolla white, 2/5–3/5 in. long, rotate; petals 5, valvate in the bud, elliptic-oblong or lanceolate-oblong, acute to linear-tipped, slightly puberulent externally or glabrous; stamens 10, filaments flat, erect, pubescent below and adnate to the corolla-base; anthers bright yellow, elongate, erect, the sacs united, basi-fixed; ovary half-inferior, 3-celled or at length 1-celled by obliteration of the septa; ovules several in each cavity, ascending; stigma 3-toothed.

FRUIT. Drupe maturing September–October, persistent, dry crustaceous, subglobose or obovoid, about 1/4–1/3 in. in diameter, finely tomentose, calyx persistent on the lower third, dehiscent into 3 thin valves; seed usually solitary, rarely 2–3, globular, erect, hard-coated.

LEAVES. Simple, alternate, deciduous, blades oval, elliptic, or oblong, sometimes ovate to obovate, length ¾–4 in., apex acute or short-acuminate, base usually acute, margin varying from entire to serrate or remotely toothed; upper surface dark green and usually glabrous; lower surface paler or somewhat puberulent to glabrous, pinnately veined; petioles glandular and slightly pubescent to semiglabrous, 1/12–1/6 in. long.

TWIGS. Slender, stellate-pubescent when young but glabrous later; bark thin, smooth, reddish brown to gray.

RANGE. Margins of swamps and streams in rich, moist soil. Arkansas, perhaps also in Texas, and Louisiana; eastward to Florida, northward to Virginia, and westward to Illinois and Missouri.

REMARKS. The genus name, *Styrax*, is the Greek name of the Old World tree producing storax. The species name, *americanum*, refers to its North American habitat. Also known under vernacular name of Spring Orange.

A variety has been segregated and named *S. americanum* var. *pulverulentum* (Michx.) Perkins on the basis of the dense hairiness of the pedicels, calyxes, and petioles. However, it is sometimes difficult to separate the species and variety with certainty because many intermediate forms are found.

Downy American Snow-bell

Styrax americanum var. *pulverulentum* (Michx.) Perkins [A, B]

FIELD IDENTIFICATION. Shrub of sandy lowlands to 12 ft tall and 3 in. in trunk diameter.

FLOWERS. March–April, borne in lateral, leafy-bracted, loosely flowered racemes from 1–4 in. long. Individual flowers 1–4, in the axils, pendent, fragrant. Pedicels ⅛–¼ in. long, scurfy-hairy. Corolla rotate, petals 5, reflexed, imbricate in the bud, white, about ¼ in. long, elliptic to oblong or elliptic to lanceolate, puberulent, apex acute or obtuse; stamens 10, adnate to the corolla-base, exserted; filaments white and threadlike; anthers nearly erect, elongate, about 1/12 in. long, linear, flattened, yellow, longer than filaments; pistil slender, filiform, exserted considerably beyond stamens; ovary nearly superior; calyx persistent, densely scurfy-hairy; shallowly 5-lobed, lobes apiculate.

FRUIT. Capsule subglobose, ¼–⅓ in. in diameter, puberulent, dry with a hard coat, 3-valvate at the summit; seed solitary.

TWIGS. Young ones slender, elongate, green to gray or brown,

densely scurfy-hairy; older ones dark gray to reddish brown, glabrous.

BARK. Rather smooth, dark gray to brown.

LEAVES. Alternate, deciduous, elliptic to oval or obovate to oblong, blades 1–2½ in. long, margin shallowly toothed, slightly revolute, apex acute to abruptly short-acuminate, base cuneate, upper surface dull green, veins impressed, with a few scattered hairs or almost glabrous, lower surface much paler and densely scurfy-hairy; petioles 1/16–1/4 in. long, densely scurfy-hairy.

RANGE. Moist places in sandy soil; east Texas, Arkansas, and Louisiana; eastward to Florida and north to Virginia.

REMARKS. The genus name, *Styrax*, is the Greek name of the Old World tree producing storax. The variety name, *pulverulentum*, refers to the scurfy indument and hairs on the lower leaf surface. Also known by the vernacular names of Powdery Storax and Snow-bell in some localities. Has been in cultivation since 1794. May be propagated by seeds, layers, or grafting.

Some authorities classify Downy American Snow-bell as a distinct species instead of a variety of American Snow-bell. However, the two are so similar that a varietal standing seems most fitting.

Ash Family (Oleaceae)

White Fringe-tree

Chionanthus virginicus L. [A, B]

FIELD IDENTIFICATION. Usually a shrub with crooked branches, but sometimes a tree to 35 ft, with a narrow, oblong crown.

FLOWERS. March–June, perfect or polygamous, in delicate drooping panicles 4–6 in. long; pedicels pubescent; bracts of panicles sessile, oval-oblong, leaflike; calyx small, 4-lobed, persistent, lobes ovate-lanceolate and acute, green, glabrous; petals 4–6, linear, acute, about 1 in. long, white with purple spots near the base, barely united at base, longer than the tube, fragrant; stamens 2; filaments short, adnate to corolla-tube; anthers 2, ovate, light yellow, subsessile; ovary ovoid, 2-celled; style short, thick, 2-lobed; staminate flowers sometimes with sterile pistils.

FRUIT. August–October, drupe borne in loose clusters; bracts leaflike, oval or short-oblong, some 2 inches long; drupe bluish black, glaucous, globose-oblong, ½–¾ in. long, pulp thin, 1-celled, 1–3-seeded; seeds about ⅓ in. long, ovoid, brown, somewhat reticulate. Plants 5–8 years old begin to produce seed.

LEAVES. Simple, opposite, deciduous, oval to oblong or obovate-lanceolate; apex obtuse, acute or acuminate; base wedge-shaped; margin entire or wavy; 4–8 in. long, 1–4 in. wide, dark green and glabrous above, paler below with hairs on veins; petioles ½–1 in. long, puberulent.

TWIGS. Stout, pubescent, light brown to orange, later gray.

BARK. Brown to gray, thin, close, appressed, broken into small thin scales.

WOOD. Light brown, sapwood lighter, hard, heavy, close-grained, weighing about 39 lb per cu ft.

RANGE. Oklahoma, Arkansas, Texas, and Louisiana; eastward to Florida and northward to Pennsylvania and New Jersey.

REMARKS. The genus name, *Chionanthus*, is a combination of two Greek words meaning "snow flower," and the species name, *virginicus*, refers to the state of Virginia. Vernacular names are Flowering Ash, Old Man's Beard, Grandfather-graybeard, Snowflower-tree, Sunflower-tree, Poison Ash, White-fringe, Shavings, and Graybeard-tree. The bark has medicinal uses as a diuretic and fever remedy. The tree is cultivated to some extent for the fragile panicles of flowers in spring and for the dark green foliage. It has been cultivated since 1736. The staminate plants display the attractive delicate, drooping flowers but bear no fruit. The leaves are persistent in winter in the Gulf Coast area, but farther north fall after turning bright yellow.

Downy Forestiera

Forestiera pubescens Nutt. [A, B, C]

FIELD IDENTIFICATION. Sometimes a small tree to 15 ft, and

5 in. in diameter, but usually only a straggling, irregularly shaped shrub.

FLOWERS. Polygamo-dioecious, appearing before the leaves in spring from branches of the preceding year; clusters lateral, from bracts which are obovate, 1/12–1/8 in. long, ciliate, densely pubescent; staminate fascicles greenish; sepals 4–6, small, early-deciduous; petals absent; stamens 2–5; pistillate clusters on slender pedicels of short spurs; ovary 2-celled, 2 ovules in each cell, style slender, stigma capitate or somewhat 2-lobed.

FRUIT. June–October, drupes pediceled, clustered, bluish black, glaucous, ellipsoid, 1/4–1/3 in. long, fleshy, 1-seeded; stone oblong to ellipsoid, ribbed.

LEAVES. Simple, opposite, deciduous, 1/2–1¾ in. long, varying from elliptic to oblong or oval, margin obscurely serrulate, apex obtuse or rounded, base cuneate or rounded; dull green and glabrous or slightly pubescent above; lower surface densely soft-pubescent; petioles short, yellowish green, pubescent.

TWIGS. Green to yellowish and pubescent when young, older ones light to dark gray and glabrous.

RANGE. Mostly in rich moist soil along streams. New Mexico, Texas, and Oklahoma; eastward to Florida.

REMARKS. The genus name, *Forestiera*, honors the French physician and naturalist, Charles Le Forestier, and the species name, *pubescens*, refers to the soft-hairy leaves. Also known under the vernacular names of Devil's-elbow, Chaparral, Spring-herald, Spring-goldenglow, and Tanglewood. The shrub has no particular economic value but has been recommended for erosion control and wildlife cover. It has been cultivated since 1900. About 20 species of *Forestiera* are known, these being distributed in North America, the West Indies, and Central to South America. The various species are propagated by cuttings and seeds, and some are rooted by layering.

Wright Forestiera

Forestiera wrightiana C. L. Lundell [B]

FIELD IDENTIFICATION. Shrub to 6 ft, with short lateral branches.

FLOWERS. Staminate flowers unknown; pistillate flowers lateral, fasciculate or borne in reduced racemes, usually glabrous, sometimes sparsely to densely hirtellous, pedicels 1/25–1/12 in. long; bracts elliptic, ciliate, 1/12–1/10 in. long; calyx small, usually 2–4-lobed, the lobes unequal; petals not evident; staminodia usually 4, reduced; ovary 2-celled, with 2 ovules in each cell; style slender.

FRUIT. Bluish black, glaucous, subglobose, 1/4–2/5 in. long, depressed apically.

LEAVES. Opposite, crowded at the tips of the spurlike branchlets; petioles pubescent, slender, canaliculate; blade subcoriaceous, elliptic or ovate-elliptic, 1/2–2 in. long, 3/4–1 in. wide, apex obtuse, rounded or acutish, base acute, slightly decurrent, margin serrulate, densely pilose beneath over the entire surface, pubescent above along the midvein, primary veins and veinlets slightly impressed above, the primary veins inconspicuous beneath.

TWIGS. Usually shortened, at first pubescent, later glabrous.

RANGE. The following localities are given by Lundell: Texas, Newton County, just off U.S. highway 190, in woods above Cow Creek, September 10, 1942, C. L. Lundell and S. W. Geiser, 11878 (type in the University of Michigan Herbarium, duplicate in the herbarium of Southern Methodist University); same locality and date, Lundell and Geiser,

11879; Harris County, Houston, in low woods, Sept. 18, 1915, E. J. Palmer, 8582.

REMARKS. The genus name, *Forestiera*, is in honor of Charles Le Forestier (d. ca. 1820), French physician and naturalist at Saint-Quentin. The species name, *wrightiana*, is in honor of Charles Wright, early botanical collector of Texas. Cyrus Longworth Lundell, who described the species, remarks that *F. wrightiana*, a species closely allied to *F. ligustrina* (Michx.) Poir., grows in the southeastern region where Wright as a young man made his first collections in the state.

The author has noted a very close resemblance between specimens of *F. wrightiana* with *F. pubescens* Nutt. also. More study is needed to determine whether the two plants are the same.

Texas Forestiera

Forestiera acuminata Poir. [A, B, C]

FIELD IDENTIFICATION. Straggling shrub or tree to 30 ft, growing in swampy ground.

FLOWERS. Dioecious or polygamous; staminate in dense green fascicles subtended by yellow bracts; calyx ring narrow, slightly lobed; petals none; stamens 4; filaments long, slender, erect; anthers oblong, yellow; ovary in staminate flowers abortive; pistillate flowers in short panicles, ¾–1¼ in. long; ovary ovoid with a slender style and 2-lobed stigma, stamens usually abortive or absent.

FRUIT. Drupe ovoid-oblong, purplish, apex acute, tipped with style remnants, base rounded, fleshy, dry, about 1 in. long, young fruit somewhat falcate; seed usually solitary, ridged, compressed, light brown, about ⅓ in. long, one side often flatter than the other.

LEAVES. Simple, opposite, deciduous, elliptical or oblong-ovate, acuminate at apex, cuneate at base, remotely serrulate above the middle, 2–4½ in. long, 1–2 in. wide, glabrous and yellowish green above, paler with occasional hairs on veins beneath; petioles slender, ¼–½ in., slightly winged by leaf bases.

TWIGS. Light brown, glabrous, slender, warty, with numerous lenticels, sometimes rooting on contact with the mud.

BARK. Dark brown, thin, close, slightly ridged.

WOOD. Yellowish brown, close-grained, light, weak, soft, weighing about 39 lb per cu ft.

RANGE. In swamps or bottom lands, Oklahoma, Arkansas, Texas, and Louisiana; eastward to Florida and northward to Tennessee, Indiana, Illinois, and Missouri.

REMARKS. The genus name, *Forestiera*, is in honor of the French physician and botanist, Charles Le Forestier, and the species name, *acuminata*, refers to the acuminate leaves. Another vernacular name is Swamp Privet. It has no particular economic use, except that the fruit is considered to be a good wild duck food.

Narrow-leaf Forestiera

Forestiera angustifolia Torr. [B]

FIELD IDENTIFICATION. Evergreen, dense, stiff, intricately branched shrub. Sometimes a small tree to 25 ft, with a short, crooked trunk.

FLOWERS. Polygamo-dioecious, inconspicuous, greenish, in clusters from scaly bracts; sepals 4, minute, early-deciduous; petals absent; staminate flowers sessile or nearly so; bracts imbricate, oval to ovate, margin fimbricate, yellowish green, about 1/16 in. long; stamens 2–4 in a cluster, conspicuously exserted, erect or spreading, 1/8–3/16 in. long; anthers reddish brown, oblong, hardly over ⅛ in. long; pistil about ⅛ in. long, style slender and gradually swollen below into a 2-celled ovary, developing a stipelike base later, ovules 2 in each cavity.

FRUIT. Drupe short-peduncled, oblong-ovoid, somewhat falcate, acute, ¼–½ in. long, black, 1-seeded, edible but astringent.

LEAVES. On older twigs often clustered on short knotty spurs, on young shoots mostly opposite and more distant, persistent, linear to oblanceolate, apex obtuse, margin entire and somewhat revolute, leathery, light green and glabrous, veins obscure, somewhat porous, blade length ½–1¼ in., width 1/6–1/4 in., sessile or nearly so.

TWIGS. Gray, slender, stiff, smooth, sometimes spinescent; bark of older branches and trunk smooth and gray.

RANGE. On dry, well-drained hillsides, or along stony arroyos in Texas and Mexico. In Texas in the central, western, and southern portions. Also following the coastal shellbanks (limy soil) along the Gulf as far east as Chambers County. Rare in Harris County but found on Hog Island at Tabbs

Bay Ferry and at La Porte and Seabrook close to the bayside.
The coastal plant may be referable to *F. texana* upon more
investigation. In Mexico in the states of Tamaulipas, Nuevo
León, and Coahuila.

REMARKS. The genus name, *Forestiera*, is in honor of Charles
Le Forestier, a French naturalist and physician, and the
species name, *angustifolia*, refers to the narrow, linear
leaves. In Mexico it is known as Panalero and Chaparral
Blanco. The fruit is eaten by a number of birds and mammals, including the scaled quail and gray fox. The plant may
be propagated by seeds and layers. It has some possibility
as an ornamental in close proximity to the Gulf, in saline or
limy soil, where plants are subject to heavy buffeting by
winds.

Japanese Privet

Ligustrum japonicum Thunb. [A, B, C]

FIELD IDENTIFICATION. A much cultivated evergreen, or deciduous in cold climates, becoming a bushy shrub or small tree to 18 ft. Sometimes escaping cultivation. Bark rather smooth and gray. Sometimes confused with the *L. lucidum* Ait., but the latter has larger leaves ovate-lanceolate in shape, with an acute or acuminate apex, and not as glossy as in *L. japonicum* Thunb.

FLOWERS. Borne July–September, bisexual. Panicles terminal, to 4½ in. long. Corolla funnelform, the tube usually somewhat longer than the calyx; the 4 corolla lobes spreading; calyx campanulate, obscurely 4-toothed; stamens 2, slightly longer than the lobes, attached to the corolla tube; ovary 2-celled, with 2 ovules in each cell, or sometimes 1-seeded by abortion.

FRUIT. A drupelike berry, black, oblong or sometimes falcate.

LEAVES. Opposite; 2–4 in. long; shape roundish-ovate to ovate-oblong; base rounded or broadly cuneate; margin entire; apices acute to obtuse; texture coriaceous; color dark green and glossy; with 4–5 pairs of lateral veins, the veins rather obscure beneath; midrib and margin sometimes reddish. Petiole ¼–½ in. long.

TWIGS. Slender, gray to brown, minutely puberulous at first, but glabrous later and lenticellate.

RANGE. A native of Japan and Korea. Introduced into cultivation in 1845. A handsome, much cultivated, evergreen shrub or tree. Sometimes pruned for hedges or for rounded poodle forms.

REMARKS. The genus name, *Ligustrum*, is an ancient Latin name, and the species name, *japonicum*, is for its place of origin. Vernacular names are Privet-berry and Prim. The fruit is greedily eaten by the cedar waxwing and other birds.

A variety known as the Round-leaf Japanese Privet, *L. japonicum* var. *rotundifolium* Bl. (*L. japonicum* var. *coriaceum* Lav., *L. coriaceum* Carr.), is described as a compact shrub to 6 ft, with stiff short branches and leaves crowded; shape broad-ovate or suborbicular; length 1¼–2½ in.; margin obtuse or emarginate; surface dark green and lustrous, often curved; panicle dense, 2–4 in. long; flowers sessile; fruit subglobose, about 1/5 in. in diameter. Introduced into cultivation in about 1860.

Glossy Privet

Ligustrum lucidum Ait. [A, B, C]

FIELD IDENTIFICATION. A cultivated, evergreen, erect, large shrub or tree to 30 ft tall. The branches spreading and lenticellate. Trunk rather smooth and pale to dark gray or blotched gray or whitish.

FLOWERS. Borne July–August in terminal panicles 4–9 in. long, almost as wide. Flowers white, perfect, sessile or subsessile. Corolla salverform, with a rather short tube about as long as the calyx; lobes 4, spreading, about as long as the tube; calyx campanulate and obscurely 4-toothed; stamens 2, about as long as the corolla-lobes; style cylindric, not exceeding the stamens; ovary 2-celled, cells 2-ovuled.

FRUIT. A berrylike drupe, oblong, blue-black, about ⅜ in. long.

LEAVES. Opposite, 3¼–5 in. long; shape ovate-lanceolate; apices acuminate to acute; margin entire; base usually broad-cuneate; venation with lateral veins usually 6–8 pairs which are distinct on both sides; veinlets often impressed; surface glabrous; winter buds ovoid, with about 2 outer scales. Petioles ⅓–¾ in. long.

TWIGS. Slender, light to dark gray.

RANGE. Native to China, Korea, and Japan. Commonly planted in warm regions. Often planted for ornament in the Gulf Coast cities. Common in Houston, Texas. Introduced into cultivation in 1794.

REMARKS. The genus name, *Ligustrum*, is the ancient Latin name. The species name, *lucidum*, refers to a shiny leaf

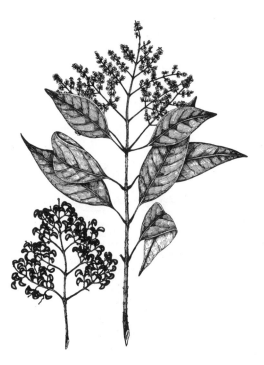

surface. However, this has caused some confusion of names
in the nursery trade, because the Japanese Privet, *L.
japonicum* Thunb., has a much more glossy leaf surface
than *L. lucidum* Ait. Both *L. lucidum* and *L. japonicum*
yield a white wax, an exudation of the branches, caused by
an insect, Pe-lah; therefore, it is cultivated in China. A
number of varieties and horticultural clones have been
named.

Chinese Privet

Ligustrum sinense Lour. [A, B, C]

FIELD IDENTIFICATION. Shrub or small tree to 20 ft, and 5 in.
in trunk diameter. Trunks often clumped and inclined,
branches slender and spreading.

FLOWERS. Inflorescence March–May, fragrant, perfect; borne
in panicles which are terminal, narrow, elongate, 2–6 in.
long and ½–3 in. wide; corolla white, tubular, limb about
⅜ in. across, 4-lobed, lobes spreading, oblong or ovate, acute;
stamens 2, filaments adnate to the corolla-tube, exserted,
longer than the prominent corolla-lobes; pistil shorter than
the stamens, stigma spatulate, flattened; calyx campanulate,

about 1/12 in. long, glabrous, shallowly 4-lobed, lobes acute; pedicels 1/16–1/8 in. long, pubescent.

FRUIT. Drupe bluish black, subglobose to oval or obovoid, seeds 1–2.

LEAVES. Opposite, oval to elliptic, apex rounded to obtuse or slightly notched, base cuneate or rounded, margin entire, length 1–2 in., width ½–1 in., main vein apparent but others obscure; upper surface dark green and semilustrous, glabrous or slightly pubescent along the main vein; lower surface paler, glabrous or slightly pubescent on the main vein; petiole ⅛–½ in., pubescent.

TWIGS. Slender, spreading, gray to brown, pubescent; older branches and trunk smooth, glabrous, and various shades of gray to brown, lenticels pale and scattered.

RANGE. A native of southeast Asia. Grown for ornament in Texas, Oklahoma, Arkansas, Louisiana, and elsewhere throughout the North Temperate Zone, sometimes escaping cultivation.

REMARKS. The genus name, *Ligustrum*, is the ancient classical name, and the species name, *sinense*, refers to its
Chinese origin. It is a handsome plant, much cultivated for
hedges and screens in the South. A number of varieties
have been listed.

Quihoui Privet

Ligustrum quihoui Carr. [A, B, C]

FIELD IDENTIFICATION. Shrub cultivated, slender, erect or
spreading, to 10 ft.

FLOWERS. April–June, heavy-scented, borne in narrow
racemes 2–8 in. long and ½–1 in. wide, lateral branches of
inflorescence ¼–½ in. long, rather densely flowered from
the axils of smaller leaves below, usually leafless above;
calyx sessile or nearly so, puberulent, shallowly 4-toothed;
corolla white, tubular, about ⅛ in. long, the tube as long as
the 4 lobes of the limb or longer, lobes ovate, acute to obtuse;
stamens 2, much exserted, anthers short-oblong, about 1/16
in. long; pistil much shorter than the stamens, included or
slightly exserted, simple, erect, stigma slightly capitate.

FRUIT. Ripening September–November, bluish black, slightly glaucous, 3/16–1/4 in. long, subglobose or slightly flattened; seeds 1–2, about 3/16 in. long, short-oblong to oval; when 2-seeded the outer surfaces are rounded and sculptured and the inner faces plane.

LEAVES. Opposite, simple, partly folded, ⅔–1½ in. long, 3/16–1/4 in. wide, linear to narrowly oblong or elliptic, margin entire; apex obtuse, sometimes slightly notched, base gradually narrowed, upper surface dark green and glabrous; lower surface paler and duller green, glabrous or barely puberulent on the midrib; leaves sessile or short-petiolate, glabrous or puberulent.

TWIGS. Younger ones green and finely pubescent, older ones gray or pale brown and glabrous; bark gray, smooth, and with numerous pale lenticels.

RANGE. A native of China, cultivated in the Gulf Coast states, sometimes escaping.

REMARKS. The genus name, *Ligustrum*, is the ancient classical name. The species name, *quihoui*, honors Antoine Quihou, a French botanist who worked in the late nineteenth century. The plant has been cultivated since 1862. It is an attractive shrub with erect or spreading stems and late-flowering habit and grows well in the Houston area.

Berlandier Ash

Fraxinus berlandieriana A. DC. [A, B, C]

FIELD IDENTIFICATION. Small round-topped tree of western distribution, seldom seen east of the Colorado River except in cultivation. Rarely over 30 ft.

FLOWERS. Dioecious, greenish, staminate and pistillate flowers on different trees; calyx of staminate flower obscurely 4-lobed; stamens 2, filaments short, anthers linear-oblong and opening laterally; calyx of pistillate flower campanulate, deeply cleft; ovary with a slender style and stigmas 2-lobed.

FRUIT. Ripening in May. Samara spatulate to oblong-obovate, 1–1½ in. long, about ¼ in. wide; wing acute or acuminate at apex, decurrent down the seed body almost to the base, set in a deeply lobed calyx; samaras sometimes 3-winged.

LEAVES. Deciduous, opposite, odd-pinnate, slender, petioled, 3–10 in. long; leaflets 3–5, petiolulate, elliptic, lanceolate or obovate, acuminate to acute at apex, cuneate or rounded at base, entire or remotely serrate, thickish, dark green and glabrous above, glabrous or a few axillary hairs beneath, 3–4 in. long, ½–1½ in. wide, petiolule of terminal leaflet longer than those of lateral leaflets. Leaflets fewer, smaller, more coarsely toothed, and more widely separated than those of White Ash or Green Ash.

TWIGS. Green, reddish, or gray, with scattered lenticels, leaf scars small, raised, oval.

BARK. Gray or reddish, fissures shallow and ridges narrow.

WOOD. Light brown, sapwood lighter, close-grained, light, soft.

RANGE. Moist canyons and stream banks. Central Texas to Trans-Pecos Texas; southward in Mexico in Coahuila, Durango, and Veracruz.

REMARKS. The genus name, *Fraxinus*, is the ancient Latin name, and the species name, *berlandieriana*, is in honor of the Swiss botanist, Jean Louis Berlandier (1805–1851), who collected extensively in Mexico and Texas. Local names for the tree are Plumero, Fresno, and Mexican Ash. The wood has no particular commercial importance, but the tree is widely planted as an ornamental in western and southwestern Texas and Mexico.

Carolina Ash

Fraxinus caroliniana Mill. [A, B]

FIELD IDENTIFICATION. Tree of deep swamps, with small branches and rounded open head, to 40 ft.

FLOWERS. Dioecious, appearing in fasciculate panicles before the leaves, yellowish green; no petals; staminate panicles dense; staminate calyx minute; stamens 2–4, with linear-

oblong, apiculate anthers opening longitudinally; pistillate flowers in slender clusters about 2 in. long; pistillate calyx campanulate, deeply cleft, persistent; ovary globose, elongated into a forked style.

FRUIT. Samara oblong-obovate to elliptic, yellowish brown, flattened, thin, smooth, 1–3 in. long, ½–¾ in. broad; seed elliptic, flattened, surrounded by the broad wing; wing pinnately veined, midvein impressed, apex acute, rounded, or emarginate.

LEAVES. Deciduous, opposite, odd-pinnately compound of 5–9 (usually 7) leaflets, 7–12 in. long, petiole elongate; leaflets long-petiolulate, the blades 2–6 in. long, ½–3 in. broad, oblong-ovate, thick, acute, or acuminate at apex, rounded or cuneate at base, serrate or sometimes entire on margin; dark green, lustrous and glabrous above; paler and glabrous or pubescent beneath.

TWIGS. Slender, terete, green, pubescent at first, later brown to gray and glabrous.

BARK. Gray, often blotched, thin, smoothish, with small scales.

WOOD. Yellowish white, close-grained, soft, weak, weighing 22 lb per cu ft, not important commercially.

RANGE. Swamplands, eastern Texas, Arkansas, and Louisiana; eastward to Florida and northward to Washington, D.C., Virginia, and Missouri.

REMARKS. The genus name, *Fraxinus*, is the ancient Latin name, and the species name, *caroliniana*, refers to the states of Carolina. Vernacular names are Poppy Ash, Pop Ash, and Water Ash.

Green Ash

Fraxinus pennsylvanica var. *subintegerrima* (Vahl) Fern. [A, B, C]

FIELD IDENTIFICATION. Spreading, round-topped tree attaining a height of 70 ft or more.

FLOWERS. Dioecious, borne in spring in slender-pediceled, terminal, glabrous panicles; no petals; staminate with a campanulate, obscurely toothed calyx; stamens 2, composed of short, terete filaments and linear-oblong, greenish purple anthers; calyx of pistillate flowers deeply cleft; ovary 2–3-celled, style elongate, with 2 green stigmatic lobes.

FRUIT. Samaras in panicles; samaras flat, 1–2 in. long, ¼–⅓ in. wide, winged; wing decurrent down the side of seed body often past the middle, spatulate or oblanceolate; end of wing square, notched, rounded or acute; seed usually 1-celled, or rarely 2–3-celled.

LEAVES. Deciduous, opposite, odd-pinnately compound, 8–12

in. long, rachis glabrous; leaflets 5–9 (usually 7) ovate to oblong-lanceolate, acute or acuminate at apex, cuneate at base, entire or irregularly serrate on margin, lustrous green on both sides or somewhat paler beneath; glabrous above, usually glabrous below or with scant pubescence on veins, 2–6 in. long, 1–2 in. wide.

TWIGS. Gray, glabrous, terete; lenticels pale.

BARK. Brown, tight, ridges flattened, furrows shallow, scales thin and appressed.

WOOD. Light brown, sapwood lighter, coarse-grained, heavy, hard, strong, weighing 44 lb per cu ft.

RANGE. Texas, New Mexico, Oklahoma, Arkansas, and Louisiana; eastward to Florida, northward to Nova Scotia, and west to Manitoba, Montana, Wyoming, Colorado, and Kansas.

REMARKS. The genus name, *Fraxinus*, is the ancient name of ash tree. The variety name, *subintegerrima*, means spaced between, with reference to the somewhat remote teeth of the leaf margin. Vernacular names are Water Ash, River Ash, Red Ash, Swamp Ash. The wood is not as desirable as that of White Ash but is used for the same purposes, such as tool handles, furniture, interior finishing, cooperage, and wagons. A number of birds eat the seeds, and the foliage is browsed by white-tailed deer and cottontail.

White Ash

Fraxinus americana L. [A, B, C]

FIELD IDENTIFICATION. Tree attaining a height of 100 ft and a diameter of 3 ft. Records show that some trees have reached a height of 175 ft and a diameter of 5 to 6 ft, but such trees are no longer to be found. The general shape is rather narrow and rounded.

FLOWERS. Borne April–May, dioecious, with or before the leaves in staminate and pistillate panicles; staminate clusters short and dense; individual flowers minute, green to red, glabrous; no petals; calyx campanulate, 4-lobed; stamens 2–3, filaments short, anthers oblong-ovate and reddish; pistillate clusters about 2 in. long, slender, calyx deeply lobed; style split into 2 spreading, reddish purple stigmas.

FRUIT. Ripening August–September. Samaras in dense clusters often 6–8 in. long; seed body terete; wing slightly extending down the body of the seed, but usually not at all, oblong or spatulate; often notched at the end, thin, smooth, flat, yellow to brown, 1–2½ in. long, about ¼ in. wide.

LEAVES. Simple, opposite, deciduous, odd-pinnately com-

pound, 8–13 in. long, leaflets 5–9, usually 7, ovate-lanceolate, acuminate or acute, rounded or cuneate at base, entire or crenulate-serrate on margin, dark lustrous green above, paler and whitish and glabrous or pubescent beneath, 3–5 in. long, 1½–3 in. wide; petiole glabrous.

TWIGS. Green to brown or gray, stout, smooth with pale lenticels.

BARK. Light gray to dark brown, ridges narrow and separated by deep fissures into interlacing patterns.

WOOD. Brown, sapwood lighter, close-grained, strong, hard, stiff, heavy, tough, weighing 41 lb per cu ft, seasons well, takes a good polish, moderately durable, shock resistant.

RANGE. Typical White Ash is distributed in Oklahoma, Arkansas, Texas, and Louisiana; eastward to Florida, northward to Nova Scotia, and west to Ontario, Minnesota, Michigan, and Nebraska.

REMARKS. The genus name, *Fraxinus*, is the ancient Latin name, and the meaning of the species name, *americana*, is obvious. Also known as Small-seed White Ash, Cane Ash, Biltmore Ash, and Biltmore White Ash. It has been known in cultivation since 1724. It is an important timber tree and is widely planted as an ornamental. It is estimated that 45 percent of all ash lumber used is from the White Ash. The center of production is now the lower Mississippi valley. No differentiation is made in the lumber trade as to the species of ash; however, the term "white ash" generally designates top quality ash. Ash wood is used for tanks, silos, toys, musical instruments, cabinets, refrigerators, millwork, sash, doors, frames, vehicle parts, farm utensils, woodenware, butter tubs, veneer, fuel, railroad cross ties, sporting goods, furniture, cooperage, handles, ships, boats, railroad cars, and frame parts of airplanes. It usually grows in association with other hardwoods in well-drained soils on slopes. It is valuable in small tracts for woodland management. Although sometimes used, it is not as valuable for shelter-belt planting as Green Ash. The fruit is known to be eaten by a number of birds, including the purple finch and pine grosbeak, and the foliage is browsed by rabbit, porcupine, and white-tailed deer.

Dogbane Family (Apocynaceae)

Common Oleander

Nerium oleander L. [A, B, C]

FIELD IDENTIFICATION. Cultivated, clumped shrub to 18 ft, 3–8 in. in diameter at the base.

FLOWERS. Odorless, blooming during summer in compound, terminal cymes; flowers variously colored, and often double; corolla-tube funnelform, dilated into a narrow-campanulate throat with crownlike appendages 3–5-toothed; limb salverform, 1½–3 in. across, 5-lobed; lobes convolute in the bud, obliquely apiculate, twisted to the right; stamens 5, alternating with corolla-lobes, filaments partly adnate to corolla-tube; anthers with 2 basal tails, apex long-attenuate, hairy, 2-celled; styles united, slender, stigma simple, ovary superior and 2-carpellate; calyx of 5 persistent sepals, imbricate in the bud, lanceolate, acuminate, 1/6–1/4 in. long.

FRUIT. The 2 ovaries forming follicles, erect or nearly so, 4–8 in. long, seeds twisted.

LEAVES. Numerous, opposite, or in whorls of 3–4, linear to elliptic, margin entire and often whitened, revolute, apex and base acute or acuminate, firm and leathery, many-nerved; dark green and glabrous with a conspicuous yellowish green main vein above; paler beneath with numerous, delicate, almost parallel lateral veins.

TWIGS. Erect or arching, young ones green, older ones light brown to gray; lenticels numerous, oval.

RANGE. Cultivated in gardens in Texas and Louisiana, sometimes escaping cultivation. A native of Asia and widely distributed from the Mediterranean region to Japan. Cultivated throughout the tropics and subtropics.

REMARKS. The genus name, *Nerium*, is from the Greek *neros* ("moist"), referring to places the wild plants grow. The species name, *oleander*, is from the Latin, meaning "olivelike," referring to the leaves. The flowers are poisonous if eaten by human beings, and the leaves have been known to kill cattle. They also contain a small amount of rubber. Oleander has been used for rat poison in Europe for many centuries. The symptoms of poisoning in human beings are abdominal pain, dilation of the pupil, vomiting, vertigo, insensibility, convulsive movements, small and slow pulse, and in fatal cases epileptiform convulsions with coma ending in death. The erratic pulsation of the heart where death has not followed has been pronounced, the pulse for 5 days remaining as low as 40 beats per minute. An infusion made from 4 ounces of the root is affirmed to have taken life. The active principle of the plant is a glycoside, oleandrin, which hydrolyzes into a gitoxigenin.

Borage Family (Boraginaceae)

Anaqua

Ehretia anacua (Mier & Berland.) I. M. Johnst. [A, B, C]

FIELD IDENTIFICATION. Half-evergreen shrub or tree with a rounded head and attaining a height of 50 ft.

FLOWERS. March–April, but occasionally in fall after rains. Panicles 2–3 in. long, fragrant; bracts linear, acute, deciduous, about ¼ in. long; corolla small, white, about ¼ in. long, ⅓–½ in. across when open, tube short and campanulate, 5-lobed; lobes oval to ovate; calyx lobes 5, ovate to linear or lanceolate, acute at apex, almost as long as the corolla-tube; stamens 5, adnate to the tube within, filaments filiform; ovary oblong, style split into 2 capitate stigmas.

FRUIT. Drupe ¼–⅓ in. in diameter, globular, yellowish orange, juicy, sweet, edible, 2-celled and 2-seeded, stone separating into 2 bony nutlets rounded on the back and plane on the inner face, seeds terete and erect. A handsome tree when laden with the yellowish orange drupes.

LEAVES. Simple, alternate, half-evergreen, oval to oblong or elliptic, margin entire or coarsely serrate above the middle, apex acute and sometimes apiculate, base cuneate or rounded, leathery, stiff, upper surface very roughened by small, crowded tubercles, upper surface dull olive green, glabrous or slightly pubescent, lower surface paler and pubescent, veins coarse, blade length 1–3½ in., width ¾–1½ in.; petiole stout, grooved, pubescent, ⅛–¼ in. long.

TWIGS. Slender, crooked, brown to gray, when young with pale or brownish hairs, older glabrous; leaf scars small, obcordate and depressed; lenticels pale and numerous.

BARK. Thick, reddish brown to gray or black, broken into narrow, flat-topped ridges and deep fissures, the platelike scales exfoliating into gray or reddish flakes.

WOOD. Light brown, sapwood lighter, close-grained, tough, heavy, hard, difficult to split, specific gravity about 0.64.

RANGE. Usually attaining its largest size in rich river valleys of central and south Texas. Only a shrub on poor, dry soil of hillsides. Southward into the Mexican states of Nuevo León,

Tamaulipas, Coahuila, Guanajuato, and Veracruz. Occasionally as far east as Houston, Texas. Abundantly planted as shade trees in Victoria, Texas.

REMARKS. The genus name, *Ehretia*, is in honor of George Dionysius Ehret (1708–1770), a German botanical artist. The species name, *anacua*, is a latinization of the vernacular name Anaqua. A scientific synonym no longer valid is *E. elliptica* DC. Other vernacular names are Anacahuite, Knackaway, Nockaway, Sugarberry, Manzanita, and Manzanillo. The wood is used for posts, wheels, spokes, axles, yokes, and tool handles. A number of birds and mammals feed upon the fruit. Anaqua is a desirable tree for ornamental planting in its native region. It forms persistent clumps by root suckers, which can be used for transplanting. It is drought resistant and comparatively free of disease. Of the 40 species of *Ehretia* known in the warm regions of the world, only a few are used in horticulture.

Black Mangrove Family (Avicenniaceae)

Black Mangrove

Avicennia germinans L. [B]

FIELD IDENTIFICATION. Shrub, or small tree, of sandy beaches with opposite, oblong or lanceolate, entire leaves.

FLOWERS. July, borne in axillary or terminal spikes; calyx campanulate, sepals 4–5, ovate, rounded or obtuse, densely tomentose; bracts 4–5, imbricate, obtuse or acute, densely tomentose; corolla fragrant, campanulate-rotate, ½–¾ in. long, creamy white, throat yellow, tube short and densely hairy; limb 4-lobed, spreading, lobes oval to obovate, densely white-hairy and ciliate, about 1/12 in. long, some lobes abruptly contracted at base; upper lobe somewhat broader, reflexed, cleft at apex; stamens 4, equal, exserted, glabrous or puberulent, filaments broadened and flattened toward base, partially adnate to corolla; anthers oblong, somewhat asymmetrical, opening below; pistil exserted, pubescent, gradually enlarged toward base; stigma 2-cleft, one lobe larger.

FRUIT. Capsule 2-valved, compressed, oblique, ovate or ellipsoid, very densely pubescent, beaked at the apex, ½–1½ in. long, ⅓–¾ in. wide.

LEAVES. Short-petiolate, entire, leathery, elliptic, oblong or lanceolate, 1½–6 in. long, ⅓–1¾ in. wide, obtuse at apex, acute or acuminate at base, shining above, densely pale-pubescent beneath.

BARK. Dark brown, thin, green when young.

WOOD. Dark brown, close-grained, hard.

RANGE. Sandy tidal flats and lagoons of the Texas coast. On the east end of Galveston Island near the stone breakwaters. East to Florida, south to Mexico, also the West Indies, and Central and South America. In South America it becomes a tree with curious aerating projections rising from superficial roots.

REMARKS. The genus name, *Avicennia*, is in honor of Abdallah Ibn Sina, Arabian philosopher and scientist. The species name, *germinans*, refers to the character of the ovary. This plant has long borne the species name of *nitida*, meaning "shiny" and referring to the leaves. It has the vernacular names of White Mangrove or Mangle Blanco. It is reported that the bark is used for tanning.

Verbena Family (Verbenaceae)

Creeping Skyflower

Duranta repens L. [A, B, C]

FIELD IDENTIFICATION. Spiny, or spineless, shrub or small tree to 18 ft with drooping or trailing branches.

FLOWERS. February–August, in long racemes, peduncles 2–5 in. long, glabrous or sparsely white-hairy; individual pedicels pubescent, 1/16–1/4 in. long; corolla tubular, 1/8–3/16 in. long, somewhat curved, greenish, puberulent, flaring into a salverform, slightly oblique, limb with 5 lobes; lobes violet or purple; lower lobe largest, about ¼ in. long, oval to suborbicular or obovate, base rather abruptly contracted, margin somewhat crisped and ciliolate; 2 lateral lobes of limb 1/8–3/16 in. long, obovate, somewhat asymmetrical, margin crisped and ciliolate; 2 upper lobes smallest, 1/16–3/16 in. long, obovate to spatulate, margin crisped and ciliolate, center usually with a dark purple stripe or spots; throat of tube usually white and hairy; 4 stamens, 2 long and 2 short, adnate to the corolla-tube, included; stigma capitate, 3–4-lobed; calyx tubular, plicate, 3/16–1/4 in. long, green, pubes-

cent or almost glabrous; sepals 5, 1/25–1/16 in. long, subulate.

FRUIT. In long, pendent, loose, heavily-fruited racemes, sometimes up to 1 ft long; pedicels ⅛–½ in. long, glabrous or nearly so; fruit body golden yellow, shiny, subglobose, formed by the accrescent calyx, sepals drawn together at the apex to form a short beak, fleshy, juicy; nutlets 4, ⅛ in. long or less, short-ellipsoid or oval, rounded and grooved on the dorsal surface, ventral surface flattened or angled and notched at one end, brown.

LEAVES. Opposite, elliptic-oblong, ovate to obovate; margin serrate along distal two-thirds, or nearly entire; apex acute, obtuse or apiculate; base gradually narrowed to form a semiwing on the petiole; upper surface dull green, glabrous, veins puberulent and impressed; lower surface paler green, glabrous or pubescent along the prominent veins; blades 2–4 in. long, ¾–1¼ in. wide; petiole short, pubescent, portion not winged by blade mostly less than ¼ in. long.

STEMS. Young stems green to brown or gray, pubescent at first but glabrous later, 4-angled; older stems mostly light brown, rather smooth; spines paired at leaf bases, straight, slender, stiff, sharp, green or brown, pubescent at first, glabrous later, ⅛–¾ in. long.

RANGE. In Texas escaping from cultivation in the lower Rio Grande Valley area. In Mexico in the states of Baja

California, Sinaloa, and Chiapas, to Puebla, Veracruz, and Yucatán.

REMARKS. The genus name, *Duranta*, is in honor of Castor Durantes, physician and botanist in Rome who died about 1500. The species name, *repens*, means "creeping," perhaps with reference to the drooping or trailing branches. Vernacular names are Golden Dewdrop, Violet Duranta, Pigeonberry, Espina Blanca, Xcambocoche, Adonis Blanco, Adonia Morado, Garbancillo, Espino Negro, Celosa, Celosa Cimmarona, Violetina, Espina de Paloma, Lluvia, Azota Caballo, Lila, Cuenta de Oro, Pensamiento, Lora, Heliotropio, and Chulada. This plant is often cultivated for ornamental purposes, and the fruit used as a domestic remedy for fevers.

Lilac Chaste-tree

Vitex agnus-castus L. [A, B, C]

FIELD IDENTIFICATION. Cultivated, aromatic tree to 30 ft, often with many trunks from base. Branches slender and spreading outward to form a wide, broad-topped crown.

FLOWERS. May–September, panicled spikes conspicuous, terminal, dense, puberulent to pulverulent, 4–12 in. long, ½–1¼ in. wide; flowers sessile or very short pediceled; corolla blue to purplish, ¼–⅓ in. long, funnelform; tube slightly curved, densely white-pubescent above the calyx; limb 1/5–1/4 in. broad, slightly oblique, ciliate, white hairs at the limb sinuses, somewhat 2-lipped, 5-lobed, upper 2 lobes and lateral 2 lobes ovate and obtuse, lower lobe largest, obtuse to rounded; stamens 4, exserted, 2 sometimes longer than the others but not always, anthers with nearly parallel, arched or spreading sacs; stigma exserted, slender, 2-cleft; ovary 4-celled and 4-ovuled; calyx campanulate, 1/12–1/8 in. long, densely white-puberulent, irregularly and shallowly 5-toothed, teeth triangular and acute; bractlets and bracteoles linear-setaceous, 1/25–1/6 in. long.

FRUIT. Small, globular, brown to black, 1/8–1/6 in. long, the persistent calyx membranous; stone 4-celled, no endosperm.

LEAVES. Internodes 1¼–4 in. long, leaves decussate-opposite, deciduous, digitately compound of 3–9 (mostly 5–7) leaflets, (blades) 1¼–5 in., central one usually largest, linear to linear-elliptic or lanceolate, apex attenuate-acuminate; base gradually narrowed into a semiwing and channeled, sessile in the smaller leaves; margin entire or plane surface undulate-repand, texture thin; upper surface dull green and glabrous or minutely pulverulent; lower surface paler or almost whitened, puberulent, veins reticulate under magnification; petioles ½–3 in. long, densely grayish or reddish brown, puberulent to pulverulent or cinereous, resinous-granular.

TWIGS. Slender, elongate, quadrangular, green to reddish brown or gray, grayish puberulent and pulverulent, pith stout.

BARK. Smooth, light to dark gray on young branches, on old trunks gray with broad ridges and shallow fissures.

RANGE. Dry, sunny situations, in various types of soils. From China and India, widely cultivated in Europe and Asia. In the United States cultivated from Texas eastward to Florida and northward to North Carolina. Sometimes escaping cultivation.

REMARKS. The genus name, *Vitex*, is the ancient Latin name. The species name, *agnus-castus*, is from *agnus* ("lamb") and *castus* ("pure, holy, or chaste"). Vernacular names are Monk's Pepper-tree, Wild Pepper, Indian Spice, Abraham's Balm, Hemp-tree, Sage-tree, Wild Lavender, Common Chaste-tree, True Chaste-tree, Tree of Chastity, Chaste Lamb-tree.

The seeds of the Chaste-tree are reported to be sedative. In Brazil a perfume is made from the flowers, and the aromatic leaves are used to spice food.

Negundo Chaste-tree

Vitex negundo L. [A, B]

FIELD IDENTIFICATION. A cultivated, deciduous, strong-scented shrub or small tree to 15 ft high. Twigs, underside of leaves, and inflorescence clothed with short gray or white tomentum. Leaves palmate or trifoliate with 3–5 leaflets.

FLOWERS. In late summer or autumn. Inflorescence in a terminal, showy, rather loose thyrsus 5–8 in. long, and nearly as wide; composed of opposite, distant, dense cymes. Flowers closely set on short branches. Corolla about ⅓–1¼ in. long, pale to rather deep blue, tubular-funnelform; bilaterally symmetrical, very hairy in the throat; 2 lobes on the upper lip and 3 lobes on the larger lower lip; often speckled, generally with a yellow horseshoelike mark on the lower lip. Calyx campanulate, small, gray-hairy; often 5-toothed, the teeth triangular or somewhat oblong, ⅓–½ as long as the tube. Stamens 4, didynamous, usually exserted; ovary 2–4-celled, 2–4-ovuled; style filiform, bifid at apex.

FRUIT. Drupe small, globose, 1/5–1/4 in. in diameter, barely longer than the calyx, indehiscent, containing a stone with 1–4 seeds without albumen, endocarp bony.

LEAVES. Opposite, trifoliate or palmate with 3–5 leaflets, 1½–4 in. long; the middle leaflet largest and distinctly stalked; leaflets lance-shaped or elliptic-ovate; apices acuminate; margin entire (in some varieties notched, toothed, or deeply lobed); dark green above; lower surface gray-tomentulose. Petiole ⅓–2 in. long.

TWIGS. Tetragonal, with short, gray or white tomentum, with age less so.

RANGE. Cultivated in the Gulf Coast states and occasionally tending to escape. Native and common and often gregarious in the plains and lower hills of India. Ascending to 5,000 ft in the Northwest Himalayas, extending west to Peshawar and Sind. In China, Malaysia, Java, and Ceylon.

REMARKS. The genus name, *Vitex*, is the ancient Latin name. The species name, *negundo*, is from the Indian plant name *nirgundi*.

Distinguished from V. *agnus-castus* L. by the loose wide

panicle and 3–5 leaflets. Also, *V. negundo* is more root-hardy northward. *Vitex* species do well in any good soil. They are propagated by seeds in spring and by greenwood cuttings under glass. In India the roots and leaves are regarded as tonic and febrifuge. A decoction of the leaves, or their juice, aids in the composition of draughts for headache, catarrh, and a pillow of leaves for a headache.

Trumpet-creeper Family (Bignoniaceae)

Southern Catalpa

Catalpa bignonioides Walt. [A, B, C]

FIELD IDENTIFICATION. Tree to 60 ft and 2–4 ft in diameter. Trunk short, crown broad and rounded, branches stout and brittle.

FLOWERS. May–July, borne in large, erect, broad-pyramidal panicles up to 10 in. long; irregular, perfect, showy and attractive; calyx deeply 2-lipped, about ½ in. long, glabrous, purplish, lips broad-concave, abruptly pointed; corolla white, bell-shaped, tube expanded into throat, 1½–2 in. long, about 1½ in. wide, channeled and keeled on lower side; limb oblique, 2-lipped, upper lip 2-lobed, lower lip 3-lobed, lobes crisped; interior of corolla with 2 rows of yellow and purple spots; fertile stamens 2 (rarely, 4), but some sterile and rudimentary; filaments filiform with spreading linear-oblong anthers; ovary sessile, 2-celled; style filiform with 2 exserted stigmas.

FRUIT. Ripening in October, capsule beanlike, linear, cylindrical, woody, 8–18 in. long, ⅜–½ in. wide, thin-walled, pointed, tardily dehiscent into 2 valves; seeds numerous, flat, about 1 in. long and ¼ in. wide, apices winged and fringed with white hairs.

LEAVES. Simple, opposite or whorled, deciduous, ovate, apex abruptly acuminate or acute, base subcordate or truncate, entire, sometimes lobed, blades 5–12 in. long, upper surface glabrous and light green, lower surface paler and pubescent, strong-scented; petioles stout, terete, shorter than the blade, 5–6 in. long, pubescent.

TWIGS. Stout, brittle, greenish purple to grayish brown, lustrous; lenticels large and pale; leaf scars suborbicular, bundle scars about 10; buds large, subglobose; pith large, white.

BARK. Thin, light brown to gray, divided into narrow scales.

WOOD. Grayish brown to lavender-tinged, sapwood lighter, coarse and straight-grained, no characteristic odor or taste, very durable, weighs about 28 lbs per cu ft, shrinks little, weak in endwise compression, soft, moderately high in shock resistance, weak in bending.

RANGE. Thought to be native from Florida and Georgia, westward into Louisiana. Doubtful whether native in Texas, Oklahoma, and Arkansas, though planted for many years and escaping cultivation in those states and elsewhere.

REMARKS. The genus name, *Catalpa*, is the American Indian name, and the species name, *bignonioides*, refers to its flowers resembling the Bignonia-vine. Abbé Jean Paul Bignon was the court librarian to Louis XV. Vernacular names for the tree are Candle-tree, Cigar-tree, Smoking-

bean, Bean-tree, Catawba, Indian-bean, and Indian-cigar.
The wood of Southern Catalpa is used for posts, poles, rails,
crossties, interior finish, and cabinet work.

Northern Catalpa

Catalpa speciosa Warder [A]

FIELD IDENTIFICATION. Tree usually less than 50 ft, with a narrow or broad head; rarely up to 120 ft and 4½ ft in diameter.

FLOWERS. May–June, borne in panicles 5–8 in. long and broad, terminal, relatively few-flowered, attractive, fragrant; pedicels slender, glabrous, green to purplish, 1–3-bracteate; calyx closed in the bud, 2/5–1/2 in. long, green to purplish, subglabrate, or pubescent, splitting irregularly into 2 broad-ovate, entire, apiculate lobes; corolla campanulate, about 2 in. long and 2½ in. wide, limb oblique and 5-lobed, posterior 2-lobed, anterior 3-lobed, lobes all spreading and margins undulate, externally white, throat marked by rows of yellow blotches with pale purplish spots spreading on lips; stamens 2, filaments flattened, anthers oblong and introrse, staminodia 3, minute or absent; ovary 2-celled, style filiform with 2 stigmatic lobes; ovules in numerous series on the central placenta.

FRUIT. Capsule maturing in October, persistent, solitary or 2–3 together, 8–20 in. long, 3/8–1/2 in. in diameter near the middle, tapering to either end, shape elongate-linear, straight or curved, terete, light brown, wall thick, splitting into 2, loculicidally dehiscent concave valves, seeds numerous, inserted in 2–4 ranks, free from the capsule wall, about 1 in. long and 1/3 in. wide, oblong, compressed, papery-thin, light brown to gray, veined longitudinally, notched at base of seed and ends fringed with hairs.

LEAVES. Involute in the bud, simple, opposite or in threes, deciduous, blades 6–12 in. long, 4–8 in. wide, broadly ovate to oval, apex long-acuminate, base cordate or somewhat rounded, margin mostly entire or with 1–2 lateral teeth, surfaces when young with whitish or brownish tomentum, later dark green and smooth above, paler and pubescent beneath, ribs rather prominent and sometimes with dark axillary glands; petioles 4–6 in. long, stout, terete.

TWIGS. Robust, terete, green to reddish brown or purplish, at first somewhat glaucous and hairy, later more glabrous; lenticels numerous; leaf scars conspicuous, large, raised, each with a circular row of fibro-vascular scars; buds large, scales imbricate, brown, ovate to obovate, acute or apiculate at apex, pubescent.

BARK. Dark gray to brown or reddish, 3/4–1 in. thick on the trunk, surface broken into irregular fissures and scaly flat-topped ridges.

WOOD. Heart light brown, sapwood nearly white, coarse-grained, not strong, soft, weighs 26 lb per cu ft, very durable in contact with the soil, moderately weak in bending, weak in endwise compression, moderately high in shock resistance.

RANGE. In woods in deep, moist, rich soil. East Texas, Lou-

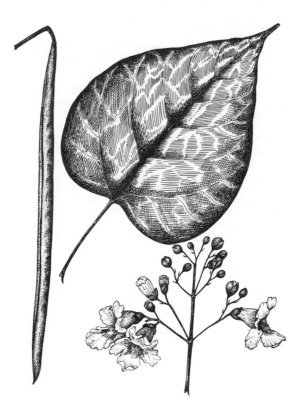

isiana, Oklahoma, and Arkansas, north to Missouri, Tennessee, Kentucky, Indiana, and Illinois. Naturalized in Virginia,
Kansas, and Ohio.

REMARKS. The genus name, *Catalpa*, is the American Indian
name. The species name, *speciosa*, is given for the large
showy flowers. It is known under the vernacular names of
Larger Indian-bean, Bois-plant, Indian-cigar, Smoking-bean,
Cigar-tree, Shawnee-wood, Hardy Catalpa, Western Catalpa,
and Catawba-tree. The wood is used for fence posts, rails,
poles, and occasionally furniture and interior finish. The tree
seems to coppice easily, is rapid growing, short-lived, easily
injured by storms, insects, and fungi. It is subject to the
attack of the catalpa sphinx, which defoliates the tree.
Northern Catalpa is distinguished from Southern Catalpa
primarily by the smaller, fewer-flowered lax panicle of the
former; by the sparser, paler spots on the corolla-throat, and
the lobes flatter, with the limb up to 2–2⅓ in. long; also by
the leaves having a less fetid odor and the pods thicker walls.

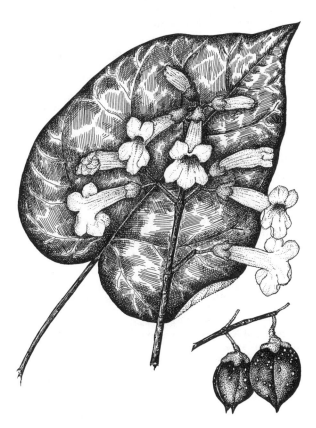

Royal Paulownia

Paulownia imperialis Sieb. & Zucc. [A]

FIELD IDENTIFICATION. Cultivated tree to 50 ft, with a diameter of 4 ft. The stout spreading branches develop into a rounded or flattened head.

FLOWERS. April–May, borne before the leaves in terminal panicles up to 10 in. long with densely tomentose pedicels; corolla 1½–2½ in. long, irregularly shaped, pale violet to blue, puberulent, corolla-tube slightly curved and spreading at the apex into an oblique, 5-lobed limb; upper corolla-lobes reflexed, lower corolla-lobes spreading, lobes unequal and shorter than the tube; corolla-throat broad and 2-ridged with spots or yellowish stripes; 4 stamens, 2 long and 2 short, included, anther sacs divergent and pendent; style slender, slightly thickened distally, stigmas distinct, plate-like, inwardly stigmatic; calyx campanulate, 2/5–3/5 in. long, nearly regular; sepals 5, united half their length, ovate to rounded, obtuse, thick, tomentose.

FRUIT. Capsule persistent, conspicuous in winter, length 1¼–1¾ in., woody, broadly ovoid, acute, beaked, longitudinally dehiscent into 2 valves; seeds numerous, about 2,000 per capsule, small, flat, striate, broadly winged.

LEAVES. Deciduous, opposite, blades 5–12 in. long, cordate to suborbicular, margin entire or 3-lobed, apex acuminate, base heart-shaped; young leaves densely short-stellate hairy, somewhat sticky, older ones pubescent above, tomentose beneath; petioles about 3–8 in. long, terete, pubescent.

TWIGS. Stout, smooth; bark thin and flaky on older branches, winter buds with several outer scales, pith segmented.

WOOD. Brown to purplish, sapwood thin, light, soft, easily worked, has a satiny finish.

RANGE. Persistent about old gardens and waste places; Texas, Louisiana, Oklahoma, and Arkansas. A native of central China. Escaping to roadsides and open woods throughout almost all of the eastern United States, north to New York.

REMARKS. The genus name, *Paulownia*, is in honor of Anna Paulownia (1795–1865), princess of the Netherlands. The species name, *imperialis*, refers to the royal name. It is also known under the names of Empress-tree, Princess-tree, Cotton-tree, and Karri-tree. The flowers are delightfully fragrant and the large catalpalike leaves are conspicuous.

Botanists differ about the family placement of the Royal Paulownia. The presence of the endosperm suggests Scrophulariaceae, while the arboreal habit and large terminal inflorescence favor the Bignoniaceae.

Madder Family (Rubiaceae)

Common Button-bush

Cephalanthus occidentalis L. [A, B, C]

FIELD IDENTIFICATION. Shrub or small tree to 18 ft, growing in low areas, often swollen at the base.

FLOWERS. June–September. Borne on peduncles 1–3 in. long, white, sessile, clustered in globular heads 1–1½ in. in diameter; corolla ¼–½ in. long, tubular with 4 short, ovate, spreading lobes; stamens 4, inserted in corolla-throat, an-

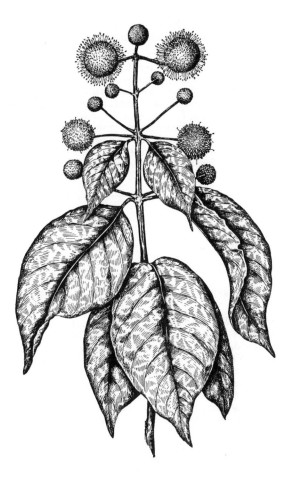

thers oblong; style slender, exserted; stigma capitate; ovary 2-celled; calyx-tube obpyramidal with 4–5 rounded sepals.

FRUIT. September–October. Round cluster of reddish brown nutlets; nutlets dry, obpyramidal, ¼–⅓ in. long.

LEAVES. Opposite, or in whorls of 3, simple, deciduous, short-petioled, ovate or lanceolate-oblong, acuminate or acute at apex, rounded or narrow at base, entire; blades 2–8 in. long, 1–3 in. wide, dark green and glabrous above or somewhat hairy beneath; petioles glabrous, stout, ½–¾ in. long; stipules small, triangular.

TWIGS. Dark reddish brown, lustrous, glaucous when young; lenticels pale and elongate.

BARK. Thin, smooth, gray to brown, later with flattened ridges and deep fissures.

RANGE. New Mexico, Oklahoma, Texas, Arkansas, and Louisiana; eastward to Florida, and throughout North America from southern Canada to the West Indies, also in eastern Asia.

REMARKS. The Greek genus name, *Cephalanthus*, means "head-flower," and the species name, *occidentalis*, means "western." Vernacular names for the shrub are Spanish Pincushion, River-brush, Swampwood, Button-willow, Crane-willow, Little-snowball, Pinball, Box, Button-wood, Pond-dogwood, Uvero, and Crouper-brush. It is frequently cultivated as an ornamental shrub and provides good bee food. According to stomach records the nutlet is eaten by at least 25 species of birds, mostly water birds. The wood is of no economic value.

Texas Randia

Randia aculeata L. [B]

FIELD IDENTIFICATION. Rigid, thorny shrub attaining a height of 12 ft.

FLOWERS. Axillary, solitary or few in a cluster, on puberulent pedicels ⅛–¼ in. long, perfect; calyx about 1/16 in. long, 4–5-lobed, lobes about 1/25 in. long, ovate to almost subulate; corolla short-tubular, flared into a 5-lobed spreading limb, white above, greenish white below; lobes about ⅛ in. long, short-oblong, elliptic or ovate, apex rounded to obtuse and mucronulate; stamens 5, adnate to the corolla-throat, short; anthers barely exserted from the hairy throat, linear; pistil about 1/25 in. long, slightly exserted, 2-lobed, flattened, granular.

FRUIT. Scattered along the stems, sessile or nearly so, globose, smooth, greenish when young, black when ripe, ¼–½ in. long; seed solitary, black, disklike, round, compressed, thin on the edges, center with a short ridge on each side, 1/8–3/16 in. wide.

LEAVES. Clustered at the nodes but essentially opposite, ½–1½ in. long, broadly-obovate, oval or suborbicular; apex rounded to truncate and often obcordate; base cuneate or gradually narrowed and continuing down the petiole; margin entire and ciliate, slightly wavy occasionally; texture leathery, papillose, pubescent on both sides but at maturity more glabrous above, with hairs mostly on the veins beneath, light to dark green, veins obscure above but more obvious beneath; petioles pubescent, semiwinged by the acuminate leaf base.

TWIGS. Young twigs densely tomentose, later glabrous, smooth, gray; conspicuously armed with opposite, stiff, stout, slender thorns ¼–¾ in. long.

BARK. Mottled gray, smooth, tight.

RANGE. South Texas along the lower Rio Grande. Also on sandy or clay loams in brushy pastures; from south and west of Corpus Christi. In Mexico in the states of Sinaloa, Tamaulipas, Oaxaca, and Veracruz; south through Panama to Colombia. Also in south Florida and the West Indies.

REMARKS. The genus name, *Randia*, is in honor of Isaac Rand, and the species name, *aculeata*, refers to the spines. *R. mitis* L. is a common synonym. Vernacular names in use in Central America and northern South America are Crucilla, Cruceto, Crucecilla de la Costa, Crucete, Tintillo, Escambron, Cambron, Palo de Catarro, Maiz Tostado, Agalla de Costa, Yamaguey, Yamoguey de Costa, Pitajoni Bravo, Pitajoni Espinoso, Espino Cruz, and Papachilla.

The crosslike paired thorns are a conspicuous feature supporting the name of Crucilla ("little cross") among the Mexican people of south Texas and adjacent Mexico. The plant is also reported to be used in domestic medicine as a remedy for dysentery and the ripe fruit is said to produce a blue dye.

Honeysuckle Family (Caprifoliaceae)

American Elder

Sambucus canadensis L. [A, B, C]

FIELD IDENTIFICATION. Stoloniferous shrub with many stems from the base, or under favorable conditions a tree to 30 ft. Stems thinly woody with a large white pith.

FLOWERS. Borne May–July in conspicuous, large, terminal, convex or flattened cymes, sometimes as much as 10 in. across. Peduncles and pedicels striate, green at first, reddish later. Corolla white, 1/5–1/4 in. wide, tube short and expanding into 5 lobes; lobes ovate to oblong, rounded, about ⅛ in. long; calyx minute, 5-lobed; stamens 5, exserted, inserted at the base of the corolla; filaments slender, white, about ⅛ in. long, anthers oblong, yellow; style short, depressed, 3-parted; ovary inferior, 4-celled and 1-seeded.

FRUIT. Drupe berrylike, deep purple or black, subglobose, 1/6–1/4 in. in diameter, bittersweet, 4-celled, seed roughened.

LEAVES. Deciduous, opposite, 4–12 in. long, odd-pinnately compound of 5–11 (usually 5–7) leaflets; rachis glabrous or pubescent; leaflets elliptic to lanceolate or ovate to oval, apex acute or acuminate, base rounded or broadly cuneate, margin sharply serrate, blades 2–6 in. long, width 1–2 in.; petiolules ⅛–¼ in. long, pubescent; upper surface lustrous, bright green and glabrous; lower surface paler, barely or copiously pubescent.

STEMS. Smooth to angular or grooved, green to red when young, older stems reddish, yellowish, or gray, bark sometimes with warty protuberances, nodes sometimes enlarged; external woody layer thin, pith large and white.

RANGE. In rich moist soil, along streams, low places, fence rows. In Oklahoma, Arkansas, Texas, and Louisiana; east-

ward to Florida and Georgia, northward to Nova Scotia, and westward to Kansas and Manitoba.

REMARKS. The genus name, *Sambucus*, is the classical Latin name, and the species name, *canadensis*, refers to Canada, where the plant grows at its most northern limit. It is also known under the local names of Elderberry, Common Elder, Sweet Elder, Pie Elder, and Elder-blow. The various parts of the plant have been used for food or medicine in domestic practice. The fruit is made into pies, wines, and jellies. The flowers are used to flavor candies and jellies, and the Indians made a drink by soaking them in water. The dried leaves have been used as an insecticide, and the bark in preparing a black dye. The stems, with the pith removed, were formerly used as drains in tapping maple sugar, and children make whistles, flutes, and popguns from them. The plant has considerable value as a wildlife food, being eaten by about 45 species of birds, especially the gallinaceous birds, such as the quail, pheasant, and prairie chicken. It is also browsed by white-tailed deer and is considered highly palatable to livestock; however, its use by livestock should be investigated further. The writer has noted that in some localities it is browsed, but in other localities the cattle refuse to touch it even under stress conditions.

Rusty Blackhaw Viburnum

Viburnum rufidulum Raf. [A, B, C]

FIELD IDENTIFICATION. An irregularly branched shrub or tree to 40 ft, with opposite, finely serrate, shiny leaves.

FLOWERS. In flat cymes 2–6 in. across with 3–4 stout rays and minute subulate bracts and bractlets; corolla small, ¼–⅓ in. in diameter, regular; petals 5, rounded orbicular or oblong, white; stamens 5, attached to the corolla, exserted, anthers oblong and introrse; pistil with style absent and stigmas 1–3, sessile on the ovary, ovary 3-celled, only 1 cell maturing.

FRUIT. Ripe July–October, in drooping clusters, drupes ⅓–½ in. long, oblong to obovoid, bluish black, glaucous; seed solitary, flattened, oval to ovate, ridged toward one end.

LEAVES. Simple, opposite, deciduous, or half-evergreen southward, dark green, leathery, shiny above, paler below with red hairs on veins, margin finely serrate, elliptic to obovate or oval, apex rounded to acute or obtuse, base cuneate or rounded, 1½–4 in. long, 1–2½ in. broad, petiole

grooved, wing-margined, clothed with red hairs, length
½–¾ in.

BARK. Rather rough, ridges narrow and rounded, fissures
narrow, breaking into dark reddish brown or black squarish
plates.

TWIGS. Young ones gray with reddish hairs, older ones reddish brown, more glabrous.

WOOD. Fine-grained, hard, heavy, strong, with a disagreeable
odor.

RANGE. In river-bottom lands or dry uplands. Oklahoma,
Arkansas, Texas, and Louisiana; eastward to Florida, northward to Virginia, and west to Kansas.

REMARKS. The genus name, *Viburnum*, is the classical name
of the Wayfaring-tree, *V. lantana* L., of Eurasia, which is
often cultivated. The species name, *rufidulum*, refers to the
rufous-red hairs on young parts. This character prompted
the use of the name V. *rufotomentosum* Small at one time.
Some vernacular names are Rusty Nanny-berry, Southern
Nanny-berry, Blackhaw, Southern Blackhaw. The tree is
worthy of cultivation because of the lustrous leaves, cymes
of white flowers in April, and bluish black fruit in October.
The wood is of no particular value.

Blackhaw Viburnum

Viburnum prunifolium L. [A]

FIELD IDENTIFICATION. Shrub or small tree to 28 ft, with a
diameter of 10 in., the stiff spreading branches forming an
irregular crown.

FLOWERS. April–June, with the leaves or slightly before,
cymes sessile or nearly so, compound, round-topped, white,
3–4-rayed, 2–4 in. wide; individual flowers 1/6–1/4 in. wide;
calyx 5-toothed; corolla-tube short, deeply 5-lobed, rotate
and spreading, lobes suborbicular; stamens 5, filaments slender, exserted, inserted on the corolla-tube; anthers oblong,
introrse; style absent; stigmas 3, minute and sessile; ovary
3-celled, 1 ovule usually maturing.

FRUIT. August–October, drupe ⅓–½ in. long, ellipsoid to
subglobose, bluish black, glaucous or only slightly so, flesh
thin and dry but sweet; seed solitary, flat, oval or elliptic, or
one side slightly convex, anatropous, embryo small, albumen
fleshy.

LEAVES. Simple, opposite, deciduous, 1–2¾ in. long, oval to
ovate or obovate, or oblong to elliptic; apex acute to obtuse
or rounded; base obtuse to rounded, margin finely serrulate;
upper surface dull green (not lustrous), smooth, lower sur-

face paler, membranaceous but later subcoriaceous; petiole green to red, slender, ¼–¾ in. long, not winged or only slightly so; buds slender, short-pointed, with small reddish fascicled hairs and whitish crystals, scales involute.

TWIGS. Slender, rigid, green to reddish or brown, some with short lateral spurs.

BARK. Gray to brown with narrow rounded ridges broken into short sections.

WOOD. Reddish brown, hard, weighs 52 lb per cu ft, of no commercial importance.

RANGE. Thickets, roadsides, borders of woods, and along streams. Oklahoma, Arkansas, Texas, and Louisiana; east to Florida, north to Connecticut, and west to Michigan and Kansas.

REMARKS. The genus name, *Viburnum,* was the Latin name applied to the Wayfaring-tree but is of uncertain origin. The species name, *prunifolium,* means "plum-leaved." It also is known under the vernacular names of Sheep-berry, Nanny-berry, Sweet-haw, Sweet-sloe, Stag-bush, and Arrow-wood. The plant has been cultivated for ornament since 1727. The fruit is sweet and edible and is known to be eaten by 12 species of birds, including bobwhite quail, and also by the gray fox and white-tailed deer.

Maple-leaf Viburnum

Viburnum acerifolium L. [A]

FIELD IDENTIFICATION. Shrub attaining a height of 2–6 ft, sometimes forming thickets. Branches erect or ascending and rather slender.

FLOWERS. Maturing May–August, in 3–7-rayed cymes which are convex or flattened and ¾–3½ in. wide; peduncles slender, ⅝–2¾ in. long, pubescent with simple or stellate hairs; corolla small, 1/6–1/4 in. wide, creamy white, 5-lobed; stamens 5, long-exserted, filaments 1/8–1/6 in. long, inserted on the corolla-tube, anthers oblong and introrse; ovary 3-celled at first, usually only 1 ovule maturing, style none, stigma sessile on the ovary summit; calyx with the 5 sepals reniform and about 1/50 in. long.

FRUIT. Maturing July–October, drupes persistent, reddish to purplish black at maturity, about ⅓ in. long, globose to oblong or ellipsoid, flesh thin and purplish; stone lenticular, flattened, crustaceous, 3-grooved on one side and 2-grooved on the other, endosperm fleshy, embryo minute.

LEAVES. Simple, opposite, deciduous, blades suborbicular to ovate, margin coarsely dentate and often also with 3 acute to acuminate lobes, base rounded or subcordate, length or width 1¼–5 in., venation palmately 3-ribbed, surfaces usually dull green and pubescent on both sides, lower surface more densely so and often conspicuously dotted, sometimes with tufted axillary hairs, thin; petioles ⅜–1 in., slender, pubescent, often stipulate at base.

TWIGS. Slender, tan to reddish brown, finely stellate-pubescent, later gray and glabrous.

RANGE. Dry sandy or rocky woods. Arkansas, Texas, and Louisiana; eastward to Florida, northward to Quebec, and west to Ontario and Minnesota.

REMARKS. The genus name, *Viburnum*, is the classical name of a Eurasian tree, and the species name, *acerifolium*, refers to the maplelike foliage. It is also known under the vernacular names of Dockmackie, Arrow-wood, Possum-haw, Squash-berry, and Guelder-rose. The plant has been cultivated since 1736. The creamy white cymes of flowers in summer and dark purple to crimson foliage in fall make it attractive. The foliage endures city smoke well. The fruit is eaten by at least 4 species of birds, including ruffed grouse, and the leaves are sometimes browsed by white-tailed deer and cottontail.

Possum-haw Viburnum

Viburnum nudum L. [A]

FIELD IDENTIFICATION. Irregularly branched shrub or small tree, rarely over 20 ft.

FLOWERS. April–June, white, perfect, borne in flat or round-topped cymes 2–4½ in. across, primary peduncles ½–1 in. long, often with ovate, acute bracts; pedicels ¼–⅓ in. long; corolla about 3/16 in. broad, 5-lobed; lobes spreading or reflexed, broad-ovate to rounded, apex obtuse to rounded; stamens 5, exserted about ⅛ in. beyond the corolla; filaments white, filiform, with short-oblong anthers; pistil short, included at anthesis; calyx about 1/16 in. long, greenish, short-tubular, lobes short-ovate, obtuse or acute.

FRUIT. Mature in autumn, in cymes 2–4½ in. across, pink

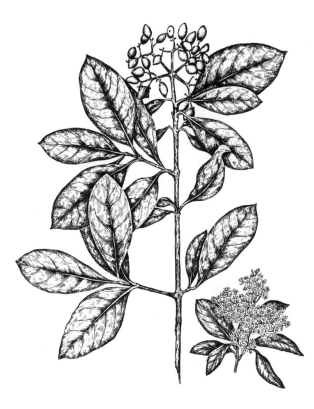

at first but glaucous-blue later, about ¼ in. in diameter,
subglobose to short-oblong or somewhat flattened, wrinkling
early, fleshy; seed black, compressed, rounded, rugose, ridged
down the middle, apices with abrupt points; fruiting peduncles with rusty brown scales, finely grooved, ½–1 in.
long, rebranched into short pedicels about ¼ in. long.

LEAVES. Opposite, leathery, shiny, variable in size, shape,
and scurfiness, oblong to elliptic or oval, blades 2–5 in. long,
1–2 in. broad, margin entire or obscurely serrulate; apex
acute, obtuse, acuminate, rounded or abruptly pointed; base
rounded or cuneate into a narrow wing on petiole; olive
green to dark green and lustrous above; lower surface paler
and with rusty brown scales; petioles slender, somewhat
winged, pubescent and brown-scaly, about ½ in. long; buds
usually acuminate, ½–¾ in. long, with reddish brown
scales.

BARK. Gray to brown, rather smooth.

TWIGS. Young ones gray to reddish brown or green, lustrous,
finely grooved, rusty brown, scaly; older twigs glabrous.

Shining Possum-haw Viburnum

RANGE. In sandy, acid swamps, usually in pinelands. East Texas, Louisiana, Oklahoma, and Arkansas; eastward to Florida and north to Tennessee and Kentucky.

REMARKS. *Viburnum* is the classical name of a Eurasian tree, and the species name, *nudum*, refers to the rather naked stems with remote leaves. Vernacular names in use are Withe-rod, Smooth Withe-rod, Naked Withe-rod, Bilberry, Nanny-berry, and Swamp-haw Viburnum. The sweet but unpalatable fruit is consumed by a number of species of birds, including the bobwhite quail.

Shining Possum-haw Viburnum, V. *nitidum* Ait., is hardly different from V. *nudum* L., but the leaves may vary to somewhat narrower, acuminate, shiny, and less coriaceous or they may be smaller. It also grows in low wet grounds and appears to have about the same distribution. However these characteristics are not constant and some authors use the names of V. *nudum* var. *angustifolium* T. & G. or V. *cassinoides* var. *nitidum* (Ait.) McAtee.

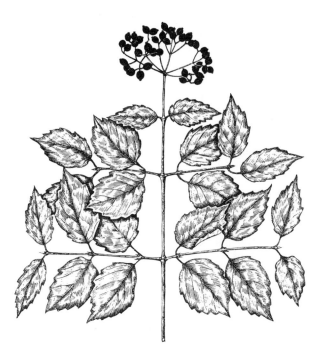

Arrow-wood Viburnum

Viburnum dentatum L. [A]

FIELD IDENTIFICATION. Shrub attaining a height of 3–15 ft. Branches slender, elongate, ascending or semipendent. Main stem either solitary or numerous from a clumped base. Very variable in size and shape of leaves and cymes and amount of pubescence, and hence divided into a number of varieties by authors.

FLOWERS. Maturing June–August, cymes terminal or on short lateral branches, flower parts more or less pubescent; cyme usually 5–7-rayed, 1¼–4½ in. broad; peduncle 1⅛–2⅜ in. long; corolla small, white, regular, spreading, rotate, 5-lobed; stamens 5, exserted; anthers oblong, introrse; style very short or mostly absent, the 3 stigmas minute and sessile; ovary 3-celled, only 1 cell with a maturing ovule.

FRUIT. Drupe ripening August–November, bluish black, subglobose to ovoid, pulp soft, 1/5–2/5 in. long; stone solitary, crustaceous, ellipsoid to ovoid, deeply grooved on the ventral side.

LEAVES. Opposite, blade 1–4½ in. long, ovate-lanceolate to rotund, apex acute or short-acuminate (in some forms rounded), base rounded to subcordate, margin serrate to dentate, the teeth rather triangular; usually thick and firm, especially in sun-exposed plants of dry situations; upper surface glabrous or nearly so, or with stellate pubescence; veins 5–11 pairs, straight or nearly so, conspicuous beneath the leaf blade; petioles very slender, ⅓–1¼ in. long, glabrous to stellate-pubescent.

TWIGS. Slender, elongate, straight or arching, young ones pubescent, older ones glabrous, bark gray to grayish brown or reddish brown.

RANGE. Arrow-wood Viburnum and its forms occur in many types of soil, but mostly in moist sandy lands. Arkansas, eastern Texas, and Louisiana; eastward to Florida and northward to Massachusetts.

REMARKS. The genus name, *Viburnum*, is the classical name. The species name, *dentatum*, refers to the coarsely toothed margins of the leaf. It is also known under the vernacular names of Southern Arrowwood, Mealy-tree, Withe-rod, and Withe-wood. Indians were known to have made arrows from the straight stems.

Diagrams

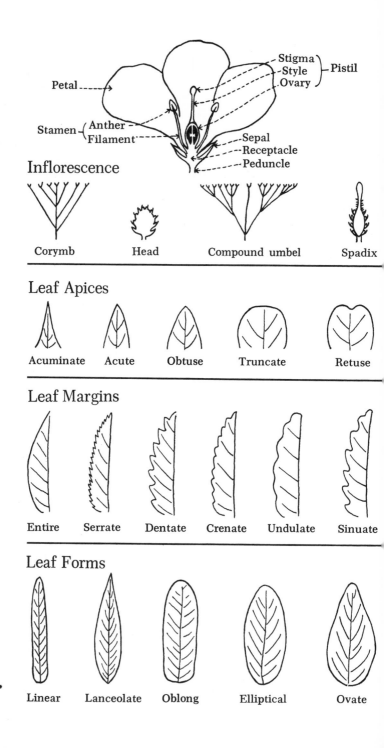

Petal

Stamen { Anther
         Filament

Stigma }
Style   } Pistil
Ovary

Sepal
Receptacle
Peduncle

Inflorescence

Corymb   Head   Compound umbel   Spadix

Leaf Apices

Acuminate   Acute   Obtuse   Truncate   Retuse

Leaf Margins

Entire   Serrate   Dentate   Crenate   Undulate   Sinuate

Leaf Forms

Linear   Lanceolate   Oblong   Elliptical   Ovate

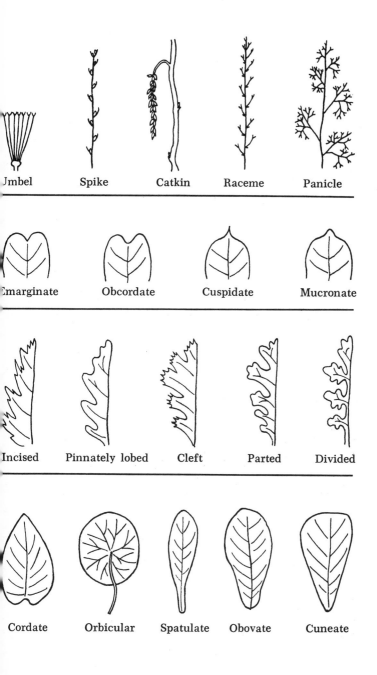

Umbel   Spike   Catkin   Raceme   Panicle

Emarginate   Obcordate   Cuspidate   Mucronate

Incised   Pinnately lobed   Cleft   Parted   Divided

Cordate   Orbicular   Spatulate   Obovate   Cuneate

Glossary

A- (prefix). Without, lacking.
Abaxial. On the dorsal side, away from the axis.
Aberrant. Not normal, atypical.
Abortive. Imperfectly developed.
Abruptly acuminate. Suddenly pointed from a rounded or
    truncate apex.
Abruptly pinnate. A pinnate leaf ending with a pair of
    leaflets; even-pinnate.
Acaulescent. Without a stem aboveground.
Accrescent. Increasing in size with age.
Accumbent. Lying against and face to face.
Acerose. Needlelike.
Achene. A small, dry, hard, one-seeded, indehiscent fruit.
Acicular. Bristlelike.
Acidulous. Slightly acid or bitter.
Acorn. The fruit of oaks.
Acotyledonous. Without cotyledons.
Acrid. Bitter or sharp tasting, usually referring to the fruit
    or sap.
Acropetal. Borne in succession toward the apex, as in cer-
    tain inflorescences.
Acuminate. Referring to an acute apex whose sides are con-
    cave.
Acute. Terminating with a sharp angle.
Adherent. Referring to two dissimilar parts or organs which
    touch but are not fused.
Adnate. Grown together; organically united.
Adventive. A recent, perhaps temporary, introduction, not
    as yet naturalized, or barely so.
Aerenchyma. Spongy respiratory tissue in stems of many
    aquatic plants, characterized by large intercellular
    spaces.
Aerial. Parts above the ground or water.
Aggregate. Referring to a type of fruit with a cluster of
    ripened coherent ovaries.
Alkaloid. An organic base produced in some plants, some-
    times with medicinal or poisonous properties.
Allergic. Subject to irritation by foreign substances.
Alpine. At high elevations; above the tree line.
Alternate. Placed singly at different levels on the axis.
Alternation of generations. Alternate sexual and asexual
    generations.
Alveola. Surface cavity of carpel or seed.
Ament. A catkin or scaly-bracted, often pendulous, spike of
    naked or reduced flowers.
Amplexicaul. Clasping the stem.
Ampliate. Expanded or enlarged.
Anastomosing. Netted; said of leaf blades with cross veins
    forming a network.

Anatropous. Referring to an ovule's position when the micropyle is close to the point of funiculus attachment.

Androecium. Stamens, in the collective sense.

Androgynous. Bearing staminate and pistillate flowers in the same inflorescence.

Androphore. Supporting stalk of a group of stamens.

Angulate. Angled.

Annulus. A ring-shaped part or organ.

Anterior. Away from the axis; the front; toward a subtending leaf or bract.

Anther. The polleniferous part of a stamen.

Anther cells. The actual chambers or locules of an anther.

Anther sac. Pollen sac of an anther.

Antheriferous. Having anthers.

Anthesis. Time of expansion of a flower; pollination time.

Anthocarp. A fruit condition in which at least a portion of the perianth is united with the ovary wall itself.

Antrorse. Directed upward.

Apetalous. Lacking petals.

Apex. The top or termination of a part or organ.

Apiculate. Ending in a short pointed tip.

Apomixis. Reproduction without sexual union.

Appendages. Various subsidiary or secondary outgrowths.

Appressed. Closely and flatly pressed against.

Approximate. Adjacent or close.

Aquatic. Growing in water.

Arachnoid. Bearing weak, tangled, cobwebby hairs.

Arboreal. Referring to trees, treelike.

Arborescent. Like trees in size and growth habit.

Arcuate. Somewhat curved.

Arenicolous. Sand loving.

Areole, areola (pl. *areolae*). An open space or island formed by anastomosing veins in a foliar organ; spine-bearing area of cactus.

Aril. An appendage or complete additional covering of the seed, arising as an outgrowth from hilum or funicle.

Aristate. With a stiff, bristlelike appendage.

Articulated. Jointed and cleanly separating to leave a scar.

Ascending. Growing upward, but not erect.

Asexual. Without sex, reproduction without sexual union, such as by cuttings, buds, bulbs, etc.

Assurgent. Ascending.

Asymmetric. Not symmetrical; with no plane of symmetry.

Atypical. Not typical.

Attenuate. Slenderly tapering.

Auricle. Earlike attachment, such as at the base of some leaves or petals.

Auriculate. Furnished with auricles.

Autophytic. Having chlorophyll, self-sustaining.

Axial. Referring to the axis.

Axil. The upper angle formed by a leaf with the stem, or veins with other veins.

Axile. Situated on the axis.

Axillary. Situated in an axil.

Axis. The center line of any organ; the main stem.

Baccate. Berrylike; bearing berries.
Banner. Upper or posterior petal of a papilionaceous flower.
Barb. A bristlelike hooked hair or projection.
Bark. External tissues of woody plants, especially the dead corky layer external to the cortex or bast in trees.
Basal. At or near the base.
Beak. A narrow pointed outgrowth of a fruit, a petal, etc.
Berry. A fruit in which the ovary becomes a fleshy or pulpy mass enclosing one or more seeds, as is seen in the tomato.
Bi- (prefix). Two or two-parted.
Bifid. Cleft into two lobes.
Biglandular. With two glands.
Bilabiate. Two-lipped, as in some irregular corollas.
Bipinnate. Twice pinnate.
Bisexual. Having both sex organs in the same flower.
Biternate. Twice ternate.
Blade. The expanded portion of a leaf.
Brackish. Partially saline.
Bract. A more or less modified leaf subtending a flower or belonging to a cluster of flowers.
Bracteole. A small bract or bractlet.
Bractlet. The bract of a pedicel.
Bud. The rudimentary state of a shoot; an unexpanded flower.
Bud scales. Modified leaves protecting a bud, often dry, resinous or viscid.

Caducous. Falling early.
Caliche. A hard calcareous soil.
Callose. Bearing a callus.
Callus. A thickened or hardened protuberance or region.
Calyculus. Usually in the Compositae, referring to the short outer sepallike phyllaries of an involucre.
Calyx. The outer perianth whorl of the flower.
Campanulate. Bell-shaped.
Canaliculate. Having one or a few prominent longitudinal grooves.
Cancellate. With cross hatching or latticed ridges.
Canescent. Hoary with a gray pubescence.
Capillary. Hairlike.
Capitate. In a head, or headlike.
Capsule. A dry dehiscent fruit composed of more than one carpel.
Carina. A dorsal ridge or keel.
Carpel. A simple pistil, or one member of a compound pistil; the ovule-bearing portion of a flower, believed to be of foliar origin.
Cartilaginous. Firm or tough tissue, suggestive of animal cartilage.
Caruncle. A seed protuberance; a small hard aril.
Catkin. A delicate, scaly bracted, usually pendulous, spike of flowers; an ament.
Caudate. Long-attenuate; taillike.

Caudex. Enlarged basal part of stems, or combined root and stem.

Caulescent. Having an evident stem, as contrasted to acaulescent.

Cauline. Borne on the stem.

Centrifugal inflorescence. Flowers developing from the center outward; a determinate type, such as a cyme.

Centripetal inflorescence. Flowers developing from the outer edge toward the center; an indeterminate type, such as a corymb.

Cespitose, caespitose. In tufts.

Chaff. A small scale, as is found on the receptacle of many Compositae.

Chaparral. A type of low scrub, commonly with dense twiggy, thorny habit and evergreen leaves.

Chartaceous. Like old parchment; papery.

Ciliate. Bearing marginal hairs.

Ciliolate. Bearing short marginal hairs.

Cinereous. Ashy gray.

Circinate. Referring to a leaf that is coiled from the tip toward the base, the lower surface outermost.

Cirrhus. A tendril.

Clambering. Leaning on other plants or objects, not self-supporting.

Clasping. Enveloping the stem partially or wholly at the base, as leaf bases, bracts, stipules, etc.

Clavate. Club-shaped.

Claw. Narrowed petiolelike base of a petal or sepal.

Cleft. Incised or cut nearly or quite to the middle.

Cleistogamous. Said of flowers that are self-fertilized without expanding; modified or reduced flowers.

Climber. Plant seeking support by twining or by tendrils.

Coalescent. Grown together, as in similar parts.

Coat. Covering of a seed.

Coherent. Having similar parts in close contact but not fused.

Column. A body formed by the union of parts, such as a union of stamens to form the staminal column in Malvaceae.

Coma. A hair tuft, usually at the apex of seeds.

Commisure. A line of coherence, such as where two carpels are joined.

Compound leaf. A leaf with the blade divided into two or more leaflets.

Compressed. Flattened.

Concavo-convex. Convex on one side and concave on the other.

Concolorous. The same in color.

Conduplicate. Folded lengthwise.

Cone. An inflorescence of flowers or fruit with overlapping scales.

Confluent. Gradually passing into each other.

Congested. Crowded, as flowers in a dense inflorescence.

Conic. Cone-shaped.

Coniferous. Cone-bearing.

Connate. Said of similar parts which are united, at least at the base.

Connective. Extension of the filament of a stamen connecting the anther lobes.

Connivent. Arched inward so that the tips meet.

Consimilar. Alike.

Constricted. Narrowed between wider portions.

Contiguous. Adjacent or adjoining similar or dissimilar parts, not fused.

Contorted. Twisted.

Contracted. Narrowed or shortened.

Convergent. Tending toward a single point, as with leaf veins approaching each other.

Convolute. Rolled together, as with petals in buds of certain plants.

Copious. Abundant, plentiful.

Cordate. Heart-shaped, as in some leaves.

Coriaceous. Leathery in texture.

Corneous. Horny, as in margins of some leaves.

Corniculate. Hornlike in appearance.

Cornute. Spurred or horned.

Corolla. The inner perianth whorl of a flower.

Corona. A crownlike structure on the corolla and the stamens.

Coroniform. Crown-shaped, applied to the pappus of certain Compositae.

Corrugate. Strongly wrinkled.

Corymb. A flat-topped or convex open flower cluster, with its marginal flowers opening first.

Costa. A thickened vein or midrib.

Cotyledon. Plant embryo leaf, usually rich in stored food.

Creeping. Referred to a trailing shoot which strikes root along most of its length.

Crenate. Dentate with the teeth much rounded.

Crenulate. The diminutive of crenate.

Crest. A crown or elevated ridge, often entirely or partly of hair.

Crispate. Crisped or crumpled.

Cross-pollination. Transfer of pollen from flower to flower.

Crown. Usually referring to the branches and foliage of a tree; or thickened bases of stems.

Cruciform. Shaped like a cross.

Crustaceous. Dry and brittle.

Cucullate. Hood-shaped.

Cuneate. Wedge-shaped.

Cupulate. Cup-shaped, as the involucre of an acorn.

Cuspidate. Having a sharp rigid point.

Cyathium. A specialized form of inflorescence of some of the Euphorbias.

Cylindric. Elongate and circular in cross section.

Cylindroid. Like a cylinder but elliptic in cross section.

Cymbiform. Boat-shaped.

Cyme. A usually broad and flattish inflorescence with its central or terminal flowers blooming earliest.

Cymose. Cymelike.

Cymule. A small cyme.

Deciduous. Not persistent, not evergreen.
Declined. Turned downward or outward, as in some stamens.
Decompound. Several times divided, as in repeatedly compound leaves and inflorescences.
Decumbent. Reclining, but ascending at the apices.
Decurrent. Extensions downward, as of some petioles or leaves along the stem.
Decurved. Curved downward.
Decussate. Leaves opposite, with each pair at a right angle to the pair above or below.
Deflexed. Bent downward.
Dehiscent. Opening regularly by valves.
Deltoid. Triangular.
Dentate. Toothed, specifically when teeth have sharp points and spreading bases.
Denticulate. Minutely toothed.
Denudate. Becoming bare.
Depressed. Flattened from above.
Dermatitis. Irritation or inflammation of the skin.
Determinate. Having fixed limits, as in an inflorescential axis ending with a bud; also referring to a cymose, or centrifugal, inflorescence.
Diadelphous. With stamens in two groups.
Dichotomous. Forked in pairs.
Didymous. Twice, two-lobed, in pairs.
Didynamous. With four stamens in two pairs of differing length.
Diffuse. Spreading.
Digitate. Said of a compound leaf in which all the leaflets arise from one point.
Dilated. Expanded or enlarged.
Dimidiate. Reduced to one-half, often by abortion.
Dimorphic. Having two forms.
Dioecious. Unisexual, with the two kinds of flowers on separate plants.
Diploid. Having the somatic number of chromosomes; twice as many as in the germ cells after reduction.
Disarticulate. Breaking at a joint.
Disc, disk. Outgrowth of the receptacle or hypanthium within the perianth, often composed of fused nectaries; central portion of the head in Compositae.
Disciform. Disk-shaped.
Discoid. Referring to a rayless head of flowers, as in some Compositae.
Discolored. Usually of two colors, as in leaf surfaces.
Dissected. Deeply cut or divided into many narrow segments, as in some leaves.
Distal. The apex of an organ, the part most distant from the axis.
Distended. Swollen.
Distichous. In two vertical ranks.
Distinct. Separate, not united.

Diurnal. Opening during the day.

Divaricate. Widely spreading.

Divergent. Spreading apart.

Divided. Lobed to near the base.

Division. Segment of a parted or divided leaf.

Dorsal. Upon or relating to the back or outer surface of an organ.

Dorsifixed. Attached to the dorsal side.

Drupe. A fleshy or pulpy fruit in which the inner portion is hard and stony, enclosing the seed.

Drupelet. A small drupe.

E- (prefix). Without or lacking a structure or organ.

Echinate. Prickly.

Ecology. Science dealing with plants in relation to their environment.

Eglandular. Without glands.

Ellipsoid. Referring to the geometric figure obtained by rotating an ellipse on its longer axis.

Elliptic. Of the form of an ellipse.

Elongate. Lengthened, drawn out.

Emarginate. Referring to a notch, usually of a leaf apex.

Embryo. A young plant, still enclosed in the seed.

Endemic. Known only in a limited geographical area.

Endocarp. Inner layer of the pericarp of the ovary or fruit.

Endosperm. Part of the seed outside the embryo; the albumen or stored food.

Ensiform. Sword-shaped.

Entire. Without toothing or divisions.

Ephemeral. Lasting for only a short period.

Epidermis. The superficial layer of cells.

Epigaeous, epigeous. Growing on the ground, or close to the ground.

Epigynous. Attached to or borne on the pistil, as in some stamens or petals.

Erose. Irregularly toothed.

Estipulate. Exstipulate.

Exalbuminous. Without albumen or endosperm, the embryo filling the seed instead.

Excavated. Referring to some pitted or channeled seeds.

Excurrent. Prolongation of nerves into awns or mucros of a leaf or fruit body; also the prolongation of the main stem or axis of a plant in certain conifers.

Excurved. Curved outward.

Exfoliating. Referring to bark separating into strips or flakes.

Exocarp. The outer layer of pericarp.

Exogenous. Growth by increase of tissue beneath the expanding bark; the cambium region in dicotyledonous woody plants; as opposed to endogenous growth by internal multiplication of tissues in monocotyledonous plants.

Expanded. Spreading, opened to the greatest extent.

Explanate. Flattened out.

Exserted. Projecting beyond an envelope, as stamens from a corolla.

Exstipulate. Lacking stipules.

Extra-axillary. Being near the axil but not truly axillary, as in some flowers.

Extrafloral. Outside the flower, as extrafloral nectaries.

Extrorse. Directed outward.

Exudate. An excretion of wax, gum, sap, etc.

Faceted. Usually applied to seeds with several plane surfaces.

Facial. On the plane surface or face rather than the margin.

Falcate. Sickle- or scythe-shaped.

Farinose. Covered with mealy or floury particles.

Fascicle. A close bundle or cluster.

Fastigiate. Having closely set erect branches.

Faveolate. Honeycombed.

Feather-veined. With secondary veins branching from the main vein.

Fertile. Applied to flowers with pistils capable of producing seeds, or to stamens with functional pollen.

Fetid. Malodorous.

Fibrilla. A very small fringe.

Fibrillose. Having fine fibers, as the leaf margins of some Yuccas.

Fibrous. Bearing a resemblance to fibers, or possessing fibers, as in fibrous roots.

Filament. The part of a stamen which supports the anther.

Filamentose. Having threadlike structures; threadlike.

Filiferous. Bearing threads.

Filiform. Thread-shaped.

Fimbriate. Fringed, frayed at the ends or on the margin.

Flabellate. Fan-shaped.

Flaccid. Lax, limp, flabby.

Flexuose, flexuous. Zigzag, or bent in an alternating manner.

Floccose. Clothed with tufts of soft woolly hairs.

Floral. Referring to flowers.

Floret. A small flower, as in the disk flowers of Compositae.

Floriferous. Having flowers, usually abundantly.

Floristic. Referring to the aggregate aspects of the vegetation, as to species, abundance, and distribution in a geographical sense.

Fluted. Regularly marked by alternating ridges and groovelike depressions.

Foliaceous. Leaflike in texture and appearance.

Foliate. Referring to leaves as opposed to leaflets.

Foliolate. Referring to the leaflets in a compound leaf, such as bifoliolate or trifoliolate.

Follicle. A dry fruit opening along the single suture, the product of a simple pistil.

Fruit. Seed-bearing part of a plant.

Frutescent. Shrubby.

Fugacious. Referring to early-deciduous parts, such as petals or sepals of certain plants.

Fulvous. Tawny, dull yellow.

Functional. Able to produce normally.

Funiculus. The stalk attaching ovule to ovary wall or
placenta.
Funnelform. Shaped like a funnel.
Fuscous. Dark brownish gray.
Fusiform. Spindle-shaped.

Gamopetalous. Referring to the petals being more or less
united.
Gamosepalous. Referring to the sepals being more or less
united.
Germinate. In pairs, twins.
Gene. A unit of inheritance which occupies a fixed place
on a chromosome.
Geniculate. Bent like a knee joint.
Gibbous. Swollen or inflated on one side.
Glabrate. Somewhat glabrous or becoming glabrous.
Glabrous. Smooth; pubescence or hairs absent.
Gland. A secreting protuberance or appendage.
Glandular. Bearing glands, or of the nature of a gland.
Glaucous. Covered with a white, waxy bloom.
Globose. Globular, spherical.
Glochid. A hair or minute prickle, often with retrorse or
hooklike projections, as in some cacti.
Glomerate. In a headlike or crowded inflorescence.
Glomerule. A small headlike inflorescence.
Glutinous. Gluelike, sticky.
Graduated. Rows or series of bracts, or phyllaries, of differ-
ent size, as on the involucre of some Compositae.
Granules. Small particles on the surface of a plant, such as
resinous granules, wax granules, etc.
Gynoecium, gynecium. The total female element of a flower.
Gynophore. The stalk of a pistil.

Habitat. The environment of a plant.
Halophyte. A plant tolerant of saline conditions.
Haploid. Possessing half of the diploid number of chromo-
somes, as in the germ cells after the reduction
division.
Hastate. Halberd-shaped; sagittate, but with the basal lobes
more or less at right angles.
Head. A spherical or flat-topped inflorescence of sessile or
nearly sessile flowers borne on a common receptacle.
Heartwood. The oldest wood, inclosing the pith; the hard
central, often deeply colored, portion of a tree trunk.
Hermaphrodite. Bisexual.
Heterogamous. Having two or more kinds of flowers with
respect to the distribution of sex organs.
Heteromorphic. Unlike in form or size, as sometimes the
length of stamens or pistils on different plants of the
same species.
Heterostylous. Having styles of different length or character.
Hexamerous. With the parts in sixes.
Hilum. The scar of a seed, marking the point of attachment.
Hip. Fruit in *Rosa*, composed of swollen hypanthium bear-
ing achenes within.

Hirsute. Covered with rather coarse or stiff hairs.
Hirsutulous. Finely or minutely hirsute.
Hispid. Beset with rigid or bristly hairs or with bristles.
Hispidulous. Minutely hispid.
Hoary. Densely grayish white pubescent.
Homochromous. Of uniform color.
Homogeneous. Of the same kind, uniform.
Homomorphic. Of uniform size and shape.
Hood. A concave organ, usually referring to certain petals.
Hyaline. Very thin and translucent.
Hybrid. Product of genetically dissimilar parents.
Hybridization. The production of a hybrid.
Hydrophilous. Referring to a tendency to grow in water.
Hydrophyte. An aquatic plant.
Hypanthium. Upward or outward extension of receptacle derived from fused basal portions of perianth and androecium.
Hypogynous. Inserted beneath the gynoecium, but free from it.

Imbricate. Overlapping.
Immersed. Submerged.
Imparipinnate. Pinnate with a single terminal leaflet; odd-pinnate.
Imperfect. Diclinous; lacking functional stamens or pistils.
Implicate. Twisted together or interwoven.
Impressed. Lying below the general surface; as, impressed veins.
Incanous. Hoary with whitish pubescence.
Incised. Cut sharply, irregularly, and more or less deeply.
Included. Not protruding, not exserted.
Incomplete. Descriptive of flowers in which one or more perianth whorls are wanting.
Incurved. Curved inward.
Indehiscent. Not opening.
Indeterminate. Applied to inflorescences in which the flowers open progressively from the base upward.
Indigenous. Native to an area.
Indument. A covering of hairs or wool.
Induplicate. Having the edges folded together.
Indurate. Hardened.
Inequilateral. Asymmetrical.
Inferior. Usually referring to an ovary being adnate to and appearing as if below the calyx.
Infertile. Not fertile or viable.
Inflated. Bladderlike.
Inflexed. Bent inward.
Inflorescence. A flower cluster; the disposition of flowers.
Inframedial. Below the middle, but not at the base.
Infrastaminal. Below the stamens.
Inodorous. Lacking odor.
Inserted. Attached to or growing out of.
Inter- (prefix). Between.
Intercostal. Between the ribs, veins, or nerves.

Internode. That portion of stem lying between two successive nodes.

Interrupted. Referring to an inflorescence with sterile intervals, mostly of varying length, between the flowers.

Intricate. Densely tangled, as in some branches.

Introflexion. State of being inflexed.

Introrse. Turned inward; facing the axis.

Intrusion. Protruding or projecting inward.

Inverted. Reversed, opposite to the normal direction.

Investing. Enclosing or surrounding.

Involucel. A secondary involucre, subtending a secondary division of an inflorescence as in Umbelliferae.

Involucral. Belonging to an involucre.

Involucre. One or more series of bracts, surrounding a flower cluster or a single flower.

Involute. With edges rolled inward.

Irregular. Said of flowers that are not bilaterally symmetrical.

Joint. A node; a unit of a segmented stem as in *Opuntia*.

Keel. The united pair of petals in a papilionaceous flower; a central or dorsal ridge.

Laciniate. Cut into lobes separated by deep, narrow, irregular incisions.

Lanate, lanuginose. Covered with matted hairs or wool.

Lanceolate. Shaped like a lance head.

Lanulose. Short-woolly.

Leaf. The usually thin and expanded organ borne laterally on the stem; in a strict sense inclusive of the blade, petiole, and stipules; but in common practice referred to the blade only.

Leaflet. A single division of a compound leaf.

Legume. A dry fruit, the product of a simple unicarpellate pistil, usually dehiscing along 2 lines of suture.

Lenticels. Corky growths on young bark.

Lenticular. Having the shape of a double convex lens.

Lepidote. Covered with minute scales or scurf.

Liana. A climbing woody plant.

Ligneous. Woody.

Ligulate. Tongue-shaped.

Ligule. Usually referring to an expanded ray flower in the Compositae.

Limb. The ultimate or uppermost extension of a gamopetalous corolla or calyx; distinct from the tube or throat.

Linear. Long and narrow.

Lingulate. Tongue-shaped.

Lip. One of the (usually two) divisions of an unequally divided corolla or calyx.

Littoral. Growing near the sea.

Lobe. Any segment or division of an organ.

Lobed. Divided into lobes, or having lobes.

Lobulate. With small lobes.

Locule. A compartment of an anther, ovary, or fruit.

Loculicidal. Longitudinally dehiscent dorsally, midway between the septa.

Loment. A fruit of the Leguminosae usually constricted between the seeds, the one-seeded indehiscent portions breaking loose.

Longitudinal. Lengthwise.

Lunate. Crescent-shaped.

Lyrate. Lyre-shaped, or a pinnatifid form with the terminal lobe usually longest.

Marcescent. Persistent after withering.

Marginal. On or pertaining to the margin of a plane organ.

Mealy. Farinose or floury.

Medial, median. Referring to or at the middle.

Membranaceous, membranous. Thin, rather soft, and more or less translucent.

Meniscoid. Concavo-convex, like a watch crystal.

Mericarp. A one-seeded indehiscent carpel of a fruit whose carpels separate at maturity.

-Merous (suffix). Referring to the number of parts; as 4-merous.

Mesophyte. Plant requiring a moderate amount of water.

Microphyllous. Small-leaved.

Midnerve. The central vein or rib.

Midrib. The main rib of a leaf.

Monadelphous. Union of all stamens by their filaments.

Moniliform. Necklacelike.

Monochasial. Applied to a cymose inflorescence with one main axis.

Monochromatic. Of one color.

Monoecious. With stamens and pistils in separate flowers, but on the same plant.

Monopodial. Applied to a stem having a single continuous axis.

Montane. Growing in the mountains.

Mottled. Spotted or blotched.

Mucilaginous. Sticky and moist.

Mucro. A short and small abrupt tip.

Mucronate. Tipped with a mucro.

Mucronulate. Diminutive of mucronate.

Multicipital. With several or numerous stems from a single caudex or taproot.

Multifoliolate. Referring to a compound leaf with numerous leaflets.

Multiple fruit. One that results from the aggregation of ripened ovaries into one mass.

Muricate. With surfaces bearing hard sharp tubercles.

Muriculate. Diminutive of muricate.

Naked. Lacking a customary part or organ; flowers without a perianth, a receptacle without chaff, a stem without leaves, etc.

Nectariferous. Producing nectar.

Nectary. A gland, or an organ containing the gland, which secretes nectar.

Nerve. An unbranched vein.
Neuter. Referring to flowers lacking stamens or pistils; or in some flowers of the Compositae having an ovary but lacking style or stigmas.
Nigrescent. Turning black.
Nocturnal. Night blooming.
Nodding. Arching downward.
Node. The joint of a twig; usually a point bearing a leaf or leaflike structure.
Nut. A hard, indehiscent, one-celled and one-seeded fruit.

Ob- (prefix). Inversely, upside down, as an obovate leaf (inversely ovate), etc.
Obcordate. Inverted heart-shaped.
Oblanceolate. Lanceolate with the broadest part toward the apex.
Oblique. Slanting; with unequal sides.
Oblong. Longer than broad and with nearly parallel sides.
Obovate. Inverted ovate.
Obovoid. Appearing as an inverted egg.
Obsolete. Not evident; very rudimentary; vestigial.
Obtuse. Blunt.
Ochroleucous. Yellowish white.
Ocrea. A tubular sheath formed by the union of a pair of stipules.
Odd-pinnate. A pinnate leaf with a single terminal leaflet.
Opposite. Opposed to each other, such as two opposite leaves at a node.
Orbicular. Circular.
Organ. A part of a plant with a definite function, as a leaf, stamen, etc.
Oval. Broadly elliptical.
Ovary. The part of the pistil that contains the ovules, or seeds after fertilization.
Ovate. Egg-shaped, with the broader end closer to the stem.
Ovoid. Referring to a solid object of ovate or oval outline.
Ovulate. Bearing ovules; referring to the number of ovules.
Ovule. The body which after fertilization becomes the seed.

Palea. A chaffy bract on the receptacle of Compositae.
Pallid. Pale or light colored.
Palmate. Said of a leaf radiately lobed or divided.
Palmatifid. Palmately cleft or lobed.
Palmatisect. Palmately divided.
Palustrine. Growing in wet ground.
Panicle. A branched raceme.
Pannose. Feltlike, covered with closely interwoven hairs.
Papilionaceous. Descriptive of the flowers of certain legumes having a standard, wings, and keel petals; resembling a sweet pea.
Papilla. A small soft protuberance on leaf surfaces, etc.
Papillate. Bearing papillae.
Pappus. Modified calyx of certain Compositae, often elaborate in the fruit, consisting of hairs, bristles, awns, or scales.

Parcifrond. A long leafy usually sterile shoot of a floricane, arising from below the ordinary floral branches.

Parietal. Attached to the wall within the ovary.

Parted. Cleft nearly to the base.

Parthenogenetic. Asexual development of an egg, without fertilization by a male sex cell.

Parti-colored. Variegated.

Pectinate. With narrow, toothlike divisions.

Pedate. Palmate, with the lateral lobes or divisions again divided.

Pedicel. The stalk of a single flower in a cluster.

Pedicellate. Borne on a pedicel.

Peduncle. Primary flower stalk supporting either a cluster or a solitary flower.

Pedunculate. Borne on a peduncle.

Pellucid. Transparent or nearly so.

Peltate. Referring to a leaf blade in which the petiole is attached to the lower surface, instead of on the margin as in the garden nasturtium.

Pendent. Hanging or drooping.

Pendulous. More or less hanging.

Pentagonal. Five-angled.

Pentamerous. Of five parts, as a flower with five petals.

Perennial. Usually living more than two years.

Perfect. Referring to a flower having both pistil and stamens.

Perfoliate. A sessile leaf whose base passes around the stem.

Perforate. Pierced with holes; dotted with translucent openings which resemble holes.

Perianth. The floral envelope, usually consisting of distinct calyx and corolla.

Pericarp. The outer wall of an ovary after fertilization, hence of the fruit.

Perigynous. Referring to petals and stamens whose bases surround the pistil, or pistils, and are borne on the margin of the hypanthium, as in some Rosaceae.

Persistent. Said of leaves that are evergreen, and of flower parts and fruits that remain attached to the plant for protracted lengths of time.

Petal. The unit of the corolla.

Petaloid. Resembling a petal.

Petiole. The stalk of a leaf.

Petiolar. Relating to or borne on the petiole, as a petiolar gland.

Petiolate. Having a petiole.

Petiolulate. Having a petiolule.

Petiolule. The footstalk of a leaflet.

Phyllary. One of the bracts of the involucre in Compositae.

Pilose. Hairy, especially with long soft hairs.

Pinnae. The primary divisions of a pinnate leaf.

Pinnate. Descriptive of compound leaves with the leaflets arranged on opposite sides along a common rachis.

Pinnatifid. Pinnately cleft, the clefts not extending to the midrib.

Pinnatilobate. Pinnately lobed.

Pinnatisect. Pinnately divided, the clefts extending to the midrib.

Pinnule. A leaflet or ultimate segment of a pinnately decompound leaf.

Pistil. The seed-bearing organ of the flower, consisting of ovary, stigma, and style.

Pistillate. Provided with pistils, but lacking functional stamens.

Pith. The central tissue of a (usually exogenous) stem, composed of thin-walled cells.

Placenta. The structure in an ovary to which the ovules are attached.

Plano-convex. Flat on one side, convex on the other.

Pleiochasium. A compound cyme with more than two branches at each division.

Plicate. Folded into plaits.

Plumose. Having fine hairs on each side like the plume of a feather.

Pluriseriate. In many series.

Pod. Any dry and dehiscent fruit.

Pollen. The male germ cells, contained in the anther.

Pollen sac. Pollen-bearing chamber of the anther.

Pollination. Deposition of pollen upon the stigma.

Polygamo-dioecious. Essentially dioecious, but with some flowers of other sex or perfect flowers on same individual.

Polygamous. With both perfect and unisexual flowers on the same individual plant or on different individuals of the same species.

Polygonal. With several sides or angles.

Polymorphic. With a number of forms, as a very variable species.

Polyploid. With chromosome number in the somatic nuclei greater than the diploid number, sometimes accompanied by increased size and vigor of the plant.

Pome. A kind of fleshy fruit of which the apple is the typical form.

Pore. A small opening, as found in certain anthers or fruits.

Porrect. Reaching or extending perpendicular to the surface, as with spines of some cacti.

Posterior. Toward the rear, behind, toward the axis.

Prickle. A rigid, straight or hooked, outgrowth of the bark or epidermal tissue.

Procumbent. Lying on the ground.

Prominent. Higher than the adjacent surface, as in prominent veins.

Prophyllum. A bracteole.

Prostrate. Flat on the ground.

Proximal. Near the base or axis, the opposite of distal.

Pruinose. Covered with a white bloom or powdery wax.

Puberulent. Very slightly pubescent.

Pubescence. A covering of short hairs.

Pubescent. Covered with hairs, especially if short, soft, and downlike.

Pulverulent. Powdered, appearing as if covered by minute grains of dust.

Punctate. Dotted with depressions or translucent internal glands or colored spots.

Pungent. Sharply and stiffly pointed; bitter or hot to the taste.

Pyriform. Pear-shaped.

Quadrangular. Four-angled.

Quadrate. Square.

Raceme. A simple indeterminate inflorescence of pediceled flowers upon a common more or less elongated axis.

Racemose. Resembling a raceme; in racemes.

Rachis. The axis of a compound leaf or of an inflorescence.

Radial. Developing around a central axis.

Raphe. In anatropous ovules, the ridge formed by the fusion of a portion of the funicle to the ovule coat; ridge often persistent and prominent in seeds.

Ray. Usually referring to the more or less strap-shaped flowers in the head of Compositae.

Receptacle. The expanded portion of the axis that bears the floral organs.

Reclining. Bending or curving toward the ground.

Recurved. Curved downward or backward.

Reduced. Not normally or fully developed in size.

Reflexed. Abruptly bent or turned downward.

Regular. Uniform in shape or distribution of parts; radically symmetrical.

Remote. Referring to leaves or flowers which are distant or scattered on the stem.

Reniform. Kidney-shaped.

Repand. Having a somewhat undulating margin.

Repent. Prostrate, with the creeping stems rooting at the nodes.

Reticulate. Forming a network.

Retrorse. Turned downward or backward.

Retuse. Rounded and shallowly notched at the apex.

Revolute. Rolled or turned downward or toward the under surface.

Rhizome. A prostrate stem under the ground, rooting at the nodes and bearing buds on nodes.

Rhombic. With equal sides forming oblique angles.

Rib. A primary vein.

Rigid. Stiff.

Rosette. A cluster of basal leaves appearing radially arranged.

Rostrate. With a beaklike point.

Rotate. Wheel-shaped, usually referring to a flattened, short-tubed, sympetalous corolla.

Rotund. Rounded in shape.

Rudiment. A vestige, a much reduced organ, often non-functional.

Rufous. Reddish brown.

Rugose. Wrinkled.

Runcinate. Sharply incised pinnately, the incisions retrorse.
Runner. A stolon.

Sagittate. Shaped like an arrowhead.
Salient. Conspicuously projecting, as salient teeth or prominent ribs.
Salverform. Referring to a sympetalous corolla, with the limb at right angles to the tube.
Samara. An indehiscent winged fruit as in the maples and elms.
Scaberulous. Minutely scabrous.
Scabrous. Rough to the touch.
Scale. A leaf much reduced in size, or an epidermal outgrowth.
Scandent. Climbing.
Scape. A flower-bearing stem rising from the ground, the leaves either basal or scattered on the scape and reduced to bracts.
Scarious. Thin and dry.
Schizocarp. Referring to a septicidally dehiscent fruit with one-seeded carpels.
Sclerotic. Hardened, stony.
Scurf. Small scales, usually borne on a leaf surface or on stems.
Secondary. The second division, as in branches or leaf veins.
Secund. One-sided.
Seed. A ripened ovule.
Segment. Part of a compound leaf or other organ, especially if the parts are alike.
Self-pollination. Pollination within the flower.
Semi- (prefix). Approximately half; partly or nearly.
Sepal. A unit of the calyx.
Septicidal. Splitting or dehiscing through the partitions.
Septum (pl. *septa*). A partition or crosswall.
Seriate. Arranged in rows or whorls.
Sericeous. Bearing straight silky hairs.
Serrate. Having sharp teeth pointing forward.
Serrulate. Serrate with small fine teeth.
Sessile. Without stalk of any kind.
Seta (pl. *setae*). A bristle.
Sheath. A tubular structure, such as a leaf base enclosing the stem.
Shoot. A young branch.
Shrub. A woody plant with a number of stems from the base, usually smaller than a tree.
Silicle. A silique broader than long.
Silique. A long capsular fruit typical of the Cruciferae, the two valves separating at maturity.
Silky. Covered with close-pressed soft and straight hairs.
Simple. In one piece or unit, not compound.
Sinuate. Deeply or strongly wavy.
Sinus. The cleft or recess between two lobes.
Solitary. Alone, single.
Somatic. Referring to the body, or to all cells except the germ cells.

Spatulate. Gradually narrowed downward from a rounded summit.

Spherical. Round.

Spike. A racemose inflorescence with the flowers sessile or nearly so.

Spine. Modification of a stipule, petiole, or branch to form a hard, woody, sharp-pointed structure.

Spinescent. Ending in a spine.

Spiniferous. Bearing spines.

Spinulose. With small spines.

Spur. A tubular or saclike projection of the corolla or calyx, sometimes nectar bearing; a short, compact twig with little or no internodal development.

Squamella. A small scale, usually as in the pappus of some Compositae.

Squamose. Bearing scales.

Squamulose. Diminutive of squamose.

Stamen. The pollen-bearing organ, usually two or more in each flower.

Staminal column. A column or tube formed by the coalescence of the filaments of the stamens.

Staminate. Bearing stamens but lacking pistils.

Staminodium (pl. *staminodia*). A sterile stamen, often reduced or otherwise modified.

Standard. Usually referring to the upper or posterior petal of a papilionaceous corolla; a banner.

Stellate. Having the shape of a star; starlike.

Stem. Main axis of the plant.

Sterile. Unproductive.

Stigma. That part of the pistil which receives the pollen.

Stigmatic. Relating to the stigma.

Stipe. A stalklike support of a pistil or of a carpel.

Stipel. The stipule of a leaflet in compound leaves.

Stipitate. Having a stipe.

Stipulate. Having stipules.

Stipule. An appendage at the base of a petiole or on each side of its insertion.

Stolon. A branch or shoot given off at the summit of a root.

Stoma. A minute orifice in the epidermis of a leaf.

Stone. The hard endocarp of a drupe.

Striate. With fine grooves, ridges, or lines.

Strict. Erect and straight.

Strigillose. Diminutive of strigose.

Strigose. Bearing hairs which are usually stiff, straight, and appressed.

Strobile. An inflorescence or cone with imbricate bracts or scales.

Style. Upward extension of the ovary terminating with the stigma.

Sub- (prefix). Under, below, less than.

Subshrub. Perennial plant with lower portions of stems woody and persistent.

Subtend. Adjacent to an organ, under or supporting; referring to a bract or scale below a flower.

Subulate. Awl-shaped.

Succulent. Juicy.

Sucker. A stem originating from the roots or lower stem.

Suffrutescent. Slightly shrubby or woody at the base.

Suffruticose. Referring to a slightly shrubby plant; especially applied to low subshrubs.

Sulcate. Grooved or furrowed.

Superior. Above or over; applied to an ovary when free from and positioned above the perianth.

Supra- (prefix). Above.

Suture. Line of dehiscence; a groove denoting a natural union.

Symmetric. Divisible into equal and like parts; referring to a regular flower having the same number of parts in whorl or series.

Sympetalous. Petals more or less united.

Sympodial. Development by simultaneous branching rather than by only a main continuous axis.

Taproot. The main or primary root.

Taxonomy. The science of classification.

Tendril. Usually a slender organ for climbing, formed by modification of leaf, branch, inflorescence, etc.

Terete. Circular in transverse section.

Terminal. At the end, summit, or apex.

Ternate. Divided into three parts.

Testa. The outer seed coat.

Tetragonal. Four-angled.

Tetrahedral. Four-sided.

Theca. Anther sac.

Thorn. A sharp-pointed modified branch.

Throat. The orifice of a sympetalous or gamopetalous corolla.

Thyrse. A shortened panicle with the main axis indeterminate and the lateral flower clusters cymose; loosely, a compact panicle.

Tomentellous. Diminutive of tomentose.

Tomentose. Densely hairy with matted wool.

Tomentulose. Slightly pubescent with matted wool.

Toothed. Having teeth; serrate.

Tortuous. Zigzag or bent in various directions.

Torulose. Cylindrical and constricted at intervals.

Torus. The receptacle, or thickened terminal axis, of a flower head, especially in the Compositae.

Toxic. Poisonous.

Trailing. Growing prostrate but not rooting at the nodes.

Translucent. Transmitting light but not transparent.

Transpiration. Passage of water vapor outward, mostly through the stomata.

Transverse. A section taken at right angles to the longitudinal axis.

Tri- (prefix). In three parts, as trilobate (3-lobed); trifid (3-cleft).

Trichome. A hair arising from an epidermal cell.

Trichotomous. Three-branched or forked.

Truncate. Ending abruptly, as if cut off transversely.

Trunk. The main stem or axis of a tree below the branches.

Tube. A hollow cylindric organ, such as the lower part of a sympetalous calyx or corolla, the upper part usually expanding into a limb.

Tuber. A thickened underground stem usually for food storage and bearing buds.

Tubercle. A small tuberlike body.

Tumid. Inflated or swollen.

Turbinate. Top-shaped.

Turgid. Swollen.

Twining. Climbing by means of the main stem or branches winding around an object.

Ultimate. The last or final part in a train of progression, as the ultimate division of an organ.

Umbel. An inflorescence with numerous pedicels springing from the end of the peduncle, as with the ribs of an umbrella.

Umbilicate. Depressed in the center.

Umbo. A central raised area or hump.

Uncinate. Scythe-shaped, sometimes referring to hooked hairs or prickles.

Undershrub. A low plant generally woody only near the base.

Undulate. With a wavy surface or margin.

Unequally pinnate. Pinnate with an odd terminal leaflet.

Uni- (prefix). Solitary or one only; such as unifoliate (with one leaflet) or unilocular (with one cell).

Unilateral. One-sided.

Uniseriate. In one series, or in one row or circle.

Unisexual. Of one sex, either staminate or pistillate only.

Urceolate. Pitcher-shaped, usually with a flaring mouth and constricted neck.

Utricle. An achenelike fruit, but with a thin, loose outer seed covering.

Vallecula (pl. *valleculae*). A channel or groove between the ridges on various organs, such as on stems or fruits.

Valve. One of the pieces into which a capsule splits.

Vascular. Referring to the conductive tissue in the stems or leaves.

Vascular bundle. A bundle or group of vascular tubes or ducts.

Vegetative. Nonreproductive, as contrasted to floral.

Veins. Ramifications or threads of fibrovascular tissue in a leaf, or other flat organ.

Velutinous. Covered with dense velvety hairs.

Venation. A system of veins.

Venose. Veiny.

Ventral. Belonging to the anterior or inner face of an organ; the opposite of dorsal.

Ventricose. Asymmetrically swollen.

Vernation. Arrangement of leaves in a bud.

Verrucose. Covered with wartlike excrescences.

Versatile. Swinging free, usually referring to an anther attached above its base to a filament.

Verticil (adj. *verticillate*). A whorl of more than two similar parts at a node; leaves, stems, etc.

Verticillate. Disposed in a whorl.

Vesicle (adj. *vesicular*). A small inflated or bladderlike structure.

Vespertine. Opening in the evening.

Vestigial. A rudimentary, usually nonfunctioning, or underdeveloped organ.

Villosulous. Diminutive of villous.

Villous, villose. Bearing long soft hairs.

Virgate. Straight and wandlike.

Viscid. Glutinous or sticky.

Viviparous. Precocious development, such as the germination of seeds or buds while still attached to the parent plant.

Whorl. Cyclic arrangement of like parts.

Wing. Any membranous or thin expansion bordering or surrounding an organ.

Woolly. Clothed with long and tortuous or matted hairs.

Xeric. Characterized by aridity.

Xerophilous. Drought resistant.

Xerophyte. A desert plant or plant growing under xeric conditions.

Index